HOLLYWOOD AT THE INTERSECTION
OF RACE AND IDENTITY

HOLLYWOOD AT THE INTERSECTION OF RACE AND IDENTITY

EDITED BY

DELIA MALIA CAPAROSO KONZETT

RUTGERS UNIVERSITY PRESS

New Brunswick, Camden, and Newark, New Jersey, and London

Library of Congress Cataloging-in-Publication Data

Names: Konzett, Delia Caparoso, editor of compilation.
Title: Hollywood at the intersection of race and identity / edited by
    Delia Malia Caparoso Konzett.
Description: New Brunswick : Rutgers University Press, [2019] | Includes
    bibliographical references and index.
Identifiers: LCCN 2019007367 | ISBN 9780813599311 (pbk.)
Subjects: LCSH: Identity (Psychology) in motion pictures. | Race in motion
    pictures. | Motion pictures—United States—History. | Intersectionality
    (Sociology)—United States.
Classification: LCC PN1995.9.I34 H65 2019 | DDC 791.43/653—dc23
LC record available at https://lccn.loc.gov/2019007367

A British Cataloging-in-Publication record for this book is available from the
British Library.

www.rutgersuniversitypress.org

To my mother for all her love and support

CONTENTS

HOLLYWOOD AT THE INTERSECTION OF RACE AND IDENTITY

INTRODUCTION

DELIA MALIA CAPAROSO KONZETT

INTERPRETING INTERSECTIONALITY IN FILM

The question may be asked why film should be studied in an intersectional context. The visual turn in recent cultural debates has made abundantly clear that social interactions are predominantly informed by iconic rather than indexical textual signs. "As the relationship between sign and its referent becomes less clear-cut," Stuart Hall notes, "meaning begins to slip and slide away from us into uncertainty. Meaning is no longer transparently passing from one person to another."[1] The immediacy of the visual image, the icon bearing visual resemblance to reality, appears to have made the act of signification more reliable and less arbitrary than the textual sign. As an extension of the visual sign into the moving reality of things, film carries this illusion of reality to an ever-greater degree. Not surprisingly, cinema's etiquette codes and fashions, its celebrities and settings draw a great deal of interest from the general public to the point of emulation and fashioning oneself in the image of film personas and their lifestyles. Given this power that film holds over its audiences, its impact as a sociological training ground for social interaction is not to be underestimated. As much as or even more so than written culture, cinema informs and relays our social perception of others and the cultural grammar we share.

Intersectionality places social justice and ethics into the forefront, reminding us that the symbolic aesthetics of classical Hollywood film are not simply formal codes used to entertain audiences but are intimately connected to social and cultural practices, especially that of representation. Take, for example, Douglas Sirk's *Imitation of Life* (1959), a radical remake of the 1934 version and a landmark film that raises intersectionality to a more self-aware engagement with its representation.[2] Formerly Detlef Sirk, the director hailed from Hamburg, Germany, and reached the United States with his Jewish wife as a refugee in 1937. *Imitation of Life*, Sirk's final Hollywood film, comes in the wake of not only Germany's horrific genocidal history exposed especially during the Nuremberg trials but also the civil rights movement trying to address a legacy of over three hundred years of slavery and oppression in the United States, a democratic nation that apparently disposed of European fascism during World War II. The social problem film, a predominant genre of 1950s Hollywood, combined with Sirk's self-conscious melodramatic style indebted to the modern theater of Bertolt Brecht known for its defamiliarization of stage and representational practices, finds a happy medium in *Imitation of Life* with its reconfiguration of traditional norms of race, gender, family, and social class. This is not to say that the film does not come with the usual Hollywood limitations. For example, the casting of Sarah Jane, the film's young black heroine who can pass for white, predictably passed over the choice of light-skinned African American actresses and settled instead on the white Jewish American child actress Karin Dicker (Sarah at age eight) and the ethnically ambiguous Susanna Kohner of Mexican and Czech Jewish descent (Sarah at age eighteen). However, given its limitations set by industry codes and conventions, the film nevertheless presents a more fluid sense of identity, anticipating intersectionality in its performative masks of costume and setting, echoing sociologist Erving Goffman's notion, articulated in the mid-1950s, of the self as a social construct of various performative masks.[3]

To give a brief illustration of Sirk's intersectional style of representation in *Imitation of Life*, let us turn to this book's cover image, which is a production still from the film released in 1959 that starts its narrative in 1948 and moves forward to its present. Filmed in the industry standard of Eastmancolor, Sirk's melodrama is highly adept in using color for its critical representation of race.[4] The scene from which this still is taken occurs early in the film and documents a gathering of two women and their two daughters in the living room during the Christmas season. It includes the lady of the house, struggling actress and white single mother Lora Meredith (Lana Turner), rehearsing her Broadway script, and her black live-in maid and confidante Annie Johnson (Juanita Moore), telling the story of the nativity to the children, her eight-year-old light-skinned daughter Sarah Jane (Karin Dicker), who is mistaken for white at school, and Lora's six-year-old daughter Susie (Terry Burnham). Through careful blocking and an orchestration of various looks aiming in different directions, the still takes on the complexity of a *tableau vivant*, a seemingly frozen image that comes alive. Lighting adds to the scene by foregrounding various shades of skin color but also by casting a degree of darkness onto Lora. Her image that is also mirrored (not shown in cover image) suggests a doubling of the character—she is of two minds in this complex setting and belongs to two different power structures. First, she finds herself in an odd and socially incongruous family gathering that lacks the traditional male signifier or patriarch (both fathers are absent), hence opening the door for a reshuffling of the matrix of power. As a consequence, the women reciprocate one another with their gazes, bypassing the law of the father. In sum, the assembled women could be said to represent a progressive image of an open society defined by the civil rights movement emerging in the postwar era. At the same time, the noticeable doubling of Lora also implies conflicted views on this progressive constellation, pointing to traits of vanity and self-absorption. The frontal position and lighting of the two white characters reveal that not all hierarchies have been suspended, particularly that of white privilege (see Figure I.1).

Susie, for instance, is placed at the center of the frame and receives the brightest lighting (high key), as if already singled out for the brightest future. The living room lamp is placed right behind Susie and points to the tradition of Hollywood lighting that is enamored with the sublime glow of white women, as discussed by Richard Dyer.[5] The three-point lighting system intensifies their whiteness, stressing especially their glowing blond hair. Even Lora's back reflected in the mirror gives off whiteness. Both Lora and Susie wear bright light-colored outfits to enhance the glow, as opposed to Sarah Jane's rusty red robe and her mother's blue patterned dress. In the seating arrangement, Sarah Jane's access to this white privilege embodied by Susie is blocked by her black mother, cast authentically with the African American actress Juanita Moore, as if to remind the audience that color boundaries may after all not be so easily subject to negotiation. Not only does the armchair in front of Sarah Jane and her mother point to hurdles in her effort to move to the front center of the frame—her sulky look points to her frustration

FIGURE I.1 Nativity Scene *in Imitation of Life* (1959).

in doing so—but her mother also protects the white privilege of Susie who sits in her lap as if she were her own child. Annie's dark arms encircle Susie, supporting and protecting her with Susie's hand touching Annie's fingers, completing a circle. Sarah Jane is outside of this circle and her head rests upon her own semi-open palm as if supporting herself. Whereas Susie looks off screen connecting her to the audience, Sarah Jane does not reciprocate anyone's gaze but stares pensively at the back of her mother's head, engaging in bell hooks's rebellious oppositional gaze.[6] This still frame leaves the viewer with the additional question as to what is beyond the frame and haunts the nontraditional family gathering. Lora's husband, a theater director who died five years prior and "taught her everything," is absent, but even more so one takes note of the haunting absence of Sarah Jane's father who, as Annie tells us, "is practically white and left before she was born." Sarah Jane's genealogy remains entirely obscured throughout the film and renders her birth and therefore her status as illegitimate. The still in its entirety thus captures the complexity and psychosis of race, class, gender, and domestic relations in the U.S. postwar era.

In the final funeral scene, however, filmed mostly in a black church, whiteness is now associated with Annie, who in death becomes a redemptive figure, thus questioning the white norms of classical Hollywood codes. The high melodramatic ending begins with a powerful cameo performance of Mahalia Jackson singing the gospel song "Trouble of the World," placing the domestic drama of Annie and Sarah Jane firmly into the historical national legacy of slavery and racism. An excess of glowing whiteness is highlighted in multiple fashion: Annie's bright white majestic casket is sumptuously decked with white gardenias. White mums similarly frame the shot of Mahalia Jackson singing with a stark white collar juxtaposed against her black choir robe and the darkness of her skin. And, finally, four white horses pull Annie's white casket "to glory." Indeed, if, as Joshua Yumibe argues, color has been used by the industry to create a "gendered spectacle" that foregrounds the woman's body and its eroticism, one can also say that in Sirk's self-conscious Hollywood melodrama color becomes a race spectacle as well, displaying particularly what Dyer calls the "politics of looking at whiteness."[7] Sirk's melodramatic spectacle not only calls into question the white upper-class lifestyle of Lora but foregrounds the mobility of color and race in the character of Sarah Jane, who passes for white. It further underscores the violence that overshadows her burdened identity, in particular the savage beating she receives from her white boyfriend upon discovery of her black roots and the cruel binary choice placed upon her, namely to either acknowledge her black mother and embrace the denigration of her race or pass for a lower-class white woman performing for ogling men in seedy bars.

The above-described nativity scene, which carries strong metaphorical overtones, can be read as the failed birth of Sarah Jane to a proper identity and citizenship. The scene highlights the birth of Susie's identity adumbrated with lighting and supporting mise-en-scène in stark contrast to Sarah Jane's sense of entrapment. This scene eventually finds its counterpart in the final funeral scene, giving belated birth to Sarah Jane's tragic identity and that of her mother in death, who is now finally adumbrated in whiteness. The film's iconography suggests the continuing social death of African Americans, while at the same time trying to move their identity toward images of rebirth as seen in the many melodramatic and humanized close-ups during the funeral. As the invisible support system of whiteness, African Americans are finally brought to the camera's full attention.

The film's intersectional representation creates a complex network of overlapping race, gender, class, and other social identities at once at odds with but also partially informing the normative social hierarchies of 1950s U.S.

culture. Intersectionality brings together formal aesthetics and praxis and points to the not always seen link between aesthetics and ethics as systems of articulated powers. In line with this demand, this anthology has assembled a highly diverse group of contributors whose work ranges over the entire history of Hollywood cinema as well as its many genres. Each era of film and each film genre, as these essays show, comes with its own intersectional dynamics, requiring careful analysis and reevaluation.

INTERSECTIONALITY, REPRESENTATION, AND HOLLYWOOD

"Intersectionality" is a term coined in black feminist civil rights advocacy and generally refers to the fact that social subjects are constituted in multiple, aggregated, and interconnected shades of identities. As Patricia Hill Collins and Sirma Bilge explain the concept, "People's lives and the organization of power in a given society are better understood as being shaped not by a single axis of social division, be it race or gender or class, but by many axes that work together and influence each other."[8] A legal term first used to address specifically systemic violence against women of color and its omission in feminist and antiracist movements, intersectionality expresses the ironic and contradictory situation of social justice being preferentially advanced for some groups while being withheld from others. As Kimberlé Crenshaw, an early pioneer of intersectionality in legal studies, observes, "Although racism and sexism readily intersect in the lives of real people, they seldom do in feminist and antiracist practices."[9] Before this terminology was actively used, however, bell hook's study *Ain't I a Woman: Black Women and Feminism* (1982) paved the way for Crenshaw's legal approach to intersectionality in social justice.[10] Both hooks's and Crenshaw's pioneering advances in intersectional theories, particularly with regard to social justice, systemic oppression, and advocacy, stress the fundamental co-construction of identity in their intersections, including race, gender, sexuality, class, and nationalism. This concern was anticipated in the work of 1960s black feminist activists and writers such as Nikki Giovanni, Audre Lorde, Michele Wallace, and Toni Cade Bambara.

While intersectionality is traditionally associated with social/legal ethics and activism, its strong link to the struggle of representation cannot be overlooked. Although representation has its immediate practical meaning in the realm of politics, namely in the election of representatives of a community or government, its figurative meaning extends into the larger structural grid of language and signification and the systemic power relations supported by it. For example, Stuart Hall, British cultural theorist and cofounder of the Birmingham School of Cultural Studies, insists that the complex ways in which we identify with one another via various forms of cultural kinship and hierarchies cannot be disconnected from representation: "Signs can only convey meaning if we possess codes which allow us to translate our concepts into language—and vice versa. These codes are crucial for meaning and representation. They do not exist in nature but are the result of social conventions. They are a crucial part of our culture—our shared 'maps of meaning'—which we learn and unconsciously internalize as we become members of our culture. This constructionist approach to language thus introduces the symbolic domain of life."[11] As Hall notes, representation as the symbolic domain of life is a constant struggle with the act of signification, one defined by a symbolic matrix from within which one has to operate and navigate the maps of meaning and power. In short, "It is not the material world which conveys meaning: it is the language system or whatever system we are using to represent our concepts."[12] Within this linguistic turn of culture, inaugurated by the modern linguistic theories of Ferdinand de Saussure and the philosophy of language of Ludwig Wittgenstein, all forms of social action are first constituted as forms of representation. Language, our ability to represent meaning, does not follow the material world but precedes it and frames it in variously articulated social codes, conventions, and positions of power.

Modernist theorists of representation in art, literature, and film have often touched upon systemic intersectional social identities, though not necessarily using the term with a consideration of race. Russian theorist Mikhail Bakhtin, for example, viewed the novel as a plurivocal and heteroglot construct, undermining the traditional notion of the monologic voice of the author.[13] Instead, the novel is said to express conflicting, overlapping, and competing class discourses simultaneously, throwing established social hierarchies into chaos. Theorists grappling with the modern mass medium of film, starting as early as Walter Benjamin, have pointed to the composite patchwork of self and character on cinema screens, one produced in postproduction through the manipulation of editing, hence usurping the actor's original performance in front of the camera and subjecting it to rearrangement and artificial assemblage.[14] Similarly, Gilles Deleuze and Félix Guattari's concept of minor literature puts forward a type of writing that undermines the existing codes of national and cultural norms from within and erodes their dominance via complex forms of parody and ironization, as given in their prime example of the modernist works of Franz Kafka.[15] More recently, interventions in postcolonial and border culture discourse, notably Frantz Fanon's groundbreaking work on black colonial identity navigating whiteness, Edward Said's study of Orientalism, Gayatri Spivak's concept of the subaltern, Gloria Anzaldúa's work on Chicana cultural theory, and Ronald Takaki and Gary Okihiro's comparative histories of Hawai'i and Asian Americans have also called the monolithic notion of nationhood and its representation into question and complicated the understanding of citizenship as one of multiple cultural affiliations.[16] Similarly, advances in queer theory by Michel Foucault, Judith Butler, and Eve Sedgwick have redefined the spectrum of sexuality and gender, challenging heteronormative cultural concepts.[17]

Bearing in mind Benjamin's discussion of film as well as Siegfried Kracauer's concept of film as the expression of a modern mass ornament, one can begin to understand that this specific technologically inflected medium with its large reach of audiences could potentially be perfect for articulating intersectional identities and systemic ideologies.[18] However, when looking closer at Hollywood film history, a history shaped by its normative codes privileging white male heterosexuality, the profile of the classic Hollywood hero, intersectionality appears to have been actively negated or rendered non-existent for the sake of pure entertainment and commodity value. Yet, as this volume argues, such exclusion can never be entirely achieved in film, with the camera functioning as an inhuman apparatus and neutral recording device that frequently refuses or sidelines the ideological manipulation to which it is subjected in the Hollywood industry. The visual Hollywood text, if read critically against its grain, will ultimately reveal the intersectional traces covered up by the industry's codes. Film scholar Miriam Hansen, for instance, challenges the typification of Hollywood as a monolithic expression of mass culture, a view advanced by Max Horkheimer and Theodor Adorno's analysis of the Hollywood culture industry as a systemic form of capitalist mass deception.[19] Its new sensorium, she claims, can accommodate a heterogeneous mass audience and reflect the constitutive ambivalence of modernity: "Whether we like it or not, American movies of the classical period offered something like the first global vernacular."[20] Classical Hollywood cinema, Hansen notes, "not only . . . attracted and made visible to itself . . . an emerging, heterogeneous mass public ignored and despised by dominant culture. The new medium also offered an alternative because it engaged the contradictions of modernity at the level of the senses."[21] In spite of Hollywood's codes and imposed hierarchies, the new sensorium embedded in the medium also cuts across these artificial boundaries and lays bare its power structures to a perceptive and critical audience. In this respect, film can be read as a map of the organization of power in society, pointing to its repressed intersectional spaces.

Our present volume builds on this critical way of looking at Hollywood film,[22] reading its visual (and sound) aesthetics in reverse, that is, in a counterintuitive and critical fashion. Maya Deren speaks of the "controlled accident" as the most successful way of making films, allowing the camera, an inhuman apparatus, its own objective discoveries not immediately apparent to the subjective human eye.[23] In this context, Hollywood films, as products of great systematic effort expressed via cinematography, acting, sound, and editing, may tell only one obvious story set out by the industry's guidelines and formulas. Intersectionality is generally concealed through its classical system that privileges single typified or idealized identities, covering up complex webs of social and cultural negotiation. While this omission is achieved through casting, editing, lighting, setting, sound manipulation, and mise-en-scène, contributing to seamless continuity and perfection of the formula, a closer critical analysis of films will also reveal how overt intersectional representations can in fact challenge such a monolithic system. The purpose, then, of this volume is to revisit significant films as well as their influence on TV and independent cinema. What lies beyond the frame? What elements contradict a film's sustained illusion of a normative world? Where do films betray their own ideology? And most important, what intersectional spaces of identity do they attempt to conceal?

SUMMARY OF ESSAYS

The various essays in this anthology should be seen as forays and experiments in the hermeneutics of intersectionality. The volume by no means claims to be inclusive of every aspect of social and cultural intersectionality depicted in Hollywood cinema; rather, the volume offers an attempt with its various contributions to establish new ways of reading film. In doing so, the readings try to comprehend the complex sensorium of cinema and its interaction with spectator and the world of social reality.

The first part of this volume, "Hollywood Formulas," challenges the developmental myth of the progressive growth of early cinema toward a closed set of codes and formulas defining classical Hollywood, hence turning its perception into a monolithic institution. Challenging this perception, Ruth Mayer's discussion of three transitional silent films, namely *All Night* (dir. Paul Powell, 1918), *Male and Female* (dir. Cecil B. DeMille, 1919), and *The Whispering Chorus* (dir. Cecil B. DeMille, 1918), pays close attention to their embedded fantasies of social mobility cutting across class and gender divides. In doing so, she claims, the films' narratives provide not only hierarchical upheavals but also lateral space for the expression of more individualized identities aggregated from multiple contexts. Class, for example, turns merely into an exchangeable costume rather than a social contingency. Gender becomes equally unstable and its inscriptions rest mostly on performance rather than biology. The films' playful and aesthetic concerns lie not with the attainment of power and control but rather with the "projection of desire onto somebody else," daydreaming in the sense of Siegfried Kracauer and not the exclusive capitalist dream of social mobility. This play with the possibilities of representation also defines the art of Lon Chaney Sr., the master of disguise in silent cinema or "man of a thousand faces." Alice Maurice's essay on Chaney focuses on his transition from silent to his first and final sound film, *The Unholy Three* (dir. Jack Conway, 1930). This film, according to Maurice, highlights "the uneasy relationship between masculinity and disguise, revealing the cultural work performed by the seeming paradox that Chaney embodied: the authenticity of disguise." As sound significantly challenges the credibility of visual disguise, the film and its surrounding publicity campaign had to resort to "racial stereotypes, fantasies of blackness, and working-class labor . . . as props for white masculinity." Chaney's final film, signaling the end of his fluid disguises, turns toward the unmasking of his art and what was left of authenticity in Chaney himself.

Ellen C. Scott's archival reconstruction of the production history of *Gorgeous Hussy* (dir. Clarence Brown, 1936) focuses on the film adaptation of Samuel Hopkins Adams's novel. In various screen treatments by MGM and RKO studios examined by Scott, elements from the novel such as a highly visible African American population in the nation's capital, slave markets, brothels for interracial sex, and an attempted lynching are still included and even embellished in lurid fashion. As Scott points out, "MGM's *Gorgeous Hussy* screenplay represented a bold, ribald experiment with suggesting the Southern woman's desire for a male slave." However, once the film enters production and undergoes PCA (Production Code Administration) censorship, the representation of slavery is entirely removed from the film and remains extant only in the film's publicity campaign. The film's conflicted production history and engagement with its representation of slavery becomes thereby a rich intersectional source.

Yellowface and minstrelsy performance, a demeaning though popular and acceptable form of race representation in Hollywood unlike slavery, undergoes, as Delia Konzett's essay on several installments from the Charlie Chan series shows, a profound transformation in the 1930s with an attempt to put it to use for liberal and progressive ideologies tied to the national interest in the conflict region of the Asia-Pacific. This new use of yellowface is promoted in films such as *The Black Camel* (1931), *Charlie Chan in Egypt* (1935), and *Charlie Chan at the Olympics* (1937) that fall somewhere in between A and B list films, hence allowing for a greater transgression of codes. Paradoxically, the result is a psychotic landscape of representations in which the lead character Charlie Chan played in yellowface by Warner Oland surrounds himself with a large family cast exclusively with Asian Americans, hence undermining the illusion of his racial minstrelsy performance as well as that of Stepin Fetchit in *Chan in Egypt*. The films' contradictory undertaking to combat racism via racist stereotyping reveals much of the representational confusion of 1930s Hollywood defined by the cultural norms of Jim Crow segregation and its conflicted attempts to move beyond it.

The second part, "Genre and Race in Classical Hollywood," explores generic conventions of the Western, musical, melodrama, and film noir and their various attempts to express the repressed question of race in the apartheid culture and cinema of the United States. In doing so, the films also rethink the entire configuration of race, gender, and class in each of their genres. Jonna Eagle, for example, discusses the unconventional Western *The Ox-Bow Incident* (dir. William Wellman, 1943), which takes up the theme of frontier justice and its miscarriage in the form of lynching. As an anti-Western foregrounding toxic rather than heroic masculinity, "the film's deviation from generic convention marks its negotiation of race, and of whiteness specifically, through and in relation to its construction of gender, ultimately suggesting both the instability and the constitutive violence of normative masculinity itself." By giving the African American preacher Sparks a central role as the narrative's moral authority, the film turns its indictment of violence into a not so thinly disguised critique of racism. Ryan Friedman's essay revisits the Hollywood musical and its African American specialty performers who at once are supposed to adumbrate the white hero/ine without getting in his or her way or stealing the limelight. Cameo performances by Hazel Scott and Lena Horne in Eleanor Powell's musical *I Dood It* (dir. Vincente Minelli, 1943) are primarily meant to lend the film production value but can now, as Friedman shows, be read against the grain of the film's narrative and publicity. Thus, "white appropriations of African American musical culture . . . [create] a platform for African American performers working Hollywood that is both unusually prominent and marked by a very specific set of intersectional constraints."

Charlene Regester's essay takes a closer look at mother-daughter relationships in the melodramas *Imitation of Life* (dir. John Stahl, 1934) and *Stella Dallas* (dir. King Vidor, 1937). Regester compares the pursuits of race and class transcendence and its various forms of social and racial masquerades. Her reading foregrounds parallelisms and asymmetries in both films, establishing a connection between forms of social passing and performance of racial identity. As Regester notes, "Regardless as to how these imitations destabilize the categories to which they aspire, Peola and Stella's performances certainly hint at the fluidity of race and class categories and demonstrate how they become parallel characters." Since women occupy the center of Hollywood melodramas, both films also refract the representation of race and class through a gendered point of view. Matthias Konzett's discussion "The Egotistical Sublime: Film Noir and Whiteness" points out that the absence or limited amount of race representations in the classic noir genre is not necessarily an indication that the question of race is not somehow addressed. However, as he suggests, this subversive anti-Hollywood Hollywood genre, instead of taking up America's dark underside of racism, becomes entrapped in desperate myths of white sublimity as given, for instance, in the iconic film *Double Indemnity* (dir. Billy Wilder, 1944). Its inbuilt self-destructive white narcissism prevents the genre from ultimately becoming as subversive as it imagined itself to be. Michael Curtiz's *The Breaking Point* (1950), a film mostly concerned with the social downfall of its white lead protagonist, hints in its unexpected final scene openly at systemic racism.

The postwar era ushered in a new take on intersectional representation by adding a more realistic social problem agenda to many of its films. The part "Race and Ethnicity in Post–World War II Hollywood" deals with the increased social awareness of the industry and examines its multifaceted push for pressing social issues concerning race, ethnicity, gender, class, and national identity. Chris Cagle's essay discusses three immigrant dramas, namely *A Tree Grows in Brooklyn* (dir. Elia Kazan, 1945), *I Remember Mama* (dir. George Stevens, 1948), and *The Lawless* (dir. Joseph Losey, 1950). Whereas the first two films mostly take a retrospective and nostalgic view on turn-of-the-century immigration, focusing on the gains and losses of assimilation, *The Lawless* addresses xenophobia and racism in the present directly. The films' shared concerns with class mobility/transcendence and cultural integration, moreover, are refracted through the perspective of women who "are the main immigrant protagonists in each" and are closely associated with the promotion of education and literacy. Dean Itsuji Saranillio's discussion of the film *Go for Broke!* (dir. Robert Pirosh, 1951), documenting the heroic conduct of the mostly Hawaiian Japanese American 442nd Regiment during World War II, critically examines its representation of nationhood, citizenship, and culture and in its intersectional focus addresses the routinely overlooked colonial status of Hawai'i. The film, as Saranillio claims, not only presented its bid for overdue Hawaiian statehood but signaled the ascendancy in Hawaiian affairs of Japanese Hawaiians, an ethnic group now pitted against native Hawaiians in the attempt of the United States to retain much of its colonial power over its territory once it transitioned to statehood. "The state," notes Saranillio, "animated by profit motives, created the conditions for an official antiracism to facilitate forms of settler colonialism under the name of statehood."

By the 1960s, the critical examination of social identity becomes more evident on screen, as, for instance, in John Frankenheimer's film *The Young Savages* (1961). Graham Cassano views this film in comparison with Jacques Lacan's skeptical notions of reification. In a crime plot that pits immigrant groups against one another, namely the white ethnic Italian and Irish Americans against the racialized Puerto Ricans, the assistant DA Hank Bell (Burt Lancaster) finds himself on both sides of the fence, articulating the film's critical engagement with norms of whiteness and coercive assimilation. As Cassano argues, "*The Young Savages* questions the concept of whiteness, recognizes race as a social construction, but pulls back from that recognition and ultimately leaves the normative racial order intact." This sense of incomplete critical engagement with white norms in the increasingly liberal Hollywood haunts this institution to the present day, quick to pay lip service to marginalized groups without fundamentally altering its established industry practices. Priscilla Peña Ovalle's essay looks at the particular use of costume and hair in the case of Rita Moreno, pointing to various exploitative practices by the film industry and Moreno's own attempt to navigate this complex terrain of limited available screen identities for Latina actresses. "The styling of her hair for different types of roles," argues Ovalle, "reveals cinematic codes that like costume and performance artificially and systematically convey information and reinforce assumptions about each character's supposed identity in terms of race, gender, sexuality, class, age, and more."

A final part, "Intersectionality, Hollywood, and Contemporary Popular Culture," highlights various films struggling with the concept of multiculturalism and whether it can account for its intersectional complexity or simply implies a naïve concept of tolerance and coexistence, while preserving the status quo. Ernesto R. Acevedo-Muñoz discusses the contemporary TV series *Glee* (2009–2015), specifically its third season that features a production of the classic Hollywood musical *West Side Story* (dir. Robert Wise, 1961). The TV series, which is scripted as a backstage musical, places the casting and audition for the role of the lead Puerto Rican character María at the center of its unfolding drama. Comparing the multicultural TV series to the original casting of *West Side Story* and various subsequent productions of the musical, Acevedo-Muñoz, an expert of the latter's production history, notes that "in the postracial fantasy of *Glee*, 'color blind casting' means 'white default'" and perpetuates "the Puerto Rican erasure from the lead part of *West Side Story*." Conversely, the lesser role of Anita is predictably cast with an ethnic Latina meant to embody all the Hollywood stereotypes of "the Latin 'spitfire' woman." As a consequence, *Glee*'s intersectional engagement of *West Side Story*, mostly focused on melodrama, "continues to blunt the impact of a theatrical property once considered edgy and controversial, and perpetuates the marginalization of its political and cultural context." Mary Beltrán likewise explores the musical genre, focusing on the multicultural dance musical of the 1980s, such as *Fame* (1980) and *Flashdance* (1983) and their updated articulations in the *Step Up* film series (2006, 2008, 2010). While the newer films address the evolving racial and class politics featured in this genre, they also posit an imaginary postracial utopia "in which a rainbow-hued group of vaguely ethnic individuals easily form a happy and harmonious community." Hip-hop, according to Beltrán, adds the "performative glue that holds the diverse community together," while also making a commercial appeal to international audiences. As with *Glee*'s appropriation of *West Side Story*, the *Step Up* franchise similarly sanitizes the political context of hip-hop, allowing for white leadership in its postracial scenarios and a street culture resembling the middle-class status quo.

Whereas commercial and popularized versions of multiculturalism on screen show a naïve tendency to proclaim prematurely a postracial society, independent films typically define themselves against the norms of Hollywood and frequently take a sober look at the difficulty of negotiating a complex landscape of identities. Jun Okada's essay revisits the 1991 LA riots in two films, *Fakin' da Funk* (1997) and *Gook* (2017), speaking to the tensions in Asian American and African American relations. Unlike the first film, a lighthearted teen comedy intended to heal the wounds of racial tension and address some of the prevalent cultural stereotypes, the second film *Gook* "offers perhaps a more measured pessimism, not only about the riots and the possibility of racial healing, but also about the viability of an independent Asian American film aesthetic." The focus of Okada's inquiry resides with the question whether a hood film, a filmic prototype in the representation of African Americans in the inner city, can also be produced from the perspective of Asian Americans (e.g., Korean Americans), sharing particularly, as in the case of the South Central LA riots, adjoining neighborhoods with African Americans, and sometimes similar experiences in spite of their asymmetrical histories in the United States. Louise Wallenberg's essay explores the intersectional space of queerness in the African American community in the films *Tongues Untied* (1989) and *Moonlight* (2016). The semi-documentary *Tongues Untied* figures in many ways as a forerunner to the Oscar-awarded *Moonlight*, as both films "[represent] a multitude of black masculinities." Whereas Marlon Riggs's *Tongues Untied* tends to be more programmatic and vociferous about embracing black gay identity, Barry Jenkins's *Moonlight* takes a quiet, poetic, and often inherently contradictory approach to the representation of black gay masculinity, stressing its changing definition in situational contexts. Pitting black hypermasculinity from the ghetto film against unexpected moments of care and empathy in *Moonlight*'s coming-of-age story of its protagonist and his embrace of gay identity, Jenkins pushes, according to Wallenberg, the representation of identity from older binary either/or formulas into a subtler articulation of intersectionality involving Stuart Hall's notion of hidden histories.

CONCLUSION: PERVERTED CINEMA OR *THE DEVIL FINDS WORK*

Slavoj Žižek comments on film's peculiar relay of our desires in *The Pervert's Guide to Cinema*: "The problem for us is not, 'Are our desires satisfied or not?' The problem is 'How do we know what we desire?' There is nothing spontaneous, nothing natural, about human desires. Our desires are artificial. We have to be taught to desire. Cinema is the ultimate pervert art. It doesn't give you what you desire, it tells you how to desire."[24] According to Žižek, cinema artificially creates and shapes our desires, a systemic network of mimetic struggle. As the central protagonist in global cinema, Hollywood frames the world for its audiences, structures its social, racial, and sexual desires, and interposes itself as a cultural grammar or matrix in all forms of interpersonal and social relationships. James Baldwin approaches Hollywood in his *The Devil Finds Work* (1976) more from within its concrete historical context as a cinema that was born in the United States marked by its legacy of slavery. Referring to Hollywood's early film icons such as Rudolph Valentino or Weissmuller's Tarzan, Baldwin notes, "Both the Sheik and Tarzan are white men who look and act like black men—act like black men, that is, according to the white imagination which has created them."[25] It is not surprising that one of the founding thinkers for the concept of intersectionality, bell hooks, similarly would turn to film criticism with an oppositional gaze. As she aptly summarizes cinema's foundational role in today's culture, "Movies do not merely offer us the opportunity to reimagine the culture we most intimately know on the screen, they make culture."[26] Discussing our entrapment in Hollywood's regime of fantasy via the film *The Matrix* (1999), Žižek demands a third pill that does away with the artificial binary choice of the blue or red pill, of either staying within fantasyland or exiting the matrix:

> The choice between the blue and the red pill is not really a choice between illusion and reality. Of course, the matrix is a machine for fictions, but these are fictions which already structure our reality. If you take away from our reality

the symbolic fictions that regulate it, you lose reality itself. I want a third pill. So what is the third pill? Definitely not some kind of transcendental pill which enables a fake fast-food religious experience, but a pill that would enable me to perceive not the reality behind the illusion but the reality in illusion itself.[27]

This third pill, somewhere between "the reel and the real," to use hooks's terms, is crucial to the understanding of cinema as the foundational grammar of our social and cultural interactions. Critical examinations of Hollywood's systemic rhetoric, as given in our intersectional approaches to its various articulations, work in this spirit of observing the inherent connection of aesthetics and ethics as given in representation and thereby trying to detect and understand the reality in illusion itself.

NOTES

1. Stuart Hall, "The Work of Representation," in *Representation: Cultural Representation and Signifying Practices*, ed. Stuart Hall (London: Sage, 1993), 20.
2. For a discussion of the original 1934 version, see Charlene Regester's essay in this volume.
3. Erving Goffman, *The Presentation of Self in Everyday Life* (Norwell, MA: Anchor, 1959).
4. See my discussion of the possibilities of color film to address race in *Hollywood's Hawaii: Race, Nation, and War* (New Brunswick, NJ: Rutgers University Press, 2017), 172–181.
5. Richard Dyer, "The Glow of White Women," in *White* (London: Routledge, 1997), 122–142.
6. bell hooks, "The Oppositional Gaze: Black Female Spectators," in *Feminist Film Theory: A Reader*, ed. Sue Thornman (New York: New York University Press, 1999), 307–320.
7. Joshua Yumibe, *Moving Color: Early Film, Mass Culture, Modernism* (New Brunswick, NJ: Rutgers University Press, 2012), 49; Dyer, *White*, 8.
8. Patricia Hill Collins and Sirma Bilge, *Intersectionality* (Malden, MA: Polity, 2016), 2.
9. Kimberlé Crenshaw, "Mapping the Margins: Intersectionality, Identity Politics, and Violence Against Women of Color," *Stanford Law Review* 43, no. 6 (July 1991): 1241–1299, 1242.
10. bell hooks, *Ain't I a Woman: Black Women and Feminism* (Boston: South End, 1982).
11. Hall, "Work of Representation," 13–74, 28–29.
12. Hall, "Work of Representation," 25.
13. See Mikhail Bakhtin, *The Dialogic Imagination: Four Essays*, trans. Michael Holquist and Caryl Emerson (Austin: University of Texas Press, 1983).
14. Walter Benjamin, "The Work of Art in the Age of Technological Reproducibility," in *Critical Visions in Film Theory*, ed. Timothy Corrigan, Patricia White, and Peta Mazaj (Boston: Bedford/St. Martin's, 2011), 230–252.

15. See Gilles Deleuze and Félix Guattari, *Kafka: Toward a Minor Literature*, trans. Dana Polan (Minneapolis: University of Minnesota Press, 1986).

16. Frantz Fanon, *Black Skin, White Masks*, trans. Richard Philcox (1952; New York: Grove, 2008); Edward W. Said, *Orientalism* (New York: Random House, 1978); Gayatri Chakravorty Spivak, *Can the Subaltern Speak?* (Basingstoke: Macmillan, 1988); Gloria Anzaldúa, *Borderland/Frontera: The New Mestiza* (San Francisco: Aunt Lute Books, 1987); Ronald Takaki, *Strangers from a Different Shore: A History of Asian Americans* (New York: Penguin, 1989); Takaki, *A Different Mirror: A History of Multicultural America* (New York: Little, Brown, 1993); Gary Y. Okihiro, *Margins and Mainstreams: Asians in American History and Culture* (Seattle: University of Washington Press, 1994); Okihiro, *Island World: A History of Hawai'i and the United States* (Berkeley: University of California Press, 2008); Okihiro, *Pineapple Culture* (Berkeley: University of California Press, 2009).

17. Michel Foucault, *The History of Sexuality* (1976, 1984; New York: Vintage, 1990); Judith Butler, *Gender Trouble* (London: Routledge, 1990); Eve Kosofsky Sedgwick, *Between Men: English Literature and Male Homosocial Desire* (New York: Columbia University Press, 1985).

18. See Siegfried Kracauer, "The Mass Ornament," *The Mass Ornament: Weimar Essays*, trans. and ed. Thomas Y. Levin (Cambridge, MA: Harvard University Press, 1995), 75–86.

19. Max Horkheimer and Theodor W. Adorno, "The Culture Industry: Enlightenment as Mass Deception," in *Dialectic of Enlightenment*, trans. John Cumming (1944; New York: Continuum, 1990), 120–167.

20. Miriam Hansen, "The Mass Production of the Senses: Classical Cinema as Vernacular Modernism," *Modernism/modernity* 6, no. 2 (April 1999): 59–77, 68.

21. Hansen, "Mass Production of the Senses," 70.

22. See bell hooks, *Reel to Real: Race, Class and Sex at the Movies* (London: Routledge, 1996); Michael Rogin, *Blackface, White Noise: Jewish Immigration in the Hollywood Melting Pot* (Berkeley: University of California Press, 1996); Dyer, *White*; Daniel Bernardi, ed., *Classic Hollywood, Classic Whiteness* (Minneapolis: University of Minnesota Press, 2001); Lester D. Friedman, ed., *Unspeakable Images: Ethnicity and the American Cinema* (Urbana: University of Illinois Press, 1991); Mary Beltrán and Camille Fojas, eds. *Mixed Race Hollywood* (New York: New York University Press, 2008).

23. Maya Deren, "Cinematography: The Creative Use of Reality," in Corrigan, White, and Mazaj, *Critical Visions in Film Theory*, 146–156, 151.

24. Slavoj Žižek, "Introduction," in *The Pervert's Guide to Cinema*, dir. Sophie Fiennes (Microcinema, 2008).

25. James Baldwin, *The Devil Finds Work* (1976; New York: Vintage, 2011), 41.

26. bell hooks, *Reel to Real: Race, Class and Sex at the Movies* (London: Routledge, 1996), 12.

27. Žižek, *Pervert's Guide to Cinema*, pt. I.

PART 1

HOLLYWOOD FORMULAS

Codes, Masks, Genre, and Minstrelsy

1 · DAYDREAMS OF SOCIETY

Class and Gender Performances in the Cinema of the Late 1910s

RUTH MAYER

Intersectional theory's insistence that the structures of social distinction and identification are entangled and overdetermined not only has left its mark on social and cultural analyses but also has affected the debates of film and media studies. Obviously, the insight that race, class, gender, age, ability, and other categories of inequality draw upon each other in complicated ways and cannot be reduced to the logic of binary distinctions bears promising implications for any approach concerned with social and cultural meaning making. With regard to the history of film, the conceptual metaphor of an expansive network of distinctions and interactions that organizes intersectional theory not only reverberates with the productivity of genre, as Janet Staiger has pointed out,[1] but may also serve to identify the ways in which difference and diversity are being enacted visually and spatially. As this essay shows, in the late 1910s, at a key period of industrial and mass-cultural mobilization, films envision class and gender negotiations in settings and plots that highlight very concrete crossings in space and time. They use visual and narrative structures of coincidence, simultaneity, parallelism, or correspondence to explore the possibilities that contemporary conceptualizations of class and gender yield.

To focus on such structures may also help to contribute to a reinterpretation of the period itself. The 1910s, the so-called transitional era between early film and the Hollywood system, have been traditionally seen in terms of linear direction and technical, formal, and narrative progression. In keeping with such a directed reading of history, film studies tended to approach the late 1910s as the end of transition and the beginning of a long period of stylistic consolidation and perfection that the cinema of the teens prepared and envisioned. More recently, this idea of a smooth development from early to classical film has been contested.[2] Ben Singer characterized the transitional period in terms of "a complex dynamic process in which disparate forces—competing paradigms and practices—overlap and interact."[3] He is thus taking recourse to a set of markers that also feature prominently in the lexicon of intersectional theory—and this conceptualization of film history in terms of competitive trends, dead ends, loops, and parallel tracks seems to capture the dynamic of development beyond the 1910s much better than the image of the ascending (or descending) line. The films of the late 1910s that I discuss may be more sophisticated than earlier films in their narration and technical realization, but they by no means abandon the spirit of trial and error that has been made out as the dominant principle of the transitional period.

This feature manifests itself on the level of style as well as in the films' plots and character mapping. While cinema has always been a vat filled with a highly volatile and instable mix of ingredients, by the late teens its capacity to juggle narrative formulas, viewer expectations, ideological agendas, and technological innovation has reached an unprecedented momentum. By then, what James Snead has identified as cinema's "polymorphic perverse oscillation between possible roles, creating a radically broadened freedom of identification" had become a refined mechanism, particularly with respect to the invocation and cross-referencing of ideologically precarious categories of social distinction.[4] I take my cue from recent critical observations on how such categories inadvertently change their shape and function through the indirect and allusive usage of genre conventions, formulaic storytelling, or the star system.[5] All of these frames impact on the ways in which narratives are received and interpreted, but their processing and recognition in turn depend heavily on factors of personal or social identification. How an instance of genre crossing, the employment of a narrative convention, or a casting decision is recognized and read hinges heavily, after all, on a spectator's cultural horizon, value system, degree of information, and awareness of all sorts of subtle implications, submerged messages, or unacknowledged biases.

This mode of reception corresponds with Siegfried Kracauer's assessment of the films of a slightly later period of time as the "*daydreams of society,* in which its actual reality comes to the fore and its otherwise repressed wishes take on form."[6] The daydream expresses a particularly pregnant reflection of possibilities, disclosing options and opportunities, figurations and forma-tions next to, above, or underneath the real. The daydream is about things that might have been or may still come about, about variations and versions, roads that were not taken, decisions that are still open, hunches that were ignored or misinterpreted. These are the worlds of the cinema, and in the films of the late teens they tend to be displayed in their fictional and fiction-alizing character: as stories told from the vantage point of the "what if." In what follows I focus on the popular narratives of masquerades of class in the films of the late 1910s. What if he was the master and not the butler? What if they were our servants rather than our friends? What if one could just disappear? Of course, none of these stories can be told on the grounds of a symbolic repertory of social status, financial assets, habitus, and class condi-tioning alone; they call up, inadvertently or explicitly, the conceptualization of race and ethnicity, of sexuality and gender, of ability and age.

The cinematic ecology of the late 1910s in the United States seems to exem-plify the intuition of intersectionality that the processes and principles of identification and identity formation overlap and interfere with each other. In particular, the assumption that categories of exclusion and distinction take effect simultaneously but unevenly resonates strongly with the filmic enact-ment of difference and diversity, as we shall see. With regard to film, the *simul-taneous* operation of all sorts of identifying factors and forces has to be addressed in the context of other features of temporal organization: duration and instantaneity, routines and ruptures, regularity, acceleration, belatedness, and, perhaps most importantly, given the predominance of the daydream mode, the *mise-en-abime* that figures forth simultaneous but bracketed events that reflect a larger order brokenly, as inversions or miniatures or distorted reflections. The fantasy of a time out is particularly pertinent for a cinematic system that responded to "the mastery of time and space by new technolo-gies" by establishing "flexible but systematic spatial and temporal relations" in its own right, as Tom Gunning writes about the transitional era.[7] In the films that I analyze, the interlinkage of larger temporal regimes and smaller framed temporal orders is addressed when exceptional situations effect the temporary inversion, suspension, or rupture of regular routines and social relations. During the time out, categories of identification and distinction are no less entangled than in their routine operation, but they enter into either disturbing or exhilarating new combinations that highlight their constructedness—although not necessarily their changeability.

I argue my case with close attention to three films: *All Night* (dir. Paul Powell, 1918), *Male and Female* (dir. Cecil B. DeMille, 1919), and *The Whispering Chorus* (dir. Cecil B. DeMille, 1918). All three films engage with the implications of social mobility and fluctuation of status and identity as means of coming to terms with change. In all of them particular attention is afforded to a subject position that is often assumed to be the least affected by intersectional dynamics: the white male middle-class perspective. *Male and Female* and *The Whispering Chorus* are social dramas, while *All Night* is a comedy, which gives me a chance to explore a range of generic procedures and techniques. Like many others of the period, these films enact identity performances as a means of reflecting their own medial status and with close reference to the larger transformations characterizing modernity.

TO BE LOOKED AT: *ALL NIGHT*

If one goes by the plot synopses of *All Night* and *Male and Female*, the films seem to address and expose the regimes of class. *All Night* enacts the scenario of a surprise visit of a potential financier to Maude and Bill Harcourt, a society couple with money problems, who just happened to have fired all of their servants. They decide to have a couple of (unmarried but courting) friends take over their role as master and mistress, and to pose as their own servants ("Since we know the house, we can manage easily!"). *Male and Female* tells a similar story in the guise of social drama: here the master/servant constellation is turned around when a family of British aristocrats on a yachting trip gets stranded on a lonely island together with their servants. In this wild and uncultivated world, the butler quickly becomes the master and king of the community, to whom all others are eager to cater. The film ends in the shipwrecked party's rescue and the restitution of the old order—which prompts the butler and maid to emigrate to the American West.

Clearly, these stories gesture to the vagaries of social rank and the arbitrary distinctions of power and submission imposed by class. It is all the more surprising, then, to see that neither film makes much of this theme. While *All Night* is much more concerned with generational difference and sexuality than with class, *Male and Female* projects the issues of class difference onto a complicated matrix of historical and geographical references. In consequence, differences are not so much effaced or suspended but rather shifted around, transposed. Especially gender and sexuality flare up as issues of contention in a manner that inadvertently highlights these factors' interlinkage in an intricate layout that is made out as horizontal, spread out rather than hierarchical. As an effect, social roles are enacted in close conjunction and interdependence—as part of an expansive grid of interlinked factors. If you change around one, everything else shifts in accordance. But eventually, this brings about stability, not disruption.

All Night stars Rudolph Valentino before his stellar career in the 1920s—and as an ethnically nonmarked character. The part also differs starkly in other respects from Valentino's later signature roles: he is a comedic figure, characterized as shy, sexually inexperienced, and easily cowed. The film's title refers to the exceptional and bracketed situation that is brought about when the visiting sponsor spontaneously decides to spend the night rather than just staying for dinner. It also signals to a second story line that explains the friends' presence in the Harcourts' home: Maude Harcourt (Mary Warren) had arranged a dinner party for her friends Dick Thayer, played by Valentino, and Beth Lane (Carmel Myers), to give Dick a chance to catch Beth alone and declare his feelings for her. Beth, who "belongs to one of Kentucky's oldest and most prominent families," is under strict orders by her exacting father, Colonel Lane, to return home before eleven. Since Bradford is staying, she's staying too, and since she is staying, her father will show up, to cause further trouble. Every move in this film elicits countermoves, and in anticipation of the situation comedy, the domestic setting with upstairs and downstairs, bedroom and guestroom, porch and hallway sets the stage for an incessant series of parallel actions, laid out in largely symmetrical fashion. Doors, windows, and staircases function as means to enter and to exit, to go up and down, in and out, leading to ever-changing scenarios of contact and contingency.

The film's plot logic relies on the discrepancy of class, status, and access, but its comic effects derive almost exclusively from what is made out as

FIGURE 1.1 Choreographed smartness in *All Night* (1918).

generational rather than economic or power differences. The two young couples, even though they affect different social roles, are presented as a tightly interlinked entity, moving about in choreographed fashion in a series of shots that punctuate the film—either the women in white to the left and the right and the men in black in the middle, or, a little later, the women to the left of the screen and the men next to each other to the right. When one or more players leave the screen, the others rearrange their positions quickly to create a new symmetry—man in the middle, women together on the side; two women; two men; and so forth. These symmetries of arrangement express a closeness based on age and habitus that seems to defy the crude categories of class, race, or gender, since it relies on fine-tuned practices, tastes, and intuitions (see Figure 1.1). These people are a smart set in the usage of the term as it was established in the 1910s: urbane, self-assured, witty, relaxed, and very well dressed.[8] Rudolph Valentino's emergent star personality is based on the aesthetic of smartness—cool, elegant, poised, and well-groomed. "He is superbly dressed in cutaway suits, coats with fur collars, and silk pajamas, so he's not that far from the Valentino we know," writes Jeanine Basinger, who is one of the few critics that sees the film in accordance with the star's impending career rather than as a stark contrast.[9]

When Beth calls home to explain that she is going to spend the night, a black servant picks up the phone ("Massa Colonel has left town, Miss Elizabeth")—and this brief cut to a world outside the Harcourt home exemplarily expresses what this film is *not* about. The difference between the African American servant in the southern mansion of the old and prominent family, and Bill Harcourt, the dapper young society man pretending to be a servant, is so absolute that it cannot be expressed in the film's relational aesthetics. In the film's logic, class is something that you have, not something that shapes or determines your existence. Only in its debilitating interlinkage with race does it surface as an imposition that cannot simply be shed or disposed of once the job is done. Before Bradford arrives, we can see Bill posing in his butler outfit for Beth and Maude, ironically distancing himself from the garb he is forced to wear. When Bradford then enters, Bill tries to shake his hand rather than take his hat.

The eccentric visitor humiliates the young men and women in every way imaginable, and he does not make much of a difference between the servants and the masters. He molests Maud, he forces a cigar in Dick's mouth, he beats up Bill, he punches Beth on the shoulder, and he insists that his hosts go to bed early and together, since they "ought to have one or two kids," entering their bedroom several times in a bizarre exaggeration of his patriarchal power position. The bedroom setting epitomizes the contrast, when Dick, who has been forced to undress, is mortified, holding up his blanket protectively, as one by one the other protagonists enter and leave, comment, command, consult, and cast amused and desiring glances: after all, the man is looking good and he's good to look at. This is the man of the future, more than the film itself knows, and Bradford's power is comic rather than threatening because it affects a position of privilege and exceptionality that is outdated and more embarrassing than Valentino's *déshabillé*. There is no indication, in all of this, of the powerful and aggressive eroticism of the Sheik, but Valentino's gender performance signals ahead to what Miriam Hansen has identified as a pivotal aspect of the later star cult—that Valentino "seemed to live out the vicissitudes of social change as they affected people's lives."[10] In *All Night*, he is part of a team, a well-rehearsed group of social players, who react rather than act, perform rather than work, and who manage and cope with the conditions as they present themselves rather than trying to shape or change them. This is something that Bradford, as the voice of an older generation, acknowledges at the end of the film, when, alerted to the ruse, he surprisingly volunteers to extend the requested loan after all because he is impressed with Bill's flexibility: "I don't know what kind of businessman you are. . . . However, you do know how to cope with any situation."

HIGH AND LOW, *MALE AND FEMALE*

All Night's "smart" flexibility is marked by the spirit of playful improvisation and wish fulfillment: the daydream, which tests out conditions rather than going up against them, and which always reaffirms the status quo by returning to it eventually. *Male and Female* operates similarly, although the time out of this film is longer and more markedly terminated at the end of this film. Moreover, this film's return to normal is critically reflected by presenting America's classless society of the West as an alternative to a British society that has by then been exposed as decadent and hypocritical. But then again, the West is presented like a clichéd afterthought, while aristocratic flamboyance and eccentricity are what the film is all about. The displays of decadence are steeped in desire for commodities and for people (as far as it makes sense to differentiate between these two in this film) to the extent that the markers of class, hierarchy, and rank all become fetishes. The film's narrative culminates in a diegetic insert that stages the Babylonian court, conflating the antique with the modern in accordance with a larger trend of the silent cinema to conjure up the "modernity of antiquity," as Pantelis Michelakis and Maria Wyke write about silent era costume dramas.[11] The film's narrative justifies the detour to the past through its repeated reference to a line from a poem by William Ernest Henley that inexplicably intrigues the key characters: "Or ever the knightly years were gone / with the old world to the grave, / I was the King in Babylon / and you were a Christian slave." The Babylonian episode is inserted to illustrate, somewhat spuriously, that the butler Crichton (Thomas Meighan), the scullery maid Tweeny (Lila Lee), and Lady Mary Lasenby (Gloria Swanson) are caught in a love triangle that reaches back to antiquity, when their lookalikes and pre-incarnations *were* an ancient king (Crichton), a slave (Mary), and the king's consort (Tweeny). The insert pretends to explain the triangulation of desire between the characters, suggesting that the present can learn from the past or that the past informs the present, but it is not clear what precisely the past teaches or how it persists in the present. Is it that the king has to atone for his cruelty vis-à-vis the slave through centuries of servitude? Is the lady's vanity exposed by the slave's virtuous resistance? Then what is the role of the South Sea island setting in all of this? Is this about differences? Or about similarities? Maureen Turim rightfully pointed out that "the doubled and trebled temporal settings help [DeMille's] films indulge and condemn in a manner that makes no sense except if we understand it through the psychoanalytic trope of denial."[12] Prefiguring DeMille's big historical dramas of the 1920s and after, the Babylonian backstory glamorizes the motif of sexual attraction across class barriers and employs the ancient setting "as a cover, sanctifying the exploration of the sensual, the decorative, the flamboyant."[13] Like in *All Night*, markers of class, status, and social rank are made out as largely performative—or, indeed, decorative—categories in the course of *Male and Female*. There is no larger logic or underlying message to the film's diverging story lines; they do not add up but spread out randomly in kaleidoscopic fashion, calling to mind D. W. Griffith's earlier, much more magisterial "conflation or cannibalization of various layers of tradition" in *Intolerance*.[14]

The film's main characters are introduced at the beginning in a similar mode. A page boy is putting polished shoes in front of a row of doors, and sneaks a look, at this occasion, through each of the keyholes, so that the spectator's first glance at the film's main players is imbued with voyeuristic stealth: each shot is marked as subjective through the use of an iris lens, and the close-ups of the sleeping or waking characters are completed by intertitles introducing the actors and roles. The last such staged intrusion presents the film's star, Gloria Swanson, and here the preceding routine is expanded into a longer sequence of shots. This glance through the keyhole first discloses an untidy pile of lingerie, then cuts to a montage shot of a peacock, the symbol of vanity, onto which the intertitle is superimposed, and then finally shows Lady Mary herself, waking up beautifully in her luxurious art nouveau bed and sounding an antique bell. This introduction, which is interspersed with shots showing the page boy's comically excited response, will then lead over into the film's most iconic scene depicting a lavish bathing routine that merges British upper-class luxury and ancient splendor before the latter even makes a diegetic appearance.

Crichton and Tweeny have been introduced before, but they clearly figure as supporting characters at this stage in the film, or rather, they are made out as spectators, very much like the voyeuristic house boy. In the first scene that presents all three together, Tweeny is transfixed by Mary's shoes that the camera presents in another close-up iris shot, which is then juxtaposed with an iris shot of Tweeny's dilapidated footwear. A little later, a shot depicting Crichton's observation of Mary's dainty eating is cross-cut with a flashback to a previous depiction of Tweeny's healthy appetite. These vignettes, in turn, signal ahead to a later scene on the island when Lady Mary relishes the soup that Crichton made and is reminded through another flashback of her picky table manners back in England. "Comparisons are odious—and sometimes dangerous," runs the intertitle that comments on Crichton's initial correlation of the lady and the scullery maid (see Figure 1.2). But the film at large employs comparisons, interlinkages, cross-cuts, and juxtapositions as its dominant narrative modes. Resemblances, associations, recollections, and

FIGURE 1.2 "Comparisons are odious." *Male and Female* (1919).

analogies organize the way in which storytelling proceeds; the film is a veritable feast of intersections. While it pretends to be about the big topic of transhistorical passion, it really tells numerous small stories of longing and desire that each have their place and time, and need to be carefully bracketed off. Early in the film, Lady Mary's friend Eileen confides in her, telling her of her passion for her chauffeur, a blasé dandy with heavily made-up eyes, who is presented in a montage iris shot, the film's favored mode of communicating desire. Lady Mary warns her not to give in to this impulse—"It's *kind* to *kind*, Eileen, and you and I can never change it." The film condones this injunction, by making Crichton and Mary come together on a lonely island, and disband and return to their "kind," once they return to civilization. But it is important to note that this is no melodramatic tale of love across the class divide, but rather a reflection of propriety, enablement, and possibility.

"His dramas are as intimate as a department store window," film critic Frederick James Smith derided DeMille's *Male and Female* in September 1919 in *Motion Picture Classic*,[15] and he thus captures well the ways in which the film distances itself from its characters' feelings, presenting social settings—the British upper-class world, the South Sea island—like experimental arrangements or display cases, each with its own conditions and regularities that may not be mixed up. *Male and Female* is hardly concerned with the issues it professes to dramatize and actually does foreground this blind spot in its intertitles: "One cannot tell what may be in a man, my Lady! If all were to return to Nature tomorrow, the same man might not be master— nor the same man servant—Nature would decide the matter for us!" muses Crichton bitterly early on in the film, and of course he will soon have a chance to show what's "in him." But what is staged as the return to nature is really just a scene change, depicting a new setting with its own codes of conduct, attire, and culinary choices. It is important to note, after all, that Crichton is not only the one character that adjusts most easily to life on the desert island. He is also the one to return most abruptly to his previous role, shifting gears effortlessly and smoothly as they return to England. It is this very versatility that marks him as superior in the end, and that allows for a happy ending with Tweeny, rather than Lady Mary, on an idealized Western frontier, where, again, he knows just what to do.

The film's title suggests that away from civilization the characters' true gender identities are coming to the fore. But given its various historical and geographical settings, the binary of true and false collapses onto itself. Once more, like in *All Night*, class and gender roles are made out as a loose grid, shifting and changing with the overall conditions and conventions, and are performative rather than essential ascriptions. But in both cases, this does not mean that the categories are made out as arbitrary or even freely negotiable. They are shown to be firmly entrenched in their social settings, and need to be rehearsed, practiced, and performed according to the social script. Miriam Hansen has shown that Rudolph Valentino's sex appeal rested on the filmic ambiguity of the scopic object in terms of the film's explicit narrative it is the woman who is looked at, but "Valentino's appeal depends to a large degree on the manner in which he combines the masculine control of the look with the feminine quality of 'to-be-looked-at-ness,' to use Laura Mulvey's rather awkward term."[16] This dynamic may be specific to the Valentino effect, but it is significant that in *Male and Female* the white male is coming into his own by becoming the *object* of projections and desire, the one who responds to impulses and events rather than actively shaping the circumstances of his sexual and social life.

The desirous glances that Crichton shoots at Lady Mary at the beginning of the film mirror Tweeny's desire for her shoes, and in consequence it might seem as if the film deliberately highlights the divide between privilege and deprivation since it addresses an audience that has probably more in common with the servants than with the masters.[17] In such a reading, films like *Male and Female* would capitalize on eliciting feelings of desire or envy. But I think that the pull of identification that is at work in the late transitional and early classical cinema is more complicated than this, and to make my case I would like to invoke once more Siegfried Kracauer's conjunction of cinematic representation and the daydream. Kracauer points to the logic of upward aspiration inscribed into the Hollywood film, referring to the cliché of the poor girl meets rich guy narrative: "In reality it may not often happen that a scullery maid marries the owner of a Rolls Royce. But doesn't every Rolls Royce owner dream that scullery maids dream of rising to his stature?"[18]

In Kracauer's gloss the dream is that of the rich man, not that of the poor girl, and this seems to me a more appropriate reading of the powers of projection that are at work here, although I doubt that the constellation is as neatly gendered as Kracauer has it. The daydream of modern mass culture, I argue, is driven by a polymorphic perverse dynamic of projection and identification; it aims to pull the viewer into the subject position of the one who is effortlessly in control and at ease, be that a "Rolls Royce owner," or a Babylonian king, or a member of the smart set. In many of these instances of identification, conventional class and gender associations merge, overlap, or intersect, as we have seen.[19] The Valentino hype provided an arena in which this rearrangement of subject positions and perspectives was blatantly cast as a renegotiation of the binaries of gender and sexuality whereas other cinematic narratives proceeded more carefully. But still, playing around with status and with class in the 1910s is no revolutionary endeavor but presents itself, rather, in the conditional terms of the fantasy, the dream, or the speculation.

The films of the late 1910s make out social settings as ever-shifting constellations of options and strictures as force fields of possibilities and forfeitures. From this vantage point, and very much in keeping with Kracauer's assessment, the cinematic mode of the daydream points not primarily to scenarios of social mobility (the poor girl's dream), but rather to phantasmatic imaginations of achieving stability. Even though these films address masquerades of class and status, their momentum hinges not so much on the desire to *become* somebody else, but rather on the *projection* of desire *onto somebody else*. To be desired, to be looked at, to be recognized, to be attended to, these are the values that rule supreme here; this is much more important than to actively command or control. By the same logic, public opinion is made out as a network of intersecting perspectives, expectations, and attitudes that may give shape to the individual or make it disappear.

DISAPPEARANCE ACT: *THE WHISPERING CHORUS*

The Whispering Chorus, DeMille's society drama of 1918, is a narrative of class masquerade only at first glance. It really records the attempt to step away from the defining reach of society altogether. Given the immense significance afforded to contexts, frames, and identifying markers in the cinema of the time, this experiment cannot but fail. Where other films about social masquerades take care to bracket their narrative, marking it as momentary and exceptional, and set it off from the regular order of things, *The Whispering Chorus* defies the mode of the *mise-en-abîme*, totalizing the daydream as it were—and thus turns it into a nightmare, at least for the white male protagonist who ends up on the electric chair for a crime he did not commit. While his story is told straight and without qualifying frame, however, the film soon branches out into two different story lines, one narrating the man's social decline, the other one tracing his wife's ascent.

The film has been discussed mostly with regard to its experimentation with modes of representing consciousness and as an art film, in contrast to DeMille's following, more commercial productions. I focus on its continuities with later productions such as *Male and Female*, however, and on the ways in which the film stages the struggle between social norms and personal inclinations that informs so many narratives of the period, as a psychic drama, projected, as it were, on the screen of the mind. The protagonist's moral predicament and troubled conscience materializes visually as a shadowy "whispering chorus": superimposed shots of faces, representing his good (female: Edna Mae Cooper) and bad (male: Walter Lynch) impulses and a mocking commentator (Gustav von Seyffertitz). Key scenes of the film are thus organized by way of the spatial layout of the intersection, showcasing crucial moments in the protagonist's life that require decisions between two or more possible options: do I go or do I stay, do I speak up or stay silent, should I do this or that? The voices of the silent chorus pinpoint different narrative trajectories, usually by forecasting the consequences of a possible action in the conditional voice or future tense ("What would Jane think of a thief?" / "Don't be a fool! No one will ever know!").

The film tells the story of a disappearance act. Its central character John Tremble (Raymond Hatton) is a small accountant who embezzles a substantial sum of money and runs away when he is about to be found out, leaving his patiently suffering mother (Edythe Chapman) and equally angelic wife Jane (played by serial film star Kathlyn Williams) behind. Living in hiding in a tramp-like existence, he happens to come across the dead body of another tramp, whom he decides to dress up in his clothes and to disfigure, so that he is taken for himself. This act, which is meant to bring about John's liberation from public prosecution, constitutes the decisive step toward his eventual undoing. As John is going down, Jane is rising. Believing her husband to be dead, she falls in love with the prosecutor of his case, who is soon elected governor of the state. At the height of its action, the film proceeds by cross-cutting ever more quickly between the narratives of husband and wife. The cross-editing culminates when Jane's glamorous wedding to the governor is contrasted with John's sad carousing with an Orientalized prostitute. Eventually, John is caught and taken for the murderer of himself. Prodded by the whispering chorus, he decides to face the electric chair rather than destroy the happiness of his wife, who is expecting the governor's child.

The Whispering Chorus differs from the films discussed above in that it does not celebrate white male flexibility but chronicles its fatal momentum. John Tremble is so good at making use of every chance that presents itself to him that he is getting lost in the twist and turns his life takes: totalized, the daydream turns into a nightmare. In keeping with the narrative logic of naturalism, the film presents the individual as heavily entrenched in social relations, in networks of labor and economy, family obligations and ambition.[20] The film's protagonist tries to master these circumstances, but keeps succumbing to larger forces and conditions, as he plunges into his actions with desperation, not elegant poise. John is no smart society man to begin with, he does not stay on top of things, and instead of being looked at, he becomes invisible in the course of the film. Leaving mother and wife behind, he enters an all-male world of physical labor, crime, homelessness, brutality, and alienation that drags him down.

His wife, Jane Tremble, exemplifies the alternative to this demise. At the end of the film, without much of her own doing, she has become "Governor Coggeswell's wife" or the "Governor's lady." She is safely ensconced in social relations, a wife (actually of two husbands), a daughter (ironically to John's mother, of whom she continues to take care), a mother-to-be. By severing his social ties, in contrast, John has also lost his social identity. He is no longer recognized by the law, and when he meets his wife again in court, she does not recognize him either: "No, I never saw him before." John is horrified and his protestations take a telling guise: "I'm John Tremble himself. Governor Coggeswell's wife is my wife." In this strange concatenation of pronouns and possessions, personal identification and distancing are syntactically interlinked to chart a process of disintegration.

When Jane does recognize him a little later, his old bearded appearance is projected on the haggard clean-shaven face of the prisoner. At this point, the filmic modes of superimposition, blurring, fading, and double exposure seem to explode into the narration, suggesting a second layer of reality that

FIGURE 1.3 The screen of the mind. *The Whispering Chorus* (1918).

pushes into view. Now for the first time John's imagination of a surveilling chorus is complemented with a similar vision on Jane's part. In her bedroom, Jane fantasizes about her first and her second husbands, facing their spectral appearances and the sight of her future child beckoning her (see Figure 1.3). Her chorus consists of close family relations, addressing her as wife or mother. In prison, meanwhile, John is haunted by a chorus that no longer consists only of the two voices representing his good and bad impulses but keeps growing in size, featuring a panoply of anonymous faces, a crowd of strangers that is mocking, admonishing, laughing, scolding, to then fade away, leaving John suspended against a black backdrop, without context, connection, interrelations. In the end, he is completely isolated, while Jane is fully immersed in a solid and safe social network.

John Tremble's fantasy of a clean slate, personal reinvention, and exculpation quickly turns into a nightmare. But this is not the film's only fantasy, although it is the only one that is acknowledged. There is also the dream of the humiliated, long-suffering, self-sacrificing wife to be rid of a husband who will never make it—Jane's dream, which needs to stay unexpressed. Seen from her vantage point, *The Whispering Chorus* is a dream come true: the difficult, criminal, gambling, lying husband disappears, another respectable, successful, honest husband shows up, and one does not even have to go to the trouble of being unfaithful to switch from one to the other—it *just happens*. An early review of the film pointed uneasily to the film's ambiguous message and the fact that Jane and her second husband "base their happiness upon a lie."[21] In fact, the film takes trouble to resolve this moral predicament but it does not manage to do away with it. More than *All Night* and *Male and Female*, it gives shape to a particularly *genteel* daydream, delineating a sphere of entitlement and privilege, in which obstacles and problems need not be actively eliminated but disappear on their own. The visualizations of inclinations and restraint in *The Whispering Chorus* figure forth cinema's different possibilities, as they trace the intersection of moral responsibility and escapist fantasy. The film's protagonist eventually turns against self-indulgence and sacrifices himself in a virtuous act of self-denial. But the film at large does not opt for responsibility over escapism but rather ends up merging these two extremes, very much in keeping with the dream factory's persistent reconciliation of moral instruction and irresponsible wish fulfillment. The film exemplifies the potential of cinema to address all sorts of audiences simultaneously and with different messages (and white lower middle-class women were as important, in this respect, as middle-class men). But it may very well also have unsettled its audiences because it highlights the fatality of the situation and the monumentality of the choice in the end rather than keeping the array of options open, as so many other narratives of the period do. Eventually, the realization of Jane's dream requires a decision, and if it is only *not* to act and let her first husband face his execution. This final plot turn, much more than the darkness and negativity of the plot, may have been the film's biggest problem and may have brought about DeMille's own verdict on the film as a failure.[22] The mass cultural imagination of the 1910s favors the mode of the daydream precisely in its indecisive status between the real and the imaginary, after all, as a state that does not require action: it just happens. To force the dream into actualization and concreteness is a dangerous thing to do, and it is so much more pleasant to stay at the threshold or linger at the intersection, where all the options are still open.

NOTES

1. Janet Staiger, "*Les Belles Dames sans Merci,* Femmes Fatales, Vampires, Vamps, and Gold Diggers: The Transformation and Narrative Value of Aggressive Fallen Women," in *Reclaiming the Archive: Feminism and Film History,* ed. Vicki Callahan (Detroit: Wayne State University Press, 2010), 32–57, 34.

2. Charlie Keil and Shelley Stamp, "Introduction," in *American Cinema's Transitional Era: Audiences, Institutions, Practices,* ed. Charlie Keil and Shelley Stamp (Berkeley: University of California Press, 2004), 1–11.

3. Ben Singer, "Feature Films, Variety Programs, and the Crisis of the Small Exhibitor," in Keil and Stamp, *American Cinema's Transitional Era,* 76–100, 76.

4. James Snead, *White Screens, Black Images: Hollywood from the Dark Side* (London: Routledge, 1994), 23. On the ways in which narratives of identity and identification enlist and disclose numerous, often mutually exclusive readings and offer various access points to different readers and readings, see also Heather Love, *Feeling Backward: Loss and the Politics of Queer History* (Cambridge, MA: Harvard University Press, 2007), 1–30.

5. See, among others, Laura Horak, *Girls Will Be Boys: Cross-Dressed Women, Lesbians and American Cinema, 1908–1934* (New Brunswick, NJ: Rutgers University Press, 2016); Jacqueline Najuma Stewart, "What Happened in the Transition? Reading Race, Gender and Labor between the Shots," in Keil and Stamp, *American Cinema's Transitional Era,* 103–130; Rob King, *The Fun Factory: The Keystone Film Company and the Emergence of Culture* (Berkeley: University of California Press, 2009); Jennifer M. Bean, ed., *Flickers of Desire: Movie Stars of the 1910s* (New Brunswick, NJ: Rutgers University Press, 2011); Jean-Anne Sutherland and Kathryn M. Feltey, "Here's Looking at Her: An Intersectional Analysis of Women, Power, and Feminism in Film," *Journal of Gender Studies* 26, no. 6 (2017): 618–631.

6. Siegfried Kracauer, "The Little Shopgirls Go to the Movies," in *The Mass Ornament: Weimar Essays,* trans. and ed. Thomas Y. Levin (Cambridge, MA: Harvard University Press, 1995), 291–306, 292.

7. Tom Gunning, "Systematizing the Electric Message: Narrative Form, Gender, and Modernity in *The Lonedale Operator,*" in Keil and Stamp, *American Cinema's Transitional Era,* 15–50, 27.

8. See Catherine Keyser, *Playing Smart: New York Women Writers and Modernist Magazine Culture* (New Brunswick, NJ: Rutgers University Press, 2010).

9. Jeanine Basinger, *Silent Stars* (Hanover, NH: Wesleyan University Press, 1999), 268.

10. Miriam Hansen, *Babel & Babylon: Spectatorship in American Silent Film* (Cambridge, MA: Harvard University Press, 1991), 267.

11. Pantelis Michelakis and Maria Wyke, "Introduction: Silent Cinema, Antiquity and the 'Exhaustless Urn of Time,'" in *The Ancient World in Silent Cinema,* ed. Michelakis and Wyke (Cambridge: Cambridge University Press, 2013), 1–36, 15.

12. Maureen Turim, "Seduction and Eloquence: The New Woman of Fashion in Silent Cinema," in *On Fashion,* ed. Shari Benstock and Suzanne Ferriss (New Brunswick, NJ: Rutgers University Press, 1994), 140–158, 154.

13. Turim, "Seduction and Eloquence," 154. On the flattening of history into style and the camp appeal of silent and sound films about antiquity, see also, next to Michelakis and Wyke, Richard Lindsay, *Hollywood Biblical Epics: Camp Spectacle and Queer Style from the Silent Era to the Modern Day* (Santa Barbara, CA: Praeger, 2015).

14. Hansen, *Babel & Babylon,* 192.

15. Quoted in Sumiko Higashi, *Cecil B. DeMille and American Culture: The Silent Era* (Berkeley: University of California Press, 1994), 195.

16. Hansen, *Babel & Babylon,* 272.

17. See Higashi, *Cecil B. DeMille,* 147.

18. Kracauer, "Little Shopgirls," 292.

19. Race is a different matter, but films like DeMille's *The Cheat* (1915) and D. W. Griffith's *Broken Blossoms* (1919) illustrate that it can be factored in, although for the purposes of this chapter this would have been too much. See Sumiko Higashi, "Ethnicity, Class and Gender in Film: DeMille's *The Cheat,*" in *Unspeakable Images: Ethnicity in the American Cinema,* ed. Lester D. Friedman (Urbana: University of Illinois Press, 1991), 112–139; Stewart, "What Happened in the Transition?"

20. On these analogies, which indeed are often so much more significant than the often-drawn analogy between silent film and modernism, see Katherine Fusco, *Silent Film and U.S. Naturalist Literature: Time, Narrative, and Modernity* (New York: Routledge, 2016).

21. Quoted in Scott Eyman, *Empire of Dreams: The Epic Life of Cecil B. DeMille* (New York: Simon & Schuster, 2013), 149.

22. Cecilia DeMille Presley and Mark Vieira, *Cecil B. DeMille: The Art of the Hollywood Epic* (Philadelphia: Running Press, 2014), 77.

2 · THE DEATH OF LON CHANEY

Masculinity, Race, and the Authenticity of Disguise

ALICE MAURICE

Known as the "man of a thousand faces" and still remembered for his iconic roles in *The Hunchback of Notre Dame* (1923) and *The Phantom of the Opera* (1925), silent film actor Lon Chaney was associated with extreme makeup effects—a repertoire of disfigurement, deformity, and disguise. He not only portrayed these various and self-effacing roles, but also pioneered the makeup effects associated with them. Many of his most famous characters (including, of course, Quasimodo and the masked phantom) had physical deformities or disabilities of one kind or another. He played more than one character with missing limbs, tying his legs behind his back, for example, to play legless characters or wearing a straitjacket to restrict his arms. These characterizations earned Chaney a reputation as a sufferer, even a masochist, who would gladly torture and punish his body to achieve an authentic disguise. In accounts of Chaney's career, scholars have aligned him with a masochistic masculinity, in which pain and sacrifice ultimately lead to a kind of redemption. Some have also argued that Chaney's repertoire of wounds and deformities allowed for coded references to World War I, and the "mass mutilation of men's bodies and the return of those men to society."[1] While I find these analyses convincing, what I am interested in this essay is not the sweep of Chaney's career but the moment of its ending. Lon Chaney's death came in 1930, the same year that saw the release of his first talkie, *The Unholy Three* (MGM, dir. Jack Conway). Taken together, the reactions to Chaney's death and the promotional and narrative strategies surrounding *The Unholy Three* highlight the uneasy relationship between masculinity and disguise, revealing the cultural work performed by the seeming paradox that Chaney embodied: the authenticity of disguise.

Focusing on this moment also allows us to see how Chaney's brand of masculinity intersected with representations of race, class, and bodily norms, and also explore how other intersections affect the intersections of gender and race on screen. Specifically, the technological and intermedial intersections at the beginning of the talkie era—when sound and image were still working out their relationship on screen—recalibrated the terms of authenticity and realism. With the transition to sound even more ambivalence about disguise arose, as the new talking picture put the believability and appropriateness of disguise, including racial, ethnic, and gender disguise, in question. Looking at Chaney in the context of early 1930s Hollywood, then, we can see how white masculinity needed to be unmasked. That unmasking was accomplished, however, through an accumulation of masks: racial stereotypes, fantasies of blackness, and working-class labor all functioned as props for white masculinity at a time of profound anxiety and change for the cinema. As I will argue, in both the commentaries on Chaney and in *The Unholy Three*, disguise is simultaneously celebrated and disavowed, as body and voice must appear to authenticate each other.

THE AUTHENTICITY OF DISGUISE

Lon Chaney died, almost too conveniently, in 1930, shortly after making his first talking picture, *The Unholy Three*, which was a sound remake of the original film, directed by Tod Browning in 1925. Chaney died shortly after filming and before the film was released. I say this was convenient because, in the wake of his death, almost all the tributes to his career seized the opportunity to eulogize Chaney and silent cinema at the same time. Eulogists treated Chaney as a relic of a bygone era, representative of silent film itself, his talents for disguise and pantomime perfect for that quaint medium but not necessary to a cinema that speaks. The accounts, including his obituary in the *Times*, typically connected his talent for pantomime to the fact that his parents were "deaf-mutes": "Possibly this is what made him one of the greatest pantomimists the world has ever known. His hands were as expressive as most people's voices."[2] The nostalgia for silent cinema is accompanied, in the testimonials, by the portrayal of Chaney as a sufferer. More than one writer suggested that his extreme disguises literally killed him and that his years of painful bodily contortion playing characters with various deformities or disabilities had crippled him, with his body finally giving out after all the torture. As in the connection to his parents, we see here how the disabilities of his characters migrate to Chaney's body. Referring to the pain Chaney endured to play Quasimodo, including taking a real flogging to make the scene look real, one critic notes, "These are the sorts of things that eventually ended his life."[3] In truth, he died of a pulmonary hemorrhage due to bronchial cancer caused by his heavy smoking. Even before his death, however, he was aligned with his characters through the suffering and sacrifices associated with makeup effects. One particularly florid account diagnosed Chaney with "a monomania of make-up and characterization" that "devoured him like a monster."[4] The same critic notes that it was as if he "mortified the flesh like a pagan priest," sacrificing himself for his roles: "He has no other interest in life but to transform himself beyond recognition."[5] This article, written three years before Chaney's death, casts this mania for disguise as a kind of death: "So Lon Chaney moves like a lonely ghost among the stark and impressive realism of the men he creates upon the shadow sheet."[6] In emphasizing Chaney's physical pain and personal sacrifice, these accounts insist on the pathos of disguise itself.

The emphasis on the pain of Chaney's process also grounds his acting in physical labor, which provides a certain reality to his characters—their pain involves his pain—and a certain working-class credibility to him. Rather than seeing his work simply as acting, Chaney's dedication to makeup sets him apart, marking him as a kind of "freak." This "freak show presentation" was a big part of Chaney's image, as Gaylyn Studlar has pointed out,[7] but at the same time these accounts tended also to testify to the authenticity of Chaney's disguises and to the truth of his portrayals. We are told that he sought his source material in the streets, and that he would "wander into obscure movie houses and look for types."[8] His death, as one memorial poem put it, "incredibly bereft us / Of many friends—each one sincere and true!"[9] Paradoxically, Chaney's talent for disguise aligned him with realism, truth and authenticity. He was less actor than craftsman, more like a member of the crew than a movie star, his working-class image boosting his claims to authenticity.

Among the many articles written on the occasion of Chaney's death was one called "Five-Fifty-and Fate," which appeared in the fan magazine *Photoplay* in 1930 (see Figure 2.1). This article tells the supposedly true but no doubt mythical story of Chaney and "one Mose Jackson."[10] Before he became a star, Walter Ramsey tells us in his anecdotal account, Chaney was working as an actor in a traveling theater troupe that went broke while on the road in Green Bay, Wisconsin. Because they were unionized, the local stage hands had to be paid first, which left no money for the actors. So, the story continues, Chaney was broke and stranded until an African American stagehand named Mose Jackson, described as a "big, strapping, six-foot Negro," lent him five dollars.[11] He did this, we are told, because Chaney, having been a former stagehand himself, had made friends with the backstage crew. Thus, while Mose needed the money himself, he "knew he must help a brother in distress."[12] That money allowed Chaney to catch a train to Chicago, in time to join a troupe there, which wound up in LA, where he decided to get into pictures and subsequently became a star. Once he made it, Chaney decides he must pay Mose Jackson back with interest, sending him fifty dollars. Later, he goes back to Green Bay and inquires about Jackson, only to find a doorman at the old theater where he worked who tells him that Jackson "got $50 in the mail one day," gambled with it and won close to a thousand dollars, but then was robbed and stabbed to death. The doorman takes a creased newspaper clipping out of his wallet, and the article ends by quoting the news report of the stabbing. It ends with that story alongside a picture of Chaney's makeup bag and his faithful dog. The story rehearses a familiar racist trope; indeed, when he decides to send only fifty dollars, it is because his associates warn him that any more might cause trouble: "It might be bad for the boy to get so much money all at once."[13] But why use Chaney's death as an occasion for telling an old racist cautionary tale?

The story dramatizes a familiar transaction that gained new currency in the early talkie era, the transaction going back at least to the 1830s, to black-

Mose really needed that money. But he knew he must help a brother in distress

FIGURE 2.1 "Five-Fifty-and Fate," *Photoplay* (December 1930).

face minstrelsy and the lore surrounding its origins whereby a white performer borrows or is gladly given something by a black man, leading to his success. One such story involves early blackface performer T. D. Rice, who popularized the "Jump Jim Crow" dance in the 1830s. In the story, which Eric Lott discusses in detail, he meets a black porter named Cuff, borrows his clothes, blacks up, and goes out to perform to a rapturous audience. Lott calls this story "probably the least trustworthy and most accurate account of American minstrelsy's appropriation of black cultural practices."[14] The story of a black man launching a white man's success hearkens back to a founding myth of American pop culture. From our contemporary perspective, the Mose story looks like a proto-buddy film, or an early example of the "magical Negro" trope, in which the black character appears and conveniently disappears once his work of helping the white character is done.[15] In her discussion of Sidney Poitier's roles, which she does not fully equate with the "magical Negro" figure, Sharon Willis notes the importance of the figure who "passes through," leaving behind a "fantasy of racial understanding . . . that requires no effort on the part of white people."[16] The Mose story, coming decades before the civil rights era, offers an even more disturbing lesson. It warns whites against helping, suggesting that gestures like Chaney's are pointless, that the black man cannot be helped. Nonetheless, the racialized exchange burnishes Chaney's image, and the working-class rhetoric functions to masculinize the whole project of disguise.

The transaction between Chaney and the mythical Mose, then, is not really about money; rather, it is about authenticity and masculinity. That is what Chaney gains through the story, what he borrows from the African American figure. Further, the working-class male bond between them transcends racial difference and functions to prove many things about Chaney. The whole account is a kind of character testimony for Chaney, in which the Mose story authenticates Chaney. The juxtaposition at the end of the article—the quotation of the newspaper account alongside a photograph of Chaney's dog with the actor's makeup bag (which we are told is "unposed")— offers another kind of testimony, backed by photographic and documentary evidence. This creates a reciprocal authentication: Chaney is an authentic, good guy, and the story about Mose is true, as evidenced by the newspaper. Together, they amount to strange relics for a movie martyr. But we must also think about this piece in the context of the early talkie era, with its changing and often paradoxical standards surrounding the performance and representation of race. While blackface performers, most notably Al Jolson in *The Jazz Singer*, but also Eddie Cantor, Freeman Gosden, and Charles Correll (radio's "Amos 'n' Andy"), brought their acts to the new talking screen to great success, African American performers were largely absent, deeply caricatured, or relegated to the background. Hollywood's short-lived experiment with black-cast talkies, with two features released in 1929, tried to exploit the perceived authenticity and naturalness of African American performers, with some producers even claiming that black voices would record better than white voices.[17] Meanwhile, racial and ethnic disguises, apart from blackface, posed potential problems and risks for visual and aural authenticity on screen.

As mentioned earlier, Chaney was not known for blackface performance. He did, however, perform in many ethnic or racial disguises, with yellowface as one of his specialties. Chinese characters were repeated more often than others, as Chaney played numerous roles, including sympathetic and villainous versions of what he called his "Orientals." Some memorable examples include *Mr. Wu* (1927) in which he plays the murderous father of Nan Ping (Anna May Wong), and his sympathetic portrayal of Chinese immigrant Yen Sin in *Shadows* (dir. Tom Forman, 1922). Chaney tended to be secretive about his techniques, but a fan magazine in 1922 featured step-by-step photos tracing his process for becoming "Chinese," with a headline offering to enlighten readers who "often wondered how the famous character actor could portray such terrifically ugly Chinamen."[18] The truth is, Chaney's methods were pretty standard and inherited from the long-established tradition of yellowface on the nineteenth-century American stage.[19] Indeed, in makeup manuals of the period, stereotypical ethnic and racial disguises are included in the category "character makeup" alongside stock types including criminals, age makeups, mythical figures, animals, and deformities. It was typical for ethnic and racial categories to offer a mix of straightforward elements of physical appearance on the one hand and characterization and mythology on the other. In general, makeup textbooks and makeup practices during this period make claims about authenticity and realism—Max Factor and others urged makeup artists to "seek out authentic sources"[20]—but because of the rampant use of stereotype and stock figures, the line between character and caricature, especially with racial and ethnic disguise, tends to disappear.

These claims had ramifications during the transition to sound, as the terms of and demands for realism were shifting, causing a potential rift between accepted stereotypes and codes for visualizing identity, whether in terms of race, ethnicity, class, or gender, and what could pass for real on screen. Sound, along with other technological changes in the late 1920s, especially the move to panchromatic black-and-white film stock and incandescent lighting, necessitated changes in makeup, including new kinds of makeup and new application techniques, while some standard methods and materials became obsolete.[21] As I noted earlier, Chaney's passing was understood as the passing of a kind of performer suited to the silent cinema. Even Chaney seemed to agree, but in a more practical sense. He resisted the talkies for some time, and then, when he reconsidered, he noted in an interview,

> The talkies necessarily will limit my characterizations. . . . Characters such as I played in *The Hunchback of Notre Dame*, *Phantom of the Opera* and others will be impossible to do now, as I can't put anything in my mouth which will interfere with my speaking. Other characters which I will have to forego now will

be those that would require a dialect. Speaking with a dialect is one thing I won't do. There is too much chance of doing it wrong and offending some persons. I am going to speak in my own natural manner in all my pictures, which I guess means that from now on my roles will have to suit my natural personality.[22]

Chaney's comments suggest the way technical questions (like what kinds of prosthetic devices one uses to change the face) broaden out into more social or ethical questions, such as who gets to represent whom, and what will appear believable and acceptable on screen. So, talking pictures require him to talk, which means he cannot use all the mouth modifications that were so important to his characterizations on the silent screen; but additionally, *when* he talks, he is fearful of offending people with his impersonations. After years of stereotypical, but silent, portrayals, he assumes that doing a "dialect" will be more offensive than simply slanting one's eyes. He suggests the talkies will require him to give up disguise to a certain extent and to opt instead for roles that "suit his natural personality." However, with *The Unholy Three*, he found a way around this restriction.

UNHOLY THREES: MASCULINITY, VOICE, AND DISGUISE

The Unholy Three was a remake of the 1925 Tod Browning film of the same name, in which Chaney also starred. For this, his first talkie, Chaney solved the problems he anticipated not by performing in his natural face and voice, but rather by performing as two different characters and in five different voices. Chaney noted that he did not want to give up the mystery that had defined him; he wanted to use many different voices "so that people won't be able to say which is my natural voice, just as I have always used make up, so that they don't quite know what my real face is like." Chaney added, "It has taken me years to build up a sort of mystery surrounding myself, which is my stock in trade, and I wouldn't sacrifice it by talking."[23] Talking, at first just a practical concern for Chaney in the sense that he wouldn't be able to put anything in his mouth to create his makeups, becomes a more existential threat, as it was for many silent actors of the day, but for different reasons. Once the voice was added to his performance, it threatened to ruin his disguise, to dispel the illusion he had created over the course of his career.

Although much is to be taken with a grain of salt as these stories were part of the publicity campaign, the *New York Times* reported that "Chaney had hesitated to sign a new contract calling for vocal efforts on his part until he had practised [*sic*] using various voices."[24] In the interview, Chaney identified the voice as a privileged place of identity and authenticity: "When you hear a person talk, you begin to know him better." And yet he also sees the talking picture as "bringing back the old style of acting," providing an opportunity for actors to immerse themselves in their roles as they do in the theater. This apparently spurred his change of heart on the question of dialects: "I want to talk in at least two voices, or dialects, in each picture."[25]

Nonetheless, the idea of the talkie as a threat to Chaney's stardom persisted and was folded into the publicity campaign for *The Unholy Three*, which seemed to pit Chaney against the microphone. One publicity shot for the film featured Chaney with a ventriloquist dummy on his lap, director Jack Conway, and costar Lila Lee on the set with a very prominent microphone. The studio caption reads, "Lon Chaney introduced to the microphone for his first scene in his first talkie looks apprehensive. His director, Jack Conway, and leading lady Lila Lee do the introducing at the start of Metro-Goldwyn-Mayer's 'The Unholy Three.'"[26] All the publicity surrounding the film was focused on the fact that it was Chaney's first talkie, and while the ad campaign built up the anticipation and suspense of hearing Chaney with banners announcing "Lon Chaney Talks!," the studio also seemed to suggest a competition between the talking picture and Chaney's acting ability. In conjunction with the film, MGM produced a series of portraits of Chaney in different poses and expressions, shot with dramatic lighting and expressive use of shadow. Each entry in the series was titled a "Talking Still Picture." The various captions for these photos emphasize Chaney's expressive abilities: "Lon Chaney almost talks through the medium of this unique portrait in which he appears in the role of the sinister 'Echo,' hero of his first talking picture 'The Unholy Three.'"[27] In addition to suggesting that Chaney can "speak" without words (or even motion), the caption claims that the photo itself is its own "unique" medium, a "talking still picture." In these photos, the studio promotes Chaney's first talkie by suggesting he does not need the talkie in order to communicate an emotion or a character. The photograph acts as a kind of fetish here, an overcompensation to parry the potential threat represented by the sound cinema: the microphone threatens to strip Chaney of his power.

But the problem, for Chaney, was not just that talking might give him away; the problem was that sound threatened the authenticity of disguise itself. The biggest obstacle to the illusion was not that his voice *could not* be disguised but rather that it *could* be. In other words, given how sound technology works in film, it would be very easy for Chaney's multiple voices to be faked by dubbing or simply by using someone else's voice, a practice that was particularly common in musicals, for example. Recognizing this threat to his act—the multiple voices must be *his*, just as the "thousand faces" are— the ads for *The Unholy Three* featured an image of a signed affidavit. In it Chaney swears that, in the movie, "all voice reproductions which purport to be reproductions of my voice, to wit, the ventriloquist, the old woman's, the dummy's, the parrot's, and the girl's, are actual reproductions of my own voice, and in no place in said photoplay or in any of the various characters portrayed by me in said photoplay was a 'double' or substitute used for my voice."[28] In this moment, Chaney, the master of disguise, needed to show himself. Chaney wanted to perform in many voices so audiences "[wouldn't] be able to say which is [his] natural voice,"[29] yet Chaney's voice not being known is of course not worth anything (and in fact makes "faking it" even easier) if it isn't paired with the certainty that he is doing the vocalizations, that is, that the vocal disguise is real. In *The Unholy Three*, Chaney plays a ventriloquist, and he must prove that his voice is the one being thrown around, that all the voices are emanating from his body. Chaney the actor must prove, in other words, that he is the ventriloquist and not the dummy.

His ventriloquism *in* the film, then, must be separated from the ventriloquism of sound cinema itself. In his early theorization of sound in cinema, Rick Altman suggested that the sound-image relationship might be likened to ventriloquism, whereby "the soundtrack is a ventriloquist who, by moving his dummy (the image) in time with words he secretly speaks, creates the illusion that the words are produced by the dummy/image, whereas in fact the dummy/image is actually created in order to disguise the source of the sound."[30] Altman is being deliberately provocative here, in an effort to flip the assumed hierarchy in film and film studies: that image is primary and sound secondary, that the soundtrack serves the image track, and so forth. Altman goes on to point out the importance of "moving lips" to sync sound. Pointing the camera at the person who speaks "convinces us that the individual thus portrayed—and not the loudspeaker—has spoken the words we have heard."[31] This fusion of image and sound helps to cover up the technological realities of the cinema, keeping the machinery of sound and image from dispelling the cinematic illusion, the unity of the fiction. Synchronization, then, is not just a technical goal, but also an ideological one. Altman goes further, finding in ventriloquism the most apt analogue for the "problem" of the sound-image relationship in Hollywood cinema:

> For the ventriloquist's problem is exactly that of the sound track—how to retain control over the sound while attributing it to a carefully manipulated lifelike dummy with no independent life of his own. Indeed, the ventriloquist's art depends on the very fact which we have found at the heart of sound film: we are so disconcerted by a sourceless sound that we would rather attribute the sound to a dummy or a shadow than face the mystery of its sourcelessness.[32]

The early sound era is a particular moment in the history of cinema, when this quirky relationship between image and sound is often inadvertently foregrounded due to technical shortcomings, and so in that context, a movie about a ventriloquist might be particularly risky. In 1930, when *The Unholy Three* was released, sound cinema was still a bit unstable, technologically and in terms of audience approval, and the talkie, as an enterprise, while fully acknowledged as the future of cinema, was still in need of a little help.[33] Even a year later, in 1931, for example, ads for RKO's big-budget release *Cimarron* declared, "The talkies are born today!" If the talkie was on shaky ground, we might say the same for disguise. With the coming of sound, disguise was also in a transitional, vulnerable moment. Chaney's calculations about using multiple voices were a result of his concerns about voice and makeup working (or not working) together. Would disguise work in sound cinema? Could he still pull it off—would it go over with audiences? By looking at *The Unholy Three*, I suggest other, related questions: How do these various performance anxieties about sound technology and about disguise affect the performance of masculinity on screen? How does the interdependence of masculinity and authenticity in Chaney's image work in a film which involves both ventriloquism and drag?

The film tells the story of a ventriloquist named "Echo" (Chaney) and three of his carnival/criminal friends: a strong man named Hercules or Herc (Ivan Linow), a little person called Tweedle-dee in the carnival but Midge by his friends (Harry Earles), and a woman named Rosie (Lila Lee) who is Echo's love interest and an accomplished pickpocket. The four are established early on as being in cahoots, while also being more than willing to betray or double-cross each other at any moment. When a fight breaks out and the police raid the carnival, Echo meets with Herc and Midge in order to unfold his plan for escaping the heat: they will leave the carnival, take on disguises, and just "fade out," leaving their carnival personas behind. When they hear his plan, which the audience doesn't hear, Midge reacts by calling the plan "unholy." Hence, Echo dubs them "the unholy three," and they set out to establish their new gig, which the audience comes to understand in the next scene, opening on a pet store named Mrs. O'Grady's. Echo is disguised as an old woman named Mrs. O'Grady (see Figure 2.2), Midge as a baby, Mrs. O'Grady's grandson, and Herc as the old woman's son-in-law and the baby's father. Rosie is there as well, playing Mrs. O'Grady's granddaughter. Using ventriloquist skills, Mrs. O'Grady throws her voice to make the parrots in the store talk. The rather baroque plan involves selling these talking birds to unsuspecting customers, who then inevitably complain that the birds don't talk when they get them home. This trick is then used as an opening to go case the customers' homes, allowing them to later break in and rob them. Meanwhile, Rosie falls for the innocent store clerk, Hector (Elliott Nugent), inciting Echo's jealous rage. When one robbery goes wrong, ending in a murder, the police investigate the pet store, and the three men agree to frame Hector for the crime. When Rosie threatens to turn them in, they abduct her and escape. With Hector on trial, Rosie begs Echo to help him, to keep him from "going to the chair." She promises that, if he helps Hector, she will renounce her love for Hector and stay with Echo. In the climactic courtroom scene, Echo ends up revealing his disguise and turning himself in. Hector goes free, and Echo lets Rosie out of her bargain. He heads off to jail and urges Hector to "take care of that girl of yours."

The film takes up the theme of masculinity with its opening lines, as a carnival barker introduces Hercules the strong man as the "mighty, marvelous, mastodonic model of muscular masculinity." A little later, the barker presents little person "Tweedle-dee" to the crowd, and a pair of women mock him as a "pocket Daddy," while a little boy taunts him. He kicks the boy in the stomach, inciting a riot. Echo is clearly the leader of the gang, and his power is tied to the threat of violence and also to his powers of disguise. His ability to become someone else allows him and, he suggests, the rest of the gang to disappear, to "just fade out." But he also repeatedly keeps the gang in line by physically threatening them. He repeatedly threatens to "sock" Herc and

FIGURE 2.2 Lon Chaney as Mrs. O'Grady in *The Unholy Three* (1930).

Midge, and when the much larger Herc gets menacing, he also threatens him with his secret weapon, the gorilla from the carnival, whom he brings along to the pet store. The gorilla hates Hercules because he has a history of taunting the animal while he was caged. When he notices that Rosie is flirting with Hector at the pet store, Echo threatens her as well, again, with a "sock in the nose," to which she replies, "No one's gonna beat me up!" Later, he makes good on his promise and hits her in a pivotal moment that marks a turning point for his character.

Throughout the film, Echo seems to be trying to figure out how to be a man and how to maintain control while dressed as a woman. His disguise as Mrs. O'Grady is a kind of half disguise, in the sense that, unlike with roles such as the Hunchback or the Phantom, Chaney's disguise is part of the story. He is fooling the people in the film, but not the audience of the film. And, in fact, he spends much of his time half in and half out of costume. When he is in the store or in public, he is Mrs. O'Grady, but in private he remains Echo. The apartment attached to the store acts as a kind of backstage space, where Mrs. O'Grady, her son-in-law, the baby, and Rosie live. A door connects the apartment to the store, and when they are behind the door, they drop their act and are themselves. For Echo, this typically means he just takes his wig off and remains in his dress, always ready to become Mrs. O'Grady quickly, when needed. These quick changes make for some incongruous humor, especially with Midge, who is sometimes seen in the apartment still dressed as a baby but smoking a cigar, for example. And yet, with Echo, these incongruities read more as menace than as humor. For example, when he threatens Rosie, he is still wearing his dress, makeup, and earrings, but no wig. Here, it looks as if his violent masculinity is peeking out from beneath his harmless old woman disguise, and Echo seems like a wolf in sheep's clothing. Indeed, through the film, there are moments when Echo slips, when he forgets to disguise his voice while in his feminine costume. This typically happens when he is angry, when his threatening male voice reflexively comes out; typically, he covers it over with a cough. On the level of plot, these little outbursts of masculinity set up the action of the climactic courtroom scene, but they also align his maleness with threat and with his natural/authentic self. Violent masculinity seems to be uncontrollable, or barely controllable, and whether this is a weakness or a strength remains in question for much of the film.

As Gaylyn Studlar has pointed out, many of Chaney's films offer "perverse version[s] of the family" in which masochism and redemption substitute for traditional patriarchal power.[34] Studlar links Chaney's perverse father-figure characters to "uncertainties regarding the paternal role at a time when the American family was going through enormous change."[35] Indeed, the unholy nature of the threesome with Echo as grandma, Midge as grandson, and Herc as son-in-law seems to lie in its perversion of the family unit, constituting an "unholy trinity." Like the holy trinity of Christianity, the unholy three is made up of only men. This seems to add to the unholiness of the three masquerading as family. Although she is part of the gang, Rosie is the fourth who is left out when they dub themselves the unholy three. This omission is given in part because she is Echo's love interest, the girlfriend who tags along. Yet she is established early on as a pickpocket and is as much a part of the criminal gang as anyone else. As the story progresses, her status as the extra or unneeded person allows her to seize another option, as her romance with Hector is framed as a chance to be part of a real family. Hector, portrayed as an innocent yokel, offers her a glimpse of a normal family life, including such things as decorating a Christmas tree, which seems ridiculous at first to Rosie and the gang. Importantly, she does not take part in the jewel heist and murder. This refusal again sets her against the unholy three, as the group flees and takes her with them against her will. Thus, by the end of the film she is no longer a criminal, and she belongs with Hector, not with Echo.

The three men's masquerade forms an unholy family unit, but it's not the only unholy three in the film. Echo, Rosie, and the dummy form another perverse family as potential husband, wife, and wooden baby. The dummy, in this sense, might be seen as a symbol of Echo's inadequacy as a love object for Rosie, and as a harbinger of the union's sterility. The dummy on Echo's lap makes for an ambivalent phallic symbol at best, stiff and lifeless at the same time. Echo may be too old or simply too criminal for Rosie, or he may simply be too multiple to be a proper man. After all, as a ventriloquist he is already "two," as his name implies, and ultimately he is "three": Echo, the dummy, and "Mrs. O'Grady." In the end, he is perhaps none of these, as he fades out in the final shot of the film, waving from the back of a train as it pulls away.

The biggest crime in the film, at least from the standpoint of masculinity, is neither robbery nor murder, but cowardice. Throughout the film, the characters repeatedly accuse each other of being "yellow." Midge uses this taunt most often, especially when he is trying to convince Herc to double-cross Echo. He accuses Herc of being afraid of Echo, and says, "Maybe you're afraid of me, too," and yells "Boo!" in his ear. Each of the male characters seem to be compensating for something that threatens their masculinity: Midge must compensate for being too small; Herc, it seems, must compensate for being too big and too dumb, a brute who is most closely aligned with the gorilla; and Echo, meanwhile, must compensate for his facility with disguise. As Herc puts it after the murder, escape is easier for Echo, who can just "get out of [his] makeup."

This idea of cowardice and accountability comes to a head when Rosie challenges Echo and offers him her bargain: "If you get [Hector] out of this . . . you can have me always." Because he knows she loves Hector, he hesitates to help him, and yet it is clear that he feels somewhat guilty for Hector's predicament. The turning point comes when Rosie screams at him, accusing him of being afraid: "You were hot stuff full of nearsighted old ladies in a parrot store, but when it comes to doing something decent, you're afraid to take the chance. You're yella!" When she tells him she hates him, Echo slaps her. Interestingly, we don't see the slap as the camera stays on Echo in a medium shot, striking out with his hand before we only cutting to Rosie in tears, her hand on her face. In this moment, Echo's masculinity is questioned: his facility with disguise is tantamount to hiding and cowardice, and at the same time, the threatened violence that was once the source of his power has exploded. Remorseful, his need to prove that he is worthy of Rosie pushes him to do the right thing.

This confrontation leads to the climactic scene in the courtroom. Echo sits in the audience, unrecognized as he is no longer in costume, and slowly realizes that Hector will almost certainly be found guilty. His only defense involves being with Mrs. O'Grady and Rosie, and they are nowhere to be found. Ultimately, Echo decides to do something, and here silent and sound versions of the film diverge. In the silent version, Mrs. O'Grady never appears in court or takes the stand, while in the sound version, she does. And surprisingly, in the silent version, ventriloquism is key to the film's climax, while in the sound version, it plays almost no role in the courtroom scene. Rather, Echo's disguise takes center stage and his disguise itself is on trial. Echo decides to take the stand as Mrs. O'Grady, after slipping Hector a note that says "Mrs. O'Grady will take the stand for you. Have faith in miracles." The prosecutor begins questioning her story in which she corroborates Hector's alibi, and as he gets more aggressive, Echo slips and speaks in his own voice. He then coughs to cover it up. But it is clear to the audience that Echo has purposefully dropped his vocal disguise, to tip off the prosecutor, who then rips Echo's wig off, revealing his disguise. After that, Echo tells the judge that he wishes to make a full confession. By revealing himself to be a man, Echo is in fact becoming a man, according to the terms of the film he proves that he's not "yellow."

Disguise had already been equated with deception and cowardice in the previous scene, when Hector receives Mrs. O'Grady's note. As we watch him silently read the note, we hear the prosecutor's voice off-screen, delivering his closing statement. He says he is "happy to know" that Hector was beloved in his hometown and that he "went to church on Sunday," and continues, as his speech hits a crescendo: "But I am horrified, as I know all of you must be, when we know that he uses this cloak of respectability to cover up his complicity in robbery and murder!" The "cloak of respectability" could well refer to Mrs. O'Grady's shawl, and Echo might be described as hiding behind his own skirts. He must become a man by emerging from his feminine disguise, but also by escaping the femininity of disguise, here aligned with the cowardice of hiding. His masculinity, formerly defined by violence, is now defined by self-sacrifice, again, fulfilling a pattern to Chaney's roles. Importantly, though, to be a man in this film, Chaney's character must be singular—in the end, he drops all of his guises, including Echo, as he is seen without his dummy, riding away on the train in the final scene, whereas the silent version of the film ends with Echo performing his ventriloquist act.

In that sense, the plot and themes of the film seem to align with the rhetoric surrounding both Chaney's death and his stakes in his first talkie. The terms and logic of his brand of authentic disguise needed to be re-made for sound. While others made successes out of sound film by putting on the blackface mask, Chaney needed to be unmasked, distanced from disguise, his stock in trade. The "man of a thousand faces" became unique by offering "all the possibilities of the freak show under 'one tent.'"[36] He performed the potential of radical transformation but also contained and domesticated that potential, keeping it all in one place, namely his body. Memorials to Chaney seemed to want his death to mark an end to his brand of performance, as if to close the Pandora's box of fluid identities and grotesque bodies he opened. But, of course, it is not as if extreme makeup effects on screen or Hollywood's penchant for ethnic and racial disguise disappeared with Chaney or the silent cinema. We might think about how the characters, stereotypes, and makeup practices created by early Hollywood remain, coded into the real and digital faces we see on contemporary screens. Those overwrought accounts of Chaney's authenticity end up revealing the multiple identities and racialized discourses propping up Hollywood's image of a self-contained, authentic white masculinity. These discourses create perhaps the most durable mask: the mask of authenticity, to which all the other masks must adhere.

NOTES

1. Karen Randell, "Masking the Horror of Trauma: The Hysterical Body of Lon Chaney," *Screen* 44, no. 2 (Summer 2003): 216–221, 216. On Chaney and the "broken faces" of World War I, see David Lubin, *Flags and Faces: The Visual Culture of America's First World War* (Berkeley: University of California Press, 2015), 41–87. For a thorough discussion of Chaney's masochism and its relationship to "transformative masculinity" in 1920s cinema and culture, see Gaylyn Studlar, *This Mad Masquerade: Stardom and Masculinity in the Jazz Age* (New York: Columbia University Press, 1996), 199–248.

2. Clarence A. Locan, "The Lon Chaney I Knew," *Photoplay*, November 1930, 58–60, 106–108, 106.

3. Locan, "Lon Chaney I Knew," 60.

4. Ivan St. Johns, "Mr. Nobody," *Photoplay*, February 1927, 136.

5. St. Johns, "Mr. Nobody," 58.

6. St. Johns, "Mr. Nobody," 136.

7. Studlar, *This Mad Masquerade*, 238.

8. Locan, "Lon Chaney I Knew," 60.

9. Margaret E. Sangster, "Lon Chaney," *Photoplay*, October 1930, 40.

10. Walter Ramsey, "Five-Fifty-and Fate," *Photoplay*, December 1930: 69–70, 69.

11. Ramsey, "Five-Fifty-and Fate," 69.

12. Ramsey, "Five-Fifty-and Fate," 69.

13. Ramsey, "Five-Fifty-and Fate," 70.

14. Eric Lott, *Love and Theft: Blackface Minstrelsy and the American Working Class* (London: Oxford University Press, 1993), 18–19.

15. For discussions of this trope in contemporary cinema, see, for example, Krin Gabbard, *Black Magic: White Hollywood and African American Culture* (New Brunswick, NJ: Rutgers University Press, 2004) and Heather Hicks, "Hoodoo Economics: White Men's Work and Black Men's Magic in Contemporary American Film," *Camera Obscura* 18, no. 2 (2003): 27–55.

16. Sharon Willis, *The Poitier Effect: Racial Melodrama and Fantasies of Reconciliation* (Minneapolis: University of Minnesota Press, 2015), 5.

17. Alice Maurice, *The Cinema and Its Shadow* (Minneapolis: University of Minnesota Press, 2013), 153–186. See also Ryan Jay Friedman, *Hollywood's African American Films: The Transition to Sound* (New Brunswick, NJ: Rutgers University Press, 2011).

18. "Lon Chaney's Make-Up," *Photoplay*, March 1922, 43.

19. Krystyn Moon, *Yellowface: Creating the Chinese in American Popular Music and Performance, 1850s–1920s* (New Brunswick, NJ: Rutgers University Press, 2005).

20. Max Factor, "The Art of Motion Picture Make-Up," *Cinematographic Annual* 1 (1930): 157–171, 162.

21. On the shift from orthochromatic to panchromatic film stock, see David Bordwell, Janet Staiger, and Kristin Thompson, *The Classical Hollywood Cinema: Film Style and Mode of Production to 1960* (London: Routledge, 1985), 518–522; on the development of makeup for the new film stock, see Fred Basten, *Max Factor: The Man Who Changed the Faces of the World* (New York: Arcade, 2008), 174–187.

22. Dan Thomas, "Lon Chaney Talks in Makeup," *Santa Cruz News*, May 10, 1930, 7.

23. "Lon Chaney's Five Voices," *New York Times*, July 6, 1930, "Amusements" sec., 2.

24. "Lon Chaney's Five Voices," 2.

25. "Lon Chaney's Five Voices," 2.

26. Publicity photographs, *The Unholy Three*, MGM Collection, Stills, Margaret Herrick Library, Beverly Hills, CA.

27. Publicity photographs, *The Unholy Three*.

28. The ad featuring the affidavit appeared in numerous magazines and newspapers and was even singled out by the October 11, 1930, issue of *Exhibitors Herald-World* (11) for being particularly effective, in part because it included Chaney's affidavit.

29. "Lon Chaney's Five Voices," 2.

30. Rick Altman, "Moving Lips: Cinema as Ventriloquism," *Yale French Studies* 60 (1980): 67–79, 67.

31. Altman, "Moving Lips," 69.

32. Altman, "Moving Lips," 76.

33. On the transition to sound, see, for example, Donald Crafton, *The Talkies: American Cinema's Transition to Sound, 1926–1931* (Berkeley: University of California Press, 1999), and James Lastra, *Sound Technology and the American Cinema* (New York: Columbia University Press, 2000).

34. Studlar, *This Mad Masquerade*, 213.

35. Studlar, *This Mad Masquerade*, 248.

36. Studlar, *This Mad Masquerade*, 241.

3 · MGM'S SLEEPING LION

Hollywood Regulation of the Washingtonian Slave in *The Gorgeous Hussy* (1936)

ELLEN C. SCOTT

On the classical Hollywood screen, American slavery was largely unrepresentable. Though dense, muted aspects of slavery's history were palpable through the elaborate and ornate dressing of plantation mythology, the history of enslaved people—aspects of their rebellions, of daily resistance practices, of the Underground Railroad, of the slave trade and slave market—was represented in very few classical Hollywood films. Despite the writings of William Still, W. E. B. Du Bois, Carter G. Woodson, and others documenting these histories, slavery as lived remained removed from the Hollywood scene.[1] More frequent were representations of slavery outside of the American landscape: in ancient Rome or in piracy (e.g., *Roman Scandals* [1933, Goldwyn], *The Crusades* [1935, Paramount], or *Last Days of Pompeii* [1935, RKO]) where temporarily enslaved white men easily throw off their chains through natural masculinity and rightful freedom.

What do production documents tell us about classical Hollywood's signature restraint upon slavery's representation, the motivations behind this restraint, and the limits of slavery's representability in that cinematic system?

It is only through exploring the gamut of texts representing slavery that a patterned repression emerges from both Hollywood self-regulators and production companies. Casting this wider net and taking into account the relevance of censorship rather than, solely, the finished film reveals that the most vital "limit texts" were often unproduced films or those that were initially plotted to depict slavery but where slavery never made it onto the screen.

ADAMS'S *THE GORGEOUS HUSSY:* SLAVERY AS AMERICA'S FOUNDING CONTRADICTION

One of the films dropping its initial inclusion of slavery was MGM's *The Gorgeous Hussy* (1936), starring Joan Crawford as the titular "hussy." Samuel Hopkins Adams, known for his short story "Night Bus" (*It Happened One Night;* 1934), provided the film's narrative with his 1933 historical novel about Peggy O'Neal, whose friendship with President Andrew Jackson supposedly influenced the construction of his cabinet, in an incident known as the Petticoat affair. Several studios showed interest in filming O'Neal's life; RKO alone attempted it on four occasions.[2] Adams's 550-page novel stuck closely to its protagonist, spending the first twelve chapters on her fourteenth year. Born in 1799, O'Neal, a Washington tavern keeper and hotelier's daughter, was known for her beauty, persuasiveness, and boldness with men, and for becoming Tennessee senator John Eaton's wife. The novel's early pages signal Adams's intention to traverse Washington's lows and highs. Adams focalizes the first scene through black enslaved people, lingering at the window to watch and comment on the president at a dance until the city's racial curfew, after which they will have to fear arrest. Adams describes Pennsylvania Avenue first not as the home to the White House, but rather as an ad hoc back-alley space populated by cooks overflowing their kitchens, street farers visiting taverns and inns, and, persistently, a "mosaic" of black faces.[3] Peggy's first decisive action in the novel causes her to travel through this complex interracial geography: she visits a Pennsylvania Avenue slave market.[4] The bored and overly managed teenager, having won $450 in a local lottery, opts to use the money to replace her black governess, Aunt Sukey, with a slave of her own, "a yellow girl, smart, young and strong, who would perhaps in time have babies" that could replace the dolls Peggy has tired of.[5] However, the market, described as "one of the capital's most popular free entertainments," shocks Peggy: abolitionists openly challenge the sale's morality and the auctioneer's gritty discourse troubles her.[6] Lacking funds and feeling for the black chattel she once thought of only for her pleasure, Peggy purchases a "broken" middle-aged woman, Charity, who in a strange spectacle of dignity and struggle for control calls out in a commanding voice to the women at the market to buy her.[7] Out of sympathy, Peggy also buys Charity's "feeble-minded" half-brother, Cree, who has an "R" for "runaway" branded into his face. The scene's arc, with Peggy becoming gradually sensitized to slavery's seriousness, provides a rare window into slavery's horrors for a popular novel. Further, Adams describes many enslaved chattels as "mulatto" or "yaller" and even makes one bidder a "woman . . . whose skin suggested a dash of the tar-brush," revealing the pervasiveness of American racial intermixture.[8]

Adams also included a racially charged attempted lynching: when one of Peggy's impetuous suitors, professor, phrenologist, and occultist Roy La Sunderland, convinces her to run away with him, Cree nearly gets lynched trying to stop him.[9] The sequence insisted on the interlaced nature of white domestic folly and black fatal trouble and also on lynching's relationship to slavery's logic: if a human is property, he can be burned. Adams's novel also candidly revealed white lust for black slaves in a scene at a Senate-patronized whorehouse between O'Neal (who naïvely awaits Sunderland) and a tragic quadroon lady of the night, a girl her own age, who warns her to leave before it is too late.[10] At the lengthy novel's end, Adams weaves slavery back into the narrative when O'Neal, now in her seventies, marries a nineteen-year-old Italian dance instructor who engages in the illegal slave trade in order to finance his romantic affair and eventual elopement with O'Neal's fourteen-year-old granddaughter, pregnant with his child. Though the slaves in this incident, referred to as "black ivory," are never named or described, it is significant that Adams methodically returns to slavery at the book's end, asserting that nineteenth-century Washington elites' reliance on slavery, both licit and illicit, continued after the Civil War, even in Federalist families.[11] At turns, Adams's New England racism rivaled his abolitionism. Even Adams's near-lynching sequence patronizingly imbues central African American characters with a folksy inanity borne of black dialect, the plantation's self-sacrificing spirit, and strong superstition. But Adams's novel subtly managed racial politics while insistently uniting America's defining racial issues: slavery, miscegenation, and lynching. Through a narrative voice of unsentimental candor one might expect from a journalist of his ilk, Adams rendered the plight of enslaved Africans in the shadow of the Capitol as brutal, the humanity and abounding presence of the enslaved black community palpable, and American slavery as a problematic axiom deeply enmeshed with American politics and government.

Adams was not alone in highlighting O'Neal's connections to slavery. Queena Pollack's biography, credited in Adams's preface, indicates that southerners preferred Peggy's father's Franklin Inn because of the abundance of enslaved black servants, who logically surrounded Peggy.[12] Alfred Henry Lewis's novel *Peggy O'Neal* (1903) links the Nullification Crisis, an issue much associated with Peggy, to slavery.[13] Adams, though, renders slavery more brutal, and Peggy's connection to slavery, at home and in the political sphere, more personal than earlier authors. Through Peggy's "innocent" slave market trip, Adams revealed contradictions of sentiment and practice—political opposition to slavery and personal reliance on it—that characterized 1820s Washingtonians.

Adams's biography explains in part his novel's unusual racial complexity. Adams was the grandson of Harriet Tubman's first white biographer and major benefactor, Sarah Hopkins Bradford. In a 1947 article for the *New Yorker*, Adams describes Tubman's regular visits to his childhood home: "While other youngsters of the late eighteen-seventies played scouts and Indians, our standard make-believe was slaves and overseers, with Harriet as the heroine." His descriptions of Tubman, whom he called "Aunt Harriet," mingle awe, stereotype, curiosity about her scars, injuries, and escapes, and palpable reverence. Tubman's voice, he claimed, "was baritone rather than contralto . . . and produced a strangely moving effect of mingled challenge and appeal."[14] Adams's *The Gorgeous Hussy* bore a subtle abolitionism; he described black characters using racist stereotypes, but he strongly suggested through unsentimental prose that slavery was a brutal American contradiction that would eventually disrupt the Union.

DEVELOPING *THE GORGEOUS HUSSY* FOR THE SCREEN

Both RKO and MGM wrote treatments of *The Gorgeous Hussy* in 1934. MGM ultimately purchased it. From reader reports to early treatments, RKO's versions downplayed enslaved people and never drafted the lynching. RKO screenwriter Jane Murfin included black characters Charity and Cree but saw them merely as Peggy's "devoted guardians," "time after time keeping her from some disastrous result of her follies."[15] MGM planned to translate much more of Adams's depiction of slavery to the screen. The MGM screenplay, written by Ainsworth Morgan and, later, Stephen Morehouse Avery, went through at least ten drafts in 1935 and 1936. The earliest known script draft, which Morgan wrote in August 1935, translated Adams's novel into the idiom of Hollywood stereotypes, with liberal use of the word "nigger," Eaton mixing with "colored riff-raff," and Cree as a "languid," unmotivated creature modeled, in Morgan's words, on "Stepin Fetchit."[16] However, his script maintained Adams's vibrant and brimming black Washington, a Washington Morgan clearly could not imagine. Early scripts opened as the book had with enslaved Washingtonians traversing Pennsylvania Avenue, commenting upon the whites at Cerfanti's dance academy. It also included a ten-page version of Adams's interracial fight sequence between Cree and Sunderland, where Sunderland returns with a lynch mob.

Morgan's second draft, written on October 28, more seriously handled slavery's violence; a frankly rendered slave market sequence that mirrored Adams's set in an auction house on none other than Pennsylvania Avenue included evidence of black concubinage and a dramatic reveal of Cree's body branded with the letter "R" for "runaway." Morgan's slave mart was a den of cruel traders bidding on no less than twenty-one African Americans, mostly families including "Old Peter-One-Arm, good for at least five more years; Pansy and family of six to be offered as a lot; Perfume, seventeen and as pretty and willing as they come."[17] Morgan also reminded viewers that this was Washington, D.C., and a legally sanctioned proceeding: "By virtue of writ of fiero facias . . . issuing from the Circuit Court of Washington, I hereby expose and offer for unrestricted sale the following slaves," Shyrock the auctioneer begins.[18] While Morgan removed the novel's protesting abolitionist, he maintained the direct treatment of family separation and underlined Peggy's auction experience as horrific. Morgan invented a sequence where, Nancy, a mother, is torn from her twin boys, bought cheaply by a "brutish" slave trader, with Peggy voicing the audience's sorrowful sentiments: "Oh! No, they mustn't separate them!" As the boys are sold, "the agonized wail of Nancy is heard off."[19] Also traded are a husband and wife, Horatius and Geranium-Lou, split apart by the same taunting trader, who, in Legree fashion, publicly recites his punishment plans to Peggy's open rebukes. MGM's intent to stress the scene's psychic brutality—for Peggy and the enslaved—is obvious from the studio's first synopsis: "[Peggy] has never dreamed it would be so terrible, and, appalled by the smiling cruelty of a slave trader who is there to buy, Peggy begins wildly and emotionally bidding against him."[20] And yet, the auction doesn't convert Peggy into an abolitionist but rather convinces her to buy slaves, "rescuing" them through paternalism rather than freedom.

Notably, Morgan excludes the "broken" Charity in this scene. Instead he amplifies the market's sexual exchange. The scene begins with sale of "Fanny" ("Lilac" in later drafts), who starts out "anxious" with "her movements awkward" as Shyrock decrees her a "buxom, healthy wench as ever I see," while "look[ing] at her attributes." Confronted with low bids, he escalates, dubbing her "a glorious specimen of unblemished ebony" and praising the "discriminating" high-bidding "men." Seemingly enjoying the mounting attention, Fanny "beams from ear to ear and wriggles coyly" for the crowd.[21] The scene openly admits that Fanny is being sold to a white man for her sexual potential. But it also indicates that Fanny welcomes the transaction without sadness or resistance. The scene's sexual spectacle climaxed with Cree, no longer Adams's novel's feebleminded soul but instead a virile man. More surprising is Peggy's intent with and reaction to Cree; rather than wanting a slave playmate, in Morgan's version Peggy announces her desire for a strong, black "protector."[22] When caught at the slave market by her love interest, the historical U.S. congressman Randolph of Roanoke who has disapprovingly followed her, Peggy reveals that she wants to buy a "nice, strong slave of my own."[23] She picks Cree gleefully after the auctioneer calls him "a fine specimen of African manhood" and affirms her decision because, as she says, "her eyes glued to Cree, ecstatically"—"He's beautiful!" This utterance comes as Randolph protests: "the boy is a rogue, a worthless runway."[24] Peggy's profession of Cree's beauty is not in the novel though; there, Peggy similarly remarks to the quadroon Marrah, during their brief brothel exchange: "Nobody would leave you. . . . If they did, they'd come back to you. You're so beautiful."[25] Though Peggy bids on Cree partly to outdo the nasty slave trader aiming to break him, it is not this desire that she decrees but rather a breathless "I must have him," one that even the auctioneer notices as "saucy."[26] Randolph, helpless against Peggy's "large, liquid eyes, aglow with desperate imploration," eventually assists the girl when her small purse fails. But Peggy's barely implicit desire for the black man is underlined when Randolph, jealous, refuses to walk Peggy home because her beautiful "slave is fully capable of accompanying" her.[27] Aunt Sukey's response further underlines interaction's carnality; Sukey is shocked and ashamed at Peggy "buying bucks off the block."[28] It wasn't until December that Morgan apparently thought about making Peggy's desire for Cree *deniable* to censors or critics. Even then the effort was weak; Morgan hastily added a quip from Peggy to a suitor her age named Rowdy: "I've just bought that [referring to Cree]—isn't it beautifully ugly?"[29] This is a thin, awkward counterpoint to her earlier, weightier passion, apparently designed solely to make her desire for Cree questionable.

The scene's erotic direction accorded with Peggy's maturation from fourteen (in the novel) to a "full-grown" seventeen and with the studio's desire to deliver on the novel's suggestive title. On the one hand, it revealed the slave trade's sexual dynamics and hinted at America's well-developed system of racial concubinage that Hollywood rarely portrayed. However, the sequence transforms Adams's sober, unsentimental slave market into an alternately sentimental and lewd one, driven by Peggy's casual impulsiveness, lust, and perverse logic: no longer does the scene arouse Peggy's moral sensibilities; instead like Frou Frou of *The Toy Wife* (MGM, 1938), Jezebel of *Jezebel* (Warner Bros., 1938), and Scarlett of *Gone with the Wind* (Selznick, 1939), the gorgeous hussy converts all spectacles to her impetuous, dangerous sexual desire's regime.[30] In Morgan's rendering, Peggy doesn't condemn the slave market; instead she becomes its most lustful consumer. Uncannily, given the Code era's penchant for condemning licentious women, Morgan's script gives Peggy free rein, enjoying throughout her wafting desires and adventures without punishing her.[31] But, probably quite by accident, with Peggy's possessive desire for the slave, Morgan hit upon a scenario where, because of the intersectional power dynamics of race and gender, the white woman's desire actually was dangerous to Cree rather than to white patriarchy alone. However, perhaps it was precisely this raw intersectional awareness of the social difference between desiring white and black men that allowed MGM to believe the scene permissible. Even in Morgan's scripts, interracial desire had limits. He removed Adams's mulatto chattels who doubly signified racial concubinage by their telltale light skin and the lusty bids that greeted them. Morgan also dampened the racial implications of the brothel, one not only frequented by politicians but whose proprietor draws Randolph's ire because her ladies visit the congressional halls; Morgan converted Marrah, who synopses called a "quadroon," into a "creole." She still warns naïve Peggy of the brothel's horrors (ostensibly caused partly by congressmen) and later kills herself.[32] But Morgan never implies that congressmen slept with "black" prostitutes. Marrah became just a "girl" in the second treatment. And later she and the brothel were entirely removed.[33]

Cree's extended interracial fight, one that nearly ended in lynching, was equally dangerous, but Morgan always intended to include it. The details indicate that studio saw little problem with showing white violence against slaves. Further, in Morgan's early drafts, Cree fights back; he effectually "leaps for Sunderland's throat. The impact sends Sunderland's knife flying from his hand. They both jump to regain the weapon. Cree unbalances Sunderland. He falls on his own knife."[34] Morgan escalated and embellished the attack in the next draft. Sunderland's lynch mob returns with a battering ram, shouting, "Hang th' dog! . . . Burn him at th' stake! Cut his black heart out!" "Oil and fire make pyres!" and "lynch th' mongrel!"[35] In the scene's final act, Morgan, like Adams, pulled some punches. Though the slaves' quarters are brimming with men who "sense the truth" of Cree's innocence, Cree is paralyzed with fear and the black mob prays rather than defending itself.[36] Indeed, it is not until the white founding fathers arrive—Randolph and Andrew Jackson among them—that Sunderland's racist mob is put down. Despite Morgan's hesitation, the runaway, rebellious, branded Cree's initial aggressiveness in fending off Sunderland opened up narrative directions—in what it suggested about Cree's attachment to Peggy and about the history of slave rebellion—both Cree's and America's. Hereafter until April when the scene was removed, writers decreased Cree's resistance and culpability: Cree would make *no* aggressive moves, instead wrapping Sunderland in a massive bear hug to restrain him from attacking.[37]

JOSEPH BREEN AND THE INDUSTRY SELF-REGULATION OF SLAVERY

A few years earlier, with MPPDA (Motion Pictures Producers and Distributors of America) representative Jason Joy's more relaxed and negotiable style of industry self-censorship, MGM might have actualized these scenes as Universal had with *Uncle Tom's Cabin* (1928). Though the Production Code barred "sex relationships between the black and white races," with films like *Imitation of Life* (1934), the PCA (Production Code Administration) established a broad interpretation of this tenet, prohibiting even hints of white-black interracial desire.[38] Similarly, as Amy Wood and I have argued, lynching was under increased Code-era scrutiny, especially when the on-screen victims were black.[39] In 1936, studios developed images of slavery's brutality that would challenge chief Hollywood censor Joseph Breen. *Slave Ship* (Twentieth Century Fox, 1937) and *Souls at Sea* (Paramount, 1937) raised Breen's apprehension with their *mise-en-abyme* scenes of whipping during the middle passage, which Breen saw as "dangerous," "likely to be offensive to average audiences" and "to be removed by political censor boards."[40] *Anthony Adverse* (Warner Bros., 1936) featured a resonant Havana scene where an enslaved black man's public beating so disturbs the onlookers that a Catholic priest stands in the whip's path. Breen warned against detail in this scene as he had earlier warned against the film's slave auction scenes, calling them "very questionable from the standpoint of audience reaction and political censorship."[41] Breen stated more forcefully "it is imperative that you do not indulge in any cruelty to the slaves" and that these scenes be "merely suggested" rather than handled with "detail."[42] In tandem, these recommendations indicate Breen's sustained efforts in 1935–1936 to soften the realities of slave procurement (kidnapping, killing, and torture) from the middle passage to the auction block.

Though the first synopsis is dated 1934, it was not until October 1935 that MGM submitted a draft of *The Gorgeous Hussy* to Breen. His first letter, of October 7, stated emphatically that the high-class brothel sequence must be dropped and that Peggy's relationships with men should be free of physical contact. Regarding slavery, Breen's judgment was candid, direct, and peppered throughout the letter: not only did brutality toward slaves have to be softened but the attempted lynching of the enslaved Cree "handled with care."[43] Breen's biggest concern was with the impact slavery's depiction had upon the nation's historical leaders: "As a matter of general caution, care must be taken with the characterization of known historical figures in order to avoid offense. Most important, of course, is the characterization of Jackson and the other well-known political figures. Care should be taken with the treatment of the slave servants. It would be wise to avoid emphasizing the existence of slavery."[44] Breen desired to remove the taint of brutal slavery from the image of America's founding fathers, its seminal political moments, and its enshrined history and admonished MGM against Adams's grim depiction of the institution. Breen's words also suggest his discomfort with slavery's *prominence* in *The Gorgeous Hussy*. Breen clearly preferred the plantation melodrama's naturalized "slave servants" and reference to slavery only as a pastoral, paternalistic axiom of southern life as he let these pass without comment in many films of the era.

In response, MGM's screenwriters subtly shifted the slave market scene but in fact increased its intensity.[45] In his February 1936 first draft, newly added screenwriter Stephen Morehouse Avery, perhaps eager to show his boldness and capability, submitted a revised auction scene amplifying its sexuality. The elongated sequence added a new opening at the Franklin Inn where Cuthbert, a white servant, tells Randolph that Peggy has gone to "buy 'erself a boy—a Black boy . . . a little black slave boy all 'er own" at the slave market.[46] This addition suggests that Peggy broadcasted her desire for a black boy to white, male servants—and sets the audience up for a later added scene where Cuthbert, surprised that Peggy bought a black man rather than a child, says "amazed": "You bought all that for forty-five dollars?" "Well," Peggy retorts, "I threw in a smile."[47] Adding to the sexual dynamics, Avery bolstered the auctioneer's masculinizing description of Cree as "a lion of strength and devotion," "broad as an ox," and a "Goliath in th' flesh."[48] The power-laden tension linking the black man (on the auction block) to Peggy and her elder white gentleman friend (among the buyers) is more pronounced in Avery's version; Peggy threatens to publicly kiss Randolph if he doesn't help her buy Cree, and when Randolph asks why he "must" help her, Peggy baldly retorts, "Because I want him—that's why. (as she looks at Cree) Look at him. He's beautiful!"[49] Her scandalous profession of longing for Cree is augmented by her instruction to look. Her control of the gaze and, further, her direction of the white masculine gaze to the black masculine subject and away from the feminine subject, who is, here, the active, desiring, *driving* sexual force, trammel the norms of Hollywood cinema's looking relations.

Given that MGM script and research materials characterized Randolph as definitely impotent and possibly gay, Peggy's pressing Randolph to see Cree's beauty as well as Randolph's decision to buy Cree for Peggy take on accrued meaning.[50] In this draft, Cree also clearly *returns* Peggy's desire, at least insofar as her buying him is concerned: while he's being auctioned, he looks "weak and spindling . . . while the brutal man bids," but "turns-like a grinning black Samson—toward Peggy, his huge hands thumping his chests." Peggy is saucier and clearly victorious, with Randolph completely succumbing to her desire's force, forgiving her "her slave and her political opinions." Avery's version brought the "beautiful slave" into Peggy's interactions with other suitors, too. Later, when Peggy meets amorous Rowdy, who says that soon they will elope, far from dissuading him, she replies: "Oh, it would be much more exciting at night, Rowdy. But, you see, (turning toward Cree) it was for protection against just such impulses I have just bought . . . CLOSE SHOT—CREE strutting and grinning and trying to look even more powerful, very proud of his new estate as Peggy's slave."[51] Though Morgan had earlier added a line where Peggy calls Cree "beautifully ugly" making Peggy's desire deniable, Avery removed it and its deniability, replacing it with "isn't it [Cree] magnificent?"[52] Avery's draft further linked the market's brutality to the lynching: among Sunderland's mob is "the brute of the slave market scene . . . grasping a black-snake whip."[53] By March 5, 1936, acquiescing slightly, Avery had shortened the lynching. But Peggy's passionate desire for the slave was intensified, as was evidence of Cree's devotion to Peggy.

Not surprisingly, the PCA's second letter, on March 10, 1936, was stronger than the first. Where before he suggested, Breen now indicated that the auction's "details" had to be "cut to a necessary minimum. There must be absolutely no objectionable or nude exposure of the persons of the slaves. Brutal treatment of the slaves must not be shown or indicated."[54] Lilac could not be suggestive. The mention of a brutish slave trader should be removed. And "in the handling of Cree" and even the "ad lib dialogue, there must be no indication of brutality. As a matter of caution," Breen even suggested "that the showing of the brand on Cree's shoulder blade and the dialogue referring to it be deleted," along with the term "lynching" later in the script. Breen also noted and sought to blunt the film's sexual desire, stating that Peggy's reference to Cree as "beautiful . . . must be removed," as did the brothel, though if it were "described as a cabaret or gambling house . . . this material might be acceptable."[55] Breen pushed MGM to remove any indications of brutality and interracial sexuality. So grave were Breen's objections that his staff officially met with producer Joseph L. Mankiewicz and the screenwriters several days later.[56] Given the PCA focus on morality, the meeting centered on how to alter the brothel scene.[57]

Bizarrely, MGM retained both the slave auction and the lynching scenes into April, despite Breen's heavy warnings. Mankiewicz's production notes called for "no brutal handling of the slaves," and still the auction scene with Lilac, the branded Cree as a "lion of devotion and strength," along with Peggy's desire for a male slave persisted into the April 7, 1936, draft that Mankiewicz okayed.[58] Perhaps this is the case because Breen stressed the brothel scene and did not belabor Peggy's implied desire for Cree. Though the writers played down a few censorable details, others, more distanced but meta-phorical, were added. For example, the draft intensified the interracial love triangle:

PEGGY: I love you—

They look at each other. Pause.

RANDOLPH: I'm sorry then. I don't love you, Peggy—

Peggy approaches him.

PEGGY: You're a liar, John Randolph—(*she puts her arms around his neck, her lips close to his*) Aren't you a liar?

RANDOLPH (*quietly*): If you don't mind—you're not buying a slave—

He disengages her arms. She looks at him for a moment. She turns quickly and leaves the room.

REVERSE ANGLE-RANDOLPH

Randolph stares at the closed door . . . his expression revealing the intensity of his self denial.[59]

Peggy's erotic force in this moment of romantic fervor reminds Randolph of that which she has visited upon male slaves and he feels himself in the position of a bought slave, hailing back to the auction block moment as a seminal one in their romantic relationship and, apparently, in defining all of Peggy's affections. MGM made some changes, however: in the April draft, the slave trader is no longer called a "brute." And in the lynching scene, Sunderland no longer cuts Cree and the mob says it will "hang" rather than "lynch" him. Further, Peggy no longer relishes elopement with Sunderland but instead begs Cree to help her escape her "kidnapper."[60] But as the writers reduced the lynching scene's racial violence, they developed a parallel scene. Bow Timberlake, Peggy's first husband, falls for the wrong brown girl on a tropical island and is drawn into a knife fight and killed.[61] The scene absorbed the lynching scene's drama, retaining the hussy (though this time a brown one) and the knife fight but transferring the racial conflict to from the nation's capital to the islands and allowing the police rather than the lynching posse to regulate the threat of racial transgression.

By mid-April, MGM's writers relented, severely altering the market sequence. While Peggy still wants a male slave, and the auction still begins with Lilac's sale, the slave she buys is no longer Cree but "Horatius," a man so tired and lazy that he falls asleep on the auction block. The auctioneer still describes the auctioned black man in virile terms as a "superb body bursting with dynamic energy," a "mountain of strength," but this draws bidders' laughter, due to Horatius's sleepiness.[62] And though characters still refer to Horatius as "beautiful," it's never Peggy but the *auctioneer* who says "there, gentlemen, is a beautiful sight!" and later Randolph dryly calls him Peggy's "sleeping beauty."[63] In buying Horatius, Peggy's plan is foiled; her desires are checked, and she is universally chided rather than triumphant. Thus, the idea of Peggy sleeping with her slave was transmuted into Peggy purchasing a sleeping slave who is "dead on his feet" and the slave auction sequence Adams designed for riots of empathy was transformed to produce riots of laughter from spectators, on- and off-screen.[64] In this draft, Sunderland tries to kidnap Peggy, but Horatius, blundering through the door with an armful of wood, falls in front of him, literally getting in his way—becoming an object, though he considers "himself quite a hero." Horatius is center of the film's running joke. In a twist symptomatic of the actual politics of racialized labor, British Cuthbert takes the role of headman and forces Horatius "comically" into labor. However, Horatius's hard work results in a rise in station. The book shows slaves being freed, but here screenwriters have Horatius ironically proclaim his increasing value while still a slave: "Horatius: (with dignity) Ah am de pussonal servant to Mr. John Eaton, de new Minister to de King 'O Spain . . . (indignantly) . . . ah ain't no nobody, now—I'se somebody."[65] Rather than the tense, violent scene with the slave quarters under siege, it included a South-friendly Negro spiritual scene in which Jackson says, "Singin' gives em the happiness they want—an' deserve. Sometimes I think they deserve more than—other folks." Despite this, Horatius contrasts with the desirable Cree, and though it shuffled more elements than it omitted, the script confirmed even the slave auction as benign and comical.

FROM SEXUAL TO SECTIONAL CONCERNS: NATHALIE BUCKNALL AND STIRRINGS BELOW THE LINE

The April draft's shifts resulted partly from MGM Research and Legal department challenges to the film's depiction of slavery and the South. Typically, research departments focused on architecture, props, and ephemera, ensuring that the film's material culture avoided anachronism. Despite the filmmakers' general ignorance about black cultural history, very little effort was typically expended verifying story lines related to slavery. With *The Gorgeous Hussy*, the research department's racial politics overtook the research process. Nathalie Bucknall's female-dominated MGM research unit generated over four hundred pages of material on *The Gorgeous Hussy*, seeking accuracy with oft-scrutinized presidential history and nineteenth-century Washington milieu. But following Adams's lead, Bucknall researched not only expected presidential particulars but also the details of black life. An early memo, for example, noted that in 1820 Washington had 13,247 residents, of which roughly 28 percent were black.[66] These research notes justify Adams's and MGM's planned brimming black cast. Bucknall also researched Washington's ten-o'clock black curfew.[67]

Bucknall researched servants' dress and living quarters but also both tested and proved Adams's account of the slave market. Bucknall asked the questions, but MGM Home office representative William D. Kelly (often known as W. D. Kelly) provided much of the research.[68] Bucknall sent out requests like "should posters of the period be printed or hand written? Check on proceedings of slave sale in that period" and "Were R's branded into runaway slaves' shoulder? If so, on what shoulder?"[69] And Kelly responded, sending images of slave markets, slave bills of sale, posters advertising slave auctions, and pictures of slave drivers and coffles.[70] Employing these photographs, Bucknall's team facilitated the construction of a largely accurate slave auction set. Bucknall also emphasized that it "should offer definite contrast" with the film's other "brick, trim and neat" buildings, making it "a clapboard construction (use old, used lumber in various colors but no positive black and white—get dingy, faded effect)."[71] Prompted by legal department libel concerns, Bucknall researched whether Shyrock, the book's auction owner, actually existed.[72] Bucknall sought to materialize slavery through correctly rendered props, including a "blacksnake whip" on a list of essentials.[73]

Bucknall's early research efforts suggest that she sought to both re-create and build on Adams's vision of early black Washington. Bucknall, an aspiring screenwriter, proposed several screenplay sequences.[74] Most involved white women characters, including tabloid publisher Anne Royall, for whom Bucknall invented a bold sequence in which she steals "reserved, pompous" John Quincy Adams's clothes during his early morning naked swim in the Potomac and holds them ransom in order to get an interview with him.[75] Notably, Bucknall also invented several additional scenes for black Washingtonians, suggesting, for example, that during a riot scene after Andrew Jackson's election, black Washingtonians would be visible "on the outskirts . . . frightened to get mixed up in the 'white folks doings,'" save "one group [of Negroes who] might come up to the Franklin inn in a *procession,* with torches, banners and signs," a scene implying at once the decorum and legitimate fear of curfewed black Washingtonians. In addition to a parading volunteer fire company, a confused drunk yelling "'Ray for George Washington!" and a group of "disgusted" women scoffing at the rioters, she also imagined "Negro boys with gamecocks . . . arguing about whose bird is the best fighter. One bird is named 'Napoleon' and the other 'General Jackson.'"[76] Knowledgeable researchers like Bucknall stood to help develop a historically accurate narrative plot.

But Bucknall would not use her research to further black-associated plotlines. In April, Bucknall underwent a change on whether the plot should consider slavery, sectional conflict, and black people, likely in response to MGM Legal Department representative Robert E. Kopp.[77] On April 25, Bucknall wrote a memo to Joseph Mankiewicz, seemingly her first to him of the film's research and production phase. The highly unusual memo stands at odds with Bucknall's earlier stance, pushing against Adams's novel subtle anti-slavery sentiment. "I feel that you should receive the comments as set out below in view of the fact that they are purely of a historical research nature and do not purport to be anything else but such research," the memo suspiciously began.[78] Raising the memo's stakes, Bucknall told Mankiewicz that these points had been thoroughly researched *and* "submitted in rough draft form to Mr. Kopp of the legal department" who "discussed the danger of criminal libel on the above production."[79] Kopp's (and now Bucknall's) "libel" concerns were not limited to a few historical figures (Jackson and John C. Calhoun, for example) as earlier documents indicated.[80] Instead they were broadened into a paragraph titled "GENERAL DISCUSSION OF STATES RIGHTS, APPLICABLE TO THE WHOLE SCRIPT":

> I think that the most serious objection is not isolated to inaccuracies but the general concept of the political situation. The difficulty is that in order to force the character Randolph into a suitor of Peggy, and in order to provide Peggy with a romantic sacrifice for the good of her country, the history of sectional conflict may be considered by the public as having been tampered with in an erroneous and objectionable manner; and I am afraid that the audience will be left with the idea that the South was plotting treason and rebellion and assas-

sination, and that slavery was a strong moral issue at the time. Furthermore, the Southern states especially and people with knowledge of history will have the feeling that the picture has mixed together the outbreak of the Civil War, the plot which resulted in the assassination of Lincoln, etc.[81]

Bucknall's words echo an earlier seven-page memo from R. E. Kopp, which stood adamantly against depicting John C. Calhoun as a proto-secessionist, challenged whether states' rights and rebellion were credibly linked, and stated as fact that "abolition was considered a crank idea of fanatics" in the 1830s.[82] Though Kopp's motives are unclear, his perspective would now be considered erroneous: current historians concede that the 1832 Nullification Crisis, in which South Carolina issued the Ordinance of Nullification, threatening to secede rather than pay certain new taxes, bore marks of the political positions that sparked Civil War.[83] And Kopp's dismissal of 1830s abolitionism contradicts modern scholarship documenting the Underground Railroad's existence by 1810.[84] Though pro-southern historians, some of whom, like Ulrich B. Phillips, found paid gigs advising filmmakers, repressed this history, a rising tide of 1930s leftists brought it to light, and Adams, born of a family with strong abolitionist roots, knew this and applied it to his novel.[85] Without a single historical citation and departing from the research she had conducted, Bucknall's memo argued doggedly for states' rights and against slavery's centrality as a "moral issue." Seemingly usurped by Kopp, Bucknall paraphrased him almost verbatim, stating that since the American Revolution, the country was divided between those supporters of centralized government or states' rights. "Up to the period of *The Gorgeous Hussy*, both of these parties had been equally inconsistent, were led by men of equal honor and patriotism, and based their party platforms on equally logical interpretations of the Constitution. . . . Webster's party was not a group of heroic defenders of their country's honor; the party of Randolph and Calhoun was *not* a group of 'dangerous and destructive' and 'treasonable' plotters to destroy their country."[86] Thus, in bold strokes under the guise of "research" and "libel" concerns, Kopp and Bucknall adopted as *fact* a southern version of this historical period. Furthermore, they suggested directly to the film's producer that Adams's view would be legally dangerous to MGM, even libelous. Bucknall opined that the script's line, spoken by Daniel Webster, "This dangerous and destructive doctrine—State's Rights—was fought and conquered by the framers of our glorious Constitution," was simply "not true; the Constitution was considered by its makers to guarantee to the individual states the utmost of sovereignty and rights consistent with the unified action on concerns of common interest. The lines immediately following the script, forecasting the Civil War, with the South portrayed in a villainous light will be considered by Southern states as in bad taste, unjustified and prejudiced."[87] By this point, Bucknall was not only disregarding the original intent of the book's author but cutting credibly accurate anti-secessionist dialogue. This seven-page memo might well have been the document that changed the course of the script. In it, Bucknall, who had earlier developed African American plot points, reversed herself—allowing her Research Department to be used to defend "states' rights," a doctrine as useful to the white South during the emerging civil rights movement as it was during the Civil War. Kopp/Bucknall's insistence that slavery was not a Jacksonian-era "moral issue" likely subtended the recasting of the slave market as comedy rather than tragedy. Notably, MGM's "libel" concerns did not extend to northern congressmen in 1942 when *Tennessee Johnson* was made, as the film's Research Department files aver. MGM showed no concern about portraying anti-slavery congressman Thaddeus Stevens unsympathetically—and even suggested incredibly that he plotted to kill Lincoln.[88]

FROM THE "BEAUTIFUL SLAVE" TO THE "SLEEPING LION"

MGM maintained the slave auction and even considered Cree's story line after the Bucknall-Kopp memo and well into the shooting of the film. The film's set reference *and* publicity photographs include the auction. Though these show Horatius rather than Cree (see Figures 3.1 and 3.2), that several of these photos ended up in magazine publicity spreads suggests slavery remained a part of the film's paratextual diegesis and further a "selling point."[89] Harry Levette, the black press's most reliable, syndicated Hollywood reporter, referred repeatedly to *The Gorgeous Hussy* in 1935–1936, calling it "the big picture of the season . . . so far as employment . . . for Race players is concerned, needing large crowds of extras and a number of bit and part players." It wasn't until July 4, less than a month before the film's release, that he reported that Central Casting had sent out possibly the film's last group of "atmosphere players."[90] Levette's sources were reliable. He often got casting

FIGURE 3.1 Horatius at the auction surrounded by a full complement of unhappy souls. *The Gorgeous Hussy* (1936). Collections of the Margaret Herrick Library.

news from African American Charles Butler, the black casting czar for Central Casting from the mid-1920s and through 1951.

Corroborating the studio's persistent fascination with Cree, Levette reported in May that the cast included not only Fred "Snowflake" Toones (Horatius in the MGM press photos) and Mildred Gover (as Lilac, the seductive woman on the auction block), but also Louise Beavers (as Aunt Sukey) and Daniel Haynes, likely as Cree.[91] Casting Haynes as Cree, if MGM had gone through with it, would have set a precedent in screen representability of both rebellious, desirable black enslaved men and, in Avery and Morgan's bold rewriting, the mistress's possessive sexual desire for the enslaved largely invisible until films like *Mandingo* (1977). Haynes, who established his rebellion and sexual potency in the safely all-black *Hallelujah* (1929), where he courts two women and escapes the chain gang, stood to further heighten Cree's intertextual association with rebellion and sex. Audiences reading Haynes through his *Hallelujah* role likely would have seen him as just the right black man to match Peggy in sexual prowess and social insurgence.[92]

FIGURE 3.2 "You bought all that for $45?," Cuthbert remarks to Peggy. *The Gorgeous Hussy* (1936). Collections of the Margaret Herrick Library.

Ultimately, MGM removed the auction and all black characters from the finished film, though the company used the auction in radio ads for the film, evincing the plotted scenes of subjection's shadowy persistence. That the removal of most black cast members came *after* the film was shot seems evident from Louis Lautier's September *Baltimore Afro-American* article complaining that though Louise Beavers was "listed as Aunt Sukey in the program of the world premiere of 'The Gorgeous Hussy'" she "nowhere appeared in the flicker." Her part, he deduced, "was cut entirely out of the script."[93] Thus, in *The Gorgeous Hussy* film, Adams's complex, subtly rendered portrayal slavery's imbrication with American politics became a sleeping lion behind MGM's muted on-screen representation. The dangerous conception of "the beautiful slave," "the lion of devotion and strength" that positioned the slave as both chattel and desirable man, straddled Hollywood's unspoken axioms about blackness as pleasurable property and gelled with the studio's scandalous hussy narrative but, when explicitly spoken as MGM attempted, was subject to self-censorship. MGM's *Gorgeous Hussy* screenplay represented a bold, ribald experiment with suggesting the southern woman's desire for a male slave. In the early sound era, with its pre-Code, sexually empowered flappers, it might have stood a better chance. The lion might have roared.

NOTES

1. William Still, *Underground Railroad* (Philadelphia: Porter and Coates, 1872); W. E. B. Du Bois, *Black Reconstruction of Democracy in America* (New York: Harcourt, Brace, 1935); Carter G. Woodson, *The Negro in Our History* (Washington, DC: Associated Publisher, 1922).

2. See the note appended to RKO's summary of galleys for *The Gorgeous Hussy*, which mentions earlier bulletins for *President Peggy* (February 12, 1934), *Andrew Jackson and the Border Capital* (February 12, 1934), and *The Cavalier of Tennessee* (January 29, 1934) and which sought to make Samuel Hopkins Adams's book into a film in July 1934. "Summary of Galleys for *The Gorgeous Hussy*," n.d., box 345S, RKO Collection, UCLA Special Collections.

3. Samuel Hopkins Adams, *The Gorgeous Hussy* (New York: Grosset and Dunlap, 1934), 3. Adams's story weaves slavery into the fabric of the lives of early nineteenth-century white Washingtonians. Indeed, the words "slave" and "slaves" appear seventy-six times through the course of the novel, not to mention the terms "Negro" and "abolitionist" and the names of individual enslaved people (there are at least six such named characters in the novel). In the first part of the three-part novel, *every* chapter is introduced through the activities of the enslaved people.

4. There were several slave pens, owned respectively by Robey, Williams, and Neale, near the Capitol Building at that time, and slave coffles were brought across the National Mall to the disgust of foreign travelers. See Sabiyha Prince, *African Americans and Gentrification in Washington, D.C.: Race, Class and Justice in the Nation's Capital* (New York: Routledge, 2016), 38–39.

5. Adams, *Gorgeous Hussy*, 21.

6. Adams, *Gorgeous Hussy*, 44.

7. Adams, *Gorgeous Hussy*, 52–53.

8. Adams, *Gorgeous Hussy*, 50.

9. Adams, *Gorgeous Hussy*, 92–102.

10. Adams, *Gorgeous Hussy*, 80–83.

11. Adams, *Gorgeous Hussy*, 506, 510.

12. Queena Pollack, *Peggy Eaton: Democracy's Mistress* (New York: Minton, Balsch and Company, 1931), 8–10.

13. Lewis, like Adams, includes central black characters and an extended discourse between the novel's major characters blaming the Nullification Crisis on slavery. Alfred Henry Lewis, *Peggy O'Neal* (New York: American News Company, 1903), esp. 178–179, 456–458.

14. Samuel Hopkins Adams, "The Slave in the Family," *New Yorker*, December 13, 1947, 32–33.

15. See Jane Murfin Treatment, July 14, 1934, box 345S, UCLA. Even the plot descriptions from the galleys downplay the lynching sequence. "The faithful Cree comes upon him and drives him off. In the struggle he is wounded; a band of mechanics drunk in celebration find him as he is fleeing and he tells of having been attacked by a negro. They follow him back to the inn in riotous manner, to get Cree and a hand-to-hand battle occurs between the guests of the house and the rowdies. The guests are victorious; Peggy, convinced that her Sunderland is despicable, abandons all thoughts of romance with him; and her father, realizing that matters have gone too far, sends her away to school." "RKO Summary of Galleys for *The Gorgeous Hussy*," n.d., box 345S, RKO Collection, UCLA Special Collections.

16. "Languid niggers shuffle along the dirt streets or gather in small groups under the shade of trees, talking their small talk or gambling their pennies away to the tune of superstitious jargon." Ainsworth Morgan, First Draft Treatment of Gorgeous Hussy, 1; see 22 for Stepin Fetchit reference. August 30, 1935, folder G-909, Turner/MGM Collection, Academy of Motion Picture Arts and Sciences (AMPAS).

17. Ainsworth Morgan, Dia. Cont., October 28, 1935, 4, folder G-910, Turner/MGM Collection, AMPAS.

18. Ainsworth Morgan, Dia. Cont., October 28, 1935, 4, folder G-910, Turner/MGM Collection, AMPAS, 3.

19. Ainsworth Morgan, Dia. Cont., October 28, 1935, 4, folder G-910, Turner/MGM Collection, AMPAS, 8–9.

20. Lucille Sullivan, "Synopsis of Gorgeous Hussy," March 6, 1934, 3, folder G-907, Turner/MGM Collection, AMPAS.

21. Ainsworth Morgan, Dia. Cont., October 28, 1935, 5–6, folder G-910, Turner/MGM Collection, AMPAS.

22. Ainsworth Morgan, Dia. Cont., October 28, 1935, 5–6, folder G-910, Turner/MGM Collection, AMPAS, 7.

23. Ainsworth Morgan, Dia. Cont., October 28, 1935, 5–6, folder G-910, Turner/MGM Collection, AMPAS, 7.

24. Ainsworth Morgan, Dia. Cont., October 28, 1935, 5–6, folder G-910, Turner/MGM Collection, AMPAS, 11.

25. Adams, *Gorgeous Hussy*, 83.

26. Ainsworth Morgan, Dia. Cont., October 28, 1935, 10–11, folder G-910, Turner/MGM Collection, AMPAS.

27. Ainsworth Morgan, Dia. Cont., October 28, 1935, 10–11, folder G-910, Turner/MGM Collection, AMPAS, 15.

28. Ainsworth Morgan, Dia. Cont., October 28, 1935, 10–11, folder G-910, Turner/MGM Collection, AMPAS, 20.

29. Ainsworth Morgan, Dia. Cont. December 20, 1935, 12, folder 911, Turner/MGM Collection, AMPAS.

30. In all of these films, as in *The Gorgeous Hussy*, the white woman's sexual desire is associated with blackness (and in almost all of them the white woman is sidled and abetted by an enslaved character played by the beautiful black actress Theresa Harris).

31. On the image of the scandalous and fallen woman, see Lea Jacobs's excellent *The Wages of Sin: Censorship and the Fallen Woman, 1928–1942* (Madison: University of Wisconsin Press, 1991).

32. Ainsworth Morgan, Dia. Cont. October 28, 1935, 48, folder 911, Turner/MGM Collection, AMPAS.

33. Madame Strayter's house of prostitution became a "house of fortune" with girls bedecked in Oriental garb, then a house of the "seven seeresses" complete with crystal balls, and later was written out altogether. Ainsworth Morgan and Stephen Morehouse Avery, Dia. Cont., March 16, 1936, draft, 39.

34. Ainsworth Morgan, Dia. Cont., October 28, 1935, 58–67, folder G-910, Turner/MGM Collection, AMPAS.

35. Ainsworth Morgan, Dia. Cont., October 28, 1935, 58–67, folder G-910, Turner/MGM Collection, AMPAS, 60–61.

36. Ainsworth Morgan, Dia. Cont., October 28, 1935, 58–67, folder G-910, Turner/MGM Collection, AMPAS, 62.

37. "The huge, impassive black wraps his arms about the man to restrain his fury. He does not strike at Sunderland, but holds him until the latter, struggling violently, upsets the balance of both. As they fall, the knife drops from Sunderland's hand and he falls on it." Stephen Morehouse Avery, Dia. Cont., February 6. 1936, 53, folder 912, Turner/MGM Collection, AMPAS.

38. See Susan Courtney, *Hollywood Fantasies of Miscegenation: Spectacular Narratives of Gender and Race, 1903–1967* (Princeton, NJ: Princeton University Press, 2005), 147.

39. See Amy Wood, *Lynching and Spectacle: Witnessing Racial Violence in America, 1890–1940* (Chapel Hill: University of North Carolina Press, 2011); Ellen C. Scott, *Cinema Civil Rights: Regulation, Repression and Race in the Classical Hollywood Era* (New Brunswick, NJ: Rutgers University Press, 2015).

40. Memo for the files of June 5, 1936, and Breen to Joy, May 11, 1937, *Slave Ship* PCA file; Breen to Hammel, March 29, 1937, *Souls at Sea* PCA file.

41. Breen to Jack Warner, August 21, 1935, *Anthony Adverse* PCA file.

42. Breen to Jack Warner, September 10, 1935, *Anthony Adverse* PCA file.

43. Breen to Louis B. Mayer, October 7, 1935, *The Gorgeous Hussy* PCA file.

44. Breen to Louis B. Mayer, October 7, 1935, *The Gorgeous Hussy* PCA file.

45. For instance, where before the auctioneer had told spectators that with "a few strokes with the cat-o-nine tails," Cree would be a "lion of strength and devotion," in February drafts he omits mention of the whip and suggests instead that "kind, gentle treatment" would yield that result, thus reducing the auctioneer's support for punitive violence. But generally, the screenwriters failed to understand what Breen was getting at; slavery "should" be naturalized so one did not see or question it.

46. Stephen Morehouse Avery, Dia. Cont., February 6, 1936, 3, folder 912, Turner/MGM Collection, AMPAS.

47. Stephen Morehouse Avery, Dia. Cont., February 6, 1936, 3, folder 912, Turner/MGM Collection, AMPAS, 13.

48. Stephen Morehouse Avery, Dia. Cont., February 6, 1936, 3, folder 912, Turner/MGM Collection, AMPAS, 6.

49. Stephen Morehouse Avery, Dia. Cont., February 6, 1936, 3, folder 912, Turner/MGM Collection, AMPAS, 6.

50. In a memo of April 26, 1935, to Joseph Mankiewicz, Nathalie Bucknall states that "John Randolph was not an appetizing object of Peggy's romantic interest. In 1828, he was 35 years old, and prematurely aged. He was impotent, sterile, tubercular, of ruined digestion, and suffered frequent periods of insanity." The February 6, 1936, script draft written by Stephen Morehouse Avery included a scene of Randolph discussing possible suitors for Peggy and proclaiming in an oddly direct fashion that the "sailor" (Bow Timberlake) was "the best man of the lot" (65), thus helping Peggy to decide on another suitor. And when Peggy asks why he doesn't seem bothered by her flirting with other men, he silences her by sending her to bed. The scene suggests Randolph's ability to apprise men's attractiveness and leaves his lack of interest in Peggy undenied.

51. Avery, February 6, 1936, script draft, 10.

52. Avery, February 6, 1936, script draft, 10.

53. Avery, February 6, 1936, script draft, 53.

54. Breen to L. B. Mayer, March 10, 1936, *The Gorgeous Hussy* PCA file.

55. Breen to L. B. Mayer, March 10, 1936, *The Gorgeous Hussy* PCA file.

56. Ian Auster, Memo for the Files, March 14, 1936, *The Gorgeous Hussy* PCA file.

57. Ian Auster, Memo for the Files, March 14, 1936, *The Gorgeous Hussy* PCA file. Slavery did not appear to have been an issue at this meeting, according to the official memo, though we cannot assume that the memo tells all.

58. "Notes between Joe Mankiewicz, Avery, Clarence Brown, A. Morgan, Block, Levanway, and Austin," March 13, 1936, folder G-915, and Ainsworth Morgan and Stephen Morehouse Avery, Dia. Cont., folder G-918, Turner/MGM Collection, AMPAS.

59. Ainsworth Morgan and Stephen Morehouse Avery, April 7 Draft, Turner/MGM Collection, AMPAS.

60. Ainsworth Morgan and Stephen Morehouse Avery, Dia. Cont., 45–53, folder G-918, Turner/MGM Collection, AMPAS.

61. Ainsworth Morgan and Stephen Morehouse Avery, Dia. Cont., April 7, 1936, F.G-918, Turner/MGM Collection, AMPAS.

62. Ainsworth Morgan and Stephen Morehouse Avery, Dia. Cont., April 18, 1936, F.G-919, Turner/MGM Collection, AMPAS.

63. Ainsworth Morgan and Stephen Morehouse Avery, Dia. Cont., April 18, 1936, F.G-919, Turner/MGM Collection, AMPAS, 6–7.

64. Ainsworth Morgan and Stephen Morehouse Avery, Dia. Cont., April 18, 1936, F.G-919, Turner/MGM Collection, AMPAS, 8.

65. Ainsworth Morgan and Stephen Morehouse Avery, Dia. Cont., April 18, 1936, F.G-919, Turner/MGM Collection, AMPAS, 137.

66. In 1840, that percentage remained largely the same, the research files noted, though the free black population had expanded from 13 percent in 1820 to 20 percent in 1840. Bucknall cites her source as *The History of the City of Washington*, edited by Allan B. Slauson of the

Library of Congress in 1903. "Washington D.C. Architecture, 1800–1850—GORGEOUS HUSSY," undated memo, 2–3, MGM Research Files, UCLA Special Collections, box 55.

67. Bucknall confirmed this through Richard Jackson's 1878 *Chronicles of Georgetown, D.C.*, 37. "Washington D.C. Architecture, 1800–1850—GORGEOUS HUSSY," undated memo, 2–3, MGM Research Files, UCLA Special Collections, box 55. Bucknall's research was extensive, and much of it revealed a lot about the black Washington community and its history.

68. Kelly had worked on censorship concerns at MGM at least since 1927, when he helped manage the ethnic/religious debacle surrounding *The Callahans and the Murphys*. Francis Couvares, "Hollywood, Main Street, and the Church: Trying to Censor the Movies before the Production Code," in *Movie Censorship and American Culture*, ed. Francis Couvares (Amherst: University of Massachusetts Press, 2006), 129–158, 146.

69. "Special Research—GORGEOUS HUSSY," n.d., MGM Research Files, UCLA Special Collections, box 55.

70. W. D. Kelly to Nathalie Bucknall, Airmail, March 11, 1936, MGM Research Files, UCLA Special Collections, box 56; W. D. Kelly to Nathalie Bucknall, Airmail, March 13, 1936, MGM Research Files, UCLA Special Collections, box 56. According to the files, the images used to build the slave auction house set were based on creditable but public histories including *Pageant of America* III, 156 and *Photographic History of the Civil War* IX (V-13). "Washington D.C. Architecture, 1800–1850—GORGEOUS HUSSY," undated memo, 2–3, MGM Research Files, UCLA Special Collections, box 55.

71. "Architecture—Washington DC," under "General Historical Research Notes," n.d., 3, MGM Research Files, UCLA Special Collections, box 54.

72. She finally deduced that though there was no slave dealer of that name in that time, "there was but one slave dealer in Washington at a time near this period. In that case, Auctioneer Shyrock would portray that person." Bucknall to R. E. Kopp, March 19, 1936, MGM Research Files, UCLA Special Collections, box 56.

73. "Lou Crowley's Props Request for 'Gorgeous Hussy,'" n.d., MGM Research Files, UCLA Special Collections, box 55.

74. In 1939, Bucknall would write the screenplays for *Four Girls in White* (MGM) and *Five Little Peppers and How They Grew* (Columbia).

75. Nathalie Bucknall (information compiled by George Macon) to Clarence Brown (cc Mr. Dorian), "Political and Campaign Suggestions," April 6, 1936, 1, MGM Research Files, UCLA Special Collections, box 56.

76. Nathalie Bucknall (information compiled by George Macon) to Clarence Brown (cc Mr. Dorian), "Political and Campaign Suggestions," April 6, 1936, 1, MGM Research Files, UCLA Special Collections, box 56, 3–4.

77. Robert Kopp worked for the MGM Legal Department. He was Jewish and from an educated family. He and his wife were partners in a law firm. It appears that he and his wife helped people during the Blacklist. See http://dcchs.org/RobertEKopp/07182013 .pdf.

78. Nathalie Bucknall to Joseph Mankiewicz, "Historical Research Detail," April 25, 1936, MGM Research Files, UCLA Special Collections, box 55.

79. Nathalie Bucknall to Joseph Mankiewicz, "Historical Research Detail," April 25, 1936, MGM Research Files, UCLA Special Collections, box 55.

80. An undated memo titled "Remarks," likely written by Kopp, stated, "Although we do know that Andrew Jackson was a man of plain and strong words, care should be taken not to make appear his character too rough and illiterate. (To our knowledge there is a Col. Jackson living here in town who is a grandson of Andrew Jackson and locally active in the Democratic party.) After all, he was president of the US." Kopp Memo, n.d., MGM Research Files, UCLA Special Collections, box 56.

81. Nathalie Bucknall to Joseph Mankiewicz, "Historical Research Detail," April 25, 1936, MGM Research Files, UCLA Special Collections, box 55.

82. Kopp Memo, n.d., MGM Research Files, UCLA Special Collections, box 55.

83. In the Ordinance of Nullification, South Carolina states that if the government tries to collect the tariff, "the people of this State will henceforth hold themselves absolved from all further obligation to maintain or preserve their political connection with the people of the other States; and will forthwith proceed to organize a separate government, and do all other acts and things which sovereign and independent States may of right do." William MacDonald, ed., *Selected Documents Illustrative of the History of the United States, 1776–1861* (London: McMillan Press, 1898), 271.

84. For a discussion of the longue durée of Abolition, see Eric Foner, *Gateway to Freedom* (New York: Norton, 2015). Foner's work suggests that the national discourse in support of emancipation extended back to the 1780s with the initiation of the New York Manumission Society (40). For a statistic citing mass escapes of slaves from the South beginning in 1810, see John Hope Franklin, *From Slavery to Freedom: A History of African Americans* (New York: McGraw-Hill, 2000), 210.

85. Phillips advised on *Uncle Tom's Cabin* (1927). See John David Smith, *Introduction to Ulrich B. Phillips's Life and Labor in the South* (Columbia: University of South Carolina Press, 2007), xix. As for leftist histories coming out in the mid-1930s, many of these were associated with the Popular Front. Important among these historians was Herbert Aptheker. See Aptheker, "American Negro Slave Revolts," *Science and Society* 1, no. 4 (Summer 1937): 512–538.

86. Nathalie Bucknall to Joseph Mankiewicz, "Historical Research Detail," April 25, 1936, MGM Research Files, UCLA Special Collections, box 55.

87. Nathalie Bucknall to Joseph Mankiewicz, "Historical Research Detail," April 25, 1936, MGM Research Files, UCLA Special Collections, box 55.

88. "Andrew Johnson or Man on America's Conscience, An Original Story, In Screen Play Continuity by Alvin Meyers and Lowell Brodaux," June 23, 1939, Turner/MGM Script Collection, folder T-458, AMPAS. And "Notes for Alvin Meyer 7/18/39 . . . Andrew Johnson or The Man on America's Conscience (Lowell Brodaux)," Turner/MGM Script Collection, folder T-459, AMPAS. A note on the script of July 15, 1940, stated, "NOTE: Two things that made life endurable for Thaddeus Stevens: hate and gambling. His violent hatred of the world and most of the men and women in it arose from a bitter inferiority over his club foot. Drinking he considered a weakness, and never touched a drop. His sex life was confined to relations with a negro housekeeper-mistress. His single safety

valve in the society of his own kind was gambling. He was an intense, all night player and often enough, as dawn broke over Washington, he hobbled to bed loser of more than a thousand dollars." Turner/MGM Script Collection, folder T-465, AMPAS. See also "Notes from Sloan Nibley 5/17/41" for a lengthy and damning note describing Stevens. Turner/MGM Script Collection, folder T-470, AMPAS.

89. See, for example, "'Gorgeous Hussy' Tells All," *Motion Picture Herald*, August 1, 1936.

90. Harry Levette, "Thru Hollywood: Follow the Movie Stars and Players Weekly with Harry," *Chicago Defender*, July 4, 1936, 10. Levette also noted that "they will be dressed in the costumes of the period, the women in those voluminous dresses with half a dozen underskirts . . . and the men with the tight fitting trousers and gaiter shoes." Levette, "Thru Hollywood," *Chicago Defender*, May 9, 1936, 8.

91. "Stage Shorts," *Baltimore Afro American*, May 23, 1936; "Chicago Defender Back on the Air in California," *Chicago Defender*, May 23, 1936, 10.

92. Though Haynes's casting in *So Red the Rose* (1935) as Daniel Veal, an enslaved butler who struggles to keep plantation order during a slave rebellion, in some ways tamed his *Hallelujah* image, *The Gorgeous Hussy* could be read as an intertextual *play* on the powerful Veal's devotion to his young white mistress, using it as grounds for audiences to imagine hidden dynamics in the mistress-slave connection in *So Red the Rose*.

93. Louis Lautier, "Capital Spotlight," *Afro-American*, September 19, 1936, 3.

4 · YELLOWFACE, MINSTRELSY, AND HOLLYWOOD HAPPY ENDINGS

The Black Camel (1931), *Charlie Chan in Egypt* (1935), and *Charlie Chan at the Olympics* (1937)

DELIA MALIA CAPAROSO KONZETT

A widely popular Hollywood character of the 1930s and 1940s, Charlie Chan is an uncanny hybrid figure and represents a society marked by the contradiction of a racist nation looking to lead the world as a democratic force. A Chinese character played by a white European actor in yellowface and a second-class U.S. citizen who hails from the periphery of the nation, namely the U.S. territory of Hawaii, Chan resides in the *unheimlich* space of modern national myth. This myth, as Benedict Anderson has pointed out, is that of a community passionately imagined into existence, explaining why people are willing to die and kill in its name. Nationalism, a communal story of love, home, identity, belonging, hate, exclusion, and radical othering, is not so much an ideology, says Anderson, but a modern form of kinship that becomes possible with print capitalism. The reading of daily newspapers in which citizens routinely consume the same information at set times, notes Anderson, is a national performance, an "extraordinary mass ceremony," thereby "creating that remarkable confidence of community in anonymity which is the hallmark of modern nations."[1] Similarly, the regular consumption of Hollywood films and its representations by roughly sixty to eighty million viewers on a weekly basis during the 1930s and 1940s is likewise a national performance of a "community in anonymity," what Siegfried Kracauer calls the mass ornament, the simultaneous partaking in a mass narrative and pastime.[2]

This national performance embodies an ambivalent inclusiveness in its psychotic doubling of national myth defining both insiders and outsiders. The Charlie Chan series similarly articulates at once utopian ideals mixed with racist and provincial values. How does a white Hollywood actor in yellowface spouting fictive Confucian sayings, aka "Chanograms," strangely create a bridge to Asia and the rest of the world, becoming a beloved national myth of U.S. expansionism and global reach, while belittling minority Americans? More specifically, I examine classical Hollywood conventions in the context of intersectional representation in the popular Charlie Chan series released by Fox Film Corporation and Twentieth Century Fox.

Intersectionality is analyzed in the contradictions between the classical Hollywood system and its less regulated antecedent developed in the early "cinema of attractions" with its pre-narrative focus on spectacle and excess. Early cinema (1896–1906), as Tom Gunning claims, "displays its visibility, willing to rupture a self-enclosed fictional world for a chance to solicit the attention of the spectator."[3] As we will see, B film, and its related genre of the programmer, regularly partakes in pre-narrative forms of excess, undermining and challenging the totalization of the Hollywood classical narrative. In terms of the theorist Mikhail Bakhtin, it could be said that the B film provides the antithetical *heteroglossia*, a diversity of socially repressed voices, to the monologic stylization of the A-film narrative with its established and streamlined hierarchy of identity.[4] It is this B-film rupture of Hollywood codes that proves most productive for intersectional readings that give expression to the repressed, regulated, and manipulated representations of the cultural margins.

As a programmer, the Chan series is linked to the B picture, known for its low production value and overt, disruptive, unpolished, even lurid narratives. Tino Balio places major-studio programmers such as the Chan series into the category of B production, noting however that they "operate between A and B" film production, "appearing in either category."[5] Balio argues, "Although formula mysteries, running less than eight reels, and shot in under a month on modest budgets, the Chan movies were designed as programmers, but attracted major audiences and box-offices on a par with A's."[6] The foil to the A picture with its sanitized cultural rhetoric, B film crudely violates silent majority consensus and lays open Hollywood's hierarchical codes. If, as Daniel Bernardi has argued, classical conventions as found in A film "[systematize] the popularization of American whiteness," B film offers a farcical mirror of excess, especially in the representation of race, gender, sexuality, nationality, and class.[7] The B picture thus invites a critical analysis of its peculiar manipulation and reshuffling of classical Hollywood codes.[8] This analysis focuses on the conflicting A and B rhetoric meeting up in the Chan series, giving us a better idea of Hollywood's classical codes and its internal contradictions, particularly its reflection of a national sense of disorientation concerning the geopolitical significance of the Asia-Pacific region in contrast to the devalued and racist perceptions of Asian and African Americans.

Three Fox Chan films that involve various code deviations, representations of race/ethnicity, gender, sexuality, and nationality, are of interest for this inquiry. In *The Black Camel* (1931), for instance, Warner Oland's yellowface performance as the Honolulu detective Charlie Chan is curiously brought into a paradoxical intersection with his large family, one cast exclusively with Asian Americans rather than white impersonators and designed to be "progressive." When our hero visits the Middle East in *Charlie Chan in Egypt* (1935), the representational confusion of identity is heightened with the minstrel performance of Stepin Fetchit and the Egyptian impersonation by Margarita Cansino (later Rita Hayworth), creating an excess of intersecting racial/ethnic/national identities on screen that cannot be contained and eventually displace the white heteronormative couple formation in the film's ending. Finally, the Chan Olympics installment offers a strange cooperation between Nazi Germany's police force and Detective Chan representing the United States in solving an international case of military technology theft. A parallel plot features documentary footage of famed African American athlete Jesse Owens in the hundred-meter track relay at the 1936 Berlin Olympics, while Chan's "number one son" fictively also wins Olympic gold on the U.S. swimming team in a reprise of Hawaii's Duke Kahanamoku's Olympic gold medal wins of 1912 and 1920, completing the film's happy ending.[9] This very American convention of the Hollywood happy ending in all three films stresses the excess of representation with its intense condensation of national ideology. Thus, while the discussed films heavily draw from racist traditions of yellowface and minstrelsy, they also simultaneously carnivalize or invert the order of representation on which they are built via B-film forms of mimicry and farce.

The Black Camel (1931) was produced with a higher budget comparable to A-list films and shot on location in Honolulu at a time when all foreign or exotic locations were generally assembled on Hollywood backlots. The film offers extensive footage of the Royal Hawaiian, a luxury hotel that had recently opened on February 1, 1927, and quickly became known as the vacation home of famous international and cosmopolitan guests. This second Charlie Chan film starring Warner Oland (the first installment, *Charlie Chan Carries On*, released in 1930, is lost) maintains its series launch in grand fashion, demonstrating Fox Film's attempt to establish the Chan series as a major studio programmer in which B production is mixed with A-list characteristics. The strategy was successful with the Charlie Chan series becoming "one of Fox's biggest attractions."[10] Placing Detective Chan into the elite international environment of the Royal Hawaiian in which he investigates and exposes white upper-class crime breaks with the traditional Hollywood representation of minorities featured only in low and subservient positions. Earl Derr Biggers loosely based his famous detective on the real-life celebrated Honolulu detective Chang Apana. While Apana's cases also took him around the world, he bears little resemblance to the cosmopolitan fictive detective. To be sure, Apana was not even permitted to handle cases involving Hawaii's white colonial elites and, as a former *paniolo* (Hawaiian cowboy), was known for handling common criminals with his bullwhip.[11] Biggers conceived of Chan as a modern replacement, a heroic and "amiable Chinese" to oppose what he called "the old stuff," namely the prevalent villainous yellow-peril stereotypes of the 1920s.[12] In creating a modern Chinese hero, Biggers expressed the geopolitical climate of the 1920s United States and its fear of a militarized Japan. The United States had been long concerned over Japan's aggressive expansion in East Asia, particularly in China, and its rejection of the Open Door Policy, which kept China open to all trade. *The Black Camel* was released in the summer of 1931 as things boiled to a crisis point with Japan invading Manchuria in September and establishing the Manchukuo puppet state. The final two-shot in *The Black Camel* with Chan and his silly Japanese assistant

Kashimo (the butt of all jokes and badly treated by Chan) challenges the 1930s geopolitical Asian order with the Japanese in power, placing instead Chan, an American Chinese hero, in the dominant role.

As a modern representation of an amiable and cosmopolitan Chinese hero hailing from the U.S. territory of Hawaii, the gateway to the East, could the series have intended to present new ideals of American internationalism via its offshore Hawaiian detective? The U.S. Jim Crow norms of the 1930s demanded that a white actor in yellowface portray the lead role; however, Chan is firmly placed within a large Asian family (eleven children and growing eventually to fourteen, not counting grandchildren) who are played by Asian actors and who are featured increasingly as the series continues.[13] As Philippa Gates notes, Chan's "appeal to American audiences was the fact that he was a polite, soft-spoken, well-groomed, family man who had adopted middle-class, American values."[14] His sons usually accompany him on his trips around the world, and his number one son Lee (Keye Luke) would become popular as the sidekick of his father, starring opposite in seven of the Warner Orland Chan installments.

The usual critical response to this remarkable phenomenon is to draw attention to the yellowface performance of Warner Oland, which follows in the racist vein of minstrelsy or caricature and contains the screen image of the Asian hero protagonist. While not disputing the intent of the long-established racist traditions of U.S. yellowface inherited from European drama, operas, and operettas, one must ask how effective this performance is in its effort of racial/ethnic containment in the case of Chan. Unlike his successor Sidney Toler, Oland did not use extensive makeup or tape his eyes but instead conveyed Chan theatrically with stereotypical representations such as emphasis on social decor and honorifics, polite language and demeanor, and laughable Confucian wisdoms rendered in an accented English. Makeup was applied minimally, eyebrows were brushed upward, and hair was slicked back, allowing Oland to appear relatively natural. This toned-down version of yellowface still keeps the stereotypes intact but ultimately refrains from using highly demeaning caricatures of appearance, as commonly seen in more overt racist minstrelsy. As previously mentioned, the film offers an unusual family environment for Chan and embeds him within a large family entirely played by Asian actors. His children are fluent in the American idiom and use slang expressions. Family dinner scenes and outings are a frequent staple of the series alongside Chan's more prominently featured older sons who help in the investigation. This portrayal of Chan in yellow-face surrounded by actual Asian actors begs the question as to who is impersonating whom. While the surface appearance of Chan may suggest the yellowface stereotype, it can also be read in reverse fashion with the Asian character slowly subsuming the white actor and revealing a two-way assimilation. While his family can be viewed as assimilating to white American norms, Warner Oland can be likewise seen as assimilating to Asian immigrant culture. And for a white mainstream film audience living in segregated neighborhoods unaccustomed to interactions with racial/ethnic/religious others, Chan may be seen as a gateway to Asian/Asian American culture. In Jim Crow Hollywood, this representational strategy offers a remarkable deviation from the norm and only superficially appears to accommodate segregationist codes. To be sure Hollywood had already successfully engaged with Asian villains à la Fu Manchu, but it had never so boldly advanced an Asian hero protagonist.

Nevertheless, yellowface in this context becomes uncannily estranged to the point of psychosis. It appears that in a Jim Crow society, the representation of race, even in the context of a progressive outlook, can be addressed only in racist terms. This psychosis leads to a doubling and disconnection of all representations from their intended meanings. The Chan series is thus curiously progressive if read against the grain, struggling to keep the old order in place but failing to do so. Yet it also remains profoundly racist in its attempt to code progressive ideas in the regressive racist performances of yellowface and minstrelsy. In significant ways, then, Chan's cosmopolitanism, modernism, objectivity, respectfulness, and honesty challenge an America still marked by its parochial and racist inwardness, stressing instead the need to explore its nascent role as an emerging world power and leader of the free and democratic world. In this sense, Chan represents a popular and pedagogical mythical national figure, a guiding democratic ideal and the embodiment and promise of a better future for a racist nation. However, this positive representation is performed via the racist use of yellowface. While the use of a white European lead actor in yellowface is predictable in apartheid Hollywood, the excess of idealization that transforms the detective into a beloved representative and ambassador of the United States via yellowface performance makes it radically incompatible with its intent and thereby reveals the fundamentally psychotic nature of U.S. race relations. In the intersection of A and B film, of highbrow rhetoric and low mimetic representation, this contradiction of the national discourse on race becomes visible as psychosis, a doubled language that in a pathological approach attempts to solve the question of racism via racism.

Another interesting feature of *The Black Camel* is its self-reflexive or meta-cinematic quality that does away with the popular genre of the South Pacific film in which Hawaii and its natives are traditionally featured in premodern, first-contact scenarios and/or as sexual fetishes. The opening scene provides an example of this metacinematic aspect in which a Hollywood film produc-tion set in Hawaii provides the setting. In the scene, we witness an interra-cial encounter on the beach with a white woman and a younger local Hawaiian man, suggesting in pre-Code fashion a type of sex tourism, before the cam-era pulls back and exposes the scene simply as part of the ongoing film pro-duction. In doing so, however, it draws unusual attention to the race codes and the increasingly prohibited representation of interracial romance. Also, the fact that the woman approaches the exotic local young man subverts the codes of the South Seas fantasy with its white male beachcombers usually indulging in local women and interracial affairs. The film indeed features such an affair, but the beachcomber (Archie Smith) is killed and hence the film aborts the older genre with an emphasis on a new Hawaii, thereby breaking with the tradition of representing the Pacific with first encounter narratives depicting Polynesians in pretechnological and premodern worlds. While the film cleans up older stereotypes pertaining to premodern Polynesian cultures in the Pacific, it follows at the same time the newly advanced Production Code, phasing out the interracial romance and establishing more firmly seg-regated worlds that can be crossed only by Chan. The criminal activity in fact never touches on the local population but is exclusively perpetrated from within its circle of white elites and their servants, including the major Hol-lywood star who is a murderer. Hawaii is thus depicted as modern, urbane, and international via the exquisite cinematography of Joseph August, who worked on John Ford's *Battle of Midway* (1942), foregrounding the new tech-nologies of camera mobility and sound recording as given in the early stage of sound cinema. *Black Camel* was no doubt influenced by King Vidor's *Hal-lelujah* (1929), the first all-black cast film by a major studio (MGM) that pioneered the combined sound on location and postproduction sound recording.

Hollywood's self-reflexive foregrounding of its own technological achieve-ments would subsequently become more deeply embedded in the Chan series with its emphasis on modern scientific forensic techniques. As R. John Williams argues, the Chan series countered the prevalent technophobia of a Depression era America reluctantly accepting its modernization and advocated a more confident embrace of modern technology: "In addition to the novelty of having a Chinese detective hero, technology is central, perhaps even the central concern of the film series. Consider, for instance, how many of the Charlie Chan films feature some kind of techno-trick at the center of the narrative."[15] Technology hence becomes associated with modernism and a new mode of Asian representation, taking Hawaii and Asians into a position of modernity that challenges premodern and parochial views, especially U.S. racial binary thinking of black and white at home and its isolationism in world affairs.[16]

The installment, *Charlie Chan in Egypt* (1935), was no doubt inspired by the commercial success of *The Mummy* (dir. Karl Freund, 1932) and the fascination with Egypt since the stunning discovery of King Tutankhamun's tomb in 1922, which in itself inspired many of the Orientalist art deco movie palaces of the 1920s. The film looks more toward British colonialism and Orientalism in the Middle East and North Africa, expanding the reach of Hollywood's imperial fantasy. It opens on an Oriental motif combining Pacific Orientalism (framing palm leaves) with Africanism (pyramids). Vast aerial shots of the pyramids and the Sphinx dissolve into a shot with Chan riding on a donkey, falling off, losing his hat, which is then recovered and worn by Snowshoes (Stepin Fetchit). Snowshoes is in fact always referred to as "Effendi Snowshoes" by Chan, who insists upon using the Arabic honorific of Master, establishing a close connection between the two characters. As the comedic sidekick to Chan, Snowshoes also figures in an important two-shot with Chan at the end of the film. The film overall presents a carnivalesque reshuffling of Hollywood codes via an excess of otherness as seen in the exotic foreign location, the many nonwhite (though mostly impersonated) characters, and the negative portrayal of its white archeologists who cannot lay claim to the film's narrative as either grand villains or ingenious scientists. The film instead offers an upside-down world where the cultural minorities take center stage.

Often debated as ineffective, Stepin Fetchit's subversive minstrelsy is better served in this film as it amounts to comedic excess and B-film farce that uses minstrelsy's subservience to mock middle-class ideals. Whereas in films such as *Judge Priest* (dir. John Ford, 1934) and its remake *The Sun Shines Bright* (dir. John Ford, 1953) Stepin Fetchit's humor is framed by the traditional black and white binary of Hollywood and the southern plantation genre, permitting individuality only to its main white characters but containing black characters as representatives of an inferior group identity, his pairing with Oland and Hayworth (impersonating nonwhite characters) alongside other impersonated Egyptian characters works to the advantage of his subversive minstrelsy. In *Chan in Egypt*, where respectable white characters turn out in fact to be the criminals, and where the Asian detective, the Egyptian police officers, and Snowshoes restore order by the film's end, the hierarchy of classical Hollywood is inverted and disorients the audience to a degree that it cannot view the film simply at face value. Stepin Fetchit's biographer Mel Watkins explains the dilemma of his comedic act: "Many blacks were perfectly aware of the running in-joke (puttin' on old massa) that Fetchit *deliberately* enacted. . . . Many whites, on the other hand, laughed at what *appeared* to be a confirmation of a venerable Negro stereotype. For most blacks, it was ironic farce; for many whites, it was sociological verity."[17]

In *Chan in Egypt*, however, Stepin Fetchit's comedic routine benefits from a nonbinary environment located outside the United States, becoming a sophisticated satire or farce. For instance, he brags to his African girlfriend that he can easily find her employment in the United States: "I'll just carry you back to Mississippi with me. You don't have to worry about no job there cause I know a lot of white folks who will keep you working." The absurdity of this comment made in Egypt leaves no doubt about its satirical intent. Effendi Snowshoes is also looking for the genealogical roots of his "great-great-great-great-great-great grand pappy" but abandons this pursuit as soon as danger is involved. This joke ironically and significantly links Snowshoes to a nonwhite civilization that precedes white Western civilization. In defiance of his white employers, he further flaunts his laziness by smoking hookahs in a lounge chair and openly avoiding any risky situation that could endanger his life, while sending whites to their potential demise. Stepin Fetchit, despite his name stressing active subservience, was billed as the laziest man in the world and called by critics the master of slow motion. As his subversive comedic act shows, drawing on a mixture of linguistic perplexity and deliberate slow comprehension when it suits his purpose, Stepin Fetchit refuses to fetch anything or be at anyone's command. Instead, his parodic act points to the psychotic landscape of U.S. race relations with which he has made an ironic arrangement, pretending to go along with its rules, while at

FIGURE 4.1 Costume and blocking create an ethnic solidarity between the minority characters. *Charlie Chan in Egypt* (1935).

the same time undermining them. Mainstream film audiences likewise enter into a pact, laughing at his subversive antics, while finding comfort in his minstrelsy performance that places whites in the superior position. The film also shows Chan as aloof when dealing with the deaths of the white Arnold family that is engaged in an internecine struggle over treasures found in the tombs of Amati and using superstition to cover up their crimes. Rather than consoling the victims' relatives, Chan works with cold detachment and advanced scientific methods (using radiology, chemistry) to reconstruct hidden crimes. For example, a goddess of vengeance who is said to kill invaders of the ancient tombs is invoked whenever a suspicious death occurs. Chan is undisturbed by these maneuvers and follows his leads with the methods of modern forensics and chemistry/physics. Chan is also deferential toward the Egyptian chief inspector and draws close to Nadya, the Egyptian help played by Margarita Cansino / Rita Hayworth. In blocking and two-shots, the film establishes a solidarity among the ethnic minorities in the film, isolating the white agents in their own drama of deception and self-deception (see Figure 4.1).

The film offers an unusual excess of minority characters, casts no doubt on the host country of Egypt, and demystifies the Orientalism of *The Mummy* and its demonic take on the subject matter. Effendi Snowshoes, along with the Egyptian police, contributes to the film's happy ending by assisting Chan with laying a trap for the elusive murderer and catching him during his flight attempt. While a young innocent white heterosexual couple conventionally offers the happy ending shot, it is alternated with the two-shot of Chan and Effendi Snowshoes. After helping to catch the murderer, Snowshoes asks Chan, "Where will you go from here?" Chan answers with one of his Confucius-like wisdoms: "Journey of life like feather on stream—must continue with current." To which Snowshoes replies, "I guess you're right but I'm going with you," following Chan off-screen left and thus forming another type of couple that anticipates the ending of *Casablanca* (1942) and its "beginning of a beautiful friendship." A product of Hollywood codes, *Charlie Chan in Egypt* succeeds in undermining its hierarchy and establishes an alternate hierarchy with the internationally renowned detective in the leading role. Thus, what was construed by Hollywood as a controlled environment of managing nonwhite minorities via yellow-, brown-, and blackface performances ironically comes undone during the film and offers up instead a farcical satire of Hollywood's obsession with whiteness.

This progressive reading of *Chan in Egypt* nevertheless must be taken with the caveat and context of the race psychosis prevalent in the Jim Crow era with its overt systemic racism. White audiences installed in this system viewed the farce as insignificant, regarding the entire film series as an entertaining minstrelsy piece with minorities mimicking the significant roles traditionally assigned to white characters in Hollywood. However, since a majority of minorities are impersonated by white characters, the game of mimicry is carried to the absurd. We are now dealing with white characters mimicking minorities mimicking white characters. Suffice it to say, the traditional rules of representation in classical Hollywood appear to be broken, challenging a monolithic system yet without providing a viable alternative. Instead, absurdity and the psychosis of race relations are exposed. The Chan series precedes in this sense the more radical World War II combat genre with its imagined multiethnic combat teams, negating the reality of segregation in U.S. armed forces of the era. This utopian vision was realized eventually by Truman's Executive Order 9981, calling for the desegregation of the military in 1948 and becoming a crucial benchmark for the civil rights movement.

Intersectionality also proves productive in *Charlie Chan at the Olympics* (1937), establishing new types of patriotic solidarities. The film features an espionage plot that starts in Honolulu and takes the honorable detective to Berlin, with Chan now officially representing the United States in retrieving a stolen radio device that allows military planes to fly via remote control. Anticipating military conflicts on the horizon in Europe and Asia, Chan's detective work is now directly placed at the service of U.S. geopolitical interests. In keeping with the progressive formula of the Chan series, the traitor is to be found within the ranks of white Americans. *Charlie Chan at the Olympics* resembles future combat films such as *Flying Tigers* (1942) and *Bataan* (1943), depicting non-Japanese Asian populations (especially Chinese and Filipinos) in strong solidarity with U.S. national interests.[18] The film further features two of his sons in the formula of many Chan films, paying greater attention to his ever-growing family. Layne Tom Jr. stars as Charlie Chan Jr. in the Honolulu sequence alongside the Hawaiian actor Al Kikume as a young boy aspiring to follow in the footsteps of his father. Keye Luke stars as his oldest son, representing the U.S. Olympic team as a swimmer and amateur detective who helps recover the device (see Figure 4.2). The plot unveils treason on the part of the white American inventor Cartwright, who wants to sell this crucial military device to high bidders from abroad. By contrast, Chan and his family are shown as true patriots, risking their lives in securing the stolen device and topping it off with a gold-medal win by Lee Chan just a day after having been kidnapped by a hostile spy ring and almost killed along with his father.

The film also features stock footage of the American four by hundred-meter track relay race with famed African American sprinters Jesse Owens and Ralph Metcalfe in the lineup. In the re-created audience reaction shot featuring the American track team cheering on their athletes, the film includes a female African American athlete, possibly a reference to Tidye Pickett, the first African American woman athlete to compete in an Olympics. Much like the World War II combat genre with its utopian emphasis on all races and ethnicities contributing to the war effort, Chan's Olympic adventure insists on a similar national inclusivity. It is interesting to note that this film, which was released one year after the 1936 Olympics, pays public homage to Jessie

FIGURE 4.2 Chan's number one son Lee (Keye Luke) on his way to the 1936 Berlin Games as a member of the U.S. Olympic team. *Charlie Chan at the Olympics* (1937).

Owens's achievement in a manner that the Roosevelt administration failed to do by not offering its multiple gold-medal winner and superstar of the Berlin Games an invitation to the White House reception, one extended to all white medal winners. This paradox of U.S. liberal propaganda disseminated via Hollywood to national and international audiences and blatant racist discrimination on national soil perpetuates the doubled language of U.S. race psychosis.

The depiction of Germany remains surprisingly neutral and shows cooperation in police matters with the Prussian officers once again using new technology, as is the case in most Chan films. It is also interesting to note that the film now places Honolulu at the center of global affairs and validates its military significance for the United States. Keye Luke is allowed to take on a much stronger role in becoming the film's action hero, a role he would repeat in subsequent installments. Since Oland's Chan does his detective work for the most part in cerebral fashion, the action image provided by Keye Luke complements the detective and expands and complicates the portrayal of Asian Americans. It would appear that Hollywood is just a step away from casting an Asian American in a lead role and transitioning its audience to this new casting strategy. However, as is so often the case, the promises of wartime crisis are quickly retracted after the war, and post–World War II Hollywood proved rather resistant to casting Asian Americans in lead roles other than as exotic foreigners.

In fact, the practice of yellowface was resumed in performances such as Marlon Brando's character Sakini in *The Teahouse of the August Moon* (1956), Yul Brynner's King Monkgut of Siam in *The King and I* (1956), and Jennifer Jones's Eurasian character Dr. Han Suyin in *Love Is a Many-Splendored Thing* (1955). It extended to David Carradine's popular 1970s TV role as the Eurasian Kung Fu master Kwai Chang Caine, leading to a growing frustration among Asian Americans with this updated racist practice inspired by the success of the Chan series.[19] In fact, even Uma Thurman's performance in Tarantino's *Kill Bill* shows residual traces of yellowface practices, working in a more self-aware and liberal updated version of cultural appropriation.

The persistent continuity of yellowface rather than evolution in the representational practices of Hollywood concerning Asian Americans before and after World War II alerts one to the fact that progressive lessons can be quickly unlearned or simply never carried the weight they claimed to possess. Looking at other Chan examples from the 1930s and 1940s, one is struck by the overt race pedagogy inserted into some of the films. For example, in *Chan at the Opera* (1936) with Boris Karloff as Gravelle, an opera singer presumed dead in a fire and suspected for two revenge killings, the film draws attention to the police's racism with a detective constantly using racial slurs (Egg Foo Young, Chop Suey) when addressing his colleague Chan. The film has the audience side with Chan and son Lee against the narrow-minded detective. In one humorous and instructive scene, the white detective chases Lee as a possible suspect who is disguised as a knight in the opera performance. The racist police detective demands that the entire chorus consisting of knights line up and remove their helmets. To his surprise (and that of the audience) the entirety of the large chorus is cast with Chinese male actors (Lee's college fraternity brothers), allowing Lee to go undetected as the detective is unable to distinguish between them. The film thus toys with the xenophobic and racist perspective of parochial audiences and pedagogically leads them to an adjusted perspective of Asian Americans represented by Chan and family. In *Charlie Chan in the Secret Service* (1944), another revelatory scene points to the psychosis of U.S. race relations. When a small replica of the Statue of Liberty is delivered to the lady of the house (who is in fact a traitor), she comments on its beauty. Chan smartly replies that the idea behind the statue is also beautiful and hands the statue to the black servant Birmingham Brown (Mantan Moreland) in a not so subtle indictment of the racial status quo. While this ironical remark leaves the overall system in place, it chips away at its codes by exposing the system's mendacity to the audience.

Additional pedagogical moments in the Chan series concern the convention of the happy ending and the casting of the action hero. Both conventions are key pillars of the classical Hollywood system with its inbuilt ideology of white patriarchal superiority. Again, the Chan series boldly breaks with these conventions and supplies audiences with unconventional happy endings and an unconventional action hero in the performance of Keye Luke. The conventional Hollywood happy ending predominantly features the white male action hero, who, after having met his challenges and trials, wins "the girl" and frequently enters into a contract of marriage. Two-shots usually dominate the happy endings and are open to some variation when romance is less emphasized. For example, the closing two-shot of *Casablanca* features Rick and the French Captain as newfound buddies, while dropping during the midpoint of the film Sam, the black pianist and former close confidant of Rick. This surprising ending in which Rick teams up with the coercive rapist Captain Renault also makes sure at all costs that Sam duly takes his place in the racial hierarchy of Hollywood and does not usurp the exclusivity of the white couple. In the Chan programmer series, less bound by the A-film formula, this convention is seriously undermined with various two-shots featuring nonwhite characters at the closing moments of the film, with Chan as its central hero. While Oland or Toler's yellowface performance may stress the whiteness of the character underneath the costume, the partners in the two-shots happen to be nonwhites: Kashimo (*The Black Camel*), Stepin Fetchit (*Chan in Egypt*), Chan's son Lee being congratulated by Chan on his gold medal win (*Chan at the Olympics*), Lee and Chan in a two-shot being escorted by police to catch a ship to Honolulu (*Chan at the Opera*), and Chan shown celebrating the news of the birth of his grandchild with shots alternating between his daughter in the hospital and Chan listening intently on the phone to the sound of the newborn family member (*Chan in Honolulu*).

The second convention the Chan series strongly revises is that of the action hero. In the established Hollywood formula, this privileged position is tra-

ditionally assigned to the white male hero with his mobility and agency structuring the narrative. In addition, with his controlling gaze that dominates all
others (he controls the camera), he also becomes the identifying focus for
the audience that views the events and other characters from his perspective.
The Chan series quickly discovered that Chan's central role needed more
physical mobility, though Chan can be seen on occasion drawing a gun. However, with the character of Lee, his number one son played by Keye Luke,
the series found the much-needed action component. In analogy to the white
action hero, Lee frequently dabbles in youthful romance but dominates the
screen predominantly via comedic action and heroic stunts. Lee launches
himself down a flight of stairs to prevent an attack on his father (*Charlie Chan
in Shanghai*), scales buildings at dangerous heights, engages in fist fights,
breaks chairs on his opponents' heads, drives in chase scenes, and, as mentioned, wins Olympic gold. His physical talents are enhanced by his skills in
the visual arts, earning him an invitation to an international art exposition
in Paris. While Lee, with his fluency in English and his multiple skill sets,
clearly foreshadows the Asian American model minority stereotype, he can
also be seen as an experimentation in casting a nonwhite actor in a stronger
secondary lead role, paving the way to a future casting in the lead role. As
mentioned, this utopian vision was never fully realized in the postwar era and
led only to compromised lead roles as given in Nancy Kwan's Suzie Wong or
Pat Morita's Miyagi, the mentor of the white karate kid. More recent examples of Asian American actors in the lead role with blockbuster billing are
those of mixed race, including Keanu Reeves (Asian Hawaiian and white),
Dwayne "The Rock" Johnson (black and Samoan), and Lucy Liu (Chinese
American), all who clearly follow the action formula. Nevertheless, they are
still singular or token exceptions rather than the norm in the casting of Asian
Americans.

Cedric J. Robinson recounts the history of American cinema in a tellingly
different manner, one usually summarized as leading from early cinema's
experimental advances to its paradigmatic systemic vertical integration into
a corporate enterprise:

> Most histories of the early American film industry adhere to the notion that
> the anarchy of production, distribution, exhibition, and content of films which
> characterized the industry until 1908 or so was brought to order by the logic of
> economics. But there is also compelling evidence that cohesion and control of

American motion pictures was spurred by the powerful interests implicated in the formulation of a new racial regime. . . . The new racial regime would coalesce with American nationalism as the two master narratives instituted to reassert political control over an American order frayed by domestic rebellion and social diversity.[20]

What our discussion has shown here is Hollywood's continuing struggle to articulate a racial regime while updating it to the geopolitical concerns of the 1930s. Although the programmer and the B film may have provided openings for breaking with the industry's codes of racial representation and representation of Asians and Asian Americans, they have not been able to do so successfully without invoking new racist stereotypes to combat its older expressions. Similarly, A film has mostly sanitized the question of racism via representational strategies of omission, typification, and coded taboos, thus preserving the status quo of the racial regime. Reading the Chan series at the intersections of race and identity alerts us to the deep inscription of Jim Crow legislation into the cultural institution of Hollywood. At the same time, the more anarchic B genre, harking back to early cinema before its systemic integration into a capitalist economy and a cultural expression of the racial regime, hints more openly at the artificiality of the industry's codes that promote the systemic oppression of minorities via its interlocking forms of representation.

It is no wonder that Jessica Hagedorn, in her introduction to the 1993 anthology *Charlie Chan Is Dead*, writes dismissively of this former national and cinematic icon: "Charlie Chan is indeed dead, never to be revived. Gone for good his yellowface asexual bulk, his fortune-cookie English, his stereotypical Orientalist version of the Chinese family."[21] However, in her follow-up anthology, *Charlie Chan Is Dead 2* (2004), she concedes, "Is Charlie Chan really dead? Probably not. According to the critic and scholar David Eng, Charlie's merely in a coma."[22] This adjusted position by Hagedorn points to the continuing problematic representation of Asian Americans in Hollywood and minorities in general. If kinship rather than ideology, as Benedict Anderson claims, constitutes national myth, underrepresentation in Hollywood points to a hegemonic national discourse, a racial regime articulated via problematic visual and cinematic representation. Intersectional readings of film history and failed attempts at articulations of diversity in Hollywood help us shed some light on the dynamics of tribal mythmaking with its interdependent roles of belonging and exclusion, but even more so, on the powerful acts of representation that shape Hollywood narratives and its consumers.

NOTES

1. Benedict Anderson, *Imagined Communities: Reflections on the Origin and Spread of Nationalism* (New York: Verso, 1983), 36.
2. Siegfried Kracauer, "The Mass Ornament," in *The Mass Ornament: Weimar Essays*, trans. and ed. Thomas Y. Levin (Cambridge, MA: Harvard University Press, 1995), 75–86.
3. Tom Gunning, "The Cinema of Attraction: Early Film, Its Spectator and the Avant-Garde," *Wide Angle* 8, nos. 3–4 (Fall 1986): 63–70, 64.
4. See Mikhail Bakhtin, *The Dialogic Imagination: Four Essays*, trans. Michael Holquist and Caryl Emerson (Austin: University of Texas Press, 1983). Bakhtin refers in this context to "local fairs" and "buffoon spectacles" for the formation of lower genres and their *heteroglossia*: "Heteroglossia, as organized in these low genres, was not merely heteroglossia vis-a-vis the accepted literary language (in all its various generic expressions), that is, vis-a-vis the linguistic center of the verbal-ideological life of the nation and the epoch but was a heteroglossia consciously opposed to this literary language. *It* was parodic and aimed sharply and polemically against the official languages of its given time" (273).
5. Tino Balio, *Grand Design: Hollywood as a Modern Business Enterprise, 1930–1939* (Berkeley: University of California Press, 1995), 317. Balio breaks down B-film production into four categories "in order of prestige": (1) major-studio programmers, (2) major-studio Bs, (3) smaller-company Bs, (4) the quickies of Poverty Row. According to Balio, "The term *programmer* indicates its principle characteristic: its flexibility in playing any part of the program, operating in between A and B and appearing in either category."
6. Balio, *Grand Design*, 317.
7. Daniel Bernardi, ed., *Classic Hollywood, Classic Whiteness* (Minneapolis: University of Minnesota Press, 2001), xv.
8. See my discussion of World War II B film pertaining to the Pacific theater in *Hollywood's Hawaii: Race, Nation, and War* (New Brunswick, NJ: Rutgers University Press, 2017), 124–134.
9. Duke Kahanamoku, of Native Hawaiian descent, often called the father of modern surfing, is arguably the first Asian American Olympic gold medalist, winning gold in the hundred-meter freestyle at the 1912 Stockholm Olympics and two golds at the 1920 Olympics in Antwerp. Depending on the inclusiveness of the term "Asian American," some consider Sammy Lee, platform gold medalist at the London Olympics of 1948, the first Asian American Olympic champion.
10. Balio, *Grand Design*, 316.
11. See Yunte Huang, *Charlie Chan: The Untold Story of the Honorable Detective and His Rendezvous with American History* (New York: Norton, 2010), 3, 35–36.
12. Earl Derr Biggers, quoted in Jinny Huh, *The Arresting Eye: Race and the Anxiety of Detection* (Charlottesville: University of Virginia Press, 2015), 114.

13. The first two film adaptations of Bigger's Chan novels, *House Without a Key* (1926) and *The Chinese Parrot* (1927), were cast with Asian actors, George Kuwa and Kamiyama Sojin, respectively, in the lead. Both adaptations were unsuccessful at the box office.

14. Philippa Gates, "The Assimilated Asian American as American Action Hero," *Canadian Journal of Film Studies* 22, no. 2 (Fall 2013): 19–40, 22.

15. R. John Williams, *The Buddha in the Machine: Art, Technology, and the Meeting of East and West* (New Haven, CT: Yale University Press, 2014), 156.

16. See here my discussion of "The Belated Tradition of Asian-American Modernism," in *A Companion to the Modern American Novel*, ed. John T. Matthews (Oxford: Wiley-Blackwell, 2009), 496–517. Interestingly enough, the techno-modernism of the Chan series predates literary Asian American modernism triggered by the events of World War II and the attack on Pearl Harbor.

17. Mel Watkins, quoted in Richard Schickel, "Serving Up Subversion," *Wilson Quarterly* 29, no. 4 (Autumn 2005): 114–116, 115.

18. World War II marks a moment in American history in which the artificial grouping of Asians and Asian Americans required a more nuanced differentiation. Military pamphlets, for example, such as "How to Spot a Jap," provided a racist road map to distinguish the Chinese ally from the Japanese enemy based on physical and physiognomic features, much like Nazi Germany's attempt to give racial descriptions of Jews. See Huh, *Arresting Eye*, 104–108. In World War II combat film, a similar pedagogical attempt is evident, although with less emphasis on racist features in compliance with the Office of War Information guidelines, stressing rather political categories such as fascist enemy versus democratic ally. See my discussion of *Bataan* (1943) in *Hollywood's Hawaii*, 105–116.

19. Interestingly enough, Keye Luke stars in this series as his mentor Master Po. Other recent yellowface performances that drew criticism were Jim Sturgess's character Hae-Joo Chang in *Cloud Atlas* (2012) and Scarlett Johansson's Major in *Ghost in the Shell* (2017).

20. Cedric J. Robinson, *Forgeries of Memory and Meaning: Blacks and the Regime of Race in American Theater and Film before World War II* (Chapel Hill, NC: University of North Carolina Press, 2007), 180–181.

21. Jessica Hagedorn, "Introduction," in *Charlie Chan Is Dead: An Anthology of Contemporary Asian American Fiction*, ed. Jessica Hagedorn (London: Penguin, 1993), xiii.

22. Jessica Hagedorn, "Introduction," in *Charlie Chan Is Dead 2: At Home in the World (An Anthology of Contemporary Asian American Fiction—Revised and Updated)*, ed. Jessica Hagedorn (London: Penguin, 2004), xxvii.

PART 2

GENRE AND RACE IN
CLASSICAL
HOLLYWOOD

5 · "A QUEER, STRANGLED LOOK"

Race, Gender, and Morality in
The Ox-Bow Incident (1943)

JONNA EAGLE

The Ox-Bow Incident is a queer film, and an even queerer Western. Directed by William Wellman and starring Henry Fonda, the up-and-coming Dana Andrews, and a collection of other familiar faces, it was released in 1943 to considerable critical acclaim and general popular disparagement. In a genre defined through its action-based set pieces—its charges and stampedes, assaults and rescues, fist fights and gun fights—the film is remarkably static, its mise-en-scène mostly studio-bound, its frames emptied out of rousing on-screen motion. There are exceptions to this general de-emphasis on dramatic action, including a brief barroom brawl, a mounted posse in pursuit of three rustlers and presumed murderers, and, finally, a lynching. But these incidents work more to emphasize than moderate the film's generic deviations. The posse charges across the screen not as an embodiment of frontier justice but as a signifier of its miscarriage, for instance, a miscarriage played out in the queasy spectacle of the lynching to follow.

The film's stillness is coupled by its relative quiet. After the opening sequence, it turns away from dramatic scoring almost completely. Between the film's opening and its close, there are very few instances of non-diegetic sound, though the exceptions are significant. The posse's ride, for one, is accompanied by a rare dramatic outburst on the soundtrack, though rather than an upbeat and energetic score, there are ominous overtones, and the insistent, rising pitch and clash of cymbals carry an anxious sense of foreboding. While visually the sequence appears entirely conventional, featuring the posse as they gallop across vast rugged landscapes and up through a high mountain pass, the score unsettles any easy assignment of moral authority to the action image. In contrast, two other instances of non-diegetic sound work to amplify rather than undercut the production of moral authority, as twice the stirring sounds of an angelic choir rise alongside the African American preacher Sparks (Leigh Whipper), as he moves to take a position against the posse. For all its relative simplicity then, the soundtrack does a considerable amount of work, a point to which I will return.

A very brief outline of *The Ox-Bow Incident*'s plot begins to suggest how these stylistic deviations relate in central ways to the film's thematic disruptions. Set among the small community of Bridger's Wells, Nevada, in 1885, the film is based on Walter Van Tilburg Clark's successful 1940 novel of the same name (adapted for the screen by Lamar Trotti). It follows the efforts of a hastily convened posse to track down and bring to justice three men suspected of rustling and the murder of a local rancher. In an eager effort to revenge the crime, the posse apprehends a trio of men in possession of a small herd of the rancher's cattle. Based on tenuous circumstantial evidence—and over the vociferous objections of a few—following a night of pleading and delay, the posse lynches the three men. Directly after, they learn of the men's innocence—the supposedly murdered rancher is still alive and the actual rustlers have been apprehended elsewhere—a revelation met with varying degrees of remorse and distress. The film is bookended by the arrival and departure of two cowboys into Bridger's Wells, one of whom, Gil Carter (Henry Fonda), provides as close to a main protagonist as the film offers. At the film's close, Gil and his buddy, Art Croft (Harry Morgan), depart the town on a mission to deliver a letter penned by the leader of the doomed men, Donald Martin (Dana Andrews), to his wife.

On its most explicit level, *The Ox-Bow Incident* is concerned with violence and its legitimacy and with the dangers of mob mentality. Both at the time of its release and since, it has most often been interpreted as a sober cautionary tale issued in an age of fascism overseas and conformist impulses at home.

Contemporary critics heralded the film's seriousness of purpose and tone, while acknowledging its lack of easy pleasures. Bosley Crowther, for instance, writing admiringly in the *New York Times*, praised the film's unflinching representation of the mob's brutality "unrelieved by any human grace" and credited its refusal to bow to commercial pressures, calling *Ox-Bow*'s release "as brazen a gesture as any studio has ever indulged."[1] Despite the film's low-budget soundstage sets and lighting, Crowther attributes to it "a realism that is as sharp and cold as a knife"—gesturing not toward a particular style of filmmaking but rather toward the film's revelation of an "uncompromising truth" in its image of the posse's violence.[2]

Audiences, in contrast, were more put off by the film's evacuation of conventional generic pleasures; as predicted by some, it was a commercial flop. A lobby card heralding the film as "Tough! True! Terrifying!" attempts to put a positive spin on this reaction, daring viewers to rise to the film's challenge to generic expectation by asserting, "It took nerve to make it! You'll need nerve to 'take it'!" Though it was nominated for Best Picture in 1944, however (losing out to *Casablanca*), popular response ran more along the lines of critic Robert Warshow's rather resentful classification of the film a decade later as an "anti-Western," one whose superficial generic trappings belied the disruptions at its core.[3] To consider how *The Ox-Bow Incident*, at once brazen and disappointing, both engages and refuses the conventions of the Western, we must turn specifically to the film's representation of race and gender. Or, more precisely, we must turn to its negotiation of the intertwined construction of these terms. For, as it turns out, *The Ox-Bow Incident* is a suggestive film through which to explore the interarticulation of categories such as race and gender in the context of Hollywood cinema.

Warshow's discomfort with *Ox-Bow*'s generic disruptions is precisely what renders the film useful for this purpose, for the disturbance to generic form is a register and a measure of the film's ideological turbulence. More precisely, the film's deviation from generic convention marks its negotiation of race, and of whiteness specifically, through and in relation to its construction of gender, ultimately suggesting both the instability and the constitutive violence of normative masculinity itself: a queer project indeed, for a 1940s Western. In his 1954 essay on "The Westerner," Warshow identifies the moral authority of the Western hero as founded in the specifically cinematic elements of the genre, including "the wide expanses of land, the free movement of men on horses."[4] The Westerner, according to Warshow, originates in a place "where men are men," and the moral clarity of this figure is expressed through the genre's conventional action: the hero's ability to "ride a horse faultlessly, keep his countenance in the face of death, and draw his gun a little faster and shoot it a little straighter than anyone else he is likely to meet."[5] His dissatisfaction with *The Ox-Bow Incident* makes sense in this regard, as he understands that the film's stylistic deviations signal a pivot away from the genre's image of white masculinity as the locus of both thrilling action and moral authority on-screen. Rather than strong action across an expansive landscape, the conventional terms through which white masculinity is produced in the Western, in *Ox-Bow* we get the claustrophobia of a studio set and men standing around talking amid the heavy shadows of film noir.

As Warshow's outline of the Westerner and his objections to *Ox-Bow* suggest, morality is at the center of the genre's construction of whiteness and masculinity. Indeed, when we are thinking about the intersectional construction of social identity and difference, morality is always in play, alongside race, class, gender, and nation. In the context of the Western, morality has been conventionally produced through the conjunction of decisive, thrilling on-screen action with the spectacle of innocence imperiled, mainstays of the melodramatic tradition from which the genre derives.[6] In this tradition, innocence itself is constructed as a specifically racialized and gendered identity, conventionally embodied as both white and female. In focusing on the travesty of frontier justice and the futility of moral objection, and offering its few instances of energetic action only as confirmation of these, *The Ox-Bow Incident* rips at threads that have long held together the Western's traditional certainties.

The film's move away from conventional pleasures relates to broader shifts within the genre, which undergoes a significant stylistic and thematic reassessment starting in the 1940s. By the 1950s, the traditional Western hero, once defined through his vigorous on-screen action, has grown more anxious and constrained in his movements. The genre's mise-en-scène, once associated with wide open spaces, has become more claustrophobic, as the hero is more often restricted to interior spaces or to the retreading of familiar ground (though the open landscapes that had once signified the potential and promise of white Westward expansion were always far from empty). There is an inward turn across the genre, away from strong action and toward more psychologically driven dramas. Stylistically, and in this regard as in others, *The Ox-Bow Incident* is a forerunner to the Western noir, with the dark shadows and low-key lighting of noir beginning to seep into its settings, signaling the new moral and emotional unsteadiness of its hero.[7]

This generic reassessment is conditioned by the geopolitical pressures of World War II and subsequently the Cold War, in the context of which explicit manifestations of white supremacist sentiment and action were increasingly cast as anti-American. Fighting "the good war" against fascism and racism in Europe, and later heralding the virtues of a "free" and democratic society in contrast to the specter of Soviet communism during the Cold War, official discourse in the United States came to embrace a rhetoric of tolerance and to distance itself from images of racially motivated violence. These shifts posed a stark representational challenge to the Western, a genre founded on the dictates of Manifest Destiny. They take as their animating principle the superiority of Anglo-American cultural traditions, histories, and subjects that celebrate white violence. In the face of this challenge, the Western moves away from unapologetic representations of white supremacy to refigure the moral authority of the white Western hero through a revised set of terms, including an alignment with the figure of the Indian and a new emphasis on the hero's own status as one who suffers. This evolution forms an important backdrop to understanding *The Ox-Bow Incident*'s stylistic deviations as well as its ideological instabilities. For while the lynching around which the narrative revolves is not represented as racially motivated, the film in other ways highlights the significance of race to the moral dilemma it stages.

As is so often the case in the studio era in particular, the film's engagement with race and racism operates outside any explicit narrative content, but registers instead across its mise-en-scène and on its soundtrack. As John Calhoun suggests in a review of the film on the occasion of its DVD release in 2004, *The Ox-Bow Incident* is "as notable for what it omits as for what it states."[8] We see this most significantly in the figure of Sparks, the African American preacher whose prominence on both the sound and image tracks underscores his centrality to the film's indictment of violence. It is through Sparks that the film inscribes the history of lynching as a mode of white racial terrorism, a history to which only one overt reference is made, when Sparks mentions very briefly that he witnessed as a child the lynching of his own brother. In its impulse, both to highlight and to deny the significance of race, the film expands the original role of Sparks in the novel while refusing that text's more explicit engagement with racism. In contrast to the film, which makes no direct reference to race, the novel is shot through with racist rhetoric, though even in this context, Art Croft, who serves as the novel's narrator, evidences a guilty discomfort with his own racist bias against Sparks.

Stylistically, the film announces Sparks's moral function in ways that stand conspicuously apart from its otherwise spare sound and image tracks. This impulse is consistent with the historical project of melodrama, which works to produce legible signs of goodness and evil in the face of a changing and unsteady world. The introduction of Sparks features the first non-diegetic sound since the film's opening sequence, as he is urged to join the lynching party by the sadistic town drunk, Monty Smith (Paul Hurst). The angelic choir sounds a quiet, mournful note as Monty leeringly calls out to Sparks, and grows louder and more insistent as Sparks rises to take a place among the posse as a conscientious objector. In a film noteworthy for its static compositions, the camera moves along with Sparks as he walks slowly forward. We hear the chorus again that night at the Ox-Bow, as the party waits until dawn to lynch the condemned men. In this second instance, the mournful angels once again accompany the figure of Sparks, as he is the first to rise and counted for his opposition to the hanging. Though six other men will join him (including Gil Carter and Art Croft), the camera rests first on his lone figure, standing straight and centered in the frame, backlit against the hazy glow of a breaking dawn. As the chorus is heard at no other time in the film—indeed, as noted, the film runs almost completely without score—its presence and function in these sequences is hard to ignore. Isolated in the frame at these key moments, with the film's score sounding its assent, Sparks serves as a locus of spiritual enlightenment and integrity, standing in gentle yet unyielding opposition to the will of the mob.

Just after the hanging, the film offers its final and most affecting association of the lynching at the Ox-Bow with the history of racialized violence. Once again, Sparks is mobilized at the level of the mise-en-scène and soundtrack to inscribe a history the film otherwise works to repress or deny. The singing this time is Sparks's own, as he breaks into the traditional spiritual "Lonesome Valley," just after the men are lynched. The song cuts in as the camera begins a pan from the spot where the horses have been whipped out from under the noosed men, to the figure of Sparks kneeling in the dust, his face uplifted toward the bodies, which remain off screen. Sparks's song carries across the shot as it rests upon him for a moment before moving past to reveal the lynching party filing out of the valley, the shadows of the hanged men dangling in the foreground (see Figure 5.1). Off screen, Sparks's song

FIGURE 5.1 The shadows of the three lynched men dangle as the hanging party exits the valley, accompanied by Sparks' singing. *The Ox-Bow Incident* (1943).

continues to accompany the men as they ride, up the slope and away from the Ox-Bow.

Interestingly, in a review critiquing the film's self-consciousness, James Agee, writing for the *Nation* in July 1943, identifies the "angelic soprani" as one of the film's few "flagrant mistakes," alongside the "phonily gnarled lynching tree" itself. His discomfort with these elements suggests something of their ham-handed quality. In contrast to Crowther's conception of the film's realism, Agee is struck by the affectations of its style. Though he praises the film as "one of the best and most interesting pictures I have seen for a long time," his review is focused on the "sort of double focus" through which the film both represents its story and registers the nature of its own representations, "like off-printing in a comic strip."[9] In the example of the angelic choir and the hanging tree, it is the melodramatic aspects of the film to which Agee seems to object. The film, striving to express a "moral truth," encodes the history of white supremacist violence at the level of soundtrack and mise-en-scène, a history it is unable or unwilling to represent it more directly.

In diagnosing what Agee refers to as the film's "complicatedness of attitude," we must consider more closely how *The Ox-Bow Incident* negotiates the constructions of race and gender at the genre's core. In the example of Sparks, we begin to see how the moral bankruptcy of the mob is signified through its alignment with the specter of racialized violence, however veiled. It is not simply mob mentality the film critiques but the implication of the mob in white racial terrorism. Importantly, while the issue of race remains visible and audible yet bracketed at the level of plot and dialogue, the moral transgression of the mob is coded in quite explicit ways through the category of gender. And here the film's queerness comes to the fore, as masculine deviance provides the language through which the film negotiates whiteness as both a gendered and a moral identity. *The Ox-Bow Incident* circles around what is the central paradox of the Western in this period, namely how its critique of white supremacism "softens" the normative image of white masculinity at the genre's core.

Three key figures of masculine deviance work to link the film's representation of white supremacist violence to the image of masculine hardness: the bullish Jenny ("Ma") Grier (Jane Darwell), a zealous member of the lynching party, and its only woman; the militant and sadistic Major Tetley (Frank Conroy), who becomes the group's de facto leader; and Tetley's nervous and cowardly son Gerald (William Eythe), whose ultimate indictment of his father will prove definitive. Ma Grier and Major Tetley both embody and confirm the perversity of the "he-man lynch mob," while highlighting the film's intersectional construction of gender, sexuality, and race.[10] In each of these two figures, traditional virtues of masculine hardness—action, strength, resolve—are revealed as morally suspect, though the particular calculus is distinct in each case. In the context of the film as in the novel, the abstractions of such characters into types speak in part to the melodramatic impulses of the film's source material.

Ma Grier, a big, boisterous butch, is one of the most eager and enthusiastic of the posse, seeming to hunger for the violence it promises. Calhoun refers to her as a "cackling old shrew," a feminized classification that quite misses the mark.[11] As Clark's book makes explicit, Ma is a leader among men, more a man than many of the men themselves, in Kenneth Andersen's 1970 evaluation of the novel. Andersen identifies Ma in the novel as "recklessly strong" and in this strength as "unnatural": "merely a strong man in woman's clothing"[12] (though in the film as in the novel, Ma is dressed in flannel and jeans, no differently than the other men). Queerness is not a term in Andersen's 1970's lexicon, and as his general reliance on an uncritical notion of the natural suggests, a lack of insight around the construction of gender shapes his argument. Nonetheless, he identifies correctly how Ma's queerness, the "unnatural" relationship between her masculine persona and her assignment as female, aligns in the novel with her positioning outside, or even opposed to, the category of the moral.

In the film likewise, it is Ma's embodiment of female masculinity that gives the form to her perversity, and her zealous support of the mob's violence that gives this perversity its content. Thus, the masculinity of Ma Grier registers as both a gendered and a moral transgression, her queerness a figure of both non-normative gender and moral laxity. And while the film greatly truncates her leadership role as compared to the novel, pushing her to the margins of its action, it emphasizes in other ways her importance to the problematic it stages. As in the case of Sparks, the soundtrack does significant work in this respect, as the persistence of Ma's raucous off-screen laughter continues to signal her role in the film's gendering of moral transgression. Ma's laughter underscores the disturbing disjunction between the boisterous affect of the mob and the murderous implications of their actions. In assigning this inappropriate affect to Ma, the film like the novel works to queer the disjunction itself, as the moral misalignment appears as deviant rather than part of business as usual.[13] The gesture is an important one, as it makes way for the film's ultimate recuperative impulses, leaving space open for a rehabilitated white Western hero by implying racialized violence as precisely that which falls outside the parameters of normative masculine performance.

In the case of Major Tetley, the association of masculine hardness with the specter of racialized violence is made more explicit. It is anchored by Tetley's status as an ex-Confederate officer or, in the film in contrast to the novel, as a faux-ex-Confederate, an alteration made in deference to the film's southern audience. In line with dominant discourses of race and region in American culture, the film mobilizes Tetley's southern association to signify his position as morally backward, a point that highlights how region, too, enters into the intersectional construction of social identity. The Major functions as the default leader of the lynching party and the single character who most clearly and persistently drives its action forward. Under his direction, the mob embodies "decay, sin, evil, guilt, and hatred," a pantheon of moral transgressions associated with his southern provenance.[14]

As with Sparks, in its treatment of Tetley, the film encodes through the mise-en-scène a history of white supremacist violence it refuses to engage on a narrative level. This strategy is first suggested by Tetley's visual introduction near the beginning of the film, as he stands ramrod straight outside his plantation-style southern Greek Revival home, shadowed by the slightly slouching figure of his son Gerald in the background. From the edge of his property, Tetley has watched the posse form in the street beyond, and as Fonda's Gil Carter hurries by in search of the sheriff—in an effort to make the posse "regular," as shopkeeper Arthur Davies (Harry Davenport) pleads—Tetley turns and walks toward the house, readying himself to join the group. The novel describes the house as "a white, wooden mansion, with pillars like a Southern plantation home."[15] In mirroring the pillars of the house with the figure of Tetley himself, this introductory shot creates a strong visual link between the structure of the plantation home and the man who rules over it (see Figure 5.2).

Through this image we are introduced to Tetley and his son as significant in relation both to each other and to the racialized violence signified by the house itself, in its function as a metonym for the South. This connection is emphasized across the film both in cuts back to the house as well as through the conspicuous presence of a Confederate insignia on the uniform into which Tetley changes once he joins the posse, riding, in an ironic underscoring of the hijacking of conventional justice, on the lone white horse amid the pack.[16] The insignia, clearly visible in medium close-ups throughout the long night at the Ox-Bow, make visual reference to Tetley's association with racial violence even as the film avoids this history, in contrast again to the novel, in which Tetley is identified as "the son of a slave owner."[17] By linking the posse's commitment to violence with the visual suggestion of white supremacist sympathies, Major Tetley implicates both his and Ma's positions, casting manliness in both contexts as a sign of moral laxity. While Tetley's relationship to racial violence remains indirect, his engagement with a discourse of manliness is made central and explicit. Indeed, with Tetley, the film hints at racialized violence itself as a mechanism through which normative masculinity is produced and maintained, as the Major badgers his reluctant son Gerald to take on an active role in the posse's pursuit, and later in the lynching itself, in the hope that "this will do what I've obviously failed to do, make a man of you." When Gerald is unable to bring himself to whip the horse out from underneath one of the noosed men, standing instead frozen in hor-

FIGURE 5.2 Major Tetley and his son Gerald in front of their plantation-style home. *The Ox-Bow Incident* (1943).

ror, Tetley pistol-whips the boy, before ordering one of the other men to finish the doomed man. As the camera slides down toward the crumpled figure of Gerald lying in the dust, the soundtrack breaks in with Sparks's singing. Gil and Davies drag the limp Gerald away, passing the kneeling figure of Sparks, on whom the camera rests before panning to the dangling shadows of the hanged men to his right. The film's focus, which turns to Sparks on both image and soundtracks at this moment, serves again as a link between Major Tetley's concern with manliness and the issue of racialized violence, casting the violence Tetley demands of his son as reprehensible on multiple levels.

The intra- and extratextual echoes of this manly imperative are interesting to note, as in the novel the character of Gil Carter himself becomes sick with the memory of a lynching he witnessed. And though this incident is excised from the film, Fonda's work on *Ox-Bow* reportedly stirred up his own traumatizing childhood memory of being brought by his father to witness the lynching of an African American man. That *Ox-Bow* ultimately proved cathartic for Fonda in working through this memory contributes another dimension to the racialized spectacle of lynching the film both rehearses and represses. In the case of Fonda, this biographical detail circulates as a signifier of his own sensitivity and enlightenment, a point that is not irrelevant to the film's representation of masculine softness. Just as a repudiation of masculine hardness becomes the primary rhetoric through which the film decries the mob's violence, the genre's traditionally mocked or marginalized representations of masculine softness and domesticity—Sparks, the preacher; Davies, the shopkeeper; as well as Gerald himself—provide the most explicit arguments against injustice, their association with the feminine animating rather than circumscribing their authority. Though the objections of these characters remain ineffectual in the end, the construction of moral authority through them stands in significant contrast to the Western's more conventional assignment of righteousness to decisive masculine action on screen. In contrast to the image of masculine hardness and toughness, *Ox-Bow* offers us Davies as the most articulate of the posse's dissenters, as he urges the group to conduct itself "in a reasoned and legitimate manner, not like some lawless mob." That the men who chide Davies for his caution or cast it as a feminized weakness are themselves among the most eager for the violent spectacle of a "necktie party" adds to the integrity accruing to Davies' position.

Whereas Davies gives the most articulate arguments against the posse's violence, Gerald contributes an affective intensity to these arguments through the silent anguish of his gaze. Though he is timid and speaks little, the film positions him as a site of identification, aligning the audience, likewise powerless before the will of the mob, with Gerald's own distress. Such is the case in a sequence in which Gerald is shown solemnly surveying the three condemned men, gathered around the campfire during a brief reprieve, while a mournful harmonica plays in the background. The film cuts from Gerald to the men, back to Gerald, and then to three horses as they graze beneath three nooses dangling from the hanging tree. As his gaze and the camera's pans over the doomed men, their lack of awareness helps to solidify the audience's identification with Gerald as a point of both voyeuristic observation and, as the sequence comes to rest on his anguished face, of conscience. It is Major Tetley who has introduced Gerald into the sequence, drawing him forward from the background of the shot, where he had stood shuffling his feet. The final shot of Gerald's anguished face fades out onto an image of Sparks administering to the condemned men, bookending the sequence with the starkest embodiments of moral polarity that the film has to offer, and marking Gerald's alignment with Sparks.

In considering *Ox-Bow*'s depiction of manliness, it is useful to note that the association of moral authority with the feminine is not in itself something new, even as *Ox-Bow* extends this figuration in novel ways. Genre studies have often argued that moral authority in the Western is identified with values and figures of the feminine, classically embodied as a cultivated woman from the East, who provides a contrast to the freewheeling and male-identified morality of the West, as in *My Darling Clementine* (dir. John Ford, 1946), featuring Henry Fonda. I would suggest a somewhat different reading of the Western's conventional construction of righteousness, arguing that it accrues most definitively around the spectacle of white male action. Clementine, for instance, heads back home at the movie's end. Even in films that do herald the civilized virtues of the feminine, however, this positive valuation does not conventionally extend to the representation of male figures on screen. Instead, in the context of soft or sensitive men, femininity conventionally connotes a weakness both moral and physical, and often a sexualized deviance as well, identified in the studio era as an explicitly moral transgression. Villains themselves are frequently feminized along these lines and are, we might note, almost invariably better dressed than their heroic counterparts, suggesting a feminized attention to appearance that serves again as a signifier of moral weakness.

Clark's novel itself highlights a preoccupation with queerness and womanishness in more or less these terms. As offered in the novel, the physical softness and gendered "deterioration" of Gerald (a "female boy," in his father's terms), as well as of Arthur Davies, are what make their attempts to intervene in the lynching ultimately ineffectual. In contrast to the film, effeminate or sensitive men retain their stigma of weakness in the novel. Characters are chastised for their "womanish" countenance or behavior, for tears or strong emotional responses, or for any sign of timidity, even as the novel links the imperative of gender conformity to the violence of the mob. As Gerald himself identifies, to "keep from looking queer to the pack," men will evacuate positions of principle and align themselves with violence, in part to avoid becoming its object.[18]

Moral weakness is identified here with normative masculine performance most particularly. Yet at the same time, the novel casts Gerald's own queerness as a signifier of his maladjustment, and at no point more forcefully than when he makes this speech about the violence of pack mentality. Art Croft as narrator regards Gerald in this moment with disgust. Even though "queerly, weak and bad-tempered" as Gerald's social analysis might be, Art suspects it is correct ("You could feel what he meant").[19] In the novel, Gerald's moral condemnation of the pack is intermixed with the suggestion of his own homosexuality, in keeping with a heteronormative logic that reads softness or any suggestion of feminine gender identity as the sign of a male object choice. And while the novel is more suggestive on this point, the film, too, makes a veiled gesture toward what it cannot reference directly under the prevailing Production Code, namely in a freighted exchange of looks between Gerald and the captive Juan Martínez (Anthony Quinn), as the former tries and fails to dig a bullet out of Martínez's leg.

While Gerald's queerness in the novel serves to bracket his critique of the posse's violence, the film casts him in a more sympathetic light. He is weak to the extent he is unable to take a stand against his father's tyranny and is thus resigned to the lynching, but it is Gerald who serves as the mouthpiece for the film's final indictment of Major Tetley. And while Gerald hangs himself at the novel's conclusion, he is spared this fate in the film. Major Tetley does not fare so well, in the film or in the novel. In the latter, he falls on his own sword upon hearing of Gerald's suicide. In the film, however, Gerald lives to taunt his father through the locked door of his plantation home, calling him out for his sadism, his cruelty, his lust for power, the pleasure he took in the doomed men's suffering, and his need to make Gerald a witness: "How does it feel to have begot a weakling, Major Tetley?," Gerald cries. "Does it make you afraid that there may be some weakness in you, too, that other men may discover and whisper about?" The off-screen gun shot that rings out in retort makes violently explicit the film's critique of white masculine hardness as an imperative that, in the final count, is as untenable as it is immoral. When the film cuts to Gerald's face after, a small smile pulls at the edges of his mouth, one of deliverance and relief, intermixed perhaps with satisfaction, as he lifts his gaze upward.

Queerness is an unstable signifier in *The Ox-Bow Incident*. Female masculinity may circulate in the film as a sign of perversity, while male femininity helps to secure the image of whiteness in its moral claims. One implication of the shifting assignment of moral authority in the Western away from the image of manliness is thus a revision in the gendered contours of whiteness itself. Whereas the traditional figure of masculinity as active, hard, and resolute, served as the genre's representative embodiment of whiteness, *Ox-Bow* suggests a shift wherein the construction of a normative whiteness relies upon its alignment with figures of blackness and femininity. In the end, the queer-est thing about the film may be its emphasis on both the imperative and the impossibility of heteronormative masculinity, here recognized in rela-tion to the racialized violence at its core. Men must be men, which is to say, within the generic universe of the Western, they must be hard, but to be so is to be implicated in a morally unsupportable position. As we see in Ger-ald's indictment of his father, the denial of a softness or weakness within entails a brutality toward self as well as others. Men, Gerald maintains in the novel, are "the bullies of the globe"—a suggestive rebuke of both nor-mative masculinity and the imperialist impulse that informs the Western at its core.[20]

Ultimately, the different valuations of masculine softness in the novel as compared to the film relate to this indictment of manliness. Less concerned with resuscitating a sense of moral purpose or holding out for the possibil-ity of heroic action, the novel has no particular impulse to distance manli-ness from the suggestion of racialized violence, and thus no need to herald masculine softness as a signifier of moral renewal. While the novel concludes on a bleak note of resignation, however, the film evidences a significant recu-perative impulse, despite its generic and ideological disruptions and the challenges they represent. In the novel, for instance, the sheriff upon whom the lynching party stumbles just after the hanging, bearing news of the appre-hended rustlers and in the company of the supposedly deceased rancher, indicates his intention to overlook the posse's murder of the three men. In the film, in contrast, the sheriff—though his arrival carries neither the thrill of a rescue "in the nick of time" nor the pathos of a failed one "too late"—does at least promise a vigorous prosecution of the men responsible for the crime. Eschewing the more familiar satisfactions of melodrama then, the film nonetheless works to restore some amount of faith in justice and the law, indi-cating a degree of reinvestment in traditional institutions and the ideologies that uphold them.

The film holds out the hope, or perhaps even the promise, of a white mas-culinity constituted as at once moral and manly.[21] The doomed men's leader, Donald Martin, embodies something of this hope. Dana Andrews's com-ments on the role, one he identified as the most satisfying of his career due to the challenging opportunity it offered to "play a character who was sensitive without making him seem weak,"[22] suggest an attempt to provide a model of masculinity that stands apart from either the stigma of softness or the troubled imperative of hardness. However, it is through the rejuvenated figure of Fonda's Gil Carter, a character almost entirely removed from the novel's action, that the film's recuperative impulse is most clearly embodied. In the novel Gil and Art are not even among the handful of men who rise in objection to the lynching. In the film, conversely, Gil is aligned with the forces of good from the start. He is often framed alongside Sparks, Davies, and Gerald, the film's primary representatives of both softness and goodness. He resists the false deputizing of the posse and seeks out the judge at Davies' behest to try and forestall the lynching. He offers his coat to the chattering Sparks during the bitter night's cold and is quick to jump to the defense of the less powerful. Most significantly, he rises to be counted against the lynching and finally, after the posse has returned to town, reads aloud to the bar full of dejected men the letter Martin has penned to his wife, giving voice to the film's own conscience.

By assigning to Gil this set of functions not found in the novel, the film concludes on a note of resuscitation. Gil and Art, who arrive in Bridger's Wells devoid of particular purpose or direction, depart on a mission to deliver themselves and the murdered Martin's letter to his freshly made widow and her children. As Mary Beth Crain identifies, "Gil now becomes endowed with a sense of moral decency which makes the pill we, as the audience, must take easier to swallow."[23] In granting Gil a nobler purpose in his departure from Bridger's Wells than the one with which he arrived, the film adumbrates a connection between the indictment of racialized violence and the revitalization of the Western hero, a point relevant to the rise of the so-called pro-Indian Westerns in the decade to follow.[24] Understanding the film's recuperative impulse, and the intersectional constructions of race, gender, and sexuality this impulse negotiates, helps us to appreciate better the "complicatedness of attitude" James Agee diagnosed at the time of *The Ox-Bow Incident*'s release. In closing on the more stable and familiar image of the white Western hero endowed with a moral mission, the film evidences the "double focus" Agee strains to emphasize, reinscribing something of what it has critiqued. Nonetheless, like the men left dangling at the Ox-Bow, the film's stark accounting of the production of white masculinity through the threat and promise of racialized violence casts a dark and very long shadow, one we may well still recognize today.

NOTES

1. Bosley Crowther, "The Screen," *New York Times*, May 10, 1943, 15.

2. Crowther, "Screen," 15.

3. Robert Warshow, "Movie Chronicle: The Westerner," in *The Immediate Experience: Movies, Comics, Theatre and Other Aspects of Popular Culture* (Garden City, NY: Doubleday, 1962), 135–154, 142.

4. Warshow, "Movie Chronicle," 139.

5. Warshow, "Movie Chronicle," 139.

6. For a discussion of the melodramatic foundations of the Western, as well as *Ox-Bow*'s participation in it, see Jonna Eagle, *Imperial Affects: Sensational Melodrama and the Attractions of American Cinema* (New Brunswick, NJ: Rutgers University Press, 2017).

7. For further discussion of this shift, see my "Western Weepies: The Power of Pathos in the Cold War Western," in Eagle, *Imperial Affects*, 101–141; and Thomas Pauly, "The Cold War Western," *Western Humanities Review* 33 (1979): 265–273.

8. John Calhoun, "*The Ox-Bow Incident*," *Cineaste*, Summer 2004, 55–56, 55.

9. James Agee, *Agee on Film*, vol. 1 (New York: Grosset & Dunlap, 1967), 44.

10. The phrase comes from Max Westbrook's discussion of the novel in "The Archetypical Ethic of *The Ox-Bow Incident*," *Western American Literature* 1 (Summer 1966): 105–118, 110.

11. Calhoun, "*Ox-Bow Incident*," 55.

12. Kenneth Andersen, "Character Portrayal in *The Ox-Bow Incident*," *Western American Literature* 4 (Winter 1970): 287–298, 294.

13. In a somewhat different formulation, Clark's novel acknowledges the violence that underwrites normative masculinity, though deviance is at the same time suggested as central to the performance of this normativity.

14. Andersen, "Character Portrayal," 288.

15. Walter Van Tilburg Clark, *The Ox-Bow Incident* (New York: Modern Library, 2001), 87.

16. In Clark's novel, the uniform itself is described as a "Confederate field coat . . . and a Confederate's officer's hat." Clark, *Ox-Bow Incident*, 97.

17. Clark, *Ox-Bow Incident*, 87.

18. Clark, *Ox-Bow Incident*, 115.

19. Clark, *Ox-Bow Incident*, 117.

20. Clark, *Ox-Bow Incident*, 111. For a discussion of imperialist ideology and the Western, see my *Imperial Affects*, esp. 59–141.

21. *Imperial Affects*, 111–115.

22. Dana Andrews, "The Role I Liked Best," *Saturday Evening Post*, March 16, 1946, 94.

23. Mary Beth Crain, "The Ox-Bow Incident Revisited," *Literature/Film Quarterly* 4 (July 1976): 240–248, 244.

24. For a discussion of the pro-Indian cycle, see *Imperial Affects*, chapter 3.

6 · BY HERSELF

Intersectionality, African American Specialty Performers, and Eleanor Powell

RYAN JAY FRIEDMAN

In his July 1943 review of MGM's *I Dood It*, *Motion Picture Herald*'s William R. Weaver applauds one sequence that features a pair of popular African American performers: "Set into the picture, without disturbing the course of the narrative and considerably profiting the enterprise, are Hazel Scott, who does with a piano all the things there are to do and some that approach the impossible, and Lena Horne, leading a Negro chorus in a massive production number."[1] Weaver's choice of words is revealing: *I Dood It* greatly benefits from Scott and Horne's contribution to it, and yet these women are not fully a part of it, nor of the larger studio enterprise whose purpose it is to profit. In spite of the sublimity of their creative work, Scott and Horne's presence is merely tolerated—and only insofar as it is not "disturbing."

In *I Dood It*, Scott and Horne find themselves in a bind that in the 1930s, as Miriam Petty has argued, began to define the plight of African American performers in Hollywood. The studios were in search of actors to play distinctive, memorable bit roles in feature films, increasingly extending such opportunities to African American actors.[2] Petty points out, however, that "the larger racialized structure of the American film industry" ensured that, whatever gains in terms of increased "visibility" or minor stardom might accrue to these actors, the primary function of their screen roles was "to 'improve the property' of the Hollywood studios" that employed them.[3]

The production history of *I Dood It* bears out this essential imbalance and the quandary that it posed for Scott and Horne. Bringing them onboard in the late stages of the production, MGM employed an established practice, whereby black "entertainment talent" was used to "add excitement" and "value" to "movies that needed a boost."[4] Limited to set-piece, "specialty" numbers that were sometimes edited out when the films were exhibited in certain southern jurisdictions, the resulting performances existed under the shadow of Jim Crow. Moreover, as established professionals with flourishing careers as night-club and recording artists, Scott and Horne did not feel that they needed Hollywood's patronage and were highly circumspect about the loss of control over their own self-representations that signing a studio contract might entail. Refusing the sorts of typecasting that permitted black women's access to the fictional story world, they were forced to use the fact of their playing "themselves" as a hedge against exploitation and a loss of personal prestige.

Weaver's uniformly positive review of *I Dood It* portrays the film as a fluid showcase, in which the featured performers, competing aggressively for the viewer's attention, reach dazzling new heights of virtuosity. Although any-one can, it seems, "steal the show," to use Petty's phrase, the film is clearly a vehicle for its white, male star, Red Skelton.[5] Weaver reserves his greatest praise for Skelton's skills as a pantomime comedian. Weaver duly recognizes the talents of Eleanor Powell: she "danc[es] her head off in a series of pro-duction numbers, acting over her previous best."[6] But his description of her role—"opposite Skelton in the billing and the story"—masks the fact that, despite being the film's costar, her presence is relatively marginal. A remake of a Buster Keaton picture, *Spite Marriage* (MGM, 1929), with an added war-time subplot about Nazi saboteurs, *I Dood It* struggles to expand the Pow-ell's character—she plays a famous stage actor, Connie Shaw, with whom Skelton's character, Joe Rivington Reynolds, is obsessed—into a suitable vehicle for Powell's prodigious talents as a tap dancer. After Powell's initial performance, an astonishing Western-themed number, in which she dances with and over a variety of lassos, she is very much underutilized, for reasons that also have everything to do with race and gender.

In this essay, I analyze *I Dood It* using as a point of comparison a slightly earlier MGM musical, *Lady Be Good* (1941), which also stars Eleanor Powell and also prominently features a group of African American specialty performers, the "flash" dance trio, the Berry Brothers. Beginning with *Lady Be Good*, each of the last seven films in which Powell appeared involves African American musical performers in stand-alone musical numbers. Following on the heels of Powell's blackface impersonation of Bill Robinson in *Honolulu* (MGM, 1939)—a performance that she intended as an homage to her friend and mentor—this unprecedented series of films indicates a white star whose career is crucially dependent upon black performance.[7] Extending but beginning to move past the tradition of white appropriations of African American musical culture, this series creates a platform for African American performers working Hollywood that is both unusually prominent and marked by a very specific set of intersectional constraints.

This essay examines the show-stealing moments created by these performers, "moments in which [they] take distinct advantage of the peculiar and fleeting high-relief visibility afforded to them by racial difference."[8] Highlighting the extent to which such seemingly small instants can act as sites of struggle over cultural meaning, Petty's approach offers a useful corrective to the predominant treatment of African American specialties in academic film criticism, which has tended only to reinforce their marginal status. By virtue of their positioning within what black feminist scholars like Patricia Hill Collins term "interlocking structures of oppression," Scott and Horne have unique purchase over the central themes of the larger works in which they occupy a seemingly marginal place.[9] And this knowledge informs their artistic practice, which, in turn, contributes to the demystification of the workings of power in this body of films, as well as the larger worlds of entertainment and commodity culture depicted therein.

Scholars have defined the African American specialty number as a cameo that has no role in advancing the plot: it is a scene in a Hollywood musical featuring popular black performers, who appear, entertain a diegetic audience for the duration of the scene, and then disappear from the film. These performers do not have any spoken dialogue or other markers of fictional-character status and are typically billed in the films' "Cast" as "Specialty"/ "Specialties" or as "Herself"/"Himself"/"Themselves."[10] The disconnection of these cameos from the films' narratives represents an apparent concession to racist censors in the Jim Crow South, who refused to tolerate nonservile images of African Americans on the screens they controlled.

I say "apparent concession" to signal the fact that more research is needed to determine how widespread this censorship practice was and to what extent the studios deliberately catered to it. Since the 1970s, it has been a commonplace among scholars of African American representation in Hollywood film that southern jurisdictions consistently cut black specialties and that the studios structured the scenes in order to facilitate such excision. Donald Bogle's summary statement is indicative: "Because musical numbers were not integrated into the script, the scenes featuring blacks could be cut from the films without spoiling them should local (or Southern) theater owners feel their audiences would object to seeing a Negro."[11]

The censorship of black specialties in one southern jurisdiction, Memphis, Tennessee, is, indeed, well documented, owing largely to the African American press's coverage of that city's notorious, hardline white-supremacist censor Lloyd Binford.[12] We know that Binford harbored particular animosity toward individual black performers, including Horne, cutting her numbers from *Broadway Rhythm* (MGM, 1944)—though not, it appears, Scott's number in that same film—and *Ziegfeld Follies* (MGM, 1945) when exhibited locally.[13] It is highly plausible that this sort of cutting occurred in other Jim Crow jurisdictions with empowered city- (Atlanta) or state-level (Virginia) censor boards, where, we know, on-screen representations of African Americans and interracial contacts were most heavily policed. But further research is needed to establish its frequency, not to mention any causal linkage between local censorship practice and studio script practices.

Existing accounts likely overstate the importance of cutting somewhat, and in any event, evidence of it needs to be weighed against indications that black specialties circulated widely and were popular among audiences of diverse racial backgrounds. A range of anecdotal evidence testifies to this fact, from accounts of audiences demanding that specialties be replayed and of specialty performers being given top billing on theater marquees to film trailers and trade-press reviews that highlight appearances by these performers. The degree to which specialty numbers could be excised without disrupting the continuity of the film likely has also been exaggerated.[14] In the most interesting examples of films with black specialties from this period (like *I Dood It* and *Lady Be Good*), these scenes are longer, more numerous, more consequential in their placement, and/or more embedded in the diegesis than conventional accounts suggest.

A specialty composed of two songs, Scott and Horne's appearance in *I Dood It* acts as an interlude in a scene where Joe (Skelton) goes to the Martinique Theatre, in search of the actor he has, effectively, been stalking since the start of the film, Connie (Powell). In a ploy to elicit the jealousy of her ex-boyfriend and costar, Larry West (Richard Ainley), Connie has previously decided to marry Joe, whom she mistakenly believed to be a wealthy gold mine owner. In fact, Joe is a pants-presser in a hotel valet service who has been masquerading as high-class. He borrows the formal attire that customers leave in his shop to be cleaned and pressed, wearing it to the theater each night to watch Connie. After Connie's caper backfires and Joe is unmasked, she refuses to see him again. Joe goes to the theater in a desperate effort to win her back, and the stage manager tells him that he has been banned from the premises. At this moment, Scott, wearing "a full-length fur coat and black sequined gown" and accompanied by a group of elegantly attired musicians and singers, enters through the stage door.[15] Wearing a borrowed black top coat and top hat, Joe uses the commotion caused by their entrance to slip past the stage manager, inserting himself into a cluster of similarly dressed African American men and walking by unnoticed.

In the brief bit of dialogue that precedes the musical performance, the producer, Mr. Lawlor (Thurston Hall), explains to a group of prospective investors (also white) that Scott, Horne, and company are there to audition for "a new revue," which, he feels, will be a surefire hit. Before Horne herself arrives, Scott takes a seat at the piano and begins improvising on "Taking a Chance on Love," carrying the tune through a number of stylistic registers and shifting tempo dramatically along the way (see Figure 6.1). She plays it at first as a "languid" ballad, then as a rollicking "stride" piano solo, adding in brief, classical-sounding passages, as if it were a sonata.[16] With a crane moving the camera to show both sides of the keyboard and even providing an overhead view, a single, uninterrupted shot highlights the dazzlingly quick runs of Scott's right hand and her percussive, left-handed rhythm playing. Showing that nothing is being faked, the cinematography recalls Powell's first dance in the film, the "Western Rope Dance." In that scene too, fluid camera movements and a long take authenticate the performer's seemingly impossible technical skill.

As soon as Scott finishes this prelude, Horne makes her entrance and apologizes for being late, citing an inability to find a cab. Lawlor takes her black fur coat and helps her get into position at the center of the sparsely adorned stage. Spotlighted under a tree and in front of a backdrop that looks like the

FIGURE 6.1 Hazel Scott improvises on "Taking a Chance on Love" in *I Dood It* (1943).

night sky, Horne begins to sing "Jericho," accompanied by Scott and the other musicians. After "Jericho" ends, the stage manager discovers and forcibly removes Joe, who has watched the entire performance, concealed inside a prop box. Scott and Horne's presence in *I Dood It* is restricted to this one sequence, after which the focus of the action shifts back to the frustrated white romance plot; Connie is noticeably absent from this part of the film. Given the ways in which the African American specialty has conventionally been treated, these details might not seem significant. But we need only compare Scott and Horne's placement in *I Dood It* to the Berry Brothers' in *Lady Be Good* to dispel this impression.

The Berry Brothers perform two complete specialties and appear in a mid-film montage in *Lady Be Good*. Their second specialty is an integral component of the film's massive, Busby Berkeley–directed finale, in which they perform immediately before Powell appears. After a white singer (Connie Russell) introduces "Fascinating Rhythm," the Berry Brothers take the stage, wearing full evening dress in tailcoats and white ties. Set to an up-tempo, instrumental version of the Gershwin tune, their routine combines acrobatics with intricate passages of unison tap, while they impressively twirl, throw, and catch walking canes. As they wind down their dance, what appears to be a single, uninterrupted crane shot establishes a sense of an unbroken line, a transfer of energy or musical sensibility across several sets of feet.[17] The view shifts from a close-up of the three Berry Brothers' dancing feet, to those of a man working the pedals of a piano embedded in the huge stage, to those of Powell's character, the dancer, Marilyn Marsh. Clad in what the black-and-white film stock renders as a gray one-piece tuxedo, matching patent-leather tap shoes, and a shiny top hat, Powell proceeds to interpret the music in her inimitable style of precise, ultra-quick footwork, making occasional nods to Robinson's mannerisms.

Throughout the scene, staging and costuming work to both evoke and cancel out the possibility of a Powell–Berry Brothers collaboration. As Powell moves about the dance floor, Berkeley's characteristic combination of moving camerawork and stage machinery bring in and out of view a series of five stylized baby-grand pianos, each one played by an African American man, as diaphanous curtains further break up the performance space.[18] The scene emphasizes the linkage between Powell's taps and the pianist's percussive lefthanded playing, while also giving the Berry Brothers a continued, phantom presence in the scene; in their costuming and facial expressions, the pianists bear a clear resemblance to the dancers.

As Adrienne McLean has argued, "Hollywood's own [Production] Code-regulated racist sexual politics" forbade any kind of on-screen interplay between Powell and the Berry Brothers.[19] Forbidding the depiction of "sex relationship[s] between the white and black races," the Code's so-called "miscegenation clause" was construed so broadly as to make impossible any kind of mixed-gender, cross-racial interaction that could be construed as romantic in nature.[20] Barring the opportunity to have Powell trade steps or do a challenge dance with the Berrys, the film has recast them as backing musicians. This alternate arrangement seems acceptable under the Code's terms because the men playing the pianos are seated and, unlike the Berry Brothers, are stationary. Likewise, the pianos themselves act as physical barriers, mediating these men's physical relationship to the white female dancer. Berkeley's production design ultimately takes the male dancers' dynamic physical presence and reduces it to a kind of racialized mass ornament, a backdrop for Powell's visual whiteness.[21] The Berry Brothers are, in this way, subtly subordinate to Powell: she incorporates the cultural capital they bring to the scene (and to the film as a whole) and then uses it to her advantage, setting herself apart as a white performer who has access to a valorized, but othered space of performance.[22]

By contrast, Powell is nowhere near the "Jericho" scene, and *I Dood It*'s finale excludes Scott and Horne. Having elicited rapturous applause with their audition, these talented African American women should logically be cast in that second show within the show, *Star Eyes*, a single scene that concludes the film. This scene is a version of the standard Powell solo dance with large male chorus, staged on a set that looks like the deck of a battleship. But if Scott and Horne are meant to feature in this imaginary revue, the film never says so. A single shot of the Martinique's marquis sets the stage for Powell's/ Shaw's dance, and only her name, the names of the producers, and Jimmy Dorsey and His Band are listed there.

Powell's character's distance from Scott and Horne is symptomatic, in light of both her relationship with the only other black woman in the film and how she is deployed in the first show within the show, *Dixie Lou*. Shaw has a black maid, Annette, played by Butterfly McQueen, whom we first see attending to the star in her dressing room. With this pairing, *I Dood It* partakes of a stock device in classical Hollywood cinema, the deployment of an African American maid as an "adornment" meant to glamorize the white female star.[23] Small though it is, McQueen's role in the film seems designed entirely to enhance the perception of Connie's beauty, grace, and intelligence, through invidious comparison.[24]

Just before Joe goes to the theater, he runs into Annette, who is out walking Connie's dog. Now wearing his own, comparatively shabby suit, Joe sits forlornly on a park bench, in the shadow of a fountain topped by a classical-style statue of a seminude woman, which clearly acts as a stand-in for the Connie who exists for him mainly as an object of visual pleasure. After entering the scene, Annette sits down on the bench at Joe's left, while the dog, a black poodle, sits at his right. After expressing her sympathy for the dejected Joe, Annette begins describing her own experience of "tragic romance." Looking down at the ground initially, absorbed in his own thoughts, Joe suddenly takes an interest in Annette's story. He looks up and turns to his right toward the dog, asking how Annette recovered from her heartbreak. Quickly realizing his error, he turns back toward to Annette, and repeats the question. With the motif of white womanhood hovering over the scene, Joe's supposed confusion of an African American woman for a dog with black fur serves clearly to mark Annette as the abject other, physically and intellectually interchangeable with the pet for whom she is tasked with caring.

Just as Annette acts as a buffer in this scene between the Broadway star and the white man whose working-class status has been unmasked, so does she help to guarantee Connie's privileged white femininity. Annette's presence mediates any implicit comparison that might arise between Connie and the prodigiously smart, skilled, and sophisticated Horne and Scott. Moreover, Annette's symbolic function in the backstage narrative is reinforced by *Dixie Lou*'s investment in historical structures of domination. Described as a "romantic musical saga of the old South," *Dixie Lou* is a "lost cause" melodrama set on a Georgia plantation during the Civil War, with Shaw playing the eponymous character, a Scarlett O'Hara type. The film gently burlesques *Dixie Lou*, stressing that it is a "revival" and hinting at the shopworn state of its myriad plantation tradition clichés. Nonetheless, it reinforces an antebellum social hierarchy, surrounding Lou with a retinue of loyal African American "mammies" and "uncles," who celebrate at the end of the play, when the Confederacy wins the battle.[25] While portraying these proceedings as faintly ridiculous, the film must maintain the premise that it is a suitable vehicle for someone as glamorous as Joe's romantic idol, Connie, whose magazine clippings decorate the walls of his workplace.

It seems that whereas a Powell character can accommodate an association with black male dancers, any kind of association with their female peers is impossible. Sustaining the prestige of white womanhood at the expense of black women, this zero-sum logic makes Scott and Horne's position within the world of the film especially precarious. The entire structure of "Jericho" is determined by Scott and Horne's refusal to being placed in McQueen's position: its length, its staging, and its narrative complexity but also its occurring in a sort of diegetic vacuum, limited to a single portion of the film and having no bearing on anything that happens afterward.[26] The fact that they remain clearly separate from the ideologically constructed social world of the film is both necessary and a sign of profound resistance.

Scott and Horne's biographers note that each woman negotiated for a clause in her studio contracts indicating that she refused to play maids.[27] In her memoir, Scott expressed intense displeasure over the fact that black actors such as McQueen and Robinson had to play domestic servants to secure character parts in Hollywood films. It was imperative for her to maintain control over her image on screen, precisely to overcome the industry's perception of herself as on par with a domestic animal.[28] Scott found the maid stereotype so degrading as to write in her memoir that, until MGM cast Horne as a screen idol in her cameo in *Thousands Cheer* (1943), "as far as Hollywood was concerned the women of her race were a bunch of dogs."[29] As a result, she demanded "final approval of her musical numbers" and the ability to choose "her own clothes" and even insisted on always being billed "as herself."[30] Therefore, Hazel Scott plays "Hazel Scott" in *I Dood It*, the "role," she claimed was her "favorite," just as Lena Horne plays "Lena Horne."[31] Significantly, *I Dood It*'s closing credits lists the performers' names where character names appear, while the capitalized phrase, "BY HERSELF," appears in the actor's name column.

In *I Dood It*, we see Scott and Horne mount a challenge not only to a particular, class-inflected stereotype of black femininity that they found especially degrading but also, more generally, to what black feminist scholars have called "controlling images."[32] Their appearance in the "Jericho" sequence represents an effort at radical "self-definition and self-valuation," against the "externally-defined . . . images of Afro-American womanhood" that have served, historically, to "circumscribe . . . Black women's lives."[33] All of the trappings of "Jericho" follow from the performers' insistence on controlling their own images: from Lawlor's respectful, solicitous manner to the women's elegant costuming and the way in which their professionalism serves to contextualize the performance.[34]

The fact that *Dixie Lou* is presented as outdated entertainment serves to make it an implicit foil for the "Jericho" sequence (a number auditioned for the revue is supposed to replace it). "Jericho," in turn, seems to allegorize the Hollywood studios' wartime efforts to improve African American casting patterns, in that it thematizes musical performance as a means of breaking down barriers and entering into a heavily guarded preserve.[35] The number is an extensive reworking of a white-authored early jazz tune, which featured in RKO's talkie *Syncopation* (1929), where it was sung by Morton Downey, accompanied by Fred Waring's Pennsylvanians, all white performers.[36] That version is a fanciful retelling of chapter 6 of the book of Joshua, where the Israelites seize Jericho, following God's instructions to shout and blow trumpets and rams' horns, toppling the great wall that surrounds the city. In the

Downey-Waring version, the Bible story is said to foreshadow the 1920s "craze for jazz," in which the titular city becomes a "jazzy old town," once its residents come to appreciate "what a kick the coronet" has.

Expanding and extensively reworking this source material, Kay Thompson, MGM's multitalented composer and vocal coach (also white), has created something much more complex, both lyrically and musically, for *I Dood It*.[37] Working with the large choral ensemble and members of Count Basie's band, Horne and Scott collaborate with Thompson to realize what one critic calls "a dizzying [combination] of musical genres, from opera to swing [and] boogie-woogie."[38] This mini-narrative in song builds toward a climax in which Horne exhorts the trumpeter (likely Fred Trainer) to blow down the wall, literalized here as a painted scrim, and then ascends the riser, once he faints.[39] Connecting the highly resonant imagery of musical self-expression, war, and triumph with a reminder of cultural provenance, the song brings back into view the musical antecedent that the original tune obscures: the African American spiritual, "Joshua Fit the Battle of Jericho," which Horne identifies with her final line.[40] Like that and other spirituals, the film's "Jericho" uses an Old Testament story of liberation to deliver a coded message about actual conditions (see Figure 6.2).

Emphatically playing herself, Horne narrates the entire segment in song, ultimately resuming her place, alongside Scott, at the head of the group. And her powerful vocal accompaniment of the trumpet cadenza—the way she *challenges* the horn player to match her high notes—provides a fitting bookend to Scott's virtuosic display at the beginning of the sequence. Contesting this history of appropriation and speaking back to *Dixie Lou*'s mythologized vision of plantation slavery, Horne and Scott offer a highly situated display of extreme competence, which challenges the intersectional structures of oppression visible in the film and in its production history.

At the same time, as Krin Gabbard has noted, "Jericho" partakes of the "phallic symbolism" of the trumpet so prevalent in Hollywood films that feature jazz music.[41] Horne shares her position as group leader briefly with the trumpeter, who stands in for the warrior-patriarch from the biblical source text. Women lead the charge here, but only through the vehicle of a male centered narrative about social change, which, in an early civil rights era context, reinforces the twin misperceptions that only black men can "speak for the race" and that sexism has no bearing on black women's oppression.[42]

FIGURE 6.2 Lena Horne leads the chorus at the end of "Jericho" in *I Dood It* (1943).

To the plea of "Jericho" for access or inclusion, the remainder of *I Dood It* succinctly replies "not yet." The remaining twenty-five or so minutes of the film are dominated by the white male star's slapstick comedy, as Joe is forced to substitute for *Dixie Lou*'s male lead (John Hodiak). We get an endless dressing room scene of him struggling to affix a false beard to his face, followed by an extended depiction of his inept performance on stage. As a viewer, it is hard not to see this turn of events amounts to the simple replacement of the most exciting, impressive material in the film with a tedious mediocrity. However one might feel about Skelton's comedy, though, the result is that the audience is subjected to much more *Dixie Lou* before the film ends.

In an amazing deus ex machina, which fuses personal gain with patriotic duty, the film's plot allows Joe to realize his dreams of romance and upward mobility. He figures out that saboteurs have planted a time bomb in the theater and transforms himself from bumbling idiot to manly hero, when he prevails in a physical fight with the head Nazi agent. After he finds and defuses the bomb, Joe earns a "big reward," which he then uses to help finance Lawlor's next show (the aforementioned *Star Eyes*), becoming the rich benefactor whom Connie and her circle mistakenly believed him to be earlier. Over the course of this scene, he also impresses Connie, asserting his authority as her husband—they are still legally married—and ordering her to flee from the danger of the bomb. She spontaneously declares him "wonderful" and professes her true love.

The romantic clinch feels forced, in a way that, McLean explains, typifies Powell's characters' outcomes. Although "Powell always has a nominal male suitor . . . and usually ends up with paired with him" at the end of film, these conclusions are "rote," paying mere "lip-service" to the musical's conventional heterosexual romance plot.[43] In typical fashion, *I Dood It* navigates a tension between Powell's casting as an object of male romantic interest and her work as a dancer, which is very much an individual affair.[44] In the finale, Powell performs a lengthy, athletic solo, costumed in a feminized and glamorized version of men's formal wear and backed by an enormous, all-male marching and dancing band. Following but only tenuously connected to the just-resolved plot, this dance coda allows Connie to escape the passivity that defines her role in the main plot. If the typology of the white "southern belle" elevates Connie in a specific, ideological sense, then it also markedly holds her back, with respect to the things that Powell herself cared about as a performer: choreography and technical competence.[45] Showcasing what Jerome Delamater calls Powell's "aggressive individuality," the finale allows her to return as a sort of specialty performer in her own star vehicle, exploring what are, for her, the liberating possibilities of this otherwise marginal status.[46]

As "Fascinating Rhythm" makes clear, Powell's individuality depends in large part on the fact that she works in the same kinesthetic tradition as Hollywood's "eccentric dancers," who, Delamater notes, were "in general" African American men like Robinson, the Berry Brothers, and the Nicholas Brothers.[47] Within the world of 1940s Hollywood, Scott and Horne were also eccentrics, "sell[ing] themselves on the [basis of] their individual styles," and working within the same set of aesthetic traditions as Powell, despite not being dancers (or, in Horne's case at least, not primarily). One can only imagine what Powell and Scott, especially, could do together, were the film to afford a serious opportunity for them to explore their musical kinship.

In a 1974 interview, Powell would cite Fats Waller as a major influence on her practice as a dancer. She describes discovering "the off-beat" (i.e., syncopation) by listening to the boogie-woogie sides that he cut for the race record label, Okeh, in the early 1920s. Given her intense affinity for this style of music, she speculates that "there must be some coloured blood in me somewhere": "I often used to kid my mother, asking her, 'Did you have a coloured milkman or something?' Because it's a black sound—you see, a tap dancer is nothing but a frustrated drummer. You're a percussion instrument with your feet. You're a musician."[48] Powell's linkage between tap dancing and percussive, syncopated piano playing is precisely the one that the "Fascinating Rhythm" sequence explores: the first musician who appears, replacing the Berry Brothers, introduces a slow, boogie-woogie version of the tune, to which Powell then dances.

Powell's fantasy of "blood" inheritance makes sense of her relationship to African American expressive culture in a biologically essentialist way, coding true dance artistry as black and male. Ironically, though, Scott had a much more direct linkage to Waller: he was family friend who treated her like a niece, Waller helped Scott hone the boogie-woogie technique on display in *I Dood It*.[49] As one of the most accomplished interpreters of the "black sound" that Powell so revered, Scott seems to be the only other performer in the cast at her level of technical brilliance. And yet in her fluency across musical idioms, Scott's practice productively challenges Powell's assumptions about the links between race, gender, and cultural expression. In particular, Scott was known for mastering and transforming the "white sounds" of classical music, incorporating them into a jazz idiom. This approach earned her criticism both from those who felt that she was diluting the authenticity of African American "folk" styles and from those who felt that she was overstepping her bounds, merely pretending cultural sophistication.

To imagine a scene of collaboration and competition between Scott and Powell is to recognize simultaneously that they hold certain musical properties in common and that the manner in which they are empowered to use these properties is irreducibly different. In order to preserve and normalize this difference, *I Dood It* must keep at bay the sense of comparison that such a scene would afford. At the same time, however, with its story of barrier-smashing through musical virtuosity, Scott and Horne's "Jericho" begins to speak back to the intersectional structures that, albeit in very different ways, limit their own and Powell's trajectories in Hollywood.

Juxtaposing African American specialty performance to white eccentric dance, then, offers a way of illuminating how specific constructs intertwine to define and value individuals within the 1940s musical. To borrow Petty's language, black specialty performers like Scott and Horne "create performances that are bounded by the strictures of American racism," sexism and classism, "yet resonate and Signify in ways that exceed these same boundaries."[50] The signifying potential of these moments lies in their ability to evoke the performers' "distinctive standpoint[s]" on the material they have been given to interpret, both the musical material that constitutes the number and the elements composing the film's narrative at large.[51] By virtue of their positioning as "outsiders within" this narrative, black specialty performers are privy to the innermost workings of the intersecting hierarchies of race, gender, and class that structure cinematic musical performance.[52] Implicit in these specialties is a profound understanding of and critical response to the classical Hollywood cinema's ways of handling difference, the recording and annotation of which remain a project to be taken up by academic film criticism.

NOTES

1. William R. Weaver, "Skelton Starts Here," review of *I Dood It, Motion Picture Herald* 152, no. 5 (July 31, 1943): 1453.
2. Miriam J. Petty, *Stealing the Show: African American Performers and Audiences in 1930s Hollywood* (Berkeley: University of California Press, 2016), 5.
3. Petty, *Stealing the Show*, 5.
4. Barney Josephson, with Terry Trilling-Josephson, *Café Society: The Wrong Place for the Right People* (Urbana, University of Illinois Press, 2009), 145. Josephson was the white entertainment impresario who launched New York's Café Society, where both Scott and Horne were fixtures, and who served as Scott's agent in her studio contract negotiations. On the struggle to "salvage" the production of *I Dood It*, see Charlene Regester, *African American Actresses: The Struggle for Visibility* (Bloomington: Indiana University Press, 2010), 223; and Mark Griffin, *A Hundred or More Hidden Things: The Life and Films of Vincente Minnelli* (Cambridge, MA: Da Capo Press, 2010), 70.
5. Petty, *Stealing the Show*, 2. Petty argues that the power relations of the studio system in the 1930s as well as its systems of racial representation were conditioned by the larger histories of African Americans' enslavement and resistance to enslavement, which give the theft marked by "stealing the show" a special resonance.
6. Weaver, "Skelton Starts Here," 1453.
7. Margie Schultz, *Eleanor Powell, A Bio-Bibliography* (Westport, CT: Greenwood, 1994), 15.
8. Petty, *Stealing the Show*, 9.
9. Patricia Hill Collins, "Learning from the Outsider Within: The Sociological Significance of Black Feminist Thought," *Social Problems* 33, no. 6 (October-December 1986): S14–S32, S23.

10. Sometimes the performer's/performers' names simply appear in both columns. For instance, in the opening credits of *Lady Be Good*, "The Berry Brothers" are listed in the column where character names appear, and the list of the names of the men who compose the trio, James, Warren, and Nyas Berry, appears on the opposite side of the screen, enclosed by a curly bracket.

11. Donald Bogle, *Toms, Coons, Mulattoes, Mammies, and Bucks: An Interpretive History of Blacks in American Films* (New York: Viking, 1973), 121.

12. See Regester, *African American Actresses*, 199; and Arthur Knight, "Star Dances: African-American Constructions of Stardom, 1925–1960," in *Classic Hollywood, Classic Whiteness*, ed. Daniel Bernardi (Minneapolis: University of Minnesota Press, 2001), 386–414, 405.

13. "More Negro Scenes Cut Out in Dixie Set New Problems for Pix Producers," *Variety*, July 12, 1944, 1, 32. See also Laurie B. Green, *Battling the Plantation Mentality: Memphis and the Black Freedom Struggle* (Chapel Hill: University of North Carolina Press, 2007), 154; and Lester Velie, "You Can't See That Movie: Censorship in Action," *Collier's*, May 6, 1950, 11–12.

14. The *Variety* article cited in the previous note mentions Binford's excision of the Cab Calloway Band's presence from Powell's *Sensations of 1945*, by way of saying that the deletion of this long, complex sequence (intercut with scenes featuring the main, white characters) left the film seeming "'patched up' and 'confusing'" to local reviewers (1). It explains that Binford and his counterpart in Atlanta are willing to make these cuts regardless of their effect on continuity and that they have recommended that the studios find ways of making them easier to cut (not that the studios have already adopted such practices).

15. Karen Chilton, *Hazel Scott: The Pioneering Journey of a Jazz Pianist, from Café Society to Hollywood to HUAC* (Ann Arbor: University of Michigan Press, 2008), 78.

16. Chilton, *Hazel Scott*, 78.

17. Jane Gaines, "*Lady Be Good*: Do Dogs Dance?," *Jump Cut: A Review of Contemporary Media* 31 (March 1986): 19–23, 22.

18. The piano player as well as the men on stage, who appear to play pianos, are uncredited.

19. Adrienne McLean, "Putting 'em Down Like a Man: Eleanor Powell and the Spectacle of Competence," in *Hetero: Queering Representations of Straightness*, ed. Sean Griffin (Albany: State University of New York Press, 2009), 89–110, 100.

20. Susan Courtney, *Hollywood Fantasies of Miscegenation: Spectacular Narratives of Gender and Race, 1903–1967* (Princeton, NJ: Princeton University Press, 2005), 103; and McLean, "Putting 'em Down Like a Man," 100.

21. There are numerous precedents for this sort of effect in Berkeley's work. See Martin Rubin, *Showstoppers: Busby Berkeley and the Tradition of Spectacle* (New York: Columbia University Press, 1993), 94.

22. A film about the travails of a married, white songwriting duo, *Lady Be Good* positions the Berry Brothers as representatives of an African American, "hep" subculture existing around swing music and dance; each of their performances is framed (with

varying degrees of explicitness) as a translation of one of the main characters' tunes into a swing idiom.

23. Robyn Wiegman, "Black Bodies/American Commodities: Gender, Race, and the Bourgeois Ideal in Contemporary Film," in *Unspeakable Images: Ethnicity and the American Cinema*, ed. Lester D. Friedman (Urbana: University of Illinois Press, 1991), 308–328, 313.

24. Regester, *African American Actresses*, 2, 191. To her credit, Powell later criticized this sort of arrangement. Looking back at her career on stage in the 1930s, Powell said in a 1981 public appearance, "Back in those days a black person was not allowed to be on the stage with a white person unless they were in [one] subservient form or another, which was disgusting." Quoted in Schultz, *Eleanor Powell*, 9.

25. The film on which *I Dood It* is based, *Spite Marriage*, features a similar production, except, there, the African American roles are played by white actors in blackface.

26. That *I Dood It* encompasses both a scene that compares a black woman to a dog and the highly glamorized presentation of Scott and Horne speaks to the contours of white liberal racism in Hollywood during World War II and to the contradictions of director Vincente Minnelli's "Africanism." "Africanism" is James Naremore's term for Minnelli's view of black expressive culture as simultaneously "savage" and "cultivated." Working within these parameters, Minnelli could both promote Scott and Horne in Hollywood in terms of the sophisticated personae that they had cultivated at Café Society and respond with incredulity when some viewers called him on racial slur in the McQueen-Skelton scene. See James Naremore, *The Films of Vincente Minnelli* (Cambridge: Cambridge University Press, 1993), 59–60; and Griffin, *Hundred or More Hidden Things*, 70.

27. Chilton, *Hazel Scott*, 72–73; and James Gavin, *Stormy Weather: The Life of Lena Horne* (New York: Atria Books, 2009), 104. On Scott's contract negotiations, see also Josephson, *Café Society*, 13, 146.

28. Chilton, *Hazel Scott*, 72–73.

29. Chilton, *Hazel Scott*, 78. I cite Scott's language here to give an indication of the intensity of her feelings on this point. It is important, at the same time, to heed Regester's caution to "understand the struggles" of an actor like McQueen and "to recognize the milieu within which she was forced to work" (5), rather than conflating her with her characters and, thus, heaping more opprobrium on her. This is especially significant in the case of McQueen, who felt that she was treated with contempt by many of her African American contemporaries, even stating decades after the fact that Horne had called her a "dog" in 1944; the allegation remains unsubstantiated. Stephen Bourne, *Butterfly McQueen Remembered* (Latham, MD: Scarecrow Press, 2008), 49–50.

30. Chilton, *Hazel Scott*, 73.

31. Chilton, *Hazel Scott*, 87.

32. Collins, "Learning from the Outsider Within," S17.

33. Collins, "Learning from the Outsider Within," S16.

34. Were more space available, I would want to examine the reception history of Scott's and Horne's performances (here and elsewhere), which illustrates the limits of their ability to control their own images. Even when occupying a highly elegant, glamorous mise-en-scène such as this, both women were often viewed through intersecting sexist, racist,

and classist lenses. Scott in particular was often treated by critics as primitive and hyper-sexualized (in the way that she moved and displayed her body) and/or as putting on airs (because she incorporated classical elements into her repertoire).

35. Beginning in 1940, NAACP executive secretary Walter White began lobbying white liberals in Hollywood for more and better parts for African Americans. White's efforts began to gain traction after the United States entered the war and the federal government created the Office of War Information (OWI) in late 1942. The OWI began to encourage the studios to portray the nation as egalitarian and inclusive through casting choices, as a way of putting into relief what was at stake in the struggle against Nazism. Arguing that stereotyped portrayals of African Americans and other so-called minorities would alienate these groups from the war cause, the OWI's motion picture office in Hollywood allied itself with White's efforts to improve screen representation. See Petty, *Stealing the Show*, 217–219; and Thomas Cripps, *Making Movies Black: The Hollywood Message Movie from World War II to the Civil Rights Era* (Oxford: Oxford University Press, 1993), 35–63.

36. "Jericho's" music was written by Richard Myers, the lyrics by Leo Robin.

37. On Thompson's work at the studio, see Steven Cohan, *Incongruous Entertainment: Camp, Cultural Value, and the MGM Musical* (Durham, NC: Duke University Press, 2005), 48–49.

38. Kristin A. McGee, *Some Liked It Hot: Jazz Women in Film and Television, 1928–1959* (Middletown, CT: Wesleyan University Press, 2009), 129.

39. Gavin, *Stormy Weather*, 152.

40. At the high point of the Hollywood musical's swing craze, the number talks back to an earlier moment in American film history, when white recording artists working in the new medium of the talkies appropriated and popularized African American jazz.

41. Krin Gabbard, *Jammin' at the Margins: Jazz and the American Cinema* (Chicago: University of Chicago Press, 1996), 147.

42. On the reinforcement of this "single-axis framework" in different historical phases of the black liberation struggle, see Kimberlé Crenshaw, "Demarginalizing the Intersection of Race and Sex: A Black Feminist Critique of Antidiscrimination Doctrine, Feminist Theory, and Antiracist Politics," *University of Chicago Legal Forum* 8, no. 1 (1989): 139–167, 160.

43. McLean, "Putting 'em Down Like a Man," 95–96.

44. Because Skelton was not a dancer (like most of Powell's male costars), there are no duets in the film. The only number they share is a comedic sequence in which Connie is unconscious, having accidentally ingested sleeping tablets dissolved in a glass of champagne intended for Joe. Joe attempts with great difficulty to lift Connie and place her in bed, her body constantly sliding out of his grasp. Although on the level of performance the scene showcases Powell's kinesthetic skill, it tends rather disturbingly to reinforce her character's passivity.

45. McLean, "Putting 'em Down Like a Man," 91.

46. Jerome Delamater, *Dance in the Hollywood Musical* (Ann Arbor, MI: UMI Research Press, 1988), 78.

47. Delamater, *Dance in the Hollywood Musical*, 78.

48. John Kobal, "Interview with Eleanor Powell," *Focus on Film* 19 (Autumn 1974): 24–31, 26.

49. Chilton, *Hazel Scott*, 36, 88.

50. Petty, *Stealing the Show*, 9.

51. Collins, "Learning from the Outsider Within," S25.

52. Collins, "Learning from the Outsider Within," S14.

7 · DISRUPTIVE MOTHER-DAUGHTER RELATIONSHIPS

Peola's Racial Masquerade in *Imitation of Life* (1934) and Stella's Class Masquerade in *Stella Dallas* (1937)

CHARLENE REGESTER

E. Ann Kaplan argues that many film narratives that emerged in the 1930s show "increased attention to the ... Mother's need to sacrifice herself."[1] Her analysis of maternal sacrifice includes the films *Imitation of Life* (dir. John Stahl, 1934) and *Stella Dallas* (dir. King Vidor, 1937). Although Kaplan's essay mostly analyzes white motherhood, she extends her critique to the black mother-daughter relationship in her discussion of *Imitation of Life*.[2] Building on Kaplan's views, I compare the two films in their partial intersectionality, focusing on the light-complexioned daughter (and black mother) in *Imitation of Life* who escapes her blackness in pursuit of whiteness and the white mother (and white daughter) in *Stella Dallas* who escapes her lower-class position to secure an upper-class position for her daughter. A closer examination shall determine how these characters engage in racial and class masquerades.

Racial passing "in American history," according to Elaine Ginsberg, can be defined as "racial difference ... [which assumes] a fraudulent 'white identity by an individual culturally and legally defined as 'Negro' or black."[3] As for class passing, Gwendolyn Audrey Foster suggests, it refers to "class mobility" and often "involves marrying up, marrying down, and moving through social positions."[4] Critiquing race in one instance and class in another is in no way intended to suggest that they are necessarily synonymous or equal, but they become useful vehicles for examining racial and class masquerades, particularly since both films "involve close Mother-daughter bondings, and violate the Master Mother discourse in addition by showing the [white] Mother stepping outside of her allotted place."[5] To launch this inquiry it is necessary to examine (1) parallels between *Imitation of Life* and *Stella Dallas*, (2) black daughter and white mother as internally conflicted characters, (3) problematized motherhood—insofar that good mothers, becoming self-sacrificial characters, are blamed for their daughters' inability to achieve a desired racial or class position and are punished for not conforming to acceptable standards of motherhood; and (4) polarized fatherhood—absent father, good father, and bad father, whose paternal absence/presence impacts the daughter's self-formation.

PARALLELS BETWEEN *IMITATION OF LIFE* AND *STELLA DALLAS*

The parallels between *Imitation of Life* and *Stella Dallas* are most apparent in specific scenes. For example, Peola (Fredi Washington), the black daughter, arrives at her mother's funeral nearly "too late," to use Linda Williams's term, to alter her strained relationship with the mother whom she abandons to liberate herself from blackness to pursue whiteness.[6] This scene bears a striking resemblance to Stella (Barbara Stanwyck), the white mother, who arrives at her daughter's wedding "too late" to be reunited with her daughter to affirm her maternal position. After her late arrival, Peola stands between two white women among a crowd of onlookers who sympathetically observe the funeral from afar. Similarly, Stella stands behind a wrought iron fence to observe her daughter's wedding through an open draped window to witness the ceremony from afar. Both characters are passive observers to events in which they should have been active participants rather than voyeurs to their own experiences. These characters might even represent "critical voyeurs," according to Gayle Wald, who refers to critical voyeurism as "a way of looking at and analyzing the 'other' without being observed in the process of observation."[7] Gazing at "the self-as-observer," Wald notes, "generates a tension between recognition and denial."[8] As for Peola, when she gazes at her mother's bier, she recognizes her inner blackness, which she denies in order to appropriate the whiteness her white body signifies. As for Stella, when she gazes at her daughter who marries into the upper class (a class position she is denied), she recognizes her own lower-class position into which she has descended. These scenes demonstrate how both characters confront the duality of their ambivalent or "split" identity—Peola's black/white identity and Stella's lower-/upper-class identity.

Not only do these characters possess a split identity, but they assume the dual subject position of inside/outside as articulated by Trinh Minh-Ha.[9] The inside position refers to that which the Other occupies, and the outside position refers to that which the non-Other assumes. When Peola stands outside between the two white women, she identifies with whites and therefore is associated with non-Others; however, when she moves to the inside, entering the funeral procession, she assumes a black space associated with the Other. The two white women represent the divide between whiteness and blackness as Peola's position between them affirms her likeness to whiteness yet demarcates her difference from it. As for Stella, when she stands outside the window she is positioned as the lower-class Other, but when she gazes inside the mansion to observe the wedding she vicariously and temporarily assumes the position of the upper-class non-Other. Standing outside in the pouring rain, a policeman forces Stella and others to move along but she requests, "Let me see her face when he kisses her,"[10] an affirmation of her daughter's upper-class ascension. The split identity and inside/outside subject position both characters assume suggests how they are internally conflicted and endure similar fates—Peola abandons her mother and Stella abandons her daughter.[11]

INTERNALLY CONFLICTED CHARACTERS WHO MASQUERADE RACE AND CLASS

Peola and Stella can be seen as internally conflicted characters who either camouflage their racial identity or construct an upper-class façade to access privilege. It is therefore necessary to examine their internal conflicts to determine how they orchestrate their masquerade(s). Peola is internally conflicted because of her "white body" yet inner blackness, a duality that does not allow her to be classified as black, but neither is she white; it is rather her indeterminate racial status that causes her internal turmoil. Peola's identity is racially ambivalent even though both of her parents are black. Her dark mother and light-complexioned black father mark her black identity. Her conflict with her identity surfaces when Peola and her mother seek refuge in Bea's (Claudette Colbert) home where Delilah (Louise Beavers), the black mother, works as Bea's live-in maid, and Bea's daughter, Jessie (Rochelle Hudson), identifies Peola as "black." Resisting this racial marker, Peola returns home from school in tears and declares, "I am not black . . . I am not black . . . I won't be black." Peola takes offense to the term "black," which signals the beginning of her psychological demise. Though Bea chastises Jessie for her offensive deprecation of Peola, it is this racial referent that codes Peola as different and serves as a stinging reminder of her black identity. Humiliated, Peola becomes more indignant at her blackness and desirous of whiteness.[12] But it is Jessie's verbal assault that destabilizes Peola who disconnects herself from blackness and begins to pass as white. This masquerade, Lauren Berlant surmises, allows "the light-skinned body claim[s] a fraudulent relation to the privileges of whiteness."[13]

Frustrated with her black identity, Peola turns pernicious again when her mother decides to take her daughter's rain gear to her school. Delilah enters a classroom unsure if she has the right location and inquires as to whether or not Peola is enrolled. The teacher, assuming all of her students are white, insists she has "no colored children" in her class. Displaying her maternal instinct, Delilah surveys the classroom, detects Peola hiding behind a book, and disrupts her masquerade. Delilah inquires as to whether or not Peola has been passing, a double entendre referring to both her academic performance and racial masquerade. Embarrassed by her mother's exposure, Peola rises slowly from her seat while her fellow students stare and whisper, "I didn't know she was colored." Frustrated that her identity is exposed, Peola flees the classroom and declares to her mother, "I hate you . . . I hate you." It is Delilah's blackness that marks Peola's racial identity. As Susan Courtney notes, "The film forestalls the kind of rupturing of the meaning of race . . . by visually recontaining [Peola], and her contestable racial identity, in her mother's large, dark body."[14] Peola may initially not deliberately have attempted to pass as white but engaged in "inadvertent passing,"[15] where one's racial identity is simply determined by one's physical appearance. It is Delilah who marks her blackness and leads her to become more resistant to her blackness.

Realizing that her mother undermines her whiteness, Peola then makes a conscious decision to pass as white when she works in a white restaurant. Previously, Delilah recommends that she attend a "Negro" college to allow her to become more fully integrated into the black community. Unable to adjust, Peola flees the school in search of a white existence. Delilah and Bea eventually find her working in a restaurant as a cashier, taking on a type of employment that mimics Bea's pursuit of entrepreneurship, one in which she had turned Delilah's secret pancake recipe into a corporate business.[16] Since Bea represents whiteness, Peola emulates her white surrogate mother rather than her own black mother Delilah, a signifier of black subservience. Whereas Bea becomes synonymous with independence, success, glamour, and financial stability, Delilah is associated with dependence, failure, unattractiveness (according to Eurocentric standards), and financial instability. However, Delilah's relationship to Bea is much more than a work-related relationship, since she nurtures, advises, and cares for her while serving as a surrogate mother to Jessie in the absence of a genuine mother figure. As Peola observes the elevation of whiteness in the household, witnessed in Delilah's investment in the white family, and the denigration of blackness, witnessed in Delilah's divestment from black life and the black community, Peola internalizes this difference, which compels her to pursue whiteness and flee blackness (see Figure 7.1).

Discovering Peola at Jackson's restaurant, a racially segregated establishment that refuses service to blacks, Delilah confronts Peola and exposes her masquerade. In response, Peola denies and rejects her mother, insisting, "There must be a mistake . . . my name isn't Peola . . . I am sure you've got me confused with someone else. . . . I never saw you before in my life. . . . Do I look like her daughter? . . . Do I look like I could be her daughter? Why she must be crazy." These deprecating denials are demonstrative of how Peola attempts to disidentify with her mother until Bea intervenes and chastises Peola for dismissing her mother. In this scene, Peola not only denies her blackness and rejects her own mother but willingly appropriates segregated practices against those who possess the very identity she embodies. Observing Peola's rejection of Delilah, Bea emphatically reprimands, "Don't talk to your mother that way," a reprimand that allows Bea to become the voice of authority while subjugating Delilah's maternal voice of authority. Both Bea

FIGURE 7.1 Peola (Fredi Washington) and her mother Delilah (Louise Beavers) in *Imitation of Life* (1934).

and Delilah succeed in exposing Peola's disguise; though they chastise her and wish to convince Peola that she has committed a faux pas against motherhood, it furthers instead her desire for whiteness. Returning home to apologize for her inappropriate behavior, Peola makes clear that she intends to pursue whiteness no matter the cost even if it includes disowning her mother. She proposes, "I want to go away . . . and you mustn't see me or own me or claim me . . . even if you pass me on the street, you will have to pass me by. . . . But you don't know what it is to look white and be black . . . I can't go on this way any longer." This time, Peola seeks Delilah's compliance with her decision and Bea's tacit approval, a decision that marks the last time Delilah encounters Peola.

Summing up the evolution of Peola's passing, she first denies and rejects her blackness when Jessie calls her black. Peola then "inadvertently" passes as white in elementary school and realizes that in order to disconnect herself from blackness she will have to disassociate herself from her dark mother. When Peola works in a whites-only restaurant as she transitions into the white world, she not only denies and rejects her mother but disidentifies with Delilah since her mother's blackness perpetually marks her black identity. At this point, Peola realizes not only that she will masquerade as white but that she needs her mother to participate in her disguise in order to maintain her façade. Delilah strongly opposes Peola's proposition when she declares, "I ain't no white mother . . . I ain't got the spiritual strength to beat it. . . . You can't ask me to unborn my own child." Despite Delilah's insistent refusal, she relinquishes her daughter, a fatal decision that leads to her death.

As for the white mother in *Stella Dallas*, one critic claims, "Stella is passing . . . as a light-skinned black person would try to pass for white."[17] Characterizing Stella as a parallel to Peola certainly links these two passing characters. Whereas Peola flees her race, Stella flees the lower class associated with her working-class family who are employed at a local mill (Mill Hampton, MA). It is her brother, Charlie Martin (George Wolcott), who chastises Stella for her desire to pursue an upper-class lifestyle, a lifestyle reflected in the books and magazines in which Stella immerses herself. Desiring to elevate her class status, Stella dresses in a ruffled white blouse with pearls and a black skirt and stands at the white picket fence that surrounds their home while holding two books (one of which is entitled *India's Love Lyrics*) to observe the mill workers leave work so that she can attract the attentions of an upper-class potential spouse. Stella detects a well-dressed man in a suit and tie unlike the typical workers, Stephen Dallas (John Boles), and stares at him from behind her books. Observing that she intends to ascend into the upper class, her brother Charlie teases, "Stella's got a fellow—only, he don't know it. . . . What's the matter with a mill hand? I work in a mill and I am a mill hand and your father is a mill hand." Seeking to advance her class position at the expense of alienating her family, Stella disidentifies with her family (like Peola) and aspires to pursue those who can provide a more privileged lifestyle, particularly when she garners the mill manager's (Stephen) attention. Destined to capture her prey, she dresses elegantly, wearing a long-belted chiffon ruffled dress and wide brim hat with flowers attached. An "accidental" meeting leads to their courtship whereupon the young couple attends a movie theater. While attending the theater, Stella envisions herself like the characters witnessed on screen. She admits that she is attracted to Stephen and what he represents: "I want to be like all the people you have been around . . . educated, you know and speaking right . . . like the people in the movies. . . . I could learn to talk like you and act like you." In this instance, Stella hints at her desire to transition into the upper class, which she intends to achieve through speech and performance.

Following their courtship, Stella and Stephen marry, but the marriage is short-lived when she gives birth to a daughter (Laurel / Anne Shirley) and returns home from the hospital disenchanted with motherhood. Affirming her new upper-class status despite her refusal of motherhood, Stella is dressed in a fur collared coat and hat topped with feathers following her hospital stay. She employs both a nurse and maid, which are exemplary of her new status. The white nurse who accompanies Stella from the hospital holds her infant and immediately hands over the newborn to Stella's black maid, an indication that Stella is disinterested in performing her motherly duties. The black maid, Agnes (Mildred Gover), dressed in a black uniform with a white pinafore, expresses her delight in seeing the newborn and reflects Stella's class elevation. Her presence implies that while Stella refuses motherhood, she seems eager to relieve the white mother of her maternal duties. Only when Stella rejects motherhood and declines in class status, as Allison Whitney argues, does she become an embodiment of black subservience, a position that is plausible.[18]

Although Stella refuses motherhood, she desires at the same time to attend the River Club dance, but Stephen discourages her from reviving her social life. Destined to reignite her former lifestyle, Stella convinces Stephen to concede to her wishes, and they attend the dance. Stella dresses in a long sequined gown that flares at the bottom; a sheer silk fabric drapes over her back, and ostrich feathers are affixed to one shoulder of the garment. It is through her elegant attire that Stella performs her upper-class status, a reflection of Olive Higgins Prouty's (author of *Stella Dallas*) critique of fashion/style as an extension of class status.[19] The dance inspires Stella's appetite for social life, and she develops an attraction to Ed Munn (Alan Hale), a gregarious male, providing a refuge from her boring husband. When Stella and Stephen return home, they quarrel over her cheap jewelry and her attraction to the more entertaining Munn. Their relationship deteriorates further when Stephen assumes employment in New York and Stella steadfastly refuses to join him. At this point, Stella relinquishes her upper-class status to return to the lower class. She prefers Munn for entertainment purposes and neglects her spouse who reunites with his former fiancée, the wealthy aristocratic widow Helen Morrison (Barbara O'Neil).

In Stephen's absence, Stella entertains her friends and surprisingly renews her commitment to motherhood. Despite her return to motherhood, she does not deny her social life when Munn arrives with his pipe-smoking friend. Stella calls for her black maid Edna (Etta McDaniel) to answer the door, but Munn has already entered, an indication of how he imposes and intrudes on Stella. It is of note that Edna wears a printed shift and checkered apron, in stark contrast to the formal black uniform Agnes wore. Her attire conveys that even though Stella descends in class status she can still afford a maid, though not a very expensive one. Whereas Agnes was more formally dressed, Edna expresses a more liberal attitude in her behavior marked by her somewhat disheveled attire. According to Whitney, she becomes an extension of "Stella's inability to direct her servant [which] makes her appear unqualified for motherhood."[20] Her divided allegiance between motherhood and maintaining a social life is shown when Stella entertains Munn while attending to her daughter Laurel. She allows Munn to sit Laurel on his lap, and when he coaxes the child to smile, she begins to cry. At this point, Stephen returns and interrupts this raucous affair, believing that his daughter is exposed to an unhealthy lower-class lifestyle. He threatens to take Laurel away out of fear that this lower-class lifestyle will entrap his daughter.

With Stephen's increasing alienation, Stella is now positioned between the lower and upper classes, and despite her indeterminate class position she provides a birthday party for Laurel. For this occasion, Stella temporarily improves her dress in order to impress the invited upper-class guests. Her black maid Gladys (Lillian Yarbo) comments on Stella's appearance and acknowledges that her attire is much improved. Stella wears a floral print dress with fur sleeves and an enlarged corsage that cascades to her waist. While Stella's attire is demonstrative of her upper-class masquerade, unfortunately it does not encourage the invited guests to attend. Gladys assuages some of Stella and Laurel's disappointment through her sympathetic behavior. She prepares more fresh biscuits to replace the stale ones and agrees to use the formal address of "Miss" with reference to Laurel. At the same time, Gladys appears somewhat lackadaisical and reflects Stella's own confused state. Stella, "[having] discontinued the formalities of servant-employee interaction in her household," Allison Whitney claims, "suggests a continuing regression, intentional or otherwise, to a lower-class way of living."[21]

Stella's class performance becomes ever more excessive when she attempts to ensure Laurel's eventual transition into the upper class. She camouflages her lower-class identity through her excessive display of dress to enable her daughter to marry into the upper class. With money acquired from Stephen, whom she refuses to grant a divorce, Stella provides Laurel with an upper-class lifestyle when she takes her to a resort to expose her to the wealthy. During their stay, Stella lives an extravagant lifestyle and other wealthy patrons noticing her "dawdy extravagance" refer to her as a "Christmas Tree." Contrary to her intents, she becomes an embarrassment to her daughter. Stella wears a black hat that resembles a large bow with black netting hanging over her face. She dresses in a floral print dress, matching floral print shoes, and several bracelets along with a necklace accentuated with a white mink throw.[22] Stella's class masquerade is characterized as "gloriously brash and vulgar paraphernalia."[23] Putting on an excessive masquerade, Stella parades in "paint an inch thick, bells on her shoes, and bracelets up to here that clanged."[24] Based on the perversity of her performance, "Stella does not just experience her own humiliation," explains Linda Williams, but "she sees for the first time the travesty she has become by sharing in her daughter's humiliation."[25] Detecting that her excessive appearance stands in the way of Laurel's ability to marry into the upper class, Stella fakes a romantic relationship with Munn to encourage her daughter to return to her father so she can ascend into the upper class. In this instance, Stella engages in two masquerades. First, she masquerades as upper class but through her display of "classlessness" she either defies the upper class or makes a mockery of the upper-class position she once desired. Second, she masquerades as lower class when she claims a romantic relationship with Munn to deceive her daughter and to compel her to return to her father's upper-class lifestyle.

Stella's masquerade is transitory as she moves between upper and lower class. She resides in the lower class and disidentifies with her working-class family, intent on becoming a member of the upper class. Consequently, Stella marries Stephen, an upper-class symbol. When she becomes disenchanted with her marriage and bored with her spouse, she descends back gain into the lower class. Yet, when she desires an upper-class status for her daughter, Stella engages in a double masquerade—she performs as upper class (even though she does so excessively) and lower class (when she fakes a romantic relationship with Munn). Despite her masquerade, she is symbolic of the good mother who fluctuates in her maternal commitment and therefore invites further examination of the mother figure.

PROBLEMATIZED MOTHERHOOD: SELF-SACRIFICIAL, BLAMED, AND PUNISHED

While the primary focus of this discussion is related to Peola and Stella, the mother-daughter relationships deserve further discussion given the impact these relationships have upon the "passing" characters. Both Delilah and Stella are "good" mothers who are invested in their daughters. Delilah comforts Peola when she is distressed regarding her racial alienation and rejection, while Stella comforts her daughter when she is rejected due to her lower-class position. Moreover, Delilah provides for Peola when she attempts to resolve her internal conflict related to her white-looking appearance yet black racial identity and recommends that she attend a black school to come to terms with her identity. In comparison, Stella provides for Laurel when she makes her clothes and specifically, when she makes her birthday dress. However, Stella's position as a good mother fluctuates, as she becomes disinterested in motherhood and her desire for entertainment takes precedent over providing for her newly born infant. Yet she returns to motherhood and protects her daughter when Stephen threatens to take Laurel away because of the company she keeps.

In addition to providing for their daughters, Delilah and Stella are self-sacrificial characters in that Delilah willingly concedes to Peola's proposition to ignore her publicly so that she can successfully masquerade as white. Although Delilah disagrees with this request, she complies with Peola's decision, which leaves her emotionally destabilized and affects her health. As for Stella, she sacrifices her daughter when she makes arrangements for Laurel to live with her father, and even when Laurel refuses to do so, Stella fabricates a romantic relationship with Munn, which leads Laurel to return to her father. Therefore, both Delilah and Stella sacrifice their daughters and abandon them for the sake of allowing them access to a world from which they have been denied.

Moreover, these self-sacrificial mothers are blamed for their daughters' failures. For example, Delilah is blamed for marking Peola's blackness, which disavows Peola access to whiteness, and she is blamed for Peola's abandonment. The film suggests that if it were not for Delilah's blackness, Peola could live a "normal white" life. Assuming responsibility for Peola's blackness, Delilah believes she is the cause of Peola's suffering and agrees to relinquish her daughter, a sacrifice that results in her demise when she dies of a broken heart.

In comparison, Stella is blamed for Laurel's inability to transition into the upper class since she remains in the lower class. Therefore, she has to abandon her daughter in order for Laurel to ascend into the upper class. Specifically, Stella is blamed for abandoning motherhood and her daughter when she marries; Stella fails to attend the wedding. Since Stella's internal conflicts, desires, and aspirations are projected onto her daughter, she is ultimately responsible for Laurel's upper-class aspirations. It is conceivable, according to Williams, that "a mother frequently attempts to use her daughter to compensate for her own supposed inferiority by making 'a superior creature out of one whom she regards as her double.'"[26] The fact that Stella abandons her upper-class marriage to Stephen and prefers friends associated with the lower class reflects her willful descent into the lower class, a class position she rejects for her daughter. Recognizing the importance of having her daughter aspire to the upper class and acknowledging her complicity in this process, Stella becomes intent on insuring her daughter's upper-class ascension when she forces her to reside with her father and his new wife. When the upper class mocks and sneers at Stella, she realizes that she is responsible for Laurel's ability/inability to ascend into the upper class. Therefore, Stella finds it necessary to abandon her daughter so that she will no longer mark her daughter's lower-class status (see Figure 7.2).

Drawing upon Kaplan's views, these two mothers represent the "overindulgent mother" who "takes something for herself by satisfying needs for love, nurturance and merging through the child" and the "phallic mother" who "satisfies needs for power that her ideal function prohibits."[27] In the case of Delilah, she represents the overindulgent mother in that she internalizes Peola's suffering in her desire for whiteness and becomes ever more protective of her daughter.[28] Delilah constitutes the nearly perfect mother until Peola abandons her, suggesting that as the "over indulgent-mother," whose need for love is fulfilled through her investment in her daughter's love, she merges with her daughter. If, according to Kaplan, "Delilah's 'mistake' was in allowing her mulatto daughter to see at close hand what whiteness would win for her,"[29] Stella's mistake is her fluctuation in class position moving between lower and upper class even though she ultimately returns to the lower class. In transitioning from one class to another, Stella sends mixed messages to her daughter, all the while aspiring for Laurel to ascend into the upper class. Moreover, Stella desires the freedom to make her own decisions regarding her fate outside the dominant patriarchy. To what extent this

FIGURE 7.2 Stella (Barbara Stanwyck) attending the wedding of her daughter as a fence guest in *Stella Dallas* (1937).

impacts Laurel remains unknown. Yet, Kaplan argues that Stella's desire for freedom constitutes the "phallic mother" who engages in resistant behavior. Stella's resistance, Kaplan explains, "takes the forms, first, of literally objecting to mothering because of the personal sacrifices involved . . . second, of expressing herself freely in her eccentric style of dress and being unabashedly sexual; finally, of growing too attached and needful of her daughter,"[30] an attribute she shares with the "over indulgent-mother."

Regardless as to how these two mothers conform to or deviate from conventions of motherhood, both are punished for their inadequacy. Delilah is punished for abandoning Peola and Stella is punished for abandoning Laurel. Delilah's punishment is that she becomes physically ill when she disconnects from her daughter and ultimately faces death. Stella's punishment, according to Kaplan, "first . . . [turns] her into a 'spectacle' produced by the upper class [for their] disapproving gaze . . . but second, and more devastatingly, [brings] . . . Stella to the recognition that she is an unfit mother for her daughter."[31] Stella's ultimate punishment occurs when she abandons her daughter, a sacrifice necessary for Laurel's upper-class ascension.

POLARIZED FATHERHOOD: ABSENT/GOOD/BAD

While these mothers contribute to the racial desires or class aspirations of their daughters, fathers also contribute to the self-formation of daughters. In *Imitation of Life*, Peola's father remains not only absent from the film but unnamed. We are made aware of his existence only when Delilah informs Bea that Peola's father was a light-complexioned man to explain Peola's ambivalent racial identity. The absent father then is considered responsible for some of Peola's suffering due to her racial ambiguity since in a patriarchal society the father assumes a dominant role and his absence magnifies her suffering. Peola's racial uncertainty automatically problematizes her existence, and when this uncertainty is coupled with the father's absence, the film implies that she will lead an "abnormal existence." In the absence of a father figure, Delilah as the maternal figure stands in for the paternal figure.

In comparison, Stella's Laurel is provided with two paternal figures—a "good" father and a "bad" father. The "good" father (Stephen) is well spoken, well mannered, and well dressed, all signifiers of his upper-class background. Furthermore, Stephen possesses impeccable style, exhibits a strong demeanor, is educated, and displays appropriate etiquette. As a strong father figure, Stephen protects, nurtures, and guides Laurel. Furthermore, he maintains a relationship with his daughter when he separates from Stella. He visits his daughter on Christmas, sends her gifts, makes arrangements for her to visit his new home, and accommodates his daughter when she decides to live with him. He even rescues Laurel when he believes she is exposed to an inappropriate environment. His attributes as a "good" father are further evident in his relationship with Stella. As she becomes oppositional to both motherhood and marriage, Stephen exemplifies patience, cooperates with her desire for entertainment over motherhood, and pleads with her to conform to more acceptable forms of motherhood. More importantly, he never wavers in his upper-class inclinations, unlike Stella, who fluctuates between lower- and upper-class demeanor. It is Stephen's consistency that makes him a model of fatherhood, while Stella's inconsistency makes her a model of failed motherhood. And although Stephen is an embodiment of the "good father," he is not without faults and is described by Ilsa J. Bick as a "bland . . . upper-class but penniless socialite . . . [who] prefers the quiet provincial life."[32] Despite these weaknesses, Stephen stands in for the absent mother figure, who, according to Bick, "habitually appears during those moments when Stella attempts to step out of her role as a mother."[33] As the "good" father, Stephen ingratiates his daughter into the upper-class lifestyle she deserves, and although Stella provides love to her daughter, she is unable to provide the privileged lifestyle that he makes accessible.

When Stephen as the "good" upper-class father is juxtaposed to Munn, the "bad" lower-class father, the comparison makes Stephen appear even more appropriate as a father figure. Munn, as a signifier of the "bad" father, is a drinker, trickster, and deceiver; he is characterized as "raucous" and personifies the lower class.[34] Notably, Munn has no long-term aspirations and is preoccupied only with enjoying life without making a meaningful contribution. He engages in staging antics when he gives itch powder, purely for amusement to those seated on a train, and his foolhardiness becomes linked to immorality when Stella makes Laurel's birthday dress and he imposes on Laurel's privacy. While Stella fits Laurel for the dress to make final adjustments, Munn abruptly enters unannounced and chases Laurel in her undergarments, a behavior she finds immoral, distasteful, intrusive, and insulting. Munn, an alcoholic and signifier of the lower class, possesses sexual desire, but in Bick's assessment the desire he reserved for Stella is displaced onto her daughter.[35] Signifying how he constitutes the "bad" father, Munn's outrageous behavior is further exacerbated when he arrives at their house inebriated on Christmas with an unwrapped turkey for Stella to prepare and intimidates Laurel when she answers the door. He raises mistletoe above Laurel's head and solicits a kiss, but she is so thoroughly disgusted with his impertinent behavior that she exits the room. Munn's behavior, based on Bick's analysis, becomes "the main vehicle through which thinly veiled paternal . . . incestuous wishes become manifest. . . . To him, Laurel is 'Lollipops,' a delicious piece of candy to be eaten, savored, and devoured."[36] It is this vertiginous and unacceptable behavior that arouses Laurel's ire, which leads her to resent Munn and his lower-class status. As the "bad" father, Munn exemplifies Laurel's flight from the lower class and return to the upper class associated with her "good" father Stephen, while Peola's absent father serves only to exacerbate her self-hatred.

Imitation of Life and *Stella Dallas* exemplify mother-daughter relationships wherein Peola masquerades in her "white body" to conceal her blackness which she rejects to disidentify with her black mother so that she can pursue whiteness, while Stella masquerades in her "bourgeois body" to ascend into the upper class, but when she becomes disenchanted with the upper class she descends into the lower class and abandons her daughter to ensure her daughter's upper-class ascendance. While Peola is trapped in a "white body" (yet inner blackness), her mask cannot be removed, unlike Stella, who parades her "bourgeois body," a mask, as Michael Rogin claims, that "can [be] put on and take[n] off."[37] As both characters masquerade on the basis of race or class, Rogin argues that these "cultural prohibitions" frequently "generate the return of what was intended to be repressed."[38] In the case of Peola, although she desires whiteness and abandons her black mother, she returns to blackness, whereas Stella returns to the lower class after gaining access to the upper class even though she holds upper-class aspirations for her daughter. Both Peola and Stella represent the return of the repressed when they return to their place of origin. Furthermore, their performances or parodies, according to Rogin, question the boundaries of the categories to which they aspire, as they become a "copy" of a "copy," an idea borrowed from Judith Butler.[39] Butler's critique of sexuality (heterosexuality/homosexuality) has relevance for Rogin's assessment in that she suggests, "gay is to straight not as copy is to original, but, rather as copy is to copy. The parodic repetition of 'the original' . . . reveals the original to be nothing other than a parody of the idea of the natural and the original."[40] Rogin exploits these views to argue that the creation of a category is a fabrication that originated from a fabrication that certainly has applicability to the present discussion given the performance of racial and class masquerades as race and class are unstable categories. Regardless as to how these imitations destabilize the categories to which they aspire, Peola and Stella's performances certainly hint at the fluidity of race and class categories and demonstrate how they become parallel characters.

NOTES

1. E. Ann Kaplan, "Mothering, Feminism and Representation: The Maternal in Melodrama and the Woman's Film 1910–14," in *Home Is Where the Heart Is: Studies in Melodrama and the Woman's Film*, ed. Christine Gledhill (London: British Film Institute, 1987), 113–137, 130.

2. E. Ann Kaplan, *Motherhood and Representation: The Mother in Popular Culture and Melodrama* (London: Routledge, 1992), 166.

3. Elaine K. Ginsberg, ed., *Passing and the Fictions of Identity* (Durham, NC: Duke University Press, 1996), 2–3.

4. Gwendolyn Audrey Foster, *Class-Passing: Social Mobility in Film and Popular Culture* (Carbondale: Southern Illinois University Press, 2005), 2–7.

5. Kaplan, "Mothering, Feminism and Representation," 131.

6. Linda Williams, *Playing the Race Card: Melodramas of Black and White from Uncle Tom to O.J. Simpson* (Princeton, NJ: Princeton University Press, 2001), 30. Fredi Washington plays Peola as an adult, Dorothy Black plays her at age ten, and Sebie Hendricks plays her at age four.

7. Gayle Wald, *Crossing the Line: Racial Passing in Twentieth-Century U.S. Literature and Culture* (Durham, NC: Duke University Press, 2000), 155.

8. Wald, *Crossing the Line*, 171.

9. Trinh Minh-Ha, *When the Moon Waxes Red: Representation, Gender and Cultural Politics* (New York: Routledge, 1991), 65–78.

10. Ilka Brasch, "'Let Me See Her Face When He Kisses Her, Please': Mediating Emotion and Locating the Melodramatic Mode in *Stella Dallas*," *Film-Philosophy* 19 (2015): 289–303, 297.

11. Both "passing" characters have names that end in "la"—Peola and Stella; both male protagonists are named Stephen [Archer] (Warren William, *Imitation of Life*) and Stephen [Dallas] (John Boles, *Stella Dallas*); both productions end with ceremonies—a funeral or wedding; and both feature black subservience. Fannie Hurst (*Imitation of Life*, [1932]1933) and Olive Higgins Prouty (*Stella Dallas*, 1923) may have drawn upon their own life experiences to produce these works. See Jennifer Parchesky, "Adapting *Stella Dallas*: Class Boundaries, Consumerism, and Hierarchies of Taste," *Legacy* 23, no. 2 (2006): 178–198, 180–181. Parchesky suggests that Prouty's novel upon which the film was based may have reflected Prouty's own class interests, not to exclude that Prouty herself was a mother. See also Brooke Kroeger, *Fannie: The Talent for Success of Writer Fannie Hurst* (New York: Times Book, 1999), 199–200. Kroeger claims that Hurst was aware of a black teacher who passed for white. Michael Rogin, *Blackface, White Noise: Jewish Immigrants in the Hollywood Melting Pot* (Berkeley: University of California Press, 1996), 123. Rogin reports that Hurst was a Jewish novelist who "herself passed as gentile." Dan Callahan's *Barbara Stanwyck: The Miracle Woman* (Jackson: University Press of Mississippi, 2012) addresses Stanwyck's strained relationship with her son (84–85).

12. The PCA (Production Code Administration) initially rejected the film's script "because they felt that 'the main theme is founded upon the results of sex association between the white and black race (miscegenation) . . . not only violates the Production Code but is very dangerous from the standpoint both of industry and public policy.'" Cited in Patricia King Hanson and Alan Gevinson, eds., *American Film Institute Catalog of Motion Pictures Produced in the United States, Feature Films, 1931–1940* (Berkeley: University of California Press, 1993), 1013. Hollywood's attempt to represent visually the mulatto character, according to Susan Courtney, was complicated. However, when black actress Fredi Washington, who possessed a "white body" yet black identity, assumed this role, she eliminated the complexity surrounding Peola's perceived "mixed-race" identity. See Susan Courtney, *Hollywood Fantasies of Miscegenation: Spectacular Narratives of Gender and Race, 1903–1967* (Princeton, NJ: Princeton University Press, 2005), 143–149. Unlike Peola (the character), Washington unequivocally refused to pass as white off screen. See Cheryl Black, "Looking White, Acting Black: Cast(e)ing Fredi Washington," *Theatre Survey* 45, no. 1 (May 2014): 19–40, 29.

13. Laurent Berlant, *The Female Complaint: The Unfinished Business of Sentimentality in American Culture* (Durham, NC: Duke University Press, 2008), 111.

14. Courtney, *Hollywood Fantasies of Miscegenation*, 162.

15. Joel Williamson, *New People: Miscegenation and Mulattoes in the United States* (New York: Free Press, 1980), 101.

16. Berlant states, "For Bea takes Delilah's pancake recipe, her maternal inheritance, and turns it into a business" (*Female Complaint*, 125).

17. Callahan, *Barbara Stanwyck*, 89.

18. Allison Whitney, "Race, Class, and the Pressure to Pass in American Maternal Melodrama: The Case of *Stella Dallas*," *Journal of Film and Video* 59, no. 1 (Spring 2007): 3–18, 6.

19. Edie Thornton, "Fashion, Visibility, and Class Mobility in *Stella Dallas*," *American Literary History* 11, no. 3 (Autumn 1999): 426–447.

20. Whitney, "Race, Class, and the Pressure to Pass," 8–9. See Ellen C. Scott, "More Than a 'Passing' Sophistication: Dress, Film Regulation, and the Color Line in 1930s American Films," *Women's Studies Quarterly* 41, nos. 1/2 (Spring/Summer 2012): 60–86.

21. Whitney, "Race, Class, and the Pressure to Pass," 10.

22. Thornton, "Fashion, Visibility, and Class Mobility," 427.

23. Christine Gledhill, "Dialogue: Christine Gledhill on '*Stella Dallas*' and Feminist Film Theory," *Cinema Journal* 25, no. 4 (Summer, 1986): 44–48, 47.

24. Gledhill, "Dialogue," 47.

25. Linda Williams, "'Something Else Besides a Mother': '*Stella Dallas*' and the Maternal Melodrama," *Cinema Journal* 24, no. 1 (Autumn 1984): 2–27, 15.

26. Williams, "'Something Else Besides a Mother,'" 3.

27. Kaplan, *Motherhood and Representation*, 47.

28. Kaplan, *Motherhood and Representation*, 165.

29. Kaplan, *Motherhood and Representation*, 167.

30. Kaplan, *Motherhood and Representation*, 170.

31. Kaplan, *Motherhood and Representation*, 170.

32. Ilsa J. Bick, "*Stella Dallas*: Maternal Melodrama and Feminine Sacrifice," *Psychoanalytic Review* 79, no. 1 (Spring 1992): 121–145, 123.

33. Bick, "*Stella Dallas*," 126.

34. Williams, "'Something Else Besides a Mother,'" 13.

35. Bick, "*Stella Dallas*," 126.

36. Bick, "*Stella Dallas*," 127–128.

37. Michael Rogin, *Blackface, White Noise: Jewish Immigrants in the Hollywood Melting Pot* (Berkeley: University of California Press, 1996), 128.

38. Rogin, *Blackface, White Noise*, 32.

39. Rogin, *Blackface, White Noise*, 32–33.

40. Judith Butler, *Gender Trouble: Feminism and the Subversion of Identity* (New York: Routledge, 1990), 31.

8 · THE EGOTISTICAL SUBLIME

Film Noir and Whiteness

MATTHIAS KONZETT

Contrary to its reputation as a subversive Hollywood genre, classic film noir operates within rather conventional race codes established by legal and cultural Jim Crow segregation. It comes as no surprise that critical discussions of noir and race are rare and sporadic. Even the neo-noir genre was not able to change this seeming omission of race. Granted, some neo-noir films such as *Point Blank* (1967), *Chinatown* (1974), and *The Long Good-bye* (1973) reference race in passing. *Taxi Driver* (1976), with a hero that screenwriter and noir critic Paul Shrader calls "a particular kind of breed of white boy," is an anomaly.[1] More recently, neo-noirs such as *Devil in a Blue Dress* (1995), *Jackie Brown* (1997), and *Ghost Dog* (1999) deal with race more explicitly; however, ultimately it appears to be not the major concern of the noir genre built on a stylish aesthetics, low-key cinematography, and a romanticized view of crime. And yet the representation and aesthetics of race have always been a major component of Hollywood films. In noir, this representation lies in its obsession with whiteness, stylized and made over in the cool image of the American gangster.

As some critics have suggested, film noir deploys race as its repressed unconscious or dark figurative frame from within which white dramas of social corruption unfold. As Eric Lott claims, "Film noir's relentless cinematography of chiaroscuro and moral focus on the rotten souls of white folks . . . constantly though obliquely invoked the racial dimension of this figural play of light against dark."[2] Normatively, this practice could be said to violate standard classical Hollywood codes built on the U.S. legal and cultural tenets of Jim Crow segregation, leading instead to a boundary crossing between the two formerly separated worlds. As Lott states, "But with the advent of noir even the women were mostly cast into blackness, living, like the men, in shadows that suggested their racial fall from Hollywood lighting conventions."[3] However, Hollywood's concrete on-screen depictions of black characters in noirs, mostly belittling and infantilizing, do not fully seem to bear out this pervasive figurative reach suggested by Lott, as African Americans are still given only marginal representation and serve mostly as a binary prop of racial contrast. As Charles Scruggs notes, "The directors of these films either recycled the same stereotypes from other genres, or they used the 'Negro' (male or female) as a negative foil to whiteness . . . or as a 'fall from whiteness.'"[4] If directly invoked, race is mostly seen through the lens of a white perspective and placed into a pure imaginary realm, maintaining whiteness as the standard as well as the apartheid conventions of Hollywood with its limited racial interactions on screen.

Rather, noir as an anti-Hollywood Hollywood genre challenges its institutional grammar by producing no happy endings and by reverting white socioeconomic mobility into one of bankruptcy and failure: "Noir's crossings from light to dark, the indulgence of actions and visual codes ordinarily renounced in white bourgeois culture and thereby raced in the white imaginary, throw its protagonists into the predicament of abjection."[5] The final white and economically successful heterosexual couple required by the Hollywood formula appears to rebel against the very codes that frame it as the privileged result of the narrative. Whiteness, so to speak, has become a problematic race discourse unto itself in film noir as evidenced with its many white characters struggling and repeatedly failing on screen. *Double Indemnity* (1944), for example, depicts Walter Neff, a white successful insurance man bored with the American dream, leading him to betray his best friend and boss Barton Keyes and entering a plot of murder with an equally bored and greedy white femme fatale, Phyllis Dietrichson, already well provided for by her affluent husband. A telling scene in a supermarket, the paradise of consumerism, involves a troubled conversation about murder in front of a display of baby food, metaphorically aborting the offspring of the doomed couple.

Looking at two classic noir films, *Double Indemnity* (dir. Billy Wilder, 1944) and *The Breaking Point* (dir. Michael Curtiz, 1950), I argue that noir foregrounds a white sterility and an exhaustion of the myth of whiteness. Style, often associated with noir, turns into a stifling straitjacket, imprisoning characters in empty plots and rituals and providing an elaborate costume for the protagonist's self-inflated tragic exit from the world. In many noir films, the formerly safe confines of white middle-class worlds are encroached upon by newly emerging social and cultural threats, be they race, gender, nationality, real or imagined, pushing the characters to the brink of paranoid and sociopathic behavior. As a result, we see fragmentation, predatory behavior, and a decline of in-group solidarity within the very group enjoying entitlement and privilege. This antisocial behavior is heightened to a form of an egotistic white sublime, giving the hero one last chance at self-determination. This emphasis on self-agency at all cost serves as the key ingredient of whiteness, a privilege withheld from other groups, even as the white world collapses. The self-enclosed worlds of noirs require therefore an intersectional analysis to lay bare not only the disintegration of formerly privileged screen worlds but also the final stages of white entitlement and its scorched-earth approach to the question of freedom and self-agency.

While Billy Wilder, an emigrant Austrian Jewish director of the iconic noir *Double Indemnity* (1944), has been highly praised for his auteur approach to the genre with his heavy involvement in the script and production, he did not challenge the industry's racial apartheid norms, requiring that whites and African Americans live in distinctly different and separate social spheres.[6] A telling scene, for example, is given in Walter Neff's interaction with Charlie (Sam McDaniel), the black garage attendant whom he deliberately recruits without his knowledge for establishing an airtight alibi on the night of the murder.[7] The representation of Charlie resembles that of Sam in *Casablanca*, namely as one of total innocence and fidelity. In a genre known for its moral corruption, no bribe is required surprisingly as Charlie in his childlike innocence never realizes that he is being used as a cover. At the same time, Neff knows that Charlie provides the perfect alibi in his unquestioned trustworthiness and subservience. The idealization of Charlie may well remove him from the environment of white corruption, but it also virtually robs him of any agency and renders him a powerless pawn. After having carried out the murder, Neff leaves one more time through the garage making sure to meet up with Charlie and reconfirm his alibi of having stayed in all night. The scene shows Charlie dutifully polishing his car and engaging in a brief conversation as Neff claims he is running a quick errand on foot to the drugstore. After a dissolve shot we see Neff walking on the dark sidewalk commenting on this moment of successful corroboration with an onset of doubt via his hindsight voiceover narration: "Suddenly it came over me that everything would go wrong . . . I couldn't hear my own footsteps. It was the walk of a dead man." Neff realizes that he has become "a dead man walking," an interesting phrase that could also be applied to Charlie who is characterized by a legacy of social death, namely the institution of slavery that lives on in a Jim Crow society, permitting only minimal social articulation to its African American minority.[8] Indeed, the paired scenes connected via the soft edit of a dissolve seem to suggest that by becoming a murderer, Neff has assumed the position of an outsider, a dead man walking, not unlike that of Charlie.

Wilder's iconic film noir, breaking with many Hollywood conventions, follows the segregationist industry code closely in its reduction of Charlie to a flat semiotic function of reliability, invisibility, and social death. Charlie's function is akin to that of the mammy who "nurtured whites—that is, supplied material support and a symbolic, imagined community—at the expense of blacks."[9] It appears that Neff also understands this semiotic function of Charlie and hence designates him as the perfect alibi. By contrast, an encounter on the train with the white stranger Jackson creates considerable suspense for the audience during an interview with Keyes as it cannot predict what he saw or didn't see. Even though Neff mostly had his back turned to him during their brief encounter, Jackson suggests that the man on the train was not Mr. Dietrichson and triggers a deeper inquiry into the case. Charlie's gaze, conversely, is totally controlled by Neff, seeing only what Neff wants him to see. Neff and the film audience understand implicitly Charlie's Jim Crow typification of the naïve and loyal Negro, a Hollywood fiction or stereotype created to mend the cracks in its white symbolic system. In other words, within the diegetic world of the film, white characters believe Charlie at all cost as his fictively attributed honesty and loyalty provide the much-needed lie for the system to work.

Given Wilder's conventional adherence to Hollywood's normative race coding, an intersectional reading may have to recover this race pathology more fully by means of delving into its origins in the world of white characters. It is here where the film has more freedom of representation and begins to voice its own disenchantment with Hollywood's discourse of whiteness.

FIGURE 8.1 The white lead protagonists Phyllis (Barbara Stanwyck) and Walter (Fred McMurray) indulging in a dangerous and self-destructive criminal lifestyle as part of the white sublime in *Double Indemnity* (1944).

This is not to say that Wilder articulates a critique of race intentionally but rather symptomatically as a Hollywood beneficiary of white male privilege and as an auteur constrained by its system. Much like the film's lead character Neff who is bored with his white privilege, Wilder's film reveals a similar boredom with the Hollywood formula of whiteness and sends its lead characters on a self-destructive path, stopping short of addressing the cause of their symptomatic behavior (see Figure 8.1). Wilder's *auteurism* places him into the company of Hitchcock and Welles, directors striving to find a broader range of expression within the suffocating conventions of Hollywood's ameliorative vision of the American dream. In doing so, they position themselves as iconoclastic filmmakers and as a by-product deliver a critique of the Hollywood system. Somewhere in this critique, the question of whiteness emerges, what it once was and what it has since become, namely murderous, self-consuming, and perpetually discontent. It is hard to imagine that any Hollywood minority characters would ever be so willing to gamble away all the entitlements of the white characters, bent on upping the game of capitalism and self-enlargement (*Citizen Kane*) to the point of self-destruction.

Walter Neff, an accomplished insurance agent who is offered a desk-job promotion in the better paying claims department by his friend and mentor Keyes, repeats on a smaller scale Charles Foster Kane's extravagant demise as he cannot fully enjoy his secure socioeconomic standing and wishes to gamble it away for more money, "crooking the house" as he calls it, and for an illegitimate affair with a married woman. The gangster film of the 1930s, it appears, has become domesticated and now lives on in America's middle-class environment with its relentless pursuit of wealth and pleasure. To some extent, this transfer of the gangster genre is done indulgently to promote a certain degree of cool posing on the part of the main protagonist, making him the film's antihero. Neff uses idiomatic street language and wears his fedora even when hiding in the backseat of the car, ensuring that he commits a transgressive murder while stylishly dressed. Here, Neff clearly imitates the fashionable gangster types of 1930s cinema, the white ethnic fashionable mobsters Tony Camonte (Paul Muni in *Scarface*, 1931) or Tom Powers (James Cagney in *The Public Enemy*, 1931). Edward G. Robinson, once cast as lead mobster Rico in *Little Caesar* (1931), likewise returns in Wilder's film in a more respectable role but still evokes the gangster genre for the audience.[10] *Double Indemnity* ultimately shows that the fantasy space of capitalism, the American dream, is becoming increasingly disenchanted with its promised rewards and hence leads to flirtation with crime. The economic rewards offered to the successful Neff pale in comparison to the firm's boss Norton, installed by legacy, or Mr. Dietrichson, who is in the more profitable oil business. Male camaraderie as the only redemptive social bond, demonstrated between Neff and Keyes's ongoing office bromance, is ultimately betrayed in the egotistic search for the fullest economic self-realization.

The only remaining stumbling block toward this goal is the woman, the femme fatale, who has designs of her own and is no longer content in taking a back seat. One of the most memorable scenes in *Double Indemnity* is Phyllis's reaction shot at the steering wheel when her husband in the passenger seat is strangled off-screen by Neff. As her stern face slowly relaxes, it produces an enigmatic smile not unlike that of the *Mona Lisa* concealing her interior world,[11] Phyllis has reached the ultimate pinnacle of psychological self-realization, the egotistic white sublime. Slavoj Žižek speaks of the "ultimate triumph of capitalism" where everyone "becomes his own or her own capitalist, the 'entrepreneur-of-the-self.'"[12] In the logic of the ever-widening atomization and fragmentation of social bonds under capitalism, every individual is to become his or her own entrepreneur and competitive market force. Phyllis will follow this logic to the bitter end, topping even Neff in her unlimited greed and obliging him to stay on the trolley train "to the end of the line," even as he wishes to pull out of the insurance scam upon discovery of blatant inconsistencies in Phyllis's prior life. This aggressive drive for socio-economic gain, displayed even more so by Phyllis, links up with the equally important epistemic desire for the self-sufficient subject, the "entrepreneur-of-the-self," a dream of total subjective agency that haunts Western metaphysics. It is inscribed into the Hollywood film apparatus, especially in the enabling POV shots that place the spectator at the center of its cinematic fantasy and deceptively make him or her a godlike subject authorizing the film's narrative.[13] Suffice it to say, this metaphysical perspective or sublime ego is foremost meant for white characters and white audiences, with African Americans serving as the binary contrast, pointing to exclusion and a lack of agency. At best, black characters such as *Casablanca*'s Sam are allowed to support and embellish via music or vaudeville performances the white sublime.

The egotistic sublime, which has its origin in romanticism with the poet's self-enclosed world of reflection, ultimately goes back to the first articulations of the Western self during the Renaissance, as given prominently in Hamlet's self-conscious dissection of his demise. Neff's voiceover narration, which reflectively controls the interpretation of the diegesis, is an updated hard-boiled version of Hamlet's soliloquy, allowing him likewise to remain at the center of his own downfall. The famous opening scene, when Walter meets Phyllis for the first time, similarly offers a variation of Shakespeare's balcony scene in *Romeo and Juliet*, linking the tragedy of the star-crossed aristocratic lovers to their modern noir counterpart represented by a seedy middle-class couple driven by sex and greed. The highbrow pathos of uninvited tragedy has given way to lowbrow self-entrapment in criminal pursuits. Cinematically, *Double Indemnity* is structured as a male melodrama in which the hero's grand operatic exit from the narrative (death) marks both the beginning and end of the film via its circular voiceover structure. This structure is parodied or pushed to the brink of psychosis, part of what Paul Schrader calls the last phase of classic noir.[14] In *Sunset Boulevard*, for example, an already dead character speaks the voiceover while Norma Desmond (Gloria Swanson), an insane Hollywood star of the bygone silent era, still attempts to hold the public's attention. Both films betray an anxious struggle to hold on to subjective agency at all costs in the face of modern technology that challenges the integrity of the subject. The dictaphone used so ostensibly in *Double Indemnity*'s voiceover suggests that the modern subject is more a product of the postproduction assemblage of an imaginary "self" supported by the editing of image and sound rather than a natural entity. Norma Desmond's protest against the onset of sound film—"We didn't need a dialogue. We had faces"—points to the collapse of the enigmatic aura of the face that enclosed the self.[15] This epistemic crisis is further complicated by the challenge of women who wish to participate in this privileged world of male whiteness.

Another convention of film noir is that of the fall or takedown of the femme fatale. In *Double Indemnity*, for example, this fall is presented spatially as Phyllis first appears on the upper balcony clothed in a white towel bathed in bright light in her introduction but is shown descending the stairs and later at the climax is seated downstairs in the dark living room when Neff arrives to kill her. As the demonized modern woman asserting her independence and posing a serious challenge to the patriarchal order, the femme fatale is routinely subjected to punishment scenarios in the concluding sequences of noirs. In doing so, the narrative world reestablishes the balance of the status quo after having presented a world seemingly unhinged in its order. Again, it should be noted that many of the social coordinates in noir, such as the representation of race, remain stable throughout the narrative and pose no threat to the social order. Rather, the first attempt of dissent from within the privileged group is severely punished, robbing the white heroine of her voice at the moment she appears to have attained it. For example, Cora (Lana Turner) who is pregnant, meets an unexpected death in a car crash in *The Postman Always Rings Twice* (1946; Tay Garnett), thus ending her socioeconomic achievement of running her own business while at the same time also aborting any offspring.

Double Indemnity, with its telling murder plot conversation in front of the baby food section at Jerry's Market, similarly points to the impossibility of any offspring from this poisonous relationship. At the film's end, Phyllis intends to have her stepdaughter Lola killed by inciting the jealous temper of her boyfriend Zachetti. Neff initially wishes to frame Zachetti for the double murder of Mr. and Mrs. Dietrichson but then has a last-minute change of heart, suggesting a reunion of Lola and Nino, a minor happy ending within the larger darker ending. Nevertheless, sterility haunts film noir as the ultimate impasse of white privilege that fails to leave a legacy for posterity both figuratively and literally. In contrast to romantic melodramas with their happy endings expressed in marriage, the noir genre takes a sober look at the cultural and economic conditions that frame the white patriarchal self, and which cannot be integrated into a conventional union. It also appears that it cannot be placed into any dialogue with any emerging group or partner but is condemned to die a heroic lonely death in glorious self-consumption. Unlike the premodern hero of the Western genre who represents a type of freedom against the onset of modern standardization, the noir hero is trapped within the norms of modern society and chooses a self-indulgent and destructive way out rather than reconstituting this society by sharing his power with other emerging groups. The noir hero's deliberate choice of self-destruction preserves the illusion of choice, hence asserting a final grand act of white privilege. This privilege is in fact only a narcissistic social construction of self-validation. This validation is shown in *Double Indemnity*'s melodramatic exchange, "closer than that Walter—I love you too," between Keyes and Neff at the film's ending, constituting in heteronormative Hollywood an impossible white male couple and foregoing Wilder's originally intended gas chamber scene that would have removed Walter Neff's agency altogether and judged his criminal behavior to the audience's dissatisfaction. Routinely used in gangster films to warn audiences about crime and undue immigrant mobility, a gas chamber scene does not fit the WASP middle-class context of Walter Neff's world with its presupposed entitlements of fullest self-realization in the white sublime.

With their figurative black worlds, noirs contain very little of interest to black audiences other than its white pathological worlds. The descent into crime and darkness, as pointed out earlier, is inspired by the white antiheroes of the gangster genre and not associated with black street crime, which would be featured prominently in film only in the 1970s. In light of this absence of black culture in classic film noir, Manthia Diawara, for example, calls for a consideration of noirs by black authors such as Chester Himes's *Rage in Harlem* that "highlight less an aesthetic state of affairs than a way of life that has been imposed on black people through social injustice."[16] bell hooks similarly speaks of the necessity of an oppositional gaze when considering Hollywood and TV media: "When most black people in the United States first had the opportunity to look at film and television, they did so fully aware that mass media was a system of knowledge and power reproducing and maintaining white supremacy."[17] Such an oppositional gaze, or intersectional perspective, would be able to identify the much discussed fake blonde wig of Phyllis as more than the intended expression of her deception and artificiality. Instead, it appears as a parody of the angelic white glamour close-up so often given to heroines, establishing whiteness as a quasi-metaphysical quality. Richard Dyer argues that the image of the "white woman as the idealized creature of light" created with Hollywood's lighting system deliberately uses the reflective surfaces of her white skin tone to enhance the white hero: "The sense of man being illuminated by the woman is a widespread convention, established in classic Hollywood cinema."[18] The excess of the peroxide bleached wig of Phyllis unmasks this whiteness as a deliberate and cheap seductive pose meant to play up to the norms of whiteness. Wrapped up in his own white narcissism, Neff is easy prey for this display, which sexualizes whiteness and where, not unlike the horror film, "there is a frightening, disfiguring darkness to the sexuality that, moth to the flame, yearns towards the pure light of desirability."[19] The severely underlit scene created by cinematographer John F. Seitz in which Walter and Phyllis consume their sexual passion allows for the visibility of only her bleached blonde hair and her enticing white angora sweater highlighting her breasts. In their initial encounter, Neff is placed into the shadows of the hall as Phyllis appears on the upper balcony clothed by a provocatively light-reflecting white towel with the notorious blonde wig serving as icing on the cake. The femme fatale could in this sense also be critically understood as prompting the hero's fatal seduction by the myth of whiteness and its illusionary claim to superiority. This representation of the white sublime proves to be no more than a ploy of imagined norms and is at bottom sterile. Wilder, who may have taken a conventional approach to the representation of nonwhite minorities, nevertheless shows a critical perspective concerning the seduction of normative whiteness, a norm that his Jewish immigrant experience probably considered as random and unfounded.

Directed by the prolific Hollywood filmmaker Michael Curtiz of Austro-Hungarian Jewish descent, *The Breaking Point* (1950) takes us into the territory of the border noir, a subgenre focusing on questions of national identity against the southern border of the United States. As a remake of the film *To Have and Have Not* (dir. Howard Hawks, 1944), which in turn is an adaptation of Ernest Hemingway's novel from 1937, this film chooses California (San Diego) and the southern border to Mexico as its location. The earlier film is set in French Martinique to relaunch Hemingway's novel, set in Florida and Cuba, as a patriotic war propaganda piece in the style of Curtiz's *Casablanca*, starring once again Humphrey Bogart. Hawks's film uses a significant number of nonwhite African French and African American actors as a realistic demographic backdrop for Martinique, a former French slave colony, to stress the racial inclusiveness of American war propaganda vehicles. Harry Morgan (Humphrey Bogart), not unlike Rick in *Casablanca*, undergoes a conversion from a neutral bystander to becoming an active supporter of the French resistance against the Vichy government. With his charter boat, he assists the resistance in a failed attempt to rescue one of their members from a nearby prison island and later secures their escape to the United States.

The Breaking Point, conversely, set in postwar California, begins with an initial focus on white suburbia in San Diego and reduces the number of black characters drastically to a father and his son. However, the father, Wesley Park, played by African Puerto Rican actor Juano Hernandez, happens to be a longtime employee and dear friend of the hero Harry Morgan (John Garfield), who owns a charter boat service (see Figure 8.2). As such, Wesley takes a central role in the film, and his young son is shown playing with Harry's two daughters and accompanying them to school. We can see that the film has entered the era of social consciousness and the nascent civil rights movement challenging segregation. As such, this film happens to be one of Curtiz's most progressive films concerning race, given that many of his earlier films relied on minstrelsy and blackface in their representation of African Americans.[20]

With the rise of social consciousness in noir films of the 1950s and its focus on social class and disenfranchisement in contrast to the prevailing economic myth of the American dream, a new approach to race would appear to be possible. However, Hollywood's formula of the white sublime proves to be an equally persistent mythology highly adaptable to newly emerging social demands and inquiries. The self-destructive hedonism foregrounded in noirs of the 1940s, noir's aesthetic or early romantic phase, gives way to an ethical stage or noir's late romanticism, in which contingency undermines the naïve belief in agency and self. The notion of self concedes to the larger notion of history that drives its futile attempts at self-determination. However, in this larger scheme of things, the white self does not simply disappear but rather becomes more interiorized into a socially withdrawn ethical agency. Paul Schrader's notion of the psychotic noir as the final expression of its evolution

FIGURE 8.2 Harry Morgan (John Garfield) and his friend and longtime work associate Wesley (Juano Hernandez) in *The Breaking Point* (1950).

as a genre bears out this tendency. Norma Desmond's detachment from reality in *Sunset Boulevard* (dir. Billy Wilder, 1950) is driven by her delusional efforts of self-legitimation as a timeless silent movie star. Norma's concern is no longer that of hedonistic self-consumption but of accountability toward history. Her psychotic attempt to write film history stops short of nothing, including murder. In this economy of self-mastery other marginal groups or individuals may appear on the horizon—such as the young impoverished writer Joe Gillis (William Holden)—but ultimately cannot be accommodated due to the white protagonist's preoccupation with his or her impending fall from grace.

The border noir, as given in films such as *Out of the Past* (1947), *Border Incident* (1949), *Borderline* (1950), *The Breaking Point,* and *Touch of Evil* (1958), defines the prevalent corruption of the genre via nationality, attributing immorality to cultures and nations south of the border and making U.S. culture north of the border vulnerable to their influence. This binary division is shown in *Breaking Point* with the brightly lit and sunbathed location of San Diego contrasted with the dark and foggy Mexican port where Harry Morgan's charter boat lays anchor. The dark Mexico serves as the setting and space of corruption where whites can conduct their shady activities. Harry's customer, a seemingly respectable white U.S. businessman, cheats him out of his fare. He is accompanied by a striking younger blonde Leona Charles (Patricia Neal) who fulfills the normative ideals of U.S. whiteness but displays the looser morals stereotypically attributed to Mexican culture. The shady American lawyer Duncan who approaches Harry with a plan to ship human cargo across the border operates mostly from within the confines of a seedy Mexican bar and will later be shown in similar shady bars in the United States. With Harry temporarily trapped in Mexico due to the loss of his fare, the film suggests that his descent into criminal behavior stems from contingencies brought about both by the fare cheating white U.S. customer Hannagan and a more anarchic culture south of the border, undermining his moral integrity. The cargo, illegal Chinese immigrants, connects the film with the noir trope of Chinatown, a location that challenges U.S. moral norms from within.

This presentation of multiple cultural groups and individuals struggling with their economic fate, however distorted in the lenses of Hollywood, shows more social awareness in contrast to earlier noirs readily assuming white mainstream standards as the norm. The stereotypical dark or nighttime background in 1940s noirs connoting evil is now demystified and lit up as a social landscape of economic struggle. And yet the Hollywood narrative is far from abandoning its normative clichés. If the main protagonist does not possess the required white decorum, the film will chart his or her violent and desperate return to such norms. An inevitable byproduct of noirs, failure usually comes with a sense of victory or self-assertion against the forces of history. The psychotic doubling of this endeavor expresses itself in two contradictory story lines, namely social descent and seeming moral redemption or ascent. Norma's delusional demand for her close-up, which she gets, becomes a moment of triumph, however tragic or sadistic, at the point of her arrest for murder.

Unlike Walter Neff, Harry Morgan is settled well into married family life with two daughters. However, he is struggling economically and has not made a successful transition from his wartime service into civil life. The camera shows photos of Harry's earlier wartime assignments—John Garfield, known from many war films, being the perfect actor for this role—during a discussion with his wife urging him to take up a more lucrative job in her father's agricultural business in Salinas. The film's focus is that of Harry not being duly rewarded for his patriotic wartime service, which sets him on a course of criminal and reckless action. Wesley, his supportive buddy and charter boat employee, is said never to have seen a man die from a bullet, and it is implied he did not see direct military conflict. Thus, while the film promotes Wesley's character in a more well-rounded presentation, the entire melodrama stays focused on the white hero protagonist, seemingly cheated out of his due rewards for his wartime service. Factually, this melodramatic presentation is strongly misleading, as the GI Bill (Servicemen's Readjustment Act, 1944) provided huge economic, housing, and educational incentives to white GIs, rewards that were mostly withheld from African Americans.[21] Nevertheless, the film shows Harry as a white victim of circumstance and national non-appreciation.

As his plan to ship illegal Chinese immigrants to the United States goes awry and leads to the accidental death of the crooked Chinese mobster Mr. Sing (Victor Sen Yung) trying to cheat him out of his due commission, Harry returns to San Diego, where his boat is impounded by the U.S. Coast Guard. In what signals the gradual demise of his character, Harry visits a tiki bar styled with Polynesian bamboo decorations, evoking the Pacific war theater and its exotic atmosphere associated with loose military life involving booze and women. Not surprisingly, he meets up with the shady lawyer Duncan but rebuffs him and Leona, the blonde, with whom he has a drink, but resists her advances. Contrary to the viewer's expectations based on the noir genre, Harry does not succumb to temptation so easily. As he leaves the bar eventually with his wife, a seemingly innocuous scene alerts the viewer to the coming collapse of his resolve. The camera shows his young daughters playing with another friend on the boardwalk. Wesley's young son sits across from them in the foreground and frames the shot while pointing a toy gun at them. On noticing the drunk Harry, the white girlfriend giggles and shouts, "He is loaded. Your father's loaded." The scene condenses various meanings, implying, for example, that the loaded or drunk Harry is about to go off like a gun. Lucy, the mother, is surprised by the girl's use of crude street language, and it is visually implied that the bad influence may be the result of the toy-gun-wielding African American child, showing nascent signs of criminal conduct. The scene, it would appear, tacitly casts doubt on the film's initially promoted ideal of desegregation. However, it could also be stated that the film in fact teases the audience with its own stereotypical assumptions about black crime. By the film's end, no black crime has been committed. Instead, the once respectable Harry Morgan will have sunk deeper into criminal conduct, resulting in the death of Wesley, killed as an innocent bystander and leaving his young son orphaned.

Harry's wife Lucy begins to show signs of insecurity after meeting Leona at the bar and has her hair dyed blonde like Leona's to win back Harry's interest. This plot device places whiteness at the center of the film at the expense of the socioeconomic struggle. Standing in front of a mirror, Lucy is shown examining her blond hair. Later, a similar mirror shot will provide a reflection of Harry's gun as he readies himself to take up a dubious offer to ship gangsters on his boat for a getaway. The dyed blonde hair is thus linked to the corruption of the gun, and by implication the defense of whiteness. However, unlike the hedonistically motivated egotistic sublime in Walter Neff's case, Harry Morgan's sense of entitlement remains mostly ethical. In his voiceover, he explains, "I'm doing to it for her [his wife Lucy] and the reward, and I have to do it alone." As the film's ending will show, Harry is interested in not the thousand-dollar fare but rather the reward for capturing the criminals, thus remaining ethically honest to himself. At this point the film enters its psychotic narrative. The heist at the race track predictably turns violent. Harry tries to send Wesley on an errand as the gangsters are about to arrive at the boat but fails to do so in time. As Wesley warns him, "Harry, don't do it Harry," he is shot dead in front of Harry. During the boat ride, Harry callously disposes of Wesley's body by throwing it overboard with the help of one gangster, tricks the other gangsters, retrieves his hidden guns, and kills all of them. He is in turn severely wounded, mumbling to himself, "A man alone hasn't got a chance," and is rescued by the Coast Guard. In melodramatic fashion, he initially refuses to give permission to have his wounded arm amputated, which would mean certain death. After his wife pleads with him, he finally gives in and the film has apparently achieved a somber but happier ending than usually given in a noir.

At the San Diego dock, the lighting is hazy and misty and resembles the earlier shots of Mexico, suggesting that corruption has crept across the border. A medium close-up of Harry's crying daughters gives way to one of Wesley's son all by himself and isolated. After a quick cut to Leona watching the ambulance leave, the camera moves into a high crane overhead shot, providing an uncanny objective final shot of Wesley's son completely dwarfed and lost in the dock setting.[22] No questions are asked about Wesley, and no one attends to his newly orphaned son. This surreal social indifference toward

Wesley's son shown on the part of Harry's family and the involved rescue services leaves the film with a pressing open question. If Harry's masculine egotism is finally checked—the amputation standing in for his metaphorical castration—and Harry is reintegrated into the social contract, what happens to the excluded black minority? How can the film's ending even be construed as happy in the face of its disturbing lack of social empathy for the nonwhite victims?

We can see that *The Breaking Point* correctly identifies masculine narcissism, Harry's stubborn attempt of going it alone, as the hero's moral shortcoming and pulls back from its fatal consequences, thus questioning early noir's self-induced nihilism. Although Harry's individual narcissism is overcome, the collective narcissism of the white characters remains in place, resulting in a depiction of a psychotic social life with two parallel societies living side by side. The film's title, the "breaking point," offers two meanings: It depicts Harry's egotistic impasse of "going it alone" and his pride of not wanting to accept the help of the community. And the breaking point also refers to the film's *aporia* that cannot provide a successful ending in a segregated society, where the notion of community and support is not extended to everyone equally. While the exclusion of African Americans haunts the film at its center, its xenophobic treatment of Asians and Mexicans is likewise not to be overlooked, as the border noir renders them mostly in quick caricatures of morally suspect groups. The film ends with a psychotic defense of whiteness in a move that justifies Harry's moral righteousness in his double-crossing of criminals and delivering them to justice. However, somewhere in this story line of self-legitimation, Harry has lost sight of his own crime committed against Wesley.

This discussion of film noir has shown that its main focus on race has to be located with its problematic depiction of whiteness, pointing to its exclusionary logic and its cultural impasse as either an individual or collective narcissism. Surprisingly, recent neo-noirs with few exceptions do not stray far from this template. Memorable films such as *No Country for Old Men* (2007), *Drive* (2011), and *Nightcrawler* (2014) still place white self-implosion or its descent into psychosis at its center and refuse to enter the murkier terrain of a conflicted cultural landscape marked by the legacy of slavery, Jim Crow apartheid, and a persistent xenophobia involving the southern border and the Asia-Pacific region. This leads one to assume that the genre is quite comfortable with its present formula of white darkness, a narcissism that stubbornly clings to its own demise. As Sigmund Freud once poignantly observed, "Criminals . . . as they are represented in literature, compel our interest by the narcissistic consistency with which they manage to keep away from their ego anything which would diminish it. It is as if we envied them for maintaining a blissful state of mind."[23] And one could add, the white criminals of noir compel this fascination even more so.

NOTES

1. Paul Schrader, quoted in Cynthia Fuchs, "*Taxi Driver:* 'I Got Some Bad Ideas in My Head," in *Film Analysis: A Norton Reader,* ed. Jeffrey Geiger and R. L. Rutsky (New York: Norton, 2013), 748–766, 753.

2. Eric Lott, "The Whiteness of Film Noir," *American Literary History* 9, no. 3 (Autumn 1997): 542–566, 543. A similar argument is advanced in Charles Scruggs, "'The Power of Blackness': Film Noir and Its Critics," *American Literary History* 16, no. 4 (Winter 2004): 675–687.

3. Lott, "Whiteness of Film Noir," 548.

4. Charles Scruggs, "The Subversive Shade of Black in Film Noir," in *Film Noir,* ed. Homer B. Pettey and R. Barton Palmer (Edinburgh: Edinburgh University Press, 2014), 164–181, 165. Scruggs himself struggles to find explicit references to the African American experience and refers instead to possible double codings of white fugitives and maids as potentially associated with the legacy of slavery.

5. Lott, "Whiteness of Film Noir," 549.

6. Wilder had already written numerous successful screenplays such as *Ninotchka* (dir. Lubitsch, 1939) and *Ball of Fire* (dir. Hawks, 1941) before directing his own films. *Double Indemnity,* coauthored with Raymond Chandler, was his third film directed in Hollywood and won him seven Academy Award nominations. For an extensive discussion of the screen adaptation, see Richard Schickel, *Double Indemnity* (London: British Film Institute, 1992).

7. In Cain's novel from 1936, a Filipino houseboy performs this alibi function for Walter Huff, as he makes a plan to send him on his way early in the evening while also stressing that he is going to bed for the night. See Victor Bascara, "The Case of the Disappearing Filipino American Houseboy: Speculations on *Double Indemnity* and United States Imperialism," *Kritika Kultura* 8 (2007): 35–56.

8. See Orlando Patterson, *Slavery and Social Death* (Cambridge, MA: Harvard University Press, 1982), where he refers to the slave as a "social non-person" (5).

9. Michael Rogin, *Blackface, White Noise: Jewish Immigration in the Hollywood Melting Pot* (Berkeley: University of California Press, 1996), 4.

10. Wilder knew this film well and used one of its major scenes, the mob convention, in his comedy *Some Like It Hot* (1960).

11. As Jan van den Berg claims, the *Mona Lisa* is the first pictorial portrait figure "who is estranged from her landscape," thus pointing to a self-enclosed interiority or the birth of the self. *The Changing Nature of Man* (New York: Norton, 1961), 231.

12. Slavoj Žižek, *Trouble in Paradise: From the End of History to the End of Capitalism* (London: Allan Lane, 2014), 44.

13. See Jean-Louis Baudry, "The Ideological Effects of the Basic Cinematographic Apparatus," in *Critical Visions in Film Theory*, ed. Timothy Corrigan, Patricia White, and Peta Mazaj (Boston: Bedford/St. Martin's, 2011), 34–45. The cinematic apparatus, Baudry claims, "constitutes 'the subject' by the illusory delimitation of a central location— whether this be that of a god or of any other substitute" (43). In spite of Baudry's acute dissection of the transcendental subject generated by cinema, he does not see race, such as whiteness, as one of its main predicates or main ideological illusions.

14. Paul Schrader, "Notes on Film Noir," *Film Comment* 8, no. 1 (Spring 1972), 8–13, 12.

15. Walter Benjamin identifies cinema as the major apparatus that produces the loss of the human aura: "The actor performs . . . for two pieces of equipment . . . his body has lost its substance . . . his voice . . . turned into a mute image that flickers on the screen" (239). "The Work of Art in the Age of Technological Reproducibility," in Corrigan, White, and Mazaj, *Critical Visions in Film Theory*, 230–252.

16. Manthia Diawara, "Noir by Noirs: Toward a New Realism in Black Cinema," in *Shades of Noir*, ed. Joan Copjec (London: Verso, 1993), 261–278, 263.

17. bell hooks, "The Oppositional Gaze: Black Female Spectators," in *Feminist Film Theory: A Reader*, ed. Sue Thornman (New York: New York University Press, 1999), 307–320, 308.

18. Richard Dyer, *White* (London: Routledge, 1997), 140, 134.

19. Dyer, *White*, 135.

20. See Delia Malia Konzett, "Classical Hollywood, Race and Casablanca," in *Critical Insights: Casablanca*, ed. James Plath (Ipswich, MA: Salem Press, 2016), 97–113. This essay gives an extensive account of Curtiz's engagement with minstrelsy and blackface performance in his films.

21. *After the War: Blacks and the GI Bill*, an exhibit from the Smithsonian Art Museum (Washington, DC), provides the following historical information: "The GI Bill, or the Servicemen's Readjustment Act of 1944, sought to provide returning service members with many benefits. Among these benefits were low-cost mortgages, high school or vocational education, payments for tuition and living expenses for those electing to attend college, and low-interest loans for entrepreneurial veterans wanting to start a business. . . . Though the law was deemed a political and economic success, there was one segment of veterans who were denied many of the bill's benefits—African Americans."

22. See the work of Michael Civille, who discusses the ending of the film as a compromise of the historical demands of the 1950s with its progressive social consciousness movement and its regressive Cold War paranoia, undermining such liberal efforts. "'Ain't Got No Chance': The Case of *The Breaking Point*," *Cinema Journal* 56, no. 1 (Fall 2016): 1–22.

23. Sigmund Freud, "On Narcissism: An Introduction," in *The Freud Reader*, ed. Peter Gay (New York: Norton, 1989), 545–562, 555.

PART 3 # RACE AND ETHNICITY IN POST–WORLD WAR II HOLLYWOOD

9 · WOMEN AND CLASS MOBILITY IN CLASSICAL HOLLYWOOD'S IMMIGRANT DRAMAS

CHRIS CAGLE

In an early scene in the 1945 film *A Tree Grows in Brooklyn* (dir. Elia Kazan), the Nolan family is sitting in the living room of their Williamsburg, Brooklyn, apartment. As the son Neeley (Ted Donaldson) argues with his sister and mother about the worth of reading Shakespeare, his grandmother Rommely (Ferike Boros) interjects and extols the virtues of education:

> This reading will not stop. I see it this way. To this new land, your grandfather and I came, very long ago now, because we heard that here is something very good . . . but we could not find this thing. For a long time I could not understand. And then, I know. . . . In that old country, a child can rise no higher than his father's state. But here, in this place, each one is free to go as far as he's good to make of himself. This way, the child can be better than the parent. And this is the true way things grow better. And this has to do something with the learning, which is here free to all people. I who am old missed these things. My children missed these things, but my children's children shall not miss it.

What Grandmother Rommely is articulating is an ideal and an ideology of class mobility and implicit assimilation for the immigrant to the United States. The original dialogue from the 1943 novel is condensed into a monologue for the screenplay and thereby carries additional thematic weight for the film, with the character expressing a similar sentiment in the source novel.

While the ideal of class mobility has been persistent through much of U.S. history, the monologue in *A Tree Grows in Brooklyn* also speaks to a specific moment in the history of immigration. Post–World War II historian Oscar Handlin posits several competing conceptualizations of Americanization: the melting pot, cultural pluralism, and assimilation.[1] In practice, these intersected in complex ways, as they do in immigrant dramas from the 1940s and early 1950s. Films like *A Tree Grows in Brooklyn, I Remember Mama* (dir. George Stevens, 1948), and *The Lawless* (dir. Joseph Losey, 1950) made the challenges facing the immigrant the primary narrative focus. Each invoked at least the potential for assimilation, and each invoked the possibility of class mobility while depicting the economic hardships facing recent immigrants. Films about immigrants had been a staple of 1920s and 1930s Hollywood, but these mid-twentieth-century films are remarkably forthright in their thematic exploration of immigrant life and culture. In another context, Michael Ryan and Douglas Kellner use the term "class transcendence" to describe films of 1970s and 1980s Hollywood featuring working-class characters who overcome obstacles of a rigid economic and cultural stratification in order to rise into the middle class.[2] Class transcendence refers to the idea of class mobility and at the same time the inhabiting of an identity in which the putative class divisions do not matter. As such the term is useful for the earlier immigrant dramas of the 1940s and 1950s, which depict a middle-class second- or third-generation immigrant identity different from the working-class milieu of more recent immigrants.

However, these dramas deserve closer attention. While on the surface they may seem to endorse an ideology of class transcendence, they are not individualist in their view but collectivist. Their narratives serve as an allegory for immigrants at a historical juncture in which European immigrants were gaining cultural acceptance and political power while those from Latin America and Asia still faced marginalization. The two more nostalgic films, *A Tree Grows in Brooklyn* and *I Remember Mama*, are both set at the turn of the twentieth century, notably before the U.S. restrictions on immigration, especially the Immigration Acts of 1920s. *The Lawless*, with its contemporary setting, references the racial politics of the postwar United States. Each approach comments on the midcentury politics of ethnicity and immigration. Moreover, women are the main immigrant protagonists in each, and the films offer a gendered and classed understanding of ethnic and racial identity. Read side by side, the films provide a valuable case study in how overlapping lenses of interpretation (class, race, ethnicity, and gender) open up these films to a more complex view, and one more attendant to their historical context.

THE POLITICS OF NOSTALGIA

The immigrant dramas were not the only films to show nostalgia for a previous era. In the 1940s, Hollywood films showed a great nostalgia for the decades around the turn of the century: *Lillian Russell* (dir. Irving Cummings, 1940), *Meet Me in St. Louis* (dir. Vincente Minnelli, 1944), *Life with Father* (dir. Michael Curtiz, 1947), and *The Late George Apley* (dir. Joseph Mankiewicz, 1947) are just a few examples. The immigrant dramas offered two important variations to the episodic narratives popular among the nostalgic 1940s films. First, they were more specific about the economic hardships of their working-class characters, in contrast to the more prevalent middle-class settings of other nostalgic films. Second, they dramatize the tensions of assimilation for the immigrant, and the compromises that economic success brings. *A Tree Grows in Brooklyn* and *I Remember Mama* have many similarities. They are based on best-selling novels, they focus on the coming of age of young women who become writers, and they combine elements of realism and melodrama. Each uses nostalgia to broach a historical memory that is political as much as individual.

The opening of *A Tree Grows in Brooklyn* immediately signals the film's nostalgic tone. Over a pan shot of a period street scene in Brooklyn, the superimposed title reads, "For childhood, Saturday—free from school—is the most changeless of institutions—whether it is in city or village, or main street, or in those vital, teeming streets which were the Brooklyn of a few decades ago." While the opening words capture the spirit of the novel's opening chapter, they imply a more universal address in which Brooklyn is merely one instance of a general childhood experience. *A Tree Grows in Brooklyn* is the coming-of-age story of Francie Nolan (Peggy Ann Garner), who later (the film implies) becomes an author as an adult. Whereas in the novel the father

Johnny is a second-generation Irish American and Katie an Austrian American, the film makes Katie's character (played by Dorothy McGuire) ambiguous in her ethnicity. The episodic narrative creates the vantage of an adult looking back on her childhood, and looking back historically as well. By the end of the film, after Francie and Neeley get a new sister, Francie says dreamily, "Anna Lorie McShane. She'll never have the hard times we had." Neeley replies, "Or the fun either." Like many nostalgic narratives, *A Tree Grows in Brooklyn* suggests that the earlier period—in this case the years before the Great Depression and World War II—was a simpler time, but it also laments the loss of ethnic identity in the face of assimilation into a general middle class.

Similarly, *I Remember Mama* is an episodic narrative of the Hansons, a Norwegian American family in San Francisco at the turn of the twentieth century. Told in flashback, the story is the retrospective memory of the daughter Katrin, whose first winning short story doubles as the film's voiceover narration. Katrin is in her attic room working on her story. As a camera tracks in to her reflection in the mirror, the story's muttered words become her monologue, spoken aloud: "But first and foremost, I remember Mama. I remember every Saturday night I would sit at my desk by the attic window, writing down in my diary all my innermost thoughts. Mama would call up to me from the bottom of the stairs." As Katrin narrates her memory, a special effects process shot changes the mirror image to the flashback image as Katrin leaves her desk and starts down the stairs to join her family by the kitchen table. This opening literalizes the retrospective glance: older Katrin is looking at younger Katrin, Katrin the literature writer is looking at Katrin the solitary diarist (see Figure 9.1). Allegorically, the spectator of 1948 is looking at the immigrant character of the 1910s.

Like *A Tree Grows in Brooklyn*, *I Remember Mama* dramatizes the tensions of assimilation. Marta, or Mama, rebukes her sister who makes reference to Marta's Norwegianness. "You talk as if San Francisco is the world," the sister says. "It is my world," Marta replies. Her attitude carries to raising her children, and she emphasizes education and the gaining of English-language cultural capital. The character of their boarder, Mr. Hyde, emblematizes this craving for Americanization through adoption of its culture. As with Brooklyn's Nolan family, the Hansons gather around as Mr. Hyde reads canonical literature. In a montage of short vignettes, Katrin's voiceover describes how enraptured she was by the books, how important literature was, how those evenings kept Nels out of trouble, and how the books inspired her to become

FIGURE 9.1 Katrin (Barbara Bel Geddes), the literary writer is looking at herself, the solitary diarist in *I Remember Mama* (1948).

a writer. The sequence ends as Katrin recounts how her teacher disliked her short story: "she said it wasn't nice to write that way about one's own family."

This sequence shows how *I Remember Mama* invokes class transcendence yet also something else. The Hansons become both American and middle class through the adoption of a middlebrow "great books" literary canon, which can lead Nels away from juvenile delinquency and Katrin toward the future of a prestigious career. On surface, this would seem a typical fantasy of class mobility. Nonetheless, the class dynamics here are complex. Mr. Hyde has more cultural capital than actual money and is shown to be a fake who cannot pay the rent. The comic/serious tone of the family's reaction shots sends up the middlebrow affectation of the great books sensibility at the same time as it endorses it. Finally, Katrin's teacher misapprehends literature as merely something uplifting. Rather than presenting one class template, the film is pitched to a range of class positions for viewers.

Despite the seeming reactionary quality of these films' nostalgia, they address a 1940s viewer who understands the difference between then and now as a political as well as personal change. The strongest resonance is that each film is set in a time before the congressional laws of 1921, 1924, and 1929 imposed quotas on immigration. This triumph of nativist politics drastically curtailed immigration from Europe. As historian David Roediger notes, during the first decade of the twentieth century, the time period in which *I Remember Mama* and *A Tree Grows in Brooklyn* are set, nine million people immigrated from Europe to the United States. From 1921 to 1940, fewer than three million did.[3] Nativist political forces won the political war that had waged in the first two decades of the century, but the immigrants contributed to a seismic shift in American politics since they were central to the Democratic Party coalition from Al Smith's failed presidential bid through the New Deal and postwar liberalism. The late 1940s represented a broad defeat of nativist politics and the incorporation of white immigrants into a solid pillar of a post–New Deal Democratic coalition.

Neither *A Tree Grows in Brooklyn* nor *I Remember Mama* explicitly references these political shifts, but both are dramas that illustrate the hazards of the pre-welfare-state United States. The dual main conflicts of *A Tree Grows in Brooklyn* revolve around money. Johnny, because of his alcoholism and happy-go-lucky temperament, is unable to keep steady employment, so Katie must be the steady wage earner and household manager for the Nolans. Her hardened, practical nature leads to conflict with the daughter Francie, who favors her father's good nature and idealism. The film's exposition establishes the thematic preoccupation with money and security in economic fashion. While the canonical three-act structure of screenwriting manuals introduces a protagonist's internal and external conflict within the first act, *A Tree Grows in Brooklyn* has a less rigid approach. It sets up the conflict that remains implicit but has not yet fully developed:

Scene 1: Francie and Neeley go rag picking and decide how to spend their earnings

Scene 2: Katie's work is interrupted by a visit from the insurance collector

Scene 3: Following her mother's instructions, Francie negotiates with the butcher for the best cut of meat for the price

Scene 4: Francie checks out books from the library and receives reading advice from the librarian

Scene 5: Johnny returns home with the first hint of his ongoing alcoholism and discussion of the backyard tree

Very quickly, the screenplay establishes two economic conflicts. The first is between saving and consumption for the working-class immigrant. The by-the-bootstraps ideal of class mobility is often premised on the ability of the immigrant to save, but the film shows the choice to save to be one of deprivation. The thematic opposition of dreaming/practicality that Johnnie and Katie represents—"a tree never put any money in the bank," Katie says in response to Johnny's fondness of the titular tree—captures the consumption/savings dilemma.

I Remember Mama is rife with similar moments of pathos. The film also shows Mama's accounting as what provides (or denies) a winter coat or the cost of school. Throughout the film, Katrin pines for a dresser set and Marta gives it to her as a graduation present. However, Katrin learns that her mother had to sell a family heirloom brooch to afford the set and is distraught at her own selfishness and naïveté. The dresser set serves as an object of emotional pathos, the gap between want and have, daughter and mother, and childhood and adulthood. Moreover, it emblematizes the conflict between respect for heritage versus a modernizing and assimilating consumer culture.

Meanwhile, there is a second thematic conflict in both films, between an economic system in which risk falls to individual families and one in which economic risk is collective. Katie must give birth at home because she lacks the money for a hospital birth or a midwife. Similarly, *I Remember Mama* features a pivotal hospital scene as the family awaits news on whether Dagmar will live. Literary historian Michael Szalay reads the novel of *Tree Grows in Brooklyn* as a commentary on risk culture in the context of the New Deal, which adopted political measures to mitigate the risks of age, sickness, and unemployment. "Insurance is an absolute necessity for the Nolans, even though the family barely manages to provide for basic necessities," he notes, adding, "The insurance that the Nolans contribute to is markedly pre–New Deal." In contrast to a collective sharing of risk, this pre–New Deal insurance is a familial economic hedge against the death of the husband.[4] The film downplays some of the novel's emphasis on insurance, but some of this focus remains, and there are reminders of the historical improvement of working-class economic stability. In *I Remember Mama* the central conceit of Mama going to the bank is powerful because ultimately there is no bank, no institution of security. Marta explains her lie: "It's not good for little ones to feel afraid, to not feel secure." The historical memory of bank runs of the Great

Depression (a mere decade and a half before the film's release) looms in the background of the dialogue.

As with *I Remember Mama*'s maternal figure, but even more starkly so, circumstances force Katie to take on the role of an economic manager that must guide her family through the precariousness of working-class life and set up the possibility of class mobility for her children. *A Tree Grows in Brooklyn* emphasizes that a mother of the immigrant working-class family often does not have the middle-class luxury of inhabiting the ideal of true womanhood. In the labor scene, Katie's internal conflict comes to a head with a pained monologue in which she recognizes that the economic necessity of parenthood has precluded her from inhabiting the emotionally nurturing role she desperately wanted to have. Both *Tree Grows in Brooklyn* and *I Remember Mama* combine melodrama with elements of the realist drama. Here, Leon Shamroy's spotlight-heavy approach to lighting the set, Elia Kazan's long-take emphasis on blocking, and the overall lack of musical scoring all work against the stylistic excess commonly associated with melodrama. These very elements draw a parallel between Katie and Francie, whom the film has also presented in similar spot-lit compositions. The cinematography highlights a view of immigrant life as the familial bond, often fraught, between women.

Both films revolve around their women characters and are maternal melodramas, but with a difference. They are stories told by daughters about their mothers. Unlike canonical maternal melodramas like *Stella Dallas* (dir. King Vidor, 1937), the film makes a protagonist out of both daughter and mother, both of whom have central emotional conflicts, at times parallel, at times complementary. In each narrative, the young women realize the sacrifices of their working-class mothers and in the process of gaining this knowledge, grow up. The maternal melodrama thereby transposes onto a bildungsroman narrative. The films exhibit a realist sensibility means by playing against the grain of heightened dramatic conflict, with minimal scoring. The sentimental and nostalgic nature of the films means that they may not initially seem to be a productive model of political reflection. Indeed, Joanna Rapf reads *I Remember Mama*'s nostalgia as a projection of "less complicated past" for postwar audiences.[5] However, as with *Tree Grows in Brooklyn*, the film's middlebrow form encourages a different alignment with the women characters, one that productively orients the spectator to see women's experience as a crucial driver for a collective and political immigrant identity. In this historical context, nostalgia could be a critical reflection on the history of immigration at a moment in which white European immigrant communities had gained overdue integration into the national political body.

BEYOND THE EUROPEAN IMMIGRANT

European ethnic groups formed an important part of the New Deal and postwar Democratic Party coalitions. By the 1970s, however, not only did this coalition start to fray, but white ethnic groups increasingly aligned with conservatism and against civil rights. This rupture highlighted the long-standing political conflict between white immigrants and people of color, especially African Americans. As David Roediger and Noel Ignatiev have demonstrated, only gradually did an idea of ethnicity come to describe immigrants who had previously not been seen universally as white. As part of this process, European immigrant groups took on the mantle of whiteness, including discriminatory participation in important economic areas like housing and trade unionism.[6] Roediger usefully offers dual axes of understanding for the relation of immigrant ethnic identity and race in the twentieth century. Writing on Oscar Handlin, Roediger notes, "As a member of the first generation of influential non-Anglo-Saxon Protestant historians, Handlin was delivering an arresting manifesto . . . that he could change America's story because he had lived through the increased acceptance of southern and eastern Europeans in national life."[7] However, Roediger argues, the civil rights movement and more recent immigration show up the limitations of Handlin's historiography and by implication the political moment of immigrant integration.

The larger political construction of an ethnic identity as whiteness informs the cinematic depictions of ethnic identity. Reacting to the conservative versions of ethnic representation, Ella Shohat takes aim at a static ideal of ethnic identity in cinema history: "In this sense the adjective *ethnic* implies a liberal-pluralistic vision which masks the contradictions of class, race, and gender, as well as the interdependency of histories and even identities."[8] Instead, Shohat proposes that scholars forgo content-oriented readings of ethnic representations in favor of what she calls ethnicities in relation. This approach charts "not simply the relationship between a marginalized group and the 'center' . . . but also the relationship among the various on the periphery and their (potentially) dialogical interlocution with regard to the center of power."[9] Shohat's essay continues to serve as a useful touchstone for intersectional critique of classical Hollywood in proposing a model of multiple, simultaneous power vectors.

As the above analysis of *A Tree Grows* and *I Remember Mama* suggests, ethnic narratives in cinema could embrace contradictions of gender and class, but they elided rather than engaged the racial politics of the period. By looking back nostalgically to the turn of the century, they leave out African Americans' Great Migration from the historical view of the American city. Shohat's ethnicities-in-relation model points to the value of a comparative cross-genre approach. While the prestige immigrant dramas left out people of color and even the idea of race, social problem films depicted immigration politics as a matter of contemporary concern, not nostalgic retrospection.

Social problem films offer narratives of characters who face social injustices and often who crusade against them. Generally didactic in tone, they marshal both narrative form and cinematic style to position the viewer in indictment against the social problem. The variant of the *film gris* was particularly important for offering a politically engaged view of working-class immigrants. First coined as a term by Thom Andersen, the film gris is a hybrid of the film noir crime film and the social problem drama. The subgenre is set in a working-class milieu and uses individuals fighting larger forces to allegorize social structures.[10] *The Lawless* (dir. Joseph Losey, 1950), a drama about anti-Chicano discrimination in a small California town (a fictional Santa Marta) exemplifies film gris at its most explicitly political. The narrative alternates between primary and secondary protagonists: Larry Wilder (Macdonald Carey), a newspaper editor who has moved to Santa Marta to experience small-town life; Sunny Garcia (Gail Russell), who runs a Spanish-language newspaper, *La Luz*; and two young Chicano men, Paul Rodriguez (Lalo Rios) and Lopo Chavez (Maurice Jara), who face hostility from the Anglo teenagers in town. As tension between the Chicano and Anglo men escalates, Paul finds himself caught up in a spiral of accident and misunderstanding and is on the run from law enforcement. Anglo sentiment turns sour and soon the townspeople are trying to lynch Paul.

The Lawless had two immediate political contexts. First, a cycle of postwar social films about racism—including *Gentleman's Agreement* (dir. Elia Kazan, 1947), *Pinky* (dir. Elia Kazan, 1949), *Intruder in the Dust* (dir. Clarence

Brown, 1949) and *No Way Out* (dir. Joseph Mankiewicz, 1950)—were generally economically successful and prestigious. These were made at a time in which elite opinion, spurred by the publication of the sociological study *An American Dilemma* (Gunnar Myrdal et al., 1944) as well as the ideological impact of World War II, was beginning to see Jim Crow segregation as one of the central political problems facing the United States.[11] *The Lawless* was a small independent production, with a Paramount distribution deal in a period in which studios were distributing independent films as an alternative to in-house B-film productions.[12] It therefore had a lower profile than better-budgeted studio productions. Despite or because of this, its antiracist tone is starker than some other films. Ellen Scott notes, "In the mid-1940s, as the number of lynchings decreased, lynching's iconography importance for the depiction of racial problems heightened."[13] Scott points out that *The Lawless* was one of the films to depict lynching without transposing the narrative to one with a white victim. Whether the anti-Chicano sentiment is understood as ethnic or racial prejudice, *The Lawless* reflects the politics of post-1920s immigration, when U.S. immigrants were increasingly likely to come from somewhere besides Europe. Moreover, it does so in a way that connects this reality to African American civil rights politics.

At the same time, *The Lawless* was one of the films director Joseph Losey made before being blacklisted in the anticommunist wave fostered by the House Un-American Activities Committee (HUAC) in the late 1940s. The film depicts a stark class divide, literalized by the river and dividing the middle-class section of the town from the Sleepy Hollow neighborhood of largely Chicano farmworkers. Some of the dialogue implies a class solidarity. The opening dialogue, for instance, starts with a conversation between Paul and Lopo after a day of work: "There must be an easier way to make a living" / "Yeah, for Anglos." Two Anglo farm workers cross in the left of the frame, and Lopo adds, "Some of them don't do so good either." The film's racial politics made the Production Code Administration nervous about the rhetorical fodder for communist criticisms of the United States.[14]

Beyond the more immediate politics of the film, *The Lawless* offers a media critique. A year before Billy Wilder's *Ace in the Hole*, the film offers a jaundiced depiction of how a news story develops, often spinning out in vicious circle between oversimplifying journalists and an overly credulous public. The newspaperman Jonas Creel (Herbert Anderson) serves as a foil to his

FIGURE 9.2 Townspeople watching the news of Rodriguez's (Lalo Rios) arrest in *The Lawless* (1950).

editor Larry Wilder, more cynical and careerist in his outlook. In addition to writing for Santa Marta's *The Union,* he also sells stories to a bigger city newspaper. His report begins the sensationalism that will move the narrative along: "We got a riot down here," he intones at the first news of a fight at a Sleepy Hollow dance. A television news crew arrives in Santa Marta, and their presence dives much of the conflict, from the broadcast. The cut to a tracking shot into close-up of the arrested Paul Rodriguez to a long shot of townspeople watching his image on a television screen serves as a reminder that the action subplot of the film is always mediated through the news media (see Figure 9.2). In contrast, Larry and Sunny represent two positive models for the journalist: *The Union* is the elite broadsheet that has a professionalized but conscientious journalistic identity; *La Luz* represents the voice of the community and fits Antonio Gramsci's model of the organic intellectual.[15] *The Union*'s office, not Paul, is ultimately the target of Santa Marta's lynch mob. The lawlessness of the film's title is an attack on the democratic press and the values it represents.

The Lawless is more than a film about journalism, though. It seeks to question the way that racial and ethnic labels create their own reality. On seeing the news of Paul's arrest, his employer yells, "I always said he was no good. None of them are any good." Sociologists would soon develop "labeling theory" to describe how the categories of criminality applied to young people become a self-fulfilling prophesy.[16] *The Lawless* serves as an early, pop-culture version of labeling theory, adding an understanding of the racialized dimensions of labeling. Sunny introduces this motif early on when she challenges Larry on his appearance at the community dance. Asking him why he came, she wonders, "It wouldn't be because you expect something to happen, would it?" Having come in order to report any fights, Larry replies, disingenuously, "Now, why would expect that?" Sunny answers in a resigned way, "Because a lot of people do." Later, she expands on her explanation, "People were saying that we were all juvenile delinquents." Larry adopts some of her perspectives; when the television reporter asks him about the riot, Larry demurs, saying, "Let's call it a fight between a bunch of hotheaded kids." The film presents its media critique as a racialized one.

In other regards, the film is less radical. Even though *The Lawless* opens up its narrative structure to multiple protagonists, even starting with Paul's story, Larry, the Anglo male protagonist, is the only one who undergoes a major change or experiences much internal conflict. He comes to resolve this conflict in part because of his romantic interest in Sunny. Sunny herself is a strong character in many respects; a competent and independent journalist, she is also able to see through Larry's foibles. Her character makes a useful comparison to the literary protagonists of *A Tree Grows in Brooklyn* and *I Remember Mama*. Rather than an author poised between high- and middlebrow culture, she is an educated writer who lacks the prestige of Larry's character but not his journalistic ability. However, like many romantic interests in Hollywood films, Sunny arguably serves as a foil to Larry's crisis of conscience. The film only occasionally considers her subjectivity or background. She articulates the discourse of class uplift for the Chicano community, but her own identity reads as a classless cipher. Whereas the prestige immigrant dramas show how class inflects gender, *The Lawless* is more straightforward and conventional in its depiction of gendered romance. Finally, Gail Russell's brownface turn undercuts the film's use of lesser known Chicano actors for other characters.

For some time, readings of immigration in classical Hollywood have been relegated to a subfield niche, which like regional cinema studies often specializes in "images of" readings of immigrant or ethnic groups on film. The anti-immigrant policies of the 2010s in the United States and elsewhere have brought into relief the historical echoes of earlier immigrant film dramas, whether of European or Latin American immigrants, and have given renewed urgency for revisiting the representational politics of immigration in midcentury America. For this reason, Ella Shohat's ethnicities-in-relation model is so useful and her reduction of an ethnic-American identity to a liberal-pluralistic ideology (a negative one in her view) is so challenging. From the vantage of an increasingly anti-immigrant age, the pluralistic vision Shohat attacks can be useful and compatible with a more intersectional understanding of cinematic representation. There is an understandable impulse to view 1940s and early 1950s Hollywood as retrograde, but despite these films' limitations, they also offer insights into the historical experience of immigrants and the political framing by which we come to understand social class.

Depictions of white immigrants pervaded Hollywood films in the classical period, but by the late 1940s the nature of the immigrant representation in dramas changed for reasons having to do both with the changes in the prestige film and with changes in the larger politics of immigration. The immigrant dramas do not map neatly onto what we might consider a progressive politics. However, properly situating them in the discourse and politics of the 1940s opens them up to a political complexity and possibility that was always there but has been often overlooked. A comparative analysis can contrast the prestige nostalgic genres to more explicitly political social problem films in order to highlight that the ethnic or immigrant experience is not merely a white European one. Conversely, those problem films with avowed left politics complicate the viewer's understanding of some social categories while reinforcing others. If nostalgic dramas like *A Tree Grows in Brooklyn* and *I Remember Mama* focus on women characters who inhabit two stages of class mobility, *The Lawless* offers a more radical view of Latina identity as a classed one; in doing so, it presents class stasis as a political critique of economic oppression.

Each model has positive potential and political limitations. Mobility narratives were a means of figuring progressive politics even as they reinforced American exceptionalism. Stasis narratives critiqued both racial and class inequalities while romanticizing the working class as a static foil to the middle class. Undeniably Hollywood was constrained by racist representational codes that were both self-imposed and reinforced by external ideologies. Moreover, the overall temptation looking back on the postwar years is to read film representations of women as a direct path toward domestic containment, of the sort represented by the 1950s television situation comedy.[17] However, the ideological tensions in the films point to the imaginative possibilities of a period that is too easily caricatured. Ultimately, the dilemmas that women characters navigate in these films are a means by which viewers can locate themselves in objective power struggles.

NOTES

1. Oscar Handlin, *Immigration as a Factor in American History* (Englewood Cliffs, NJ: Prentice Hall, 1959), 146–147.

2. Michael Ryan and Douglas Kellner, *Camera Politica: The Politics and Ideology of Contemporary Hollywood Film* (Bloomington: Indiana University Press, 1990), 110–111.

3. David R. Roediger, *Working toward Whiteness: How America's Immigrants Became White* (New York: Basic Books, 2005), 145–146.

4. Michael Szalay, *New Deal Modernism: American Literature and the Invention of the Welfare State* (Durham, NC: Duke University Press, 2000), 163.

5. Joanna Rapf, "1948: Movies and the Family," in *American Cinema of the 1940s: Themes and Variations*, ed. Wheeler Winston Dixon (New Brunswick, NJ: Rutgers University Press, 2006), 200–221, 215.

6. Roediger, *Working toward Whiteness*, esp. chaps. 6 and 7; Noel Ignatiev, *How the Irish Became White* (New York: Routledge, 1995), 2–3.

7. Roediger, *Working toward Whiteness*, 9.

8. Ella Shohat, "Ethnicities-in-Relation: Toward a Multicultural Reading of American Cinema," in *Unspeakable Images: Ethnicity and the American Cinema*, ed. Lester D. Friedman (Urbana: University of Illinois Press, 1991), 215–250, 216.

9. Shohat, "Ethnicities-in-Relation," 217.

10. Thom Andersen, "Red Hollywood," in *Literature and the Visual Arts in Contemporary Society*, ed. Suzanne Ferguson and Barbara Groseclose (Columbus: Ohio State University Press, 1985), 141–196. See also Charles J. Maland, "*Film Gris*: Crime, Critique, and Cold War Culture in 1951," *Film Criticism* 23 (Spring 2002): 1–26.

11. Gunnar Myrdal, with Richard Sterner and Arnold Rose, *An American Dilemma: The Negro Problem and Modern Democracy* (New York: Harper & Row, 1944); for the impact on elite opinion, see David Southern, *Gunnar Myrdal and Black-White Relations: The Use and Abuse of an American Dilemma, 1944–1969* (Baton Rouge: Louisiana State University Press, 1987).

12. For the change in studios' relation to the B market, see Thomas Schatz, *Boom and Bust: The American Cinema in the 1940s*, vol. 6, *History of the American Cinema* (Berkeley: University of California Press, 1997), 341–347.

13. Ellen C. Scott, *Cinema Civil Rights: Regulation, Repression, and Race in the Classical Hollywood Era* (New Brunswick, NJ: Rutgers University Press, 2015), 59.

14. Scott, *Cinema Civil Rights.*, 59.

15. Antonio Gramsci, *Selections from the Prison Notebooks*, ed. and trans. Quintin Hoare and Geoffrey Nowell Smith (New York: International, 1971), 5–6.

16. Howard Becker, *Outsiders: Studies in the Sociology of Deviance* (London: Free Press of Glencoe, 1963).

17. See Nina Leibman, *Living Room Lectures: The Fifties Family in Film and Television* (Austin: University of Texas Press, 1995).

10 · HAWAI'I STATEHOOD, INDIGENEITY, AND *GO FOR BROKE!* (1951)

DEAN ITSUJI SARANILLIO

> The Japanese American soldiers became part of a grand story, nearly biblical in form, whose premise is that all events in U.S. history have been steps on the road to the realization of a glorious end that was in fact already foretold at the nation's beginning.... All the past is then made to contribute to the grand narrative in such a way that every moment between the beginning and the end, including anomalies such as institutional racism, can be reinscribed as minor aberrations on the path to the promised land. The problem with this narrative, of course, is that realization of the promise may be forever deferred or shifted onto different groups.
>
> —Takashi Fujitani, "*Go for Broke!*, the Movie"[1]

One of the biggest obstacles facing statehood proponents during Hawai'i's territorial period (1900–1959) was that Hawai'i contained a large population of Japanese Americans who were construed by American Orientalism as inscrutable foreign threats. Indeed, in the decades leading to World War II, and punctuated by the December 7 attack in 1941, U.S. nationalism was formed by what Moon-Kie Jung terms an "anti-Japanese Americanism."[2] Japanese Americans who were linked to a belligerent Japanese empire seizing resources and territories throughout Asia were racialized differently from other nonwhite groups in Hawai'i. Jung explains, "Anti-Japanese racism was not based on an assured belief that the Japanese were inferior but on a fear that they were *not*."[3] At the onset of the war, Japanese American men were designated 4C "enemy aliens," a classification that not only made these U.S. citizens ineligible for the draft but also cast further suspicion upon their loyalty to the United States.

Current memories of the postwar period in Hawai'i, however, are dominated by the heroics of the Japanese American soldiers in the 442nd Regiment and 100th Battalion, narrated as not just fighting valiantly in World War II but returning to defeat the last vestiges of *haole* (white) racism in Hawai'i. By tracing two mutually constitutive but colliding projects in the post–World War II period—namely the state-led project for Hawai'i statehood that required challenging the perception of Japanese Americans as "aliens ineligible for citizenship," and another project that sought to challenge the idea of *Kānaka 'Ōiwi* (Native Hawaiians) as "unfit for self-government"—we can see how U.S. Empire targeted these dissimilar groups for different ends. Such disparate representations play out intersectionally and relationally in the film *Go for Broke!*, which helped facilitate Hawai'i's admission as a U.S. state. I begin by tracing the shift from Japanese Americans as "Japs," killable populations who were obstacles to statehood, to "Japanese Americans" who became symbols of an antiracist America that embraced statehood for Hawai'i. The 1951 MGM propaganda film *Go for Broke!*, featuring the Japanese American 442nd Regimental Combat Team, stages a production of official antiracism. In it we can see the changing relations between haole and Japanese Americans, but also an attempt to reconcile two formidable empires, the United States and Japan. I juxtapose such projects with the cultural politics of Alice Kamokilaikawai Campbell, arguing that she protested statehood and effectively stalled its passage for decades by strategically playing to the racism of Congress. Kamokila, as she was publicly known, further pushed and investigated other options for Kānaka and Hawai'i besides statehood, particularly in a moment when elites aimed to deliberately contain Hawai'i's political status to statehood.

After World War II, Japan was pacified as a nonthreat and perceived as a new economic ally of the United States. Consequently, key opportunities to transform prevailing perceptions of Japanese Americans as "enemy aliens" soon appeared. Indeed, while the large Japanese population in Hawai'i provided a reason for the congressional committee in 1937, for instance, to recommend against statehood for Hawai'i, by the end of World War II the loyal military sacrifice of Japanese Americans during the war had become vital to a movement for statehood. Japanese American veterans returning from war emerged as a political vehicle for both statehood and land development.

Statehood proponents highlighted Japanese American loyalty by point-ing to the military heroism and massive casualties sustained by the 100th Infantry Battalion and 442nd Regimental Combat Team. Nicknamed the "Purple Heart Battalion," the 100th Battalion and 442 Regimental Com-bat Team received more than 18,143 decorations but also suffered an unusu-ally high number of casualties and injuries at 9,486. Indeed, the high casualty rates show how officers of the U.S. Army viewed Japanese American soldiers as expendable; even the soldiers themselves believed they were ordered on what they called "suicide missions."[4] The cultural work to convince an Amer-ican public of the trustworthiness of Japanese Americans was already done for statehood proponents by the U.S. military.

Historian Tom Coffman explains that while Japanese American soldiers faced discrimination in the military, they were key to winning the "hearts and minds" of Japan and Asia.[5] Edwin O. Reischauer, the principal architect of postwar U.S. relations with Japan (and eventual ambassador to Japan under John F. Kennedy), argued in 1942 that the internment of Japanese Americans had "unwittingly contributed" to Japanese propaganda. Such propaganda stated that Japan was fighting a war to stop the United States from spreading white supremacist domination throughout Asia. Reischauer wrote, "We should reverse this situation and make of these American citizens a major asset in our ideological war in Asia. Their sincere and enthusiastic support of the United States at this time would be the best possible proof that this is not a racial war to preserve white supremacy in Asia, but a war to estab-lish a better world order for all, regardless of race."[6] As a result of President Truman's decision to use atomic bombs against Japan, coupled with the United States' later military occupation of the country, Reischauer high-lighted the need to celebrate with vigor the wartime heroics of Japanese American veterans.

The MGM film *Go for Broke!* played one such role in combating the idea that Japanese Americans were foreign threats to be permanently excluded from the U.S. national polity. The film first screened at the national Capitol on May 24, 1951. The *New York Times* heralded the film as an expression and demonstration of Japanese American humanity: "Without fuss or feathers

FIGURE 10.1 Actual members of the Japanese American 442nd Infantry Regiment (Lane Nakano, right; Akira Fukanago, left) starring alongside Van Johnson in *Go for Broke!* (1951).

or an over-expense of preachy words, is aptly revealed and demonstrated the loyalty and courage of a racial minority group, along with the normal human qualities of decency and humor inherent in these men."[7] *Go for Broke!* challenged sentiments from around the world that the United States remained a white supremacist nation that restrained the civil rights of Japanese Americans. The film was written and directed by Academy Award–winning Robert Pirosh, who also earned an Oscar nomination for the screenplay. The protagonist Lieutenant Michael Grayson was played by Van Johnson, who had also starred in Pirosh's Academy Award–winning film *Battleground* (1949), celebrated for depicting soldiers as vulnerable and imperfect. The cast of *Go for Broke!* included actual veterans from the 442nd Regiment, notably Lane Nakano, George Miki, Akira Fukunaga, Ken Okamoto, Henry Oyasato, and Henry Hamada (see Figure 10.1). Blurring the lines between performance and historical reenactments, the casting of actual nisei (second-generation) veterans aimed to convey legitimacy, as their embodied presence verified the information expressed in the film as being both trustworthy and authentic. The Publicity Department of MGM explained, "It was their own personal story, a story, with apologies to General Stillwell, they wrote in Italy and France 'with their blood.'"[8] Major General F. L. Parks, the father of modern army public affairs, offered an official approval from the Department of the

Army. *Go for Broke!* screened nationally and internationally in parts of Europe and Asia, but most prominently it screened in Japan on December 7, 1952, the eleventh anniversary of Japan's attack on Pearl Harbor.

In the film, the heroism and valor of Japanese American soldiers, especially their unwavering loyalty and military sacrifice to the American nation, are deployed to rid the newly commissioned second lieutenant Michael Grayson of his bigoted views of Japanese Americans. From the start of the film, anti-Japanese racism is addressed through a series of pedagogical lessons on liberal racial tolerance. The film begins with a superimposed text of President Franklin Roosevelt's words over footage of the marching nisei soldiers: "The proposal of the War Department to organize a combat team consisting of loyal American citizens of Japanese descent has my approval. The principle on which this country was founded and by which it has always been governed is that Americanism is a matter of the mind and heart; Americanism is not, and never was, a matter of race or ancestry." The idea that "Americanism" is a question not of race but of "heart" provides a sentimental and overly generous view of U.S. race relations. This myopic view frames the rest of the film. Tellingly, while the film relies on the valor of the nisei—superimposed on the same scene described above is a table of their battle record: "7 Major Campaigns in Europe; 9,486 Casualties; 18,143 Individual Decorations; 7 Presidential Unit Citations"—there are many instances where the film's noble narrative of Japanese American sacrificial death serves as a backdrop for centering white life.

The issue of white racial tolerance and the project of subduing white anxiety around blurred racial lines are the focus of much of the film. In the service of teaching white Americans how to think differently about Japanese Americans, Lieutenant Michael Grayson takes center stage. Upon arrival at Camp Shelby in Mississippi, a Japanese American soldier drives a visibly disturbed Lieutenant Grayson through the camp. The script describes Grayson's discomfort with what he sees: "The distasteful expression on his rugged, handsome features leaves no doubt as to what *he* thinks of American citizens of Japanese descent. Grayson throws a glance at the jeep driver, then shifts his angular, six-foot frame to get as much space between them as possible."[9] Accordingly, the camera offers the perspective of what Grayson sees from the jeep, providing the audience with a scene where a white racial order is flipped on its head. Grayson is offended to see an American military camp overrun by Japanese, where Japanese American soldiers doing a roll call respond to their "Oriental" names being called: "Kawaguchi!" "Tsukimura!" Grayson is even more bothered by what the script describes as a "Hawaiian war chant" where so-called "Kanakas" from Hawai'i, played by Japanese actors, perform what appears to be hula, which is as contrived as the song they are dancing to. Such displays of white discomfort with "Oriental" foreignness sets the stage for Grayson to be reformed.

In the next sequence, Grayson meets with the sergeant major and immediately asks to be transferred back to the U.S. 36th Infantry, his previous Texas National Guard unit. When asked if his request isn't due to the Japanese American troops, Grayson responds, "Because they're Japs? No, sir, it isn't that at all."[10] The film then moves into its first of many disciplinary lectures on the use of the term "Japs": "They're not 'Japs,' they're Japanese-Americans—Nisei—or, as they call themselves, boodaheads [*sic*]. All kinds of boodaheads, Lieutenant. From Hawaii, Alaska, California, New York, Colorado—yes, and some from Texas. They're all American citizens and they're all volunteers. Remember that. And another thing. We officers are referred to as 'haoles'—not white men. Any questions?"

Grayson is uncomfortable because he is outnumbered by Japanese Americans and is racialized as "haole." Indeed, the older white officers at Camp Shelby, ranked higher in the white hetero-patriarchal order, lecture Grayson on his racism, demonstrating America's new inclusive position on Japanese Americans. While possessing the necessary qualities of a military officer—white, tall, blonde, and Texan—Grayson is infantilized as a newly commissioned officer. As such, his racism becomes evidence of his lack of maturity, where his superior officers consider racial tolerance of Japanese Americans necessary for masculine and democratic leadership. Such lessons of official antiracism, however, function to maintain the established hierarchy that includes senior white leadership over junior white leadership over subordinate nonwhite (Japanese American) soldiers. The take-home point for movie goers is that the inclusion of Japanese Americans can be tolerated so long as they play the role of subordinates.

In order to portray the United States as a nation founded on democratic ideals, not white supremacy, the film needed to provide sufficient reasons for why the United States interned 120,000 Japanese Americans into concentration camps. Grayson broaches the topic when he asks the captain if they use live ammunition at the rifle range, stating that all he knew was that the Japanese were placed in "relocation centers" and maybe "the army just had some surplus barbed wire they wanted to use, was that it?"[11] The captain admonishes Lieutenant Grayson by offering another forced lesson in racial tolerance: "The army was facing an emergency at the start of the war—a possible invasion by Japanese troops. So all Japanese-Americans on the West Coast were evacuated as a precautionary measure. There was no loyalty check—no screening—nothing. If there were any spies among them, I can assure you they're not in the four-four-two. Every man in the outfit has been investigated, reinvestigated and re-reinvestigated. (rising) I suggest you start getting acquainted."[12] Upon learning that he will be in charge of an all-Japanese American unit, Grayson takes his frustrations out on his platoon by maintaining strict regulations and orders. The film, and the intensity of the drama, proceeds in a series of juxtapositions of scenes featuring private conversations among the white officers and private conversations of the Japanese American soldiers. In one scene, a soldier named Sam played by Lane Nakano, who was actually interned with his family at the Heart Mountain Internment Camp, prepares a care package of canned goods. Sam explains to fellow soldier Tommy (Henry Nakamura) that the package isn't being sent to his brother who is serving in the 100th Battalion, but rather to Arizona, where his family is interned in conditions worse than Camp Shelby. Tommy asks Sam why he would volunteer to fight, given the poor treatment of his family. Sam explains that the purpose of fighting is to end discrimination against Japanese Americans. Tommy, whose family were killed in Hawai'i during the Japanese attack on Pearl Harbor, responds in pidgin: "We show 'em! We show 'em us boodaheads good soldiers, good Americans!" Sam responds, "All we need now is the casualty lists."[13]

Go for Broke! offers space for a critical assessment of the coercive forms of assimilation seemingly required to end the unfair treatment of Japanese Americans. In the transition from "Japs" to "Japanese Americans" lies a delicate play on necropolitics and biopolitics. The term "Jap" was used in wartime propaganda as a quick way to determine that a person was killable: "Let's blast the Jap clean off the map." Or magazine magnate Henry Luce's observation, "Americans had to learn how to hate Germans, but hating Japs comes natural—as natural as fighting Indians once was."[14] The transition from "Jap" to "Japanese American," an approximate relation to whiteness, still necessitated a sacrifice of "Jap" death. A kind of logic of resurrection occurs in the film, reflecting a theological dimension to settler sovereignty.[15] To end discrimination for being a sinful "Jap," one needs to be reborn as a "Japanese

American," which requires one's seeming racial sin to be sacrificed on the altar of American war.

After fighting alongside the 442nd in Italy and France, Grayson comes to respect his fellow soldiers. In a pivotal scene, which sets up the climactic rescue of the Texas Battalion by the nisei soldiers, Grayson stands up for his Japanese American regiment in the presence of his unreformed, racist friend, named Culley, who is also from the Texas Battalion. While drinking at a bar, Grayson explains that the 442nd would be the Texas Battalion's artillery, and the ensuing dialogue between Grayson and Culley provides yet another pedagogical moment for reforming prevailing social conflations of Japanese Americans with enemy "Japs":

CULLEY: They're sending us up without our own artillery? Just the Japs?
GRAYSON: They're a good outfit, Culley. Plenty good.
CULLEY: Practically winning the war single-handed, what I hear. (contemptuously) Japs!
Embarrassed as some of the Japanese American soldiers overhear their conversation, Grayson asks Culley to step outside.
GRAYSON: They're not Japs, Culley.
CULLEY: What?
GRAYSON: They're Japanese-Americans—nisei—or, if you prefer, boodaheads. But not Japs. They don't like it and neither do I.
CULLEY: What are you, a Jap-lover or something?
GRAYSON: I said, they're not Japs. I'm warning you, Culley—

Grayson proceeds to scuffle with Culley, who eventually comes to change his views of Japanese American soldiers, but only after they rescue the Texas Battalion. Popularly referred to as the "Lost Battalion," the 100th Battalion and 442nd Regiment suffered 800 casualties to save 211 of the Texan soldiers.[16] Forty years later, Daniel Inouye, one of the most famous and powerful senators on Capitol Hill personally tied to the military buildup of Hawai'i, would state forcefully, "I am absolutely certain that all of us were well aware that we were being used for the rescue because we were expendable."[17]

While Japanese Americans are shown to have the ability to be included in American culture, Japanese culture is shown to be of particular value to the United States. For example, a Japanese American soldier nicknamed Chick (played by George Miki) constantly complains about racism and the conditions of the camp. Chick explains that while most others were enlisted from internment camps, prior to the war he was in Iowa getting paid five hundred dollars a month to determine the sex of chickens. He exhorts, "Chick-sexing is a science. It was developed in Japan and it's one place a boodahead gets a break."[18] In another moment concerning "dirty tactics" hand-to-hand combat, Grayson has his sergeant, a Japanese American, in a hold from which he says there is no escape. But the sergeant suddenly flips Grayson with a judo maneuver. The idea of combining Japanese knowledge with American know-how provided the cultural groundwork for integrating Japanese American soldiers into the army.

This project of inclusion is also about integrating Asia into American political and economic hegemony at the outset of the Cold War. As Takashi Fujitani succinctly argues, "*Go For Broke* was part of a new pattern of representations and discourses in which values considered to be traditional in Asian societies were celebrated as conducive to Americanism."[19] The cultural fluidity with which Japanese Americans could be both Japanese and American also justified the disproportionate number of casualties the nisei suffered. Japan's soldiers were racialized in popular culture as "kamikaze" pilots, posing a luminous foreign threat because they were obedient to the point of death. In the context of war, the motto "go for broke," a Hawaiian reference to gambling until one loses everything, but popularized nationally by the film, continues to essentialize Japanese Americans in self-sacrificial obedience to the U.S. nation. This characterization of Japanese American soldiers as willing to "go for broke" helped to justify the disproportionately large casualty rates of Japanese American soldiers. In a scene where the exhausted soldiers are sent to rescue the Texas Regiment, Tommy and Sam speak of the need to change the attitudes of white Americans like Lieutenant Grayson toward Japanese Americans. Facing possible death, Tommy tries to encourage a disheartened Sam, "It's rough—it's plenty rough—but we know what's it all about. You bet. More bettuh we 'go for broke,' eh, Sam?" Sam eventually responds with a smile saying, "That's about it, Tommy. More bettuh we 'go for broke!'" Soon after, a shell explodes near two other soldiers, injuring one and killing the other.

Though white racism is often the brunt of many of the jokes, the film actually pivots around a fragile and delicate white masculinity that continually requires reassurance. Japanese Americans are shot in the film in ways that highlight both their sacrificial deaths and their short physical statures. These shots render them unthreatening to the white hetero-patriarchal order. In one particular montage, the soldiers are shown training for combat by running through an obstacle course, but they are unable to leap over trenches or climb a wooden wall. Their inability to perform what "normal" soldiers are routinely able to do is a symbolic form of emasculation. The racial order of the United States would symbolically become more inclusive as a multicultural nation, yet still preserve components of white supremacy. In this way, an official anti-racism also served as a developmental discourse. The camaraderie between Lieutenant Grayson and the nisei soldiers reflected a newfound prosperity that could be enjoyed with the joint efforts of Japan and the United States. This new coalition of white American and Japanese American men in the film also reflected a new possibility that Japanese American men could work alongside whites.

While Japanese American military sacrifice helped to mend U.S. relations with Japan, therefore facilitating the opening of Asian markets to American businesses, in Hawai'i it also assisted both a movement for statehood and Japanese American ascendancy. Matsuo Takabuki, 442nd veteran, major player in land development, and a once controversial trustee of the Kamehameha School Bishop Estate, recalls that their celebrated record on the battlefield "pushed" them "to the forefront of the statehood effort."[20] In his memoirs, Takabuki writes that John A. Burns told Japanese American veterans, "Do not be ashamed of who you are. Talk about your war record. . . . You have proven that you are Americans. You earned this honor under fire. Flaunt it."[21] Indeed, the Hawaii Statehood Commission would highlight the military achievements of the nisei in much of its literature.[22]

Armed with their G.I. Bills, many nisei veterans left Hawai'i to attain professional and law degrees, which upon their return bolstered the social, economic, and political power of the Japanese American community. John A. Burns helped to reorganize the Democratic Party by drawing heavily from the popularity of the Japanese American veterans, many of whom became hugely successful in political office. Some notable examples include the aforementioned Daniel Inouye and George Ariyoshi, who would become the first Japanese American governor of the state. With other elected officials like Daniel Aoki, Sakae Takahashi, and Matsuo Takabuki, they worked together with Burns to revitalize the Democratic Party in a concerted effort to unseat the Republican Party and its Big Five power base at the legislature. The Big Five were five interlocking corporations—Castle and Cooke, Charles Brewer and Company, Alexander and Baldwin, Theophilus H. Davis and Company, and Heinrich Hackfeld and Company (renamed the American Factors during World War I)—that would control nearly 95 percent of the total sugar production and dominate the surrounding industries such as banking, insurance, shipping, utilities, and retailing.

With the ideological support of returning veterans and the political support of the International Longshore and Warehouse Union (ILWU), the Democrats were able to accomplish in 1954 what is often referred to as the "Democratic Revolution," wherein political control of the legislature shifted from the Republicans to the new Democratic Party.[23] Takabuki explains, however, that the liberal Burns Faction, from its inception, was not interested in disrupting the economic power of the Big Five: "We saw the potential growth of tourism as an industry, with new and different players. We realized the Big Five were important players in Hawai'i's economy, and we did not want to destroy them. However, we did not want them to continue to dominate and be the only game in town. Tourism would open all kinds of economic avenues for the future, providing opportunities for the upcoming generation of those outside the existing economic oligarchy."[24] This new political force sought a passive revolution; they were not seeking to fundamentally reorder social relations so much as they sought to be accommodated within the economic system of the Big Five. Takabuki writes that prior to the "Democratic Revolution," returning veterans participated in creating a "financial revolution."[25]

After the attack on Pearl Harbor, many white businessmen left Hawai'i fearing further military attack and martial law. This led to an economic vacuum in which many Japanese American and Chinese American entrepreneurs were able to capitalize on abandoned businesses and wide-open markets. According to Takabuki,

The Fukunagas of Servco started a small garage in Haleiwa, which grew into a large conglomerate of auto and durable goods dealerships, discount stores, and financial institutions. The Fujieki family started a small family market that grew into the Star Supermarket chain. The Teruyas' small restaurant and market in the 1950s and 1960s eventually became Times Supermarket. Chinn Ho started Capital Investment. K.J. Luke and Clarence Ching created Loyalty Enterprises, while Aloha Airlines began with Ruddy Tongg. As the number of local professionals, lawyers, and doctors grew in postwar Hawai'i, the economic, professional, and political landscape also changed rapidly.[26]

Takabuki explains further that the major banks in Hawaiʻi, the Bank of Hawaiʻi and Bishop Bank (now First Hawaiian Bank), would not regularly offer business loans to anyone outside of the white economic circle. This led veterans Daniel Inouye and Sakae Takahashi to open two banks: Central Pacific Bank (CPB) and, later, the City Bank of Honolulu.[27] With financial and administrative support from major banking institutions in Japan, many in the Democratic Party ventured into major residential and tourist-related real estate development projects, as tourism displaced agriculture as the dominant industry in the 1950s and 1960s.

Major land development projects, particularly in hotels and shopping centers, were slowed down, however, because of a fear or lack of confidence by stateside lenders and investors in Hawaiʻi's territorial economy. This motivated many Japanese in Hawaiʻi to push for statehood, alongside those on the other end of the political spectrum who were a part of or associated with the Big Five. This emerging historical bloc would not go unchallenged by others. During the war and after it, Kamokila Campbell emerged as a leading opponent of statehood, publicly opposing this new historical bloc while fighting for other forms of self-governance for Kānaka ʻŌiwi.

In January 1946, the first congressional hearings on statehood since 1937 were held at ʻIolani Palace. Aware that Kamokila's testimony would be one of the few in opposition to statehood, the Hawaii Equal Rights Commission attempted to squeeze her into an afternoon with other witnesses. Stating that she needed more time for her graphs and charts to be prepared, she skillfully maneuvered the committee to allow her to speak on the last day, specifically January 17, 1946.[28] Aware that this date was the fifty-third anniversary of the 1893 U.S. military-backed overthrow of the Hawaiian Kingdom, Kamokila used this historic date to articulate the national dispossession of the Hawaiian people with the state-led drive for statehood.

While historians have highlighted her 1946 testimony to point out the existence of Hawaiian opposition to statehood, Kamokila's testimony was more tactical and historically precise. She charged the Big Five with orchestrating the statehood movement to expand their economic interests in tourism by attracting "outside capital and independent financial giants."[29] Striking at the heart of the avaricious desires sustaining a movement for statehood, Kamokila declared, "I do not feel . . . that we should forfeit the traditional rights and privileges of the natives of our islands for a mere thimbleful of votes in Congress, that we, the lovers of Hawaii from long association with it, should sacrifice our birthright for the greed of alien desires to remain on our shores, that we should satisfy the thirst for power and control of some inflated industrialists and politicians."[30] As a member of the political and economic elite, Kamokila knew that the Big Five desired statehood to gain access to investment money for tourism, and thus had been controlling public funds to finance a protracted opinion campaign for such private purposes. Kamokila also called attention to the links between Big Five economic domination and the fear and silence that many harbored in opposing statehood. She shared an example of one such sentiment, sent to her in private, that implored her to speak on behalf of those who could not: "We can't, Kamokila. My husband would lose his job." Those present at the hearings, however, were able express their sentiments collectively in the thunderous cheers and applause following Kamokila's comments in a packed throne room with over six hundred people in attendance. In one instance, large applause broke out after Kamokila's response to Representative Angell's question of why statehood would not be able to address the problems she cited in the territorial structure. Kamokila responded with a thinly veiled reference to the 1893 overthrow: "Who is it that has put us in the position we are today but the people who are asking you for statehood?" When asked by the congressmen what kind of government she would want instead of statehood, Kamokila responded, "an independent form of government," explaining that if others wanted to live in a U.S. state, they could simply move to any of the forty-eight states in the U.S. nation.

It is within this shifting political landscape of being squeezed between haole conservatives and Japanese American liberals that Kamokila found herself leveraging what political will she could against statehood. In her 1946 testimony, in just one example, Kamokila criticized the numerical dominance of Japanese Americans in racist terms, implying that Japanese Americans aided the attack on Pearl Harbor. She further argued that Japanese Americans moving from the plantations to small businesses could cause the Japanese to "get a hold on the islands." Kamokila's statements played to congressmen who viewed Hawai'i as unworthy of statehood because it was a largely "Asiatic" population. She thus reinforced the racist exclusion that Japanese in Hawai'i had long sought to counter. Kamokila had been arguing all along that statehood, especially as it was backed by a push for Japanese American ascendancy, was a continuation of Big Five hegemony. Her anti-Japanese statements can be read against the backdrop of the widespread circulation of heroic narratives about Japanese American loyalty during and soon after World War II. In combating the notion that Kānaka ʻŌiwi were destined to disappear and thus be replaced, she heightened fears that Japanese Americans were foreign threats "ineligible to citizenship." In hoping to prevent the latest elaboration of U.S. occupation through the vehicle of statehood, however, Kamokila appealed to a long and well-established fear among many white Americans that Japanese Americans were perpetual foreign threats; such appeals would work against her aims. In both instances, combating one's form of oppression by appealing to structures of white supremacy, either aiming to stall statehood by reinforcing the Japanese as ineligible to citizenship or fighting for statehood while casting Hawaiians as unfit for self-government, pits both marginalized groups against each other.

Speaking against both the moneyed interests of the Big Five and the ability of the numerical dominance of the Japanese in Hawaiʻi to politically marginalize Kānaka ʻŌiwi, her testimony received media coverage and editorial responses, mostly negative, for more than a month. Kamokila's testimony was printed in the *Honolulu Advertiser* the next morning, and criticism of her was published in both the *Advertiser* and the *Star-Bulletin*.[31] Lorrin P. Thurston was among the first to launch a public critique, desperately relying on sexist and racist portrayals of Kamokila's mind to prevent her arguments from gaining momentum. He wrote in his newspaper that while her testimony was "undoubtedly the high spot of the entire hearings," her logics were confused. Thurston portrayed her as lacking consistency in her loyalty to a political party or stances on statehood and said that what she lacked logically was "made up for by her utter sincerity."[32] Thurston reduced Kamokila's views to little more than emotion and sentiment, figuring her as someone who lacked the white masculine rationale to be logical and discerning. Most responses, however, criticized her for challenging Japanese American loyalty. One editorial asked, "So she thinks the AJAS [Americans of Japanese Ancestry] have received too much publicity? Well, I think they rate it. They paid for it with blood—how does she pay for her publicity? Sooner or later it should dawn on her that people are getting fed up with her line."[33] Another argued that her comments set race relations back fifty years.[34] One day after Kamokila's testimony, the *Hawaii Herald*, previously *Hawaii Hochi*, responded with an editorial titled "Kamokila Is Right!" arguing that "for the very reason that Senator Campbell deplores this undue publicity given to what she terms the AJAS, so, we believe, Japanese-Americans deplore it."[35] Stating that this publicity was initiated by army generals, not the Japanese themselves, the *Hawaii Herald* aimed to point out that the publicity was an attempt to protect Japanese Americans who had been interned in concentration camps on the U.S. continent as they reentered violently racist areas of the United States.

A few days after her 1946 testimony, Kamokila told the press that she had been asked to launch an island-wide petition to oppose statehood. This was similar to what her mother, Abigail Kuaihelani Maipinepine Campbell, had helped accomplish with the 1897 Kū'ē petitions to oppose U.S. annexation. In response, the *Maui News* published an editorial titled "Kamokila in Die Hard Fight Against Hawaii," and a few days later warned readers to "Beware of What You Sign."[36] This petition, however, did not circulate because of the risk that it could provide the Big Five with a list of names that could be immediately used to "blacklist" signers. In September 1947, however, Kamokila continued her opposition to statehood by opening an "Anti-Statehood Clearing House."[37] Designed to be a counter to the Hawaii Statehood Commission, the clearinghouse was used to collect testimony in opposition to statehood and to lobby congressional senators against statehood. Using her contacts in Washington, DC, she would send "anti-statehood information, reports and arguments to congress."[38]

On January 17, 1948, Kamokila Campbell filed a lawsuit, *Campbell v. Stainback et al.*, which challenged the legality of the financing of the Hawaii Statehood Commission. This lawsuit was timed to coincide with both the fifty-fifth anniversary of the overthrow of the Hawaiian nation and Oregon senator Guy Cordon's impromptu visit to investigate statehood.[39] In the lawsuit, Kamokila charged that the $200,000 (provided by Act 115, which established the Statehood Commission) used by the territorial government to campaign for statehood nationally and locally were "to the exclusion and detriment of citizens and taxpayers opposed to statehood."[40] Her suit targeted especially the commission's publicity campaign on three main points: "(1) A national or sectional advertising and publicity campaign is not a valid public purpose for which public funds may be expended; (2) lobbying in Washington, D.C., is not a valid public purpose for which public funds may be expended; (3) the grant of unlimited discretion to an administrative agency in the expenditure of public funds constitutes an invalid delegation of power by the legislature."[41]

In seeking to place a temporary restraining order on the governor, members of the Statehood Commission, and territorial officials before the court hearing, Kamokila hoped to stop them from spending any more taxpayer money on gaining public opinion for statehood. Circuit Court Judge Wilson C. Moore denied her request, choosing instead to withhold any action until he decided whether the financing of the Statehood Commission was unconstitutional.[42] Attorney General Walter D. Ackerman Jr. would file a demurrer against Kamokila's case. One month later, Kamokila's lawsuit was thrown out of Circuit Court by Judge Moore, who declared, "Regardless of what we think as individuals, we must bow to the will of the majority. The last plebiscite showed more than two to one in favor of statehood and the territory, as an integral part of the United States, is in its democratic realm. The basis on which we operate this government is on the will of the people."[43] But the 1940 plebiscite was "deliberately imprecise," and even the Hawaii Equal Rights Commission determined that statehood was still a debatable issue.

Kamokila appealed this ruling, and the Hawaiʻi Supreme Court returned a unanimous decision in her favor. In March 1949, Justice E. C. Peters ordered an injunction against the Statehood Commission that prohibited the use of public monies for said purposes. Justice Peters wrote, "The appellees justify the expenditure of public moneys for publicity purposes . . . upon the ground that the purposes thereof subserve the public welfare, are for a ʻpublic purpose' and hence a rightful subject of legislation. With this we cannot agree."[44] In essence, the High Court rejected the Statehood Commission's arguments, ruling instead that using taxpayer money to sway public opinion did not serve the "public" good, but instead constituted actions "purely political" in nature.

Though the court found that the territory could not "petition the public" to shape public opinion in favor of statehood, it did not, more fundamentally, go so far as to declare the commission invalid, and in fact left room for "reasonable" expenditures for the Statehood Commission to promote statehood. In this regard, the court too was prejudiced against any status other than statehood (or the status quo). This prejudicial view is best captured in the court's opinion that Hawaiʻi's territorial status was temporary and transitional, with the inevitable end goal being statehood. According to the Supreme Court, the territorial government was created specifically to promote "welfare, peace, happiness and prosperity," and thus opined that to "accelerate the evolutionary process of the political transition from a Territory to a State abstractly accomplishes the same result. Reasonable men cannot differ upon the political advantages resulting from statehood over and above those inherent in a Territory of the United States."[45]

In 1953, Kamokila wrote a letter to Congress, arguing that of the $475,000 that had been appropriated for a government-led statehood campaign since 1947, no money had been apportioned to opponents of statehood. Kamokila argued, "So much has been said and published favoring Statehood for Hawaii that it is only fair that the opposition be heard. Unfortunately, equal treatment under law is denied the opponents of Statehood."[46] By then, Kamokila had begun to campaign for commonwealth status and admitted that while the majority of people in Hawaiʻi were in favor of statehood, it was the only option being discussed and the general public "never had the opportunity of studying its merits to demerits."[47] She argued that if those in Hawaiʻi were given a choice between commonwealth status and statehood, she was confident the majority would choose the former, "provided a reasonable time were given for them to receive adequate information concerning Commonwealth Status which thus far has been suppressed."[48] Her letter to Congress in 1953 also shows how her strategies to oppose statehood had changed. Now, instead of arguing against the Japanese, she had begun to highlight two different threats: one, that statehood for Hawaiʻi would set a precedent for other U.S. territories to gain it as well; and two, that communism in the form of the ILWU, which by the mid-1930s was supporting statehood and was allied with the Democratic Party, had "crippled industry" and would pose a serious threat to the U.S. continent. By the 1950s, then, Kamokila was playing to new congressional fears of communism and the Red Scare to defeat statehood.

The state, animated by profit motives, created the conditions for an official antiracism to facilitate forms of settler colonialism under the name of statehood. Japanese Americans and their supporters challenged the view that they were perpetual foreign threats through cultural narratives of civil rights that anchored the Hawaiʻi statehood campaign. This campaign was forged deeply by the histories of Japanese American persecution and later desires to capitalize on land developments in the postwar period. These cultural narratives, however, render invisible their role in maintaining and renewing hegemonic forms of settler colonialism and occupation. At the same time, Kamokila's racist remarks should be neither justified nor taken as an invalidation of her aims to seek justice for Kānaka ʻŌiwi for the overthrow of the Hawaiian nation. In juxtaposing the politics underpinning public relations campaigns featuring *Go for Broke!* with that of Kamokila Campbell's anticolonial moves to block statehood, one can see how selected narrations of Japanese American loyal military service were set to public memory through global circulation, entertainment, and publicity, while anticolonial narratives opposing Hawaiʻi's occupation by the United States were designated for historical deletion.

NOTES

1. Takashi Fujitani, "*Go for Broke!*, the Movie: Japanese American Soldiers in U.S. National, Military, and Racial Discourses," in *Perilous Memories: The Asia-Pacific War(s)*, ed. Takashi Fujitani, Geoffrey M. White, and Lisa Yoneyama (Durham, NC: Duke University Press, 2001), 239–266, 252.

2. Moon-Kie Jung, *Reworking Race: The Making of Hawaii's Interracial Labor Movement* (New York: Columbia University Press, 2006), 98–105, 82.

3. Jung, *Reworking Race*, 82.

4. Roland Kotani, *The Japanese in Hawaii: A Century of Struggle* (Honolulu: Hawaii Hochi, 1985), 115.

5. Tom Coffman, *The Island Edge of America: A Political History of Hawaiʻi* (Honolulu: University of Hawaiʻi Press, 2003), 84–87.

6. As cited in Coffman, *Island Edge of America*, 84–87.

7. Bosley Crowther, "The Screen in Review; 'Go for Broke!,' Tribute to War Record of Nisei Regiment, Opens at the Capitol," *New York Times*, May 25, 1951.

8. Metro-Goldwyn-Mayer Publicity Department, "Facts for Editorial Reference about the Filming of M-G-M's *Go for Broke!*," University of Hawaiʻi Hamilton Library, 1.

9. Robert Pirosh, *Go for Broke!*, script, University of Hawaiʻi Hamilton Library, 2.

10. Pirosh, *Go for Broke!*, 6.

11. Pirosh, *Go for Broke!*, 7.

12. Pirosh, *Go for Broke!*, 7.

13. Pirosh, *Go for Broke!*, 13.

14. Jodi Kim, *Ends of Empire: Asian American Critique and the Cold War* (Minneapolis: University of Minnesota Press), 101.

15. For a discussion on the "theological dimension of political sovereignty," see Wendy Brown, *Walled States, Waning Sovereignty* (New York: Zone Books, 2010), 132.

16. Kotani, *Japanese in Hawaii*, 115.

17. Kotani, *Japanese in Hawaii*, 115.

18. Pirosh, *Go for Broke!*, 11.

19. Fujitani, "*Go for Broke!*, the Movie," 252.

20. Hawaii Statehood Commission, *Hawaii, U.S.A., and Statehood: History, Premises and Essential Facts of the Statehood Movement* (Honolulu: Hawaii Statehood Commission, 1948), 58–59; see also Hawaii Statehood Commission, *Hawaii and Statehood* (Honolulu: Hawaii Statehood Commission, 1951).

21. Matsuo Takabuki, *An Unlikely Revolutionary: Matsuo Takabuki and the Making of Modern Hawaiʻi* (Honolulu: University of Hawaiʻi Press, 1998), 70.

22. Hawaii Statehood Commission, *Hawaii, U.S.A., and Statehood*, 58–59; Hawaii Statehood Commission, *Hawaii and Statehood*.

23. Coffman, *Island Edge of America*, 148–153.

24. Takabuki, *Unlikely Revolutionary*, 64.

25. Takabuki, *Unlikely Revolutionary*, 79.

26. Takabuki, *Unlikely Revolutionary*, 65.

27. Takabuki, *Unlikely Revolutionary*, 81.

28. John S. Whitehead, "Anti-Statehood Movement and the Legacy of Alice Kamokila Campbell," *Hawaiian Journal of History* 27 (1993): 49–50.

29. "Text of Kamokila's Testimony: Senator Discusses Objections in Detail; Cites Racial Issues," *Honolulu Advertiser*, January 17, 1946.

30. "Text of Kamokila's Testimony."

31. "Text of Kamokila's Testimony."

32. "Kamokila's Statements before the Subcommittee Statehood Committee," *Honolulu Advertiser*, January 19, 1946.

33. George Rogers, "His Comment on Kamokila Campbell's Attitude," *Honolulu Star-Bulletin*, January 22, 1946.

34. Esther Mitchell, "Editorial: Senator Campbell and Race Relations," *Honolulu Advertiser*, January 23, 1946.

35. "Kamokila Is Right!," *Hawaii Herald*, January 18, 1946.

36. "Kamokila in Die Hard Fight Against Hawaii," *Maui News*, January 23, 1946; "Editorial: Beware of What You Sign," *Maui News*, January 26, 1946.

37. "Anti-Statehood 'Clearing House,'" *Honolulu Star-Bulletin*, September 18, 1947.

38. "Anti-Statehood 'Clearing House.'"

39. "Decision on Statehood Case Fund Reversed," *Honolulu Advertiser*, March 29, 1948.

40. "Public Funds Misused, Says Kamokila," *Honolulu Star-Bulletin*, January 17, 1948.

41. Supreme Court of Hawaii, "Opinion of the Court," *Campbell v. Stainback et al.*, 38 Haw. 310 (1949): 311–312.

42. "Court Denies Campbell Plea on 'State' Fund," *Honolulu Advertiser*, January 24, 1948.

43. "Campbell Suit against Statehood Fund Dismissed," *Honolulu Advertiser*, February 4, 1948.

44. *Campbell v. Stainback et al.*, 38 Haw. 310 (1949): 315.

45. *Campbell v. Stainback*, 321.

46. Hawaii Statehood Commission, Honolulu Office General Records, Tavares, NC—Campbell, Kamokila, 1953, Hawaii State Archives.

47. Hawaii Statehood Commission, Honolulu Office General Records, Tavares, NC—Campbell, Kamokila, 1953, Hawaii State Archives.

48. Hawaii Statehood Commission, Honolulu Office General Records, Tavares, NC—Campbell, Kamokila, 1953, Hawaii State Archives.

11 · SAVAGE WHITENESS

The Dialectic of Racial Desire in *The Young Savages* (1961)

GRAHAM CASSANO

For sociologist Patricia Hill Collins, any adequate interrogation of social domination learns from the outsider within. Like Frantz Fanon, Collins argues that disenfranchisement and repression potentially create an oppositional consciousness with the capacity to challenge mainstream, taken-for-granted fact.[1] Thus, the perspective of the outsider-within challenges modes of domination. However, Collins does not spend much time with the uncomfortable possibility that the Other within may also be the product of unconscious forces of domination and hegemony. Systems of domination intersect in a variety of ways. At times, this intersection allows for the emergence of a critical consciousness. At other moments, related axes of inequality (race, gender, class, sexuality) reinforce one another and occlude consciousness.

Between 1886 and 1925, thirteen million new immigrants came to the United States from Southern, Central, and Eastern Europe.[2] On the one hand, many of these new immigrants were recognized as legally "white," in the sense that they were considered fit for naturalization, unlike immigrants from Asia or Africa.[3] On the other, many were considered unfit for whiteness by custom, nativist prejudice, anti-Catholicism, and anti-Semitism. According to

David Roediger, these "in-between-peoples" evaded the hard color line that confronted black Americans, First Peoples, and Asian immigrants but did not necessarily find full acceptance within the normatively white community.[4] By the mid-twentieth century, racial boundaries had shifted. Italian Americans, Jewish Americans, Bohemian, Russian, and Czech Americans became "ethnic" whites. At the same time, assimilation to whiteness had a price. These new immigrant groups were pressured to accept the demands of white supremacy, and to identify with anti-black, anti-Asian, anti-Latina/o prejudices. Too often, they repressed their own ethnic identity and desired the trappings of what they imagined was the fully "white" lifestyle. Cinema dramatized this play of racial desire. In films such as *Swing Time* (1936) and *Fort Apache* (1948), immigrants find a home in the United States once they accept white supremacy and valorize white racial identity.[5]

Racial transformation requires a kind of socially constructed amnesia. As families cross into whiteness, they actively forget their prior racial status. This essay examines the traces left once such a racial trans-substantiation has taken place. John Frankenheimer's first major film, *The Young Savages* (1961), reconstructs Hank Bell's (Burt Lancaster) repressed transformation from Italian racial other into a white ethnic. In doing so, the film approaches the possibility that race itself may be a kind of social construction and explores the meaning of race in an overtly psychoanalytic language. In fact, *The Young Savages* echoes the argument of Jacques Lacan's nearly contemporaneous essay, "The Subversion of the Subject and the Dialectic of Desire in the Freudian Unconscious."[6] Lacan's paper, first delivered in 1960, and Frankenheimer's film argue that normatively socialized subjects must sacrifice an essential part of themselves in order to achieve social recognition. In Lacan's language, every subject is castrated and because of that mutilation, every subject desires completion through a symbolic phallus that itself represents an allegory of social norms. To accept castration is to live under the dominion of the Law. Hank Bell enters into this dialectic of desire and discovers his own lack (the history of his repressed racial identity) as well as his desire for the phallus (whiteness). In short, the film allows for an understanding of Lacan's dialectic as the unfolding of normative white supremacy, and Lacan allows for an understanding of the film as a dialectic of desire.

At the same time, both Lacan's essay and *The Young Savages* share the same fundamental aporia. For Lacan, the phallus is not a penis but a structural position; nonetheless, rather than renaming the phallus as male domination,

Lacan leaves the phallic language in place, and the so-called castration complex unquestioned. Even as Lacan opens a path to the interrogation of masculine domination, he essentializes patriarchal language, and paradoxically takes refuge in a developmental argument to ground the significance of the phallus as symbol. *The Young Savages* questions the concept of whiteness, recognizes race as a social construction, but pulls back from that recognition and ultimately leaves the normative racial order intact. I argue that Lacan's insistence on phallic language represents an anxious evasion of the work of Simone de Beauvoir, but also, less obviously, of Frantz Fanon. Lacan's reification of the phallus represented his anxious turn away from the possibility that revolution could overturn the Law. In the same manner, *The Young Savages* represents the Puerto Rican community as a reproduction of the Southern and Eastern Europeans arriving between 1890 and 1924, while also acknowledging the color line that keeps Puerto Ricans from full citizenship. Like Lacan's essay, the film avoids anxiety-provoking questions about race in America by turning itself into a valorization of the very whiteness it questions.

Why is the phallus the necessary emblem of the Law? Lacan could have argued that in a society dominated by men and by patriarchal traditions, mores, and everyday practices, the phallus becomes a metonymic symbol of male power. This was de Beauvoir's argument. But he does not. Indeed, as de Beauvoir says of Freud, Lacan continues to assume what he should explain. His few attempts to justify this symbology on developmental grounds are hardly convincing. In the mirror stage, he argues, the subject is captivated by an imaginary construction that misperceives the reality of the infant's dependence. This *méconnaissance* situates the subject's ego in a perpetually fictional direction. During this process, "the image of the penis . . . [as] negativity in its place in the specular image . . . is what predestines the phallus to embody *jouissance* in the dialectic desire."[7]

In order to understand Lacan's reification of terms like "phallus" and "Name-of-the-Father," consider, again, his attack upon idealism inspired by dialectics. While Lacan may have been sympathetic to certain structuralist variants of Marxism, he seems to suggest that revolution, as the Hegelian contest with the other, represents a Lost Cause: "To whomsoever really wishes to confront this Other, there opens up the way of experiencing not only his demand, but also his will. And then: either to realize oneself as object, to turn oneself into a mummy, as in some Buddhist initiation rites, or to satisfy the will to castration inscribed in the Other, which culminates in the supreme narcissism of the Lost Cause. . . . Castration means that jouissance must be refused, so that it can be reached on the inverted ladder of the Law of desire."[8] Any attempt to confront and overturn phallic law is a "Lost Cause," since in such a confrontation the revolutionary merely plays a part that the other has already written. Lacan naturalized the phallus as a symbol of social power; he naturalized male domination in the form of the Law and the Name-of-the-Father; he did so, even as he had the theoretical tools to explore the social structures of domination that inhabited those words. From a psychoanalytic perspective, it would seem that Lacan pulled away from his own insights, that a certain anxiety provoked his phallic language. While Lacan was threatened by Sartre's existentialism, he was not so threatened as to entirely repress his presence. Sartre is named often as a respondent. On the other hand, it takes some excavation to find de Beauvoir as the object of Lacan's arguments about the symbolic phallus. But the very fact that Lacan never mentions Frantz Fanon, at least nowhere in *Écrits*, suggests a deeper anxiety. I will return to this fear of the wretched of the earth after exploring a parallel argument about desire made in film.

THE YOUNG SAVAGES

First, a synthetic synopsis. *The Young Savages* is a courtroom drama, in the sense that it ends with a climactic courtroom scene. But much of the picture unfolds in poor immigrant neighborhoods, and in spaces reserved for the New York elite (high-rise apartments, well-appointed offices). It begins with the premeditated murder of a blind Puerto Rican teenager by three members of a white ethnic gang, the Thunderbirds. A politically ambitious district attorney assigns Hank Bell (Burt Lancaster) to prosecute first-degree murder charges. As the narrative progresses, a series of subnarratives and flashbacks (from gang leaders, mothers, and neighborhood residents) complicate what appears to be a simple case. The first complication is Bell himself. While he lives in an expensive high-rise apartment and has a seemingly perfect blonde wife and an obedient, poised daughter, the audience learns quickly that he came from Italian Harlem and that his family name was originally Bellini. At the same moment, the film also reveals that one of the

FIGURE 11.1 Assistant district attorney Hank Bell (Burt Lancaster) having to deal with racist ethnic gang violence and his own repressed Italian immigrant roots in *The Young Savages* (1961).

young killers, Danny Dipace, is the son of Mary (Shelley Winters), Hank's old sweetheart from the neighborhood. The reels that follow dramatize Hank's struggle with his conscience, and his wife, Karin (Dina Merrill), as he prepares the case. Throughout the film, when Karin pleads for the boys, Hank dismisses her, referring to her Vassar education ("here we go with the Vassar theories of social oppression"). Yet through Karin's arguments, and through his reconnection with Mary, Hank begins to rediscover his past, or, more correctly, to recognize the way in which his ambitions and success have caused him to repress his past (see Figure 11.1). This return of the repressed leads Hank to a further recognition: he identifies the social construction of whiteness and his marriage to the unambiguously Anglo Karin mediated his racial transformation. This recognition allows Hank to acknowledge his identification with the three murderous boys. Consequently, he intentionally sabotages his case.

At the same time, another parallel narrative explores the perspectives of the gang leaders, the white sociopath, Pretty Boy Savarisi, and the ambitious, charismatic, and intelligent Puerto Rican leader of the Horsemen, Zorro. The representation of Zorro creates central contradictions for the narrative. Unlike

Pretty Boy, Zorro is no sociopath. Indeed, he seems to have a clear understanding of the history of immigrant whiteness in the United States. Moreover, in a pivotal scene where Bell meets Zorro at home, the latter's tenement
rooms have the stereotypical look of Jewish or Italian immigrants photo-
graphed by Jacob Riis, famous for his book *How the Other Half Lives* (1890),
with an old woman in the foreground doing piecework in the central room.
Zorro never demands more than justice, even as he understands that brown
skinned peoples don't receive justice in the United States. Thus the film, while
often told from Hank Bell's point of view, also contains a metanarrative about
immigrants, race, and (in)justice. This metanarrative competes with Hank's
perspective and creates unconscious tensions. Even Bell sees the limitations
in the outcome. When the film ends with the confrontation between the
blind boy's mother and Bell, he responds to her plea for justice by saying, "A
lot of people killed your son, Mrs. Escalante."

Hank Bell's reflection upon his transition into whiteness leads him to identify with those left behind. But it does not cause him to fundamentally question whiteness itself. As I demonstrate below, the film depicts Hank's inclusion
as a member of the white race as a castration in which he sacrifices his potential identification with other, nonwhite, communities, even as he is allowed
to re-create himself through an imagined ethnicity that knits together his past
and present. In this sense, and not in this sense only, *The Young Savages* echoes
the argument Lacan makes in "The Subversion of the Subject." Just as Lacan
remains unwilling to relinquish the language of the castration complex, so
too the film deconstructs the question of race and then anxiously pulls back
from its own knowledge, finally reifying the racial categories it questioned.

RECOGNITION

The subject emerges as a social being through processes of identification and
attachment. Recognition comes into play to the extent that the boy wishes,
through identification, to be recognized as a simulacrum of his father. But
identification transforms the father, idealizing him into a symbol (the Other's desire). The boy desires the father's desire, his father's recognition. In
order to achieve that recognition, he attempts to become what he imagines
father to be. The unconscious understands that this identification is the
equivalent of patricide, and that desiring the mother will invoke the symbolic

father's rage. Thus, the symbolic father, as an ideal, desires to punish the boy. Consequently, the boy, who desires the father's desire, desires his own punishment, and fears the complexity of his desire. Freud names this complexity "ambivalence": "The little boy notices that his father stands in his way with his mother. His identification with his father then takes on a hostile colouring and becomes identical with the wish to replace his father in regard to his mother as well. Identification is, in fact, ambivalent from the very first."[9] The boy's desire for his father's desire mingles with his fear and hatred of the punishing other. And the boy's own love for himself is shaped in part by the stern judgment of this punishing father. The boy hates himself and wishes for punishment, even as he desires love and approbation.

Love and attachment produce identification, which is necessarily ambivalent. The Other is loved, and hated, desired, and feared. Those forces turn inward. The Other becomes the subject's sadistic Master. For Lacan, this Other both inhabits the subject and yet remains perpetually distant and dissatisfied, thus producing the "subjection of the subject to the signifier . . . for lack of an act in which it would find its certainty."[10] Attachment and identification are the forces of socialization. But in identifying with this symbolic father, the subject emerges as a permanent instrument of a cruel Master's desire: "The Other as previous site of the pure subject of the signifier holds the master position. . . . [One] can speak of code only if it is already the code of the Other, and that is something quite different from what is in question in the message, since it is from this code that the subject is constituted, which means that it is from the Other that the subject receives even the message he emits."[11] In a deft intellectual maneuver, Lacan moves from a subject inhabited by an unknowable, sadistic otherness, through the identification with other social subjects as objects of desire, and thus emulation, to the internalization of a normative code that speaks through the subject. Despite Lacan's dislike of Émile Durkheim's ideas, the Master's code reads remarkably like Durkheim's description of social facts:

> When I perform my duties as a brother, a husband, or a citizen . . . I fulfill obligations which are defined in law and custom and which are external to myself and my actions. . . . . The system of signs that I employ to express my thoughts, the monetary system I use to pay my debts, . . . the practices I follow in my profession, etc., all function independently of the use I make of them. . . . Thus

there are ways of acting, thinking and feeling which possess the remarkable property of existing outside the consciousness of the individual.[12]

For Durkheim, as for Lacan after him, the socialized subject is possessed by the discourse of dead others. Language, custom, and norm speak through the self. But for Lacan it is specifically the dead father who speaks.[13] When the subject identifies with an idealized, symbolic father, it reifies that identification into the "Name-of-the-Father," or "the Law."[14] Through identification (specifically with the Name-of-the-Father), the "symbolic dominates the imaginary."[15] This dominance of the symbolic over the real and the imaginary secures its force through the father's reified emblem, the phallus.

Throughout the narrative, the film projects a racial liberalism, equating the struggles of the descendants of the "new immigrants" from the 1890 to 1924 generation with the struggles faced by the newest generation of Puerto Rican Americans. Zorro understands these parallels. About the Thunderbirds, "the others are bad, but they're the worst." "You don't like 'em do you? Any of them," asks Bell. Zorro hears "any of them" as a reference to the other racial and ethnic enclaves surrounding his territory. "Well, man, put yourself in my shoes!" He starts counting on his fingers. "The niggers look down on us. The wops look down on us. The Irish were here before the Indians. Man," he puts his hand on his heart, "my people are a proud race. Puerto Rico ain't no African Jungle. And the wops, what did they ever have? Mussolini? A big stink. Michelangelo? So what. You ever hear of a guy named Picasso? Pablo Picasso, man. I went all the way down to a museum to look at his paintings. Now that cat is great. The greatest artist who ever lived, man, he sings, and you know. . . ." Zorro trails off, interrupted by one of his lieutenants, and together they step outside to beat a delivery boy late on his protection payments.

Zorro's account demonstrates that while racial liberalism may be an option for third-generation Vassar progressives and second-generation Italian Americans, new arrivals learn the hard edges of American racial hierarchy from the ground up. Race is a social fact, with real boundaries and affects. But at the very moment that Zorro recognizes the social fact of race, he also recognizes its malleability. "The Irish were here before the Indians" suggests that social status and racial classifications change over time. "And the Wops, what did they ever have?" As the most recent immigrant group to "become white," Zorro challenges Italian racial status precisely in order to assert his own claim to full Americanness, for example, to whiteness. Yet even as he challenges racial oppression, for *his* group, he uncritically accepts other forms of racism ("Puerto Rico ain't no African jungle").

Moreover, in the sequence that follows, Zorro reveals the force behind this desire for full citizenship in a white republic. "We got three square blocks here, and we're busting to get out. . . . But while we're here . . . people got to respect us." When he tells Bell that the money he took from the delivery boy isn't "the point," he emphasizes, once more, that what matters is *respect*. What Zorro seeks is recognition. What he desires is the other's desire. And, in a white republic, that desire is itself shaped by normative racial and physical boundaries ("three square blocks") that imprison those on the outside of white.

PHALLUSES

Systems of domination perpetuate themselves in multiple forms. They are social facts inscribed upon the bodily habitus of the dominated. They are modes of knowledge, epistemological practices, and ways of seeing that separate "insiders" from "outsiders." They are material classifications that mediate an unequal distribution of wealth and status within society. But all forms of symbolic and material domination require the consent of the dominated. They achieve consent through various mechanisms. Through terror. Through material coercion. And through the use of hegemonic coordinates of desire. In order to secure authority over its subjects, domination imposes, brutalizes, bribes; but it also seduces.

Lacan addresses the gendered character of his schema and, by implication, the patriarchal language of Freud's description of the Oedipus complex: "The fact that the Father may be regarded as the original representative of this authority of the Law requires us to specify by what privileged mode of presence he is sustained beyond the subject who is actually led to occupy the place of the Other, namely, the Mother."[16] Returning to a much earlier argument, Lacan posits a developmental sequence of socialization in which identification with the symbolic Name-of-the-Father supplants an original (and imaginary) identification with the mother. As Freud argues in his account of the Oedipus complex, this identification with the symbolic/social Father requires castration. In order to take the place of the Father, the little boy must accept the Father's judgement. Thus, Lacan argues, the Oedipus complex may be a myth: "But what is not a myth, and which Freud nevertheless formulated soon after the Oedipus complex, is the castration complex."[17]

Society castrates every subject (male and female) in the sense that all lack the symbolic phallus that is the emblem of the Law. This phallus thus becomes the icon of the Other's desire. It is a *jouissance* (fulfillment) that is perpetually out of reach. Because the subject desires the Other's desire, and thus to take the Other's place, the subject desires the Other's phallus. In order to achieve the Other's recognition, "the subject here makes himself the instrument of the Other's *jouissance*."[18] As in Hegel's dialectic, the Slave becomes the Master's instrument. But this instrumentality does not prefigure freedom. Instead, the Slave pursues the Master's pleasure, for the sake of the Master, and infinitely defers its own desires. The Slave obeys the Law in order to please the Master.

At the beginning of the second act, the film reveals its psychoanalytic orientation. The scene opens with a court-appointed psychiatrist on the telephone. Speaking to a disembodied other, he says, "I don't want you to run another Rorschach.—I don't care if he's faking.—I don't care! What he's faking reveals just as much as his real reaction." The doctor's remarks echo Lacan's definition of the human as the being who pretends to pretend.[19] As in "The Subversion of the Subject," the film represents the psychiatric/psychoanalytic perspective as the authentic path to the "truth" the subject pretends to seek. From the first sequence forward, *The Young Savages* puts psychoanalytic techniques of representation to work. The materialized symbolic phallus (the knife, the cane, the pool cue, the harmonica) represents those outside the Law. These materialized emblems are "transitional objects" signifying the subject's fixation upon the image of the phallus, rather than the symbol of the Law.[20] In Lacan's terminology, these phallic substitutes signify the fixation on the mirror-stage. These subjects remain captive to an imaginary *méconnaissance* that prevents their full recognition of the Law. They are members of communities, but not members of the Community. They have not accepted the Name-of-the-Father.[21]

The film's first shot: the blind Roberto Escalante, playing solo harmonica beside his sister, an idyllic scene that shifts to a plain brick wall. The camera pans, the brick wall becomes Thunderbird's territory, marked out by their emblem in paint. The harmonica fades away and there are a few moments of silence as three boys in leather march into the light. An orchestral jazz score inflected with Latin percussion announces their ominous intentions. The continuous tracking shot takes us through the streets of Italian Harlem, toward "Little Puerto Rico," until the musical climax, then cuts to a shot of the backs of three leather jackets, and three arms simultaneously pulling switchblades from their belts. The camera shows their reflection in the blind boy's dark glasses as they stab. The camera cuts to his broken glasses on the ground reflecting the boy, arms outstretched, his sister attending his dead body.

While the Thunderbirds remain cyphers throughout the picture, and their motives never revealed, the stakes involved in the struggle between the gangs is very clear. What all the gangsters want is respect, the recognition of the other. But rather than seek that recognition from the Law, they seek it from each other. They are locked in poverty, the film argues, in part because they are locked in this struggle between one another. They cannot see what they have in common; nor can they accept their common subservience in the face of the Law.

As transitional objects, the switchblades represent the penises the boys cannot admit they've lost. Nor is this metonymic connection between switchblades and penises simply an interpretive imposition. The film announces the connection quite clearly. At one point, a police lieutenant's phone call wakes Hank. The cops found the lost murder weapons. When Bell, angry, asks the lieutenant, "What could I possibly do with them at this hour of the night?" the cop responds "Want a suggestion?" The film carries this symbolism further. Both gang leaders also hold phalluses in their hands. Pretty Boy Savarisi fondles a pool cue during his conversation with Bell, while Zorro carries a cane, presumably with a blade inside, as emblem of his power. In addition, the film establishes an equivalency between the blind boy's harmonica and the murderers' blades, as they all glint in the sun.

In the climactic courtroom scene, Bell's final act of sabotage is to exonerate Danny Dipace. Lab reports show that one of the three knives used in the conspiracy had no blood. Bell wants to connect Danny to that knife, thereby demonstrating Danny's relative innocence. As he badgers the boy, he continually waves the knife in Danny's face. Bell holds the boy's symbolic penis in his hand, but, simultaneously, appears to threaten castration using that very penis. As the accused breaks down into tears, he declares, guiltily, his innocence, that he did *not* stab Roberto Escalante. This admission represents a break with his gangster community, and, through castration, and his one-year sentence in juvenile detention, a path toward acceptance of the Law.

MIRRORS

Charles Horton Cooley's discussion of the "looking glass self" attempts to explain the social force of seduction.[22] For Cooley, the subject emerges into consciousness through the gaze of the other. Put in more developmental terms, the biological infant becomes a socialized child by accepting the judgments, attitudes, and points of view imposed by caregivers. The language the child acquires comes from others. Its values and beliefs originated with others. Finally, its sense of propriety, shame, guilt, and pride come from its own imagination of the other's point of view: "The reference to other persons involved in the self of the self may be distinct and particular, as when a boy is ashamed to have his mother catch him at something she has forbidden, or it may be vague and general, as when one is ashamed to do something which only his conscience, expressing his sense of social responsibility, detects and disapproves; but it is always there. There is no sense of 'I,' as in pride or shame, without its correlative sense of you, or he, or they."[23] Socialization means coming to see oneself through the perspective of others. This basic proposition, however, contains a number of implied corollaries. First, since the subject sees itself through the (metaphorical) eyes of the other, it knows itself primarily based upon this other's point of view. The self thus has no privileged access to itself. Further, to the degree that the subject seeks self-approval, it seeks the approbation of the other. That is, the other's judgment shapes the subject's consciousness. Therefore, the subject seeks the other's recognition (as this or that kind of subject) in order to come to know itself. In more Lacanian language, desire desires the other's desire. For Cooley, that means that the social subject who desires normative approval takes on the social practices of prestigious others (caregivers, educators, ministers, political leaders, bosses) in order to gain their approbation. The subject's desire for the other's desire thus has at least two pathways: First, the subject desires the other's recognition (e.g., desire); second, the subject desires the same norms, ideas, commodities that the other desires, in order to gain that recognition. Customs, beliefs, and attitudes spread through society based upon this desire to gain imagined approbation.

In addition to metonymic phalluses, *The Young Savages* plays with mirrors in ways that reveal meaning. When two Thunderbirds threaten Karin Bell in her apartment elevator, one of the boys looks beyond her, into the elevator mirror, and combs his hair, as the other opens his switchblade. One is fixated by his own imaginary reflection, and the other compensates for his unacknowledged castration with a materialized symbol of what he lost. In another scene, Zorro pleads his case for justice as he looks into the mirror and combs his hair. Once again, the stake is recognition. The boys look into the mirror, seeking recognition from the misperception that stares back.

Some mirrors are physical; some are human. Hank Bell has mirrors. Mary represents the reflection of his past, and his longing to recover some trace of what he's repressed. But Karin represents his present and his future. And her judgment matters to him. Like the image in Escalante's broken glasses, he sees himself through her eyes, and through those eyes seeks recognition as a certain kind of person. She attempts to call him to account, and he resists, often belittling her politics and her perspective. At a political party, Karin makes a drunken scene, ending with her sarcastic remark, "and I'm proud of ole Hank Bellini." Hank then physically drags her from the party, scolding her: "You third-generation progressive, sitting up at Vassar, getting your fat checks from Daddy."

Yet, in the end, Hank's recognition of his racial transformation is also the recognition of Karin as his racial Master. His exaggerated masculine attempts to control her perspective do not work. He accepts her point of view, and understands that she is the phallus that he sought. By internalizing her voice, he symbolically surrenders his own penis, becomes the pure incarnation of the Law, now signifying white supremacy. This discovery of racial transformation begins with a beating Hank receives in the subway from a group of young gangsters. In the wake of his attack, and her earlier traumatic encounter on the elevator, Hank asks Karin, "What do you think of your little victims of social oppression now?" At first, she demurs. He cross-examines her until she admits that she meant every word when she defended the young gangsters and when she drunkenly questioned Hank's moral compass.

Hank looks down, thoughtfully: "Something else you said. Old Hank Bellini. Danny Dipace said it too. 'Wassa matter Mr. Bellini, you ashamed of being a wop?'—My old man was ignorant. He thought the way to be a good American was to change your name. It was always easy for me to explain. My father did it. Now I realize I not only went along with it, I was glad. I was secretly glad my name was *Bell* rather than Bellini. It was part of getting out of Harlem. Like marrying you." Karin responds indignantly, "You married me because you loved me." But Hank is silent, his eyes to the ground. This silent recognition shifts the course of the narrative. Whiteness was Hank's castration, and the phallus he desired, Karin, was herself a metonym of white desire.

Finally, the court case is a screen for the real stakes at play. True, the white ethnics are not killed by electric chair. But that is hardly an injustice from the perspective of the film. However, the film acknowledges, and then evades, a deeper injustice. The picture draws parallels between gang members, regardless of race. And the representation of the Puerto Rican community uses tropes from the visual history of Italian and Jewish immigrants. But these parallels have limits, and race represents an impassible barrier for Puerto Ricans. Even as he tries to convince Bell, Zorro acknowledges that his people will not get justice (here a synonym for respect) because of their "brown skin." The Thunderbirds may be rebels, but they can be castrated into law-abiding white citizens. The Horsemen will always be outlaws because they can never be white.

CONCLUSION

Both *The Young Savages* and "The Subversion of the Subject" proscribe subservience to socially constructed forms of domination. Both inscribe the inescapability of the Law. Both conclude with the reinstatement of a reified social construct (the phallus, whiteness) that represses the perspectives of the colonized and oppressed. *The Young Savages* raises the claims of the colonized, only to anxiously turn away. Lacan's most obvious unwritten opponent in dialogue was Simone de Beauvoir, but his symptomatic silence also points toward Frantz Fanon.

Like Lacan, Fanon revises Hegel's dialectic, but from the perspective of colonized desire. The colonized world is the Manichean world. The colonizer (the Master) has stripped the colonized of their culture, in exchange for a set of impossibly insatiable desires. The colonized will never receive the Master's recognition.[24] They are "disreputable" by definition.[25] Trapped by the desire for an Other's desire, yet incapable of achieving satisfaction, the colonized subject is constituted as an absence, a lack. This lack provokes "a look of lust, a look of envy."[26] At the same time, the totalitarian gaze of the colonizer puts the "colonized subject . . . in a state of permanent tension," a "muscular tension," that "periodically erupts into bloody fighting between tribes, clans, and individuals."[27] Fanon's colonized at first appear to be Lacan's castrated subjects.[28] But Fanon adds the element of embodiment, with the muscular tension produced by the Master's constant surveillance. This description of the colonized subject's envy, and tension, would seem to capture something of the gangs of New York. Unlike *The Young Savages*, however, and unlike Lacan, Fanon returns to the Hegelian notion of praxis, now in an embodied form. Recall that the Slave becomes the instrument of the Master. Through work, the Slave masters the world and so transcends slavery. Like Lacan, Fanon recognizes Hegel's idealism and attempts to correct it. Like Lacan, Fanon argues that language forms subjectivity and enforces the normative order. But it also provides resources for resistance. As Fanon notes, "The existence of an armed struggle is indicative that the people are determined to put their faith only in violent methods. The very same people who had it constantly drummed into them that the only language they understood was that of force, now decide to express themselves with force. In fact, the colonist has always shown them the path they should follow to liberation. The argument chosen by the colonized was conveyed to them by the colonizer."[29] This code is the code of the other. But colonized subjects use it to remake the world: "The work of the colonist is to make even dreams of liberty impossible for the colonized. The work of the colonized is to imagine every possible method for annihilating the colonist. On the logical plane, the Manicheanism of the colonist produces the Manicheanism of the colonized."[30] If the phallus represents the whiteness of the colonizer, the machete, or the switchblade, has the potential to cut through that fabrication. The colonized subject, lost in envy and servitude, comes to recognize its new identity through action, through force, and through violence. Violence unifies the colonized into a new people. Moreover, "violence is a cleansing force. It rids the colonized of their inferiority complex, of their passive and despairing attitude. It emboldens them, and restores their self-confidence. . . . Violence hoists the people up to the level of the leader."[31]

For Lacan, the normative subject recognizes its castration, and therefore its dependence upon a phallic Law. For Fanon, through embodied force, the empowered subject overthrows the Law and establishes a new order where the "people" become the Law. In this description of Fanon's work, I do not mean to advocate for or against his argument. Instead, I am suggesting that fear of the colonized is the hidden subtext in both Lacan's "The Subversion of the Subject" and the film *The Young Savages*. Both the essay and the film attempt to "make even dreams of liberty impossible for the colonized," because both the essay and the film fear the alternative.

NOTES

1. Patricia Hill Collins, "Learning from the Outsider Within: The Sociological Significance of Black Feminist Thought," in *The Feminist Standpoint Theory Reader: Intellectual and Political Controversies*, ed. Sandra Harding (New York: Routledge, 2004), 103–126.

2. David Roediger, *Working toward Whiteness: How America's Immigrants Became White* (New York: Basic Books, 2005), 11.

3. David Roediger, "Afterword: DuBois, Race, and Italian Americans," in *Are Italians White? How Race Is Made in America*, ed. Jennifer Guglielmo and Salvatore Salerno (New York: Routledge, 2003), 259–264, 260.

4. Roediger, *Working toward Whiteness*, 57–133.

5. Graham Cassano, *A New Kind of Public: Community, Solidarity, and Political Economy in New Deal Cinema, 1935–1948* (Chicago: Haymarket Press, 2015), 84–104, 152–182.

6. Jacques Lacan, "The Subversion of the Subject and the Dialectic of Desire in the Freudian Unconscious," in *Écrits: A Selection*, trans. Alan Sheridan (New York: Norton, 1977), 292–325. I do not mean to suggest that the filmmakers read Lacan. Rather, both film and text inscribe the social forces that constituted their shared historical moment.

7. Lacan, "Subversion of the Subject," 319.

8. Lacan, "Subversion of the Subject," 324.

9. Lacan, "Subversion of the Subject," 47.

10. Lacan, "Subversion of the Subject," 304.

11. Lacan, "Subversion of the Subject," 305.

12. Émile Durkheim, *The Rules of Sociological Method*, trans. W. D. Halls (New York: Free Press, 1982), 50–51.

13. Lacan, "Subversion of the Subject," 310.

14. Lacan, "Subversion of the Subject," 310.

15. Lacan, "Subversion of the Subject," 308.

16. Lacan, "Subversion of the Subject," 311.

17. Lacan, "Subversion of the Subject," 310, 318.

18. Lacan, "Subversion of the Subject," 320.

19. Lacan, "Subversion of the Subject," 305.

20. Lacan, "Subversion of the Subject," 312.

21. In this context, consider Danny Dipace's first utterance to Bell: "I ain't go no father."

22. See also Graham Cassano, "Critical Pragmatism's Status Wage and the Standpoint of the Stranger," in *Capitalism's Future: Alienation, Emancipation, and Critique*, ed. Daniel Krier and Mark P. Worrell (Chicago: Haymarket Press, 2017), 217–239.

23. Charles Horton Cooley, *Human Nature and the Social Order* (New York: Charles Scribner, 1902), 151. It is worth noting that despite the fact Cooley uses "his mother" as an example in the passage, he does not assign a value to the "correlative sense of" she.

24. Frantz Fanon, *The Wretched of the Earth*, trans. Richard Philcox (New York: Grove, 2004), 6–7; while Lacan may not have had the occasion to read Fanon's last work (published in 1961) before composing his paper, many of that text's arguments were introduced in *Black Skin, White Masks*, trans. Richard Philcox (1952; New York: Grove, 2008).

25. Fanon, *Wretched of the Earth*, 4.

26. Fanon, *Wretched of the Earth*, 5.

27. Fanon, *Wretched of the Earth*, 16–17.

28. At times almost literally: "With his back to the wall, the knife at his throat, or to be more exact the electrode on his genitals, the colonized subject is bound to stop telling stories." Fanon, *Wretched of the Earth*, 20.

29. Fanon, *Wretched of the Earth*, 42.

30. Fanon, *Wretched of the Earth*, 50.

31. Fanon, *Wretched of the Earth*, 51.

12 · RITA MORENO'S HAIR

PRISCILLA PEÑA OVALLE

Rita Moreno, one of the most acclaimed actors of sound, stage, and screen, has lamented that she was often cast in "barefoot parts," her shorthand for the generic Gypsies, Spanish señoritas, and Mexican/Italian peasants with broken English that she was required to play in her early studio films like *The Fabulous Señorita* (1952), *Cattle Town* (1952), and *Latin Lovers* (1953).[1] She recalls, "I used to swear there was a 'Rita Moreno Makeup Kit' that consisted of a shoebox with [makeup], which was usually dark and brown, two hoop earrings, and a wig."[2] This costuming largely stereotyped Moreno's performances according to a specific intersection of race/ethnicity, gender, and age—a combination that made the young, brown female characters she played while under contract at MGM and Fox appear (hetero)sexually available and willing. The aesthetic marker of artificially brown skin was a convenient Hollywood code that used makeup to convey nonwhiteness, often combined with markers of a character's poverty or backwardness such as bare feet.

Moreno's so-called barefoot parts epitomize Hollywood's depiction of racialized female sexuality, a version of femininity that signified looseness or "excessive" female sexuality through hoop earrings, long and wild hair, an off-the-shoulder blouse, and bad attitude.[3] The manner in which costuming encoded stereotypically nonwhite female sexuality onto Moreno's characters was especially evident in contrast to the more conservative, cleaner, and seemingly brighter costuming of the white female leads of her films.[4] As an actor, Moreno was readily typecast in these roles because her gender, ethnicity, last name, and youth obscured her from being imagined as anything else.

This essay examines the function of Rita Moreno's hair to highlight how certain hairstyles represent specific combinations of her intersectional identity as a Puerto Rican woman working in Hollywood. Analyzing the function of Moreno's hair during key moments helps us identify the industrial challenges and aesthetic choices that she has faced in her career, which spans decades and various media. I build my evidence from three case studies across her stage, film, and television career: her contract work at Fox and MGM, which produced *Singin' in the Rain* (1952); scenes from her autobiographical stage production, *Life Without Makeup* (2011); and her recent performance as Lydia Riera on the Netflix streaming series *One Day at a Time* (2017–). Observing how strategic changes to Moreno's hair facilitated her long Hollywood career—into what she has called the "equal opportunity, all round ethnic person"[5]—reveals one recurrent example of how industrialized Hollywood practices produce the cinematic codes and conventions that racialize, gender, and sexualize bodies on screen in the United States.

Every hairstyle on screen, like everything on the Hollywood screen, is a fabrication that has been developed to support the industrial demands of a film production. Recognizing the industrialized labor behind things like continuity and characterization is especially useful for understanding the significance of Hollywood hairstyles. Hair is an especially rich object of analysis; its political history and media production history equally highlight how race is socially constructed and policed in the United States. Since early cinema, racialized expectations of hair have been embedded into the symbolic and industrial systems of Hollywood.[6] Physically, hair is incredibly malleable: the length, color, texture, and style of hair can be modified with some effort and experience in real life. Symbolically, however, hair is an arbitrarily racialized cultural marker that has privileged whiteness and demonized nonwhiteness at various historical moments. In the United States, for example, hair has long been used to measure racial difference and thereby police cultural citizenship; in *Hair Story: Untangling the Roots of Black Hair in America*, Ayana Byrd and Lori Tharps found that hair was historically "considered the most telling feature of Negro status, more than the color of the skin."[7] The stakes of having the right kind of hair linger to this day.

Western cultural productions like theater, literature, and cinema have long transformed ideological assumptions (particularly negative ones) about race, gender, and sexuality into efficient codes and symbols that can other characters on the stage, page, and screen. In performances of *Hamlet*, for example, Ophelia's unkempt hair identified her character as mad, a stage trope familiar to Elizabethan audiences as an indication that a woman was mentally unwell or had been sexually assaulted.[8] In *Oliver Twist*, the child-exploiting character Fagin's red hair marked him as Jewish, a long-standing stage trope that aligned characters with Judas or the devil.[9] While Charles Dickens's novel did not originate such anti-Semitic tropes, the industrialized circulation of his writings and George Cruikshank's illustrations promulgated these stereotypical conventions beyond the Victorian period and into visual media forms like cinema.[10]

Similar hair codes are embedded in and circulated through contemporary film and television in the United States. Racial and gender hierarchies of hair are evident in the ways that certain styles are privileged, often by seeming normal on the Hollywood screen, where the blonde locks of Marilyn Monroe are still prized and close-cropped hair on men remains the norm. As Ella Shohat and Robert Stam have illustrated, media industries (and academia) have long privileged Eurocentric, patriarchal, and heteronormative ideals in terms of narrative, characterization, and more.[11] Richard Dyer's work on whiteness builds on these concepts to show how white bodies on screen have come to represent humanness, purportedly void of any racialized identity and thereby serving as a default protagonist in Hollywood narratives.[12] This symbolic and industrial tendency carries over into production practices, where normalcy is encoded through hair, clothing, and other markers to uphold conventional ideas about race and gender. In *Costume, Makeup, and Hair*, Adrienne L. McLean addresses something she calls "straight makeup," cinematic cosmetic conventions that look "normal and natural on and off the screen, manufacturing ideals of beauty that were at once special or innate but also potentialities for all (if you were white) because the ideals relied on [specific cosmetic products]."[13] This feat of normalcy was similarly true for hair. White studio stars experienced the peak benefits of this system; their version of normalcy has often been associated with glamour, an industrial demand consistent with their stardom. Character and supporting actors' looks, however, have been intentionally malleable through the use of wigs, prosthetics, and more.

When talking about hair on screen, we are often actually talking about wigs, which have historically supported the industrialized nature of film production. Because most films and television programs are shot out of order from how they appear on screen, wigs are practical: they help maintain a continuous look for an actor across several days of shooting by preventing noticeable hair changes from shot to shot or scene to scene. In addition, screen hairstyles convey the character each actor is presenting. Even here, at least in terms of stars, wigs tend to function as a practical method for maintaining and reinforcing a star's appearance (as opposed to excessively changing their look, as when a star is intentionally disrupting her persona). But whether for continuity or character, wigs are primarily intended to be invisible: hair and wigs are equally styled to suit the camera, with the audience generally expected to assume that an actor's hair, wig or not, is the character's actual hair.[14] Thus, distinguishing between real or fake hair is less significant than the function it serves for the production.

The history of Moreno's hair, her "hairstory" so to speak, provides a useful framework by helping us focus on each layer of intersectionality operating through the hair codes of Moreno's characters. Focusing on key hair moments enables us to logically narrow our case studies and effectively approach Moreno's career with an intersectional lens. These specific hair moments enable us to address both the distinct axes of her identity and the various facets of systematic oppression that shape a career according to the industrialized power of Hollywood.[15] A specific hairstyle might indicate which interlocking aspect of Moreno's intersectional identity as a woman, Puerto Rican performer, and/or aging actor is being prioritized. When Moreno wears different hairstyles, including wigs, to achieve a look, she is not only supporting the creation of a particular character, but also supporting or surpassing the limited roles typically offered to nonwhite actresses. The professional necessity of manipulating one's hair highlights how supposedly arbitrary markers like hair color and length can, in fact, make or break an actor's career. While this is true regardless of an actor's identity or background, it is more pronounced for nonwhite performers, especially nonwhite female performers.

One of the standout approaches to intersectional star studies in a Latinx context is the work of Mary C. Beltrán. The introduction of Beltrán's book *Latino/a Stars in U.S. Eyes: The Making and Meanings of Film and TV Stardom* provides an excellent overview of how performers with Latinx identities complicate the typical expectations of U.S. stardom and are constantly mediated by a preceding history of racialized representations that impacts how these performers, including Rita Moreno, are cast and promoted.[16] Beltrán notes, "Rita Moreno . . . serves as an example both of the most a Latina could achieve and how Latina actresses were viewed as not quite American in these decades, revealing the narrow parameters of Hollywood Latinidad in the 1950s and '60s."[17] In this way, industrial practices around brown stars stem directly from complex U.S. notions of Latinx identities; these practices relate to cycles of U.S.–Latin American relations with the alternating perception of Latinx communities in the United States as a good neighbor or "bad hombres" in addition to the migration in the early twentieth century of U.S. media production from the East Coast to the West Coast (near the U.S.-Mexico border).[18]

Moreno's hairstory stands out among others because she gradually resisted the carefully constructed depictions of nonwhiteness on the classical Hollywood screen. Moreno's first big break from the hoop earrings and animal skins of her early days under contract at studios like MGM and Fox was in the film *Singin' in the Rain* (MGM), a role facilitated by a change in her hair color, thanks to a red wig.[19] In the film, Moreno plays a minor yet catalytic character named Zelda Zanders. The film introduces Zanders as "that famous zip girl of the screen, the darling of the flapper set" and was one of the few parts Moreno would play that was not primarily identified by ethnicity. This change of hairstyle provided Moreno, then twenty-one, with a rare opportunity that she credits to Gene Kelly. She recalls: "[Kelly] put me in a red wig. It never occurred to him to say, 'No, she's too Latina, her name is Latina.' He just thought I'd be fine for it."[20] By casting Moreno in this small but significant role, Kelly showed great foresight and revealed his theater/vaudeville roots. Like Moreno, Gene Kelly started his career on East Coast stages and in vaudeville; he knew that Moreno could do the job and that costuming was half the battle. Indeed, Moreno praised Kelly's "theater sensibility, or New York sensibility" as the reason he was able to see beyond her ethnic type.[21] Early in his career, Kelly had himself benefitted from being cast against type: his early break and first marquee mention came by performing with the *Cab Calloway Cotton Club* act during a Pennsylvania show because the Nicholas Brothers dropped out to do a Hollywood film.[22]

Although Kelly showed great foresight by casting Moreno in a nonethnic role, it was an anomaly. Had she been a young white actress under contract, the role might have led to other roles, with a wig just one more option for expanding characterization. But because she was a young, female, and *ethnic* contract player at a major studio, the temporary modification of Moreno's hair did not have a long-term effect. (The most commercially viable Hollywood Latinas, like Rita Hayworth before Moreno and Jennifer Lopez after her, combined dance and substantial hair makeovers.) In the 1950s, studios simply did not know what to do with Moreno. She was pushed "right back to the ethnic stuff" after her few scenes as Zanders and dropped from her MGM contract immediately after the film.[23] As a young actress, Moreno would go on to do a lot more ethnic roles, the stereotypical roles of caricatured nonwhite people as a freelance actress and when she signed with Twentieth Century Fox.[24]

Moreno provides some perspective on these early studio experiences in *Life Without Makeup* (2011), her autobiographical, one-woman stage production written and directed by Tony Taccone for the Berkeley Repertory Theatre.[25] According to Taccone, the play is "about a young child who comes from a different country, doesn't speak the language, learns very quickly that it's not good thing to be who or what she is—and tries to be someone else for a major part of her life."[26] In *Life Without Makeup*, Moreno recounts key moments of her life and career; as the title suggests, Moreno's appearance (including her hair) is a feature of the show. According to the playscript, the first few scenes contextualize the intersectionality of Moreno's childhood, reenacting moments from Moreno's life as a girl who has relocated with her mom from Puerto Rico to an impoverished, multiethnic Bronx neighborhood in the 1930s. The show recounts Moreno's early professional work, starting as a six-year old dancer trained by Paco Cansino (Rita Hayworth's uncle).[27] This scene sets up a series of negotiations that Moreno would make over the length of her professional career: though her neighborhood was composed of recent immigrants with similar working-class backgrounds, it became clear that her Puerto Rican-ness ranked poorly in the multiethnic neighborhood.[28] The play subtly contrasts Moreno's identity with that of ethnically white immigrants, with Moreno recounting how she ran home from school to escape the cruel teasing of Irish immigrant kids.[29] The play reenacts how Moreno's ethnic identity shaped and constrained her life at a very young age, from the taunts she received from Irish children ("You ain't gonna learn nothing because you too stupid to learn you little spic-ity spic!") to her work as a pint-size performer in a Carmen Miranda costume on the "bar mitzvah circuit" at the age of nine.[30]

According to *Life Without Makeup* and her autobiography, *Rita Moreno: A Memoir*, Moreno was conscious of her look and its potential limits on her career by the age of ten, when she decided to change her appearance by changing her hair. One scene of the stage production dramatizes this early moment of Moreno's self-awareness: an image of Moreno's ideal (the blonde Betty Grable) is projected next to an unflattering image of Carmen Miranda, the turbaned "woman in the tutti frutti hat" that played such a significant role in her early days as a child performer. Moreno explains her plan to emulate Grable to the audience:

> And so, armed with my new strategy for success, I tried desperately to get rid of my *pelo malo*, my bad, kinky, curly hair. And there was only one place to do it: Harlem. I'd lather my scalp in Vaseline before the hench women of the Rose Meta House of Beauty would pour lye on my hair and comb it straight out while my skull burst into flames. The straighter version of my hair lasted about a month before the treatment suddenly wore off, turning me instantly back into what I was sure was the world's homeliest girl with skin that was a full shade too dark. I had to get out of this body![31]

When Moreno recounts this moment in *Rita Moreno: A Memoir*, she describes it as the point she decided to "go big time," turning her attention to mainstream venues like Broadway, a transformation that included both "paler makeup" and "straight hair."[32] But while the staged scene dramatizes Moreno's early feelings of inferiority and professional desire to meet the norms of white feminine beauty, it also aligns her with the black community in New York. To "get out of [her] body," Moreno began by changing her hair at a prominent, black-owned beauty salon.[33] This scene not only highlights the significance of straightened hair to Moreno's very early career, but also connects her as a young brown woman to an important center of the black community, where other nonwhite women modified their hair (whether to align with European standards of beauty or not). In this way, Moreno's limitations as an aspiring performer are aligned with blackness or nonwhiteness, even as she aspired to access a profession oriented around whiteness. At the intersection of youth and brownness, Moreno worked to maximize her in-betweenness, as an actor that was not quite white and not quite black. Unmodified, her so-called ethnic look limited her access to roles; but with the support of the black salon and its community, Moreno achieved something closer to the so-called right look.

With dance training and hair treatments, Moreno ultimately earned a chance at a Hollywood career and the racist, sexist practices that come with it. In anticipation of meeting MGM studio head Louis B. Mayer, Moreno worked to remake herself in Elizabeth Taylor's image. With the help of her mother, she achieved the look through cosmetics, hairstyling, and lingerie that cinched and padded all the right places to create "the impossible combination of high, creamy cleavage and a wasp waist."[34] Moreno recounts her first meeting with Mayer in a later scene from Life Without Makeup: "He held my hand firmly in his while giving me a quick once over, an inspection that took all of thirty seconds before I heard . . . [him] say the magic words 'She looks like a Spanish Elizabeth Taylor! How does a 7–year contract sound to you, young lady?' I felt my feet lift off the floor as I flew around the room. I was 16 years old. Two months later we were on the studio lot in Culver City."[35] At sixteen years old, Moreno was one of many starlets using specifically gendered tactics to seek evaluation and approval by white (or white ethnic) men in power in the hopes of landing a studio contract. Mayer may have granted Moreno a contract, but it required a lot of cosmetic manipulation and support to achieve the desired feminine look. Later, Moreno earned her contract at Twentieth Century Fox by similarly catching Darryl F. Zanuck's eye on the March 1, 1954, cover of Life magazine, captioned "Rita Moreno: An Actress's Catalog of Sex and Innocence."[36]

Such moments of sexualized evaluation by men with power in the movie industry—one of many Moreno recounts in Life Without Makeup, her autobiography, and countless interviews or press releases—highlight how gender and youth produced Moreno's precariously racialized ethnic identity. Indeed, Moreno has long been keenly aware of the female performer's burden in Hollywood: "I should note that a lot of white ingénues—not just ethnic Puerto Ricans—played Indian maidens and other slave girl roles. Which goes to show you that often it is hard to distinguish what wrong is being done to you because you're ethnic or just because you're female."[37] In other words, Moreno's access to the studio system as a young woman was initially facilitated by her specific combination of age and gender. While her specific intersection of ethnicity, age, and gender resulted in characters that

FIGURE 12.1 Googie (Rita Morena) loses her hair (*Ritz*, 1977).

were stereotypically racialized and sexualized, it is important to note that her access to roles was facilitated differently than was the case for young male actors (Latinx or not) of the same era.[38]

The theatrical stage has been an important and continued refuge for Moreno.[39] At nearly eighty years old, Rita Moreno, the "all-round ethnic," had the last laugh: in *Life Without Makeup*, she played every age, every ethnicity, and every character of her personal history.[40] Before that, the stage saved her from the flood of offers for stereotypical roles that came after her Academy Award win for *West Side Story* in 1961. The stage also earned Moreno a Tony in recognition for her 1975 performance in *The Ritz* as Googie Gomez, an outlandish Puerto Rican caricature/alter ego that Moreno conceived to entertain herself and friends on the set of *West Side Story*. Googie is an amateur entertainer with an overly enunciated Puerto Rican accent, a creation that allowed Moreno to laugh at stereotypical representations of Latinas in Hollywood.[41] In the film version of *The Ritz* (1976), Moreno highlights Googie's passionate lack of talent during one of her numbers by losing a shoe and her wig (see Figure 12.1). In addition, Moreno's work on programs like *The Muppet Show* (1976) and *The Electric Company* (1971–1977) highlight her range with their vaudeville style. Something like *The Electric Company*, complete with wigs and costumes of all kinds, beautifully showcased Moreno's acting, dancing, and singing abilities and enabled her to either play with stereotypes or ignore them altogether.[42] By working across media from studio to independent films, from stage to television, Moreno willed an impressively long career into being; career longevity is a rare for female performers, especially older, nonwhite female performers. But as Moreno notes in her autobiography, the worst was yet to come: "I had battled racism and sexism all my life. Now I had to battle the worst enemy of all: ageism."[43] Like racism and sexism, she tackled this obstacle head-first.

COMBATTING AGEISM, RACISM, AND SEXISM:
ONE DAY AT A TIME

Fast-forward many years. Moreno's latest role is a character named Lydia Riera on Norman Lear's Netflix reboot of *One Day at a Time*. Lydia is a "spunky-fierce" seventy-year-old Cuban, the mother of a Cuban American veteran daughter and grandmother of two teenagers.[44] Moreno makes full use of her comedic and dramatic repertoire for this character: Lydia is a flamboyantly vain yet family-focused immigrant matriarch. The sharp dialogue and stellar cast bring out the best in Moreno, and together they deliver deeply tender, dramatic scenes that are simultaneously funny.

The role seems to be the culmination of Moreno's work on stage and screen, and she made sure it had a larger purpose, stating,

> I asked the writers . . . before there was even a script [and] said I'd like her to be sexual. Because you don't see that. Once people turn a certain age, that gets completely ignored by writers, and it's a shame. I've always been a very sexual person. . . . I'm 85, and I'm still a sexual being, or a sensual being. And that appealed to them, and of course the audience loves that. Including, by the way, the younger people because I think unconsciously they see there's hope that it doesn't all suddenly go away, your ovaries just turn to dust overnight simply because you can no longer conceive. It doesn't mean that you don't have sexual allure or yearnings. And in Lydia's case, of course she goes so far—this woman is shameless. She will flirt with a fence post.[45]

Given Moreno's screen history and the limitations she faced, it is easy to read Lydia as a Latina stereotype: she is a sexual Cuban woman with a flair for drama that is *also* comedic and fiercely committed to her family. And this is where intersectionality reveals its potential depth as a mode of analysis for studying media. Because Moreno is a well-established actor, the inflection of her work as a sexual Latina character is different now that she is an octogenarian. On sitcoms, (white) senior sexuality is often played as a joke. Meanwhile, older nonwhite characters are often asexual, such as the stereotypical mammy roles frequently assigned to black women in early Hollywood. By advocating for Lydia to be an elderly sexual character, Moreno transformed the stereotypically *sexualized* characteristics of her younger roles into a more progressive *sexual agency* for this older one.

It is striking to note, however, that this character, unlike Moreno in real life, does not seem to have one gray hair! This detail underscores Lydia's vanity, one of her defining characteristics. (In one *One Day at a Time* episode, Lydia confesses to her family that she never goes anywhere without makeup.) But I suggest that, in addition to supporting Lydia's character, the dark brown wig that Moreno wears also serves as a reminder that age, on screen as in life, can be nothing more than a number. It may not seem significant that Moreno, now in her late eighties, portrays a seventy-year-old woman on screen. But in an industry that starts to age women over thirty into mother roles because they are presumably too old to be an ingénue, it is remarkable that Moreno is covering up her stylishly short silver hair to play a slightly younger woman.

With a straight and sleek brown bob, Lydia is a character obsessed with her beauty, Cuba, and her family. But even as Moreno challenges ageism, intersectionality further nuances our reading of her stardom and hair. At a time when Latinx migration is once again in the spotlight—this time amidst racist cries of "Build That Wall!"—it can be easy to forget how identity politics operate among Latinx populations. These politics usually point to the historic privileges that have developed with Latinx racialization in the United States, where Cuban Americans and Mexican Americans are often pitted against each other and characterized as white or nonwhite, respectively.[46] How, then, should we read the casting of Moreno, a fair-skinned Puerto Rican woman, in a Cuban American family sitcom set in Echo Park, a Los Angeles neighborhood whose Latinx-dominant demographics are predominantly of Mexican descent?[47] *One Day at a Time*, to its credit, hits on some of these underlying tensions in its second season opener, "The Turn." In one scene, the episode tackles racism, white and light-skinned privilege, passing, bilingualism, and the complex racial composition of Caribbean communities like those found in Cuba (and Puerto Rico). The scene is a series of sad-funny moments, with Moreno's performance lending gravitas and lightheartedness along the way. At one point, Lydia reluctantly utters the word that scarred her as a child: "spic," an ethnic slur that Moreno herself faced in her youth. Then Lydia proceeds to argue that Cubans are white, a humorous yet character-revealing moment that calls Lydia's look, hair and all, into focus (see Figure 12.2).

A key goal of this essay has been to highlight the contours and challenges of an intersectional approach to mainstream media by analyzing Rita Moreno's hairstory. Had this analysis of Moreno's career solely addressed race (or

FIGURE 12.2 Wigs make it so: Rita Morena as Zelda Zanders (*Singin' in the Rain*, 1952) and as Cuban American elderly mother Lydia (*One Day at a Time*, 2017).

gender, age, etc.), it would have inevitably missed the varied and complex negotiations that an actor with an intersectional identity like Moreno's has had to make in order to work in mainstream media, where being an actor of any background requires untold industry-motivated negotiations. Rita Moreno's longevity and hard-earned stardom have paid off in that she can more overtly inflect her characters with her brand of depth and humor. As opportunities for Latinx performers (and producers, etc.) expand, we have the persistence and tenacity of women like Rita Moreno to thank for giving us incredible characters, however limited their roles may have been, and whatever color their hair.

NOTES

1. Mary C. Beltrán, *Latino/a Stars in U.S. Eyes: The Making and Meanings of Film and TV Stardom* (Urbana: University of Illinois Press, 2009), 71.
2. Rita Moreno, interviewed by Marla Miller, *Television Academy Foundation Interviews*, Archive of American Television (online, chapter 2 of 6), Academy of Television Arts and Sciences Foundation, June 22, 2000, https://interviews.televisionacademy.com /interviews/rita-moreno#interview-clips.
3. Priscilla Peña Ovalle, *Dance and the Hollywood Latina: Race, Sex, and Stardom* (New Brunswick, NJ: Rutgers University Press, 2011), 105–106.
4. Ovalle, *Dance and the Hollywood Latina*, 105.
5. Moreno interview by Miller (chapter 2).
6. Miranda Banks reminds us of the "collaborative nature of production and the methods and traditions of compensation" that operate behind the scenes of any film or television production. Miranda Banks, "Gender Below-the-Line: Defining Feminist Production

Studies," in *Production Studies: Cultural Studies of Media Industries*, ed. Vickie Mayer, Miranda J. Banks, and John Thornton Caldwell (New York: Routledge, 2009), 87–98, 95.

7. Ayana D. Byrd and Lori L. Tharps, *Hair Story: Untangling the Roots of Black Hair in America* (New York: St. Martin's, 2001), 17.

8. Elaine Showalter, "Representing Ophelia: Women, Madness, and the Responsibilities of Feminist Criticism," in *Hamlet: Text of the Play, the Actors' Gallery, Contexts, Criticism, Afterlives, Resources*, ed. Robert S. Miola (New York: Norton, 2011), 281–297, 286.

9. Frank Felsenstein, *Anti-Semitic Stereotypes: A Paradigm of Otherness in English Popular Culture, 1660–1830* (Baltimore: Johns Hopkins University Press, 1995), 31.

10. Felsenstein, *Anti-Semitic Stereotypes*, 239.

11. Ella Shohat and Robert Stam, *Unthinking Eurocentrism: Multiculturalism and the Media* (London: Routledge, 1994), 3.

12. Richard Dyer, *White* (London: Routledge, 1997), 1.

13. Adrienne L. McLean, "Introduction," in *Costume, Makeup, and Hair*, ed. Adrienne L. McLean (New Brunswick, NJ: Rutgers University Press, 2016), 1–20, 6.

14. The distinction of "real" or "fake" is also fascinating in terms of the general depiction of race or ethnicity on screen. Consider, for example, that Rita Moreno was the only Puerto Rican performer among the Sharks cast in the *West Side Story* film. As Frances Negrón-Muntaner has shown, brown makeup along with a "shifting, asinine accent" was used to convey Puerto Ricanness. Negrón-Muntaner highlights that the use of brown makeup on George Chakiris was especially important to his film portrayal of Bernardo, the Puerto Rican leader of the Sharks; because he had previously played the leader of the white Jets on stage in London, brown makeup "underscored Bernardo's ethnicity" in the film and served as "a clamp to avoid any ethnic misreading of his [Puerto Rican] 'realness.'" Strikingly, Negrón-Muntaner also notes that the hair of the Jets was "dyed unnaturally blond." Frances Negrón-Muntaner, *Boricua Pop: Puerto Ricans and the Latinization of American Culture* (New York: New York University Press, 2004), 66.

15. Brenda R. Weber, "Intersectionality," in *Keywords for Media Studies*, ed. Laurie Ouellette and Jonathan Gray (New York: New York University Press, 2017), 112.

16. Beltrán, *Latino/a Stars in U.S. Eyes*, 5–10. Beltrán's chapter on Moreno, "A Fight for 'Dignity and Integrity': Rita Moreno in Hollywood's Postwar Era," is an especially compelling look at Moreno's representation and access in Hollywood in the aftermath of World War II.

17. Beltrán, *Latino/a Stars in U.S. Eyes*, 63.

18. Beltrán, *Latino/a Stars in U.S. Eyes*, 7–10.

19. Ovalle, *Dance and the Hollywood Latina*, 106.

20. Moreno interview by Miller (chapter 3 of 6). In her autobiography, Moreno elaborates on this moment, noting that Kelly originally asked her to cut her "long curly black hair" for the role, which Moreno refused, stating, "Cutting hair is not the custom in Puerto Rico. Girls and women never cut their hair; it is a point of feminine pride." Rita Moreno Gordon, *Rita Moreno: A Memoir* (New York: Celebra, 2013), 96.

21. Moreno interview by Miller (chapter 3 of 6). Moreno elaborates on this in another chapter of this interview (chapter 2 of 6), stating that live productions, such as theater or live television, tended not to typecast her in stereotypical roles. To her mind, this illustrates the "New York mentality" or "theater thinking, where you could do roles that weren't necessarily Hispanic—or if they were, they were at the very least not stereotypical roles. They just had a different take about things like that. With filmed television, I did nothing but [stereotypical roles]." Moreno interview by Miller (chapter 2 of 6).

22. Frank Cullen, Florence Hackman, and Donald McNeilly, "Gene Kelly," in *Vaudeville, Old & New: An Encyclopedia of Variety Performers in America* (New York: Routledge, 2006), 622.

23. Moreno interview by Miller.

24. Moreno interview by Miller; Ovalle, *Dance and the Hollywood Latina*, 106.

25. Tony Taccone, *Life Without Makeup* (unpublished playscript, 2011). Used with permission; playscript in author's possession.

26. Actress Rita Moreno, of *West Side Story* fame, tells her own story in *Life Without Makeup* at the Berkeley Repertory Theatre, reported by PBS NewsHour Correspondent Spencer Michels, KQED clip, www.youtube.com/watch?v=pI1geTup7qs.

27. Taccone, *Life Without Makeup*, 14.

28. In New York, Moreno's mother earned money as a seamstress and housekeeper; Rita helped supplement those earnings by making paper flowers to sell. See Gordon, *Rita Moreno*, 47.

29. Taccone, *Life Without Makeup*, 7.

30. Taccone, *Life Without Makeup*, 14.

31. Taccone, *Life Without Makeup*, 14.

32. Gordon, *Rita Moreno*, 64.

33. The shop was owned by Rose Morgan, who "encouraged young women of the 1960s to enter the beauty business because 'I was a high school drop-out and it gave me an opportunity to prove that I could go as far as those who had been to college.'" Julia Kirk Blackwelder, *Styling Jim Crow: African American Beauty Training during Segregation* (College Station: Texas A&M University Press, 2003), 151–152.

34. Gordon, *Rita Moreno*, 84.

35. Taccone, *Life Without Makeup*, 16.

36. Gordon, *Rita Moreno*, 107.

37. Gordon, *Rita Moreno*, 113.

38. As I argue in *Dance and the Hollywood Latina*, Latinos as (young) male ethnic actors have not historically had the same access to white or white ethnic roles. As a result, their racial transgressions do not necessarily enhance their status; when Latinos are able to mobilize race, it is more of a lateral move across a variety of ethnicities. See Ovalle, *Dance and the Hollywood Latina*, 10.

39. Beltrán, *Latino/a Stars in U.S. Eyes*, 84.

40. At one point, for example, Moreno takes on every kind of character of her multiethnic childhood home. See Taccone, *Life Without Makeup*, 8.

41. Ovalle, *Dance and the Hollywood Latina*, 120.

42. Moreno calls those years during which she was raising her young daughter Fernanda the "bliss years," stating, "I had never been so happy, both at home and in my career." See Gordon, *Rita Moreno*, 239.

43. Gordon, *Rita Moreno*, 242.

44. Gazelle Emami, Matt Zoller Seitz, and Jen Chaney, "Rita Moreno on Why She Asked for Her One Day at a Time Character to Be Sexual, Marlon Brando, and Her First-Ever Scene Sans Makeup," *Vulture*, January 11, 2017, www.vulture.com/2017/01/rita-moreno -one-day-at-a-time-sexuality.html.

45. Emami, Seitz, and Chaney, "Rita Moreno."

46. Arlene Dávila, *Latinos, Inc.: The Marketing and Making of a People* (Berkeley: University of California Press, 2001), 144–147.

47. About 41 percent of the neighborhood's 64 percent Latinx community is of Mexican descent. "Mapping L.A. (Echo Park)," *Los Angeles Times*, http://maps.latimes.com /neighborhoods/neighborhood/echo-park/.

PART 4 INTERSECTIONALITY, HOLLYWOOD, AND CONTEMPORARY POPULAR CULTURE

13 · "EVERYTHING *GLEE* IN 'AMERICA'"

Context, Race, and Identity Politics in the *Glee* (2009–2015) Appropriation of *West Side Story* (1961)

ERNESTO R. ACEVEDO-MUÑOZ

The Fox television network premiered its musical-based series *Glee* on May 19, 2009, to unprecedented success. The show ran for six seasons, 2009 to 2015, and was even featured in the coveted slot immediately following the Super Bowl game on Fox in 2011, an outing that garnered the highest TV ratings in the history of the series. Over the course of its run, the series averaged six to seven million viewers weekly in the much sought-after eighteen to forty-nine demographic.[1] Arguably, *Glee* helped introduce a younger generation of Americans to a significant portion of the great American songbook, to reimagined and often abridged versions of well-known Broadway musical standards, and to repurposed versions of modern and contemporary pop hits, anything from Madonna to Hall and Oates to *Wicked*. Conceivably riding the coattails of the successful Disney series of *High School Musical* films (2006–2008), the high-school-set film version of the Broadway musical *Hairspray* (Adam Shankman, 2007), and singing competition shows like Fox's own *American Idol* (2002–2016; ABC 2017–), *Glee* combined comedy, light drama, competitive singing, and catchy tunes to lure its young audiences. The series creators and producers, led by Ryan Murphy and Brad Falchuk, purposely targeted the show's setting (the fictional William McKinley High School in Lima, Ohio) and story lines—boyfriend trouble, coming out, high school theatrics—to younger demographics.[2]

On the surface, *Glee*'s main casting attempted to underscore diversity, featuring characters that were LGBTQ, differently abled, and ethnic and racial minorities, those who did not fit the dominant media standards of youth representation (e.g., a heavyset African American woman). Prominently featured story lines included a love affair between two female cheerleaders, a gay couple's development of an active sexual relationship, and a transgender football coach going through gender confirmation surgery. In fact, much of the published scholarship on *Glee* centers on its representation of marginal and repressed sexualities as central, on its efforts to represent as normative sexual and gender orientations that are typically oppressed, erased, or used as comic relief in mainstream media.[3] While these representations are not unproblematic, the show's emphasis in underscoring acceptance or centralization of often repressed sexual identities, especially in a high school setting, seemed like a breath of fresh air in the dominant media landscape.

In the introduction to their 2015 volume on *Glee*, Brian C. Johnson and Daniel K. Faill state that "*Glee* has brought a new tone of inclusion to modern television," especially when it comes to gay representations as "positive," and suggest that this inclusivity is in parallel to progressive changes in contemporary society.[4] These gestures, nonetheless, did not exist in a vacuum; a 2010 Pew Research Center study concluded that millennials were generally more progressive and tolerant in their views on race, ethnicity, LGBTQ issues, marriage choices, and personal identities than their parents' generation.[5] Scholars have also pointed out, for all the apparent aura of inclusivity that permeates the show when it comes to LGBTQ identities or nontraditional sexualities, it was not all without controversy. A *USA Today* article from November 10, 2009, cited disability advocates who criticized the show for having an able-bodied actor (Kevin McHale) play the paraplegic character Artie Abrams. Some eyebrows were raised in February 2011 when the *Today* show reported that the actor who played glee club rival Blaine Anderson, who is gay, was heterosexual.

Other scholars agree that the show's attention to race issues is potentially even more problematic. In the same volume by Johnson and Faill cited above, for instance, an essay by Margaux Lippman-Hoskins underscores *Glee*'s "postracial rhetoric" to point out how the show "actively depoliticizes questions of race and difference and steers viewers away from an engagement with structural inequality."[6] In her analysis of the season 2 episode "Born This Way," Lippman-Hoskins argues that the illusion of a postracial America embraced by the show is centered around a rhetoric of "acceptance" of who we are: Black, Latinx, Asian, Jewish, and so forth; we are all equal and it is up to each one of us to simply "come as you are." In short, Lippman-Hoskins, and others cited in her work, put forward some of the ways in which *Glee* "ignores race," making race concerns a personal choice, rather than a reflection of problematic power structures that are still firmly in place.[7] Furthermore, in her analysis of representations of race in *Glee*, Rachel E. Dubrofsky also argues that postracial assumptions on the show have neutralized the character of Mercedes Jones (Amber Riley), the lead African American woman in the cast. Mercedes was represented as a somewhat typical "sassy" black girl with a ghetto-inflected speech and attitude in the early seasons. However, she was eventually whitened through several plotlines that cemented her position as a subordinate character within the firmly established glee club hierarchy to the main diva, Rachel Berry (Lea Michele).[8] Rachel was the indisputable star of the glee club from the earliest episodes of season 1, and, Dubrofsky argues, was always represented as a typically neurotic, self-centered, and show-stealing "Jewish-American Princess."[9] Rachel's aim is always to be the star of the show, which she accomplishes almost every single time, while common story lines involved her relentless pursuit of the lead soloist position in whatever musical show or competition the glee club was involved. Furthermore, Dubrofsky argues, in *Glee*, as in other representations of Jewish Americans of Ashkenazi descent, Rachel is represented, in form and attitude, as being white. In short, in *Glee*, Jewishness is middle-class whiteness, and comes with all the privileges which that identity presumes.[10]

In its third season, the series introduced a production of *West Side Story* to its plotline in which the two main competing divas, Rachel Berry and Mercedes Jones, vie for the lead role of María, the Puerto Rican girl, in the play. The series' apparently progressive approach brought in women from two often underrepresented groups (though in *Glee*, Jewish characters are not a minority in the main cast) to contend for the part of yet another minority, the most prominent Puerto Rican lead in American musical theater history. Since its Broadway debut on September 26, 1957, *West Side Story* has been controversial for the lack of Puerto Rican talent in the leading part of María, whose original Broadway star was Italian American singer and actress Carol Lawrence. The casting of Natalie Wood, an American of Russian and Ukrainian descent, as María in the 1961 movie was not without polemic. The film's producer and director, Robert Wise, engaged a casting agent known for representing Latinx actors in Los Angeles since the 1940s, but those hired were only used in background and smaller dancing roles. The producers auditioned Italian soprano Anna Maria Alberghetti for the role of María, but the search for a name actress led to the choice of Wood, though eventually her singing would be dubbed by Marni Nixon. Alberghetti would go on to play María in a 1964 revival, directed by the original show creator and choreographer Jerome Robbins.[11] The 1980 production was criticized, too, for demanding that actress Jossie de Guzmán, who is of Puerto Rican descent, dye her hair darker than her natural shade of brown for the part of María.[12] The most prominent exceptions are the two original Anita performers, Chita Rivera in the Broadway production of 1957 and Rita Moreno in the 1961 movie. In the 1980 revival, Debbie Allen, the African American choreographer and dancer, played Anita. The 2009 revival of *West Side Story* featured the Argentinian musical theater actress Josefina Scaglione, who is of Italian descent, in the lead. Actress Karen Olivo, a "Nuyorican" with Puerto Rican, Dominican, and Native American ancestry, played Anita and won a Tony Award for her performance. This pattern of casting in major productions of *West Side Story* is rather consistent: María is more often than not white, whitewashed or light-skinned, while Anita is allowed to be darker or even have (as in the cases of Rivera, Moreno, and Olivo) actual Puerto Rican blood. The *Glee* remake thus continues, for the most part, the tradition of excluding Puerto Ricans from the lead role, while at the same time allowing for the possibility of Mercedes to play María. The casting of Mercedes as María might have been seen as a somewhat resistant move against the historically whitewashed approach to casting *West Side Story*, especially the 1961 movie, which is the most widely seen of all versions. But the producers of *Glee* stopped short of that potentially provocative, though probably controversial move by perpetuating the historic trend of a white or *whiter* María.

The announcement and call for auditions for the William McKinley High School production of *West Side Story* is introduced in the third season premiere (written by Brad Falchuk). It is Rachel Berry herself who proposes they produce *West Side Story* and announces her intention to play María. Competing diva Mercedes Jones, nonetheless, calls for open auditions for the cast, herself coveting the lead role. After several musical numbers passing as auditions, the stage is set for a battle of the divas for the leading role. Mercedes, however, is the one with her work cut out for her. Over the previous seasons, Mercedes and Rachel often compete for solos or leading parts, but Rachel always wins, except when songs or performances are squarely seen as culturally aligned with black performers or characters. In fact, Mercedes's audition number for the *West Side Story* role is the song "Spotlight" (Hermansen, Eriksen, and Smith) made famous by Jennifer Hudson, the African American Academy Award winner who reached fame as an *American Idol* finalist. Mercedes is also often featured singing songs made famous by Aretha Franklin, while one of her nicknames at school is Aretha.[13] Among her other inspirations are Whitney Houston and Patti LaBelle. Mercedes's performance at the audition is praised highly by the play's directors. They single out Mercedes as glamorous and truthful and comment on how she has come out as leading lady material. Meanwhile, Rachel Berry opts for a less risky choice. In her audition, Rachel sings "(Somewhere) There's a Place for Us," in a light purple dress. The song is from the second act of the stage version of *West Side Story*, though usually sung off-stage in the show (by Consuelo or one of the secondary characters).[14] In the 1961 movie version, however, "There's a Place for Us" is sung by Tony and María in their pre-coital scene. Yet, this song is also historically associated with performer Barbra Streisand, an inspirational figure for Rachel Berry. In her pursuit of diva status, Rachel fancies herself Streisand's next heir apparent, and vows to go to Broadway and win a Tony by age twenty-five. Furthermore, inexplicably, Rachel is joined in the audition song by her birth mother, Shelby Corcoran, played by Broadway star Idina Menzel. Shelby claims to have played María eighteen times, though no details are offered. The two sing the song outfitted in purple dresses (one light, one dark). Significantly, purple is one of the colors associated with the Puerto Rican "Sharks" in *West Side Story*, both on stage and on film.[15] Of *Rent* and *Wicked* fame, Menzel is also of Eastern European Jewish descent. The embellishment of adding Shelby/Menzel to the audition song spotlights Rachel's preferred status, particularly since Mercedes Jones sings solo, without the aid of another powerful voice helping to carry hers. Rachel's audition choice is not only the less risky but also continues her assumptions that

FIGURE 13.1 Consistent with her diva status and white privilege, Rachel Berry (Lea Michelle), right, embellishes her audition for the part of María with the help of her mother (Idina Menzel). *Glee*, season 3 (2011).

she will win the part, underscores her Jewish-white privilege, and is consistent with her typical narrative arc (see Figure 13.1).

Yet, in spite of the all advantages afforded to Rachel Berry, over the course of episode 2 (written by Ryan Murphy) and episode 3 (written by Ian Brennan), much suspense is contrived from the question of who will play María. Paradoxically, the only two contenders for the part appear to be Rachel Berry and Mercedes Jones. The directors refer to other contestants; one of them in fact asking at one time, "Are we seeing more ethnic Marías today?" But the episodes never show any other aspirants to the part on camera. By the end of the first set of auditions, another one of the directors flatly states, "I like Rachel Berry. She's Jewish, but I think that'll help with the whole Puerto Rican thing." How or why being Jewish will "help with the whole Puerto Rican thing" is never explained but is consistent with *Glee*'s historic tapping of humor from racial stereotypes, or from the characters' apparent ignorance of their own racism and microaggressions. It is, however, consistent with the long history of women of white European descent playing María. The directors claim to favor "color blind casting," a statement supported by the Asian boy, Mike Chang (Harry Shum Jr.), auditioning and winning the role of Riff. Yet when Rachel and Mercedes are both called back to try out for María, at no point does it come up that apparently no ethnic Marías are being considered.

The contest between Rachel and Mercedes is considered "too close to call" and the singers are called in for "the ultimate María-off." But when Mercedes, conscious that she gave the strongest performance (and a callback is unnecessary), confronts the glee club director on his favoritism for Rachel, she is admonished and threatened with expulsion from the club. Mercedes concedes, and both are asked to audition with the same song, "(Out Here) On My Own" (Burt Bacharach and Carole Bayer Sager), a song made famous by one of Mercedes's models, Patti LaBelle. The callback audition sequence is filmed with the two performers on the same stage, singing separately, but edited together. In continuing matching shots, the sequence creates the illusion of a merging of personalities, not only as if Mercedes and Rachel are sharing the stage but also as if they were the same person. Another shot tracks from stage left to stage right, revealing the two singers in separate solo shots, but making it seem as if Mercedes and Rachel are singing the song in duet, together on stage, clearly an attempt to show that the competition is a level playing field. In the end, even Rachel herself comes to admit that Mercedes's performance was superior. Nevertheless, the directors are reluctant to cast Mercedes, thus upholding the constant favoritism of Rachel. They decide to double-cast the part and run the show for two weeks, allowing both Rachel and Mercedes to play María in alternate performances. Indignant, Mercedes walks out with a resounding sentence: "It's always been the Rachel Berry Show around here." Rachel, thus, gets to play María by default, while the show makes a big point that this is a bittersweet win for her. But that sting does not change the facts of the racial tension involved in the casting process, nor the white default practice of privileging white women in the role of María. It also cannot hide the fact that Mercedes was considered "the riskier choice," as one of the directors puts it, for all the reasons that she is always Rachel's second: being black, being fat, being typecast. Furthermore, a black María cast opposite a white Tony would also bring forth one of the most consistent taboos in American film and television: miscegenation. Given that Tony and María end up in bed together, the insistence on a white María (in almost every major production of *West Side Story*) is consistent with that cultural taboo, as well as with *Glee*'s conspicuous avoidance, with very few exceptions, of representations of interracial dating among its characters. As with most instances of race issues being brought up in *Glee*, when they do come up, it is in superficial ways, as the producers favor plotlines involving issues of sexual rather than racial identity.[16] María is whitened in favor of Rachel's privilege, saving the audience the discomforts, or the risk, of seeing a visibly inter-racial couple in bed, regardless of who is the better singer. Yet, even more alarming is the absence of the other ethnic Marías, either from the auditions or from the diegetic space of the show itself. In the postracial fantasy of *Glee*, color blind casting means white default, and in this case the producers are perpetrating and perpetuating the Puerto Rican erasure from the lead part of *West Side Story*.

The only Latina in the main cast of *Glee* is the character Santana López, played by actress Naya Rivera. A native Californian, Rivera is of Puerto Rican, African American, and German ancestry. Tellingly, among the glee club members, Santana is squarely, inevitably, and almost always placed in the position of antagonist. Santana is a stereotypical Latin "spitfire," a historic cliché in Hollywood narrative that goes back to the 1930s. More Lupe Vélez than Dolores del Río, Santana is a hypersexualized cheerleader, defiant of authority, insolent with teachers and coaches, a loudmouth often belligerent with her peers. Her sense of entitlement appears to stem from her position as one of the alpha females and cocaptain of the McKinley High cheerleading squad, the Cheerios. Hints at some dark events in her past also evidence a chip on her shoulder for which she makes up with her attitude. Taking after the Cheerios coach, Sue Sylvester, played by Jane Lynch, Santana often uses offensive language, racial slurs, and stereotypes, is prone to bullying—especially the wheelchair-bound glee club member Artie Abrams—and is often seen as a "troublemaker." She is especially sexualized, in her tiny cheerleader uniform (the only thing she wears to school), and given special attention by the directors, who often film her derrière in close-ups, and pay much attention to her legs, her hip-grinding, and her suggestive choreographic movements. Some fan sites, as well as an inactive Twitter account in Santana's name, list her middle name as "Diabla," the Spanish word for "she-devil." As antagonist, Santana is kicked out of the glee club several times over the course of the series. In one instance, in the season 3 opener, she is banned from glee club when her loyalty to the club comes into question, after she sets a piano on fire under instructions from Sue Sylvester. At points she is referred to as "two-faced" and duplicitous and self-describes as "an insidious bitch." She is cruelly outed also in season 3. During the argument when a fellow glee club member outs Santana in front of a crowd, he tells her that she looks like "an ass-less J. Lo." This insult is especially telling. As Frances Negrón-Muntaner has argued, the commodification of Jennifer López's body, and particularly her buttocks, has been the subject of both praise and criticism, as it is seen in media culture as evidence of her excess, of being "too much," and associated with an overtly threatening Latina femininity.[17] Thus, Santana's "ass-less J. Lo" body is here taken as somewhat lacking, missing the desirable derrière that white men fancy (and fear); Santana is hence seen as less than feminine, an especially cruel comment, as it comes in the act of outing her. Feeling that she too, like Mercedes, is always relegated to Rachel Berry's background, Santana plans at one time to defect to the rival glee club directed by Shelby Corcoran. Uncharacteristic of the Latin spitfire cliché, however, Santana López is a lesbian in love with, and eventually engaged to, her best friend, another one of the Cheerios. Nevertheless, Santana acts *femme*, and, eventually, after overcoming the humiliation of the outing, seems perfectly comfortable within her sexual identity.[18]

Significantly, over the course of season 3, it never seems to be a question who is going to play Anita in the McKinley High production of *West Side Story*. While we never see her audition for any part, by the end of episode 3 Santana is announced as the choice to play Anita. The show is vague about Santana's actual ethnicity, but Naya Rivera's Puerto Rican / African American roots are a useful clue. Though she is characterized loosely as a Latina—in keeping with the show's avoidance of specific ethnic/racial identities—in season 3 Santana's grandmother is played by the Puerto Rican actress Ivonne Coll, while her mother is played by Cuban American singer Gloria Estefan, setting her maternal bloodline squarely in the Caribbean region of the Greater Antilles. As mentioned above, the historical trend in casting *West Side Story* indicates the preference for hiring white or European women to play María, while Anita is more often than not portrayed by visibly ethnic types. It is thus consistent that in *Glee* the only clearly ethnic Latina is the default choice for the role. Moreover, as I have argued elsewhere, in all major versions of *West Side Story*, especially the 1957 Broadway show and the 1961 movie, Anita, in contrast to María, is characterized as being quite sexually savvy, experienced, and clearly sexually active in her relationship with María's brother, and leader of the Sharks, Bernardo. In their exchange in the bridal shop scene, María threatens to tell her parents about sexual activity between Bernardo and Anita, causing brief tension between the two best friends. María wears a gold crucifix around her neck and a charm with an image of the Virgin Mary pinned to her white slip and is seen praying at various points in the film, aligning her with a more pious, virginal personality than that of

Anita.[19] Anita is, by contrast, yet another incarnation of the Latin spitfire woman, which Rosa Linda Fregoso, in her work on Lupe Vélez, describes as "hot blooded, volatile, sexually promiscuous."[20] Fittingly, Santana's place as one of the contemporary heirs of the spitfire tradition makes her a shoo-in for the part of Anita without even having to audition for the role, certainly not on camera. We know from Santana's back story, which emerges sporadically in several episodes, that she is from Lima Heights, presumably a tough neighborhood; when provoked, she has been known to threaten to "go all Lima Heights" on her opponent and claims to have been abused by her grandmother. That is to say, singing or acting talents aside, Santana's ethnic, cultural, and social background qualify her for the part of Anita in ways that are directly opposite to Rachel Berry's natural claim as white diva to the part of María. The lead's virginal status is directly and indirectly implied in *West Side Story*, not only by her demeanor, her youth, her naïveté, and her white dress ("I will be the only one there in a white dress" she complains) but by her own admission that she yearns for "excitement." It is directly stated that, so far, in her courtship activities with would-be boyfriend Chino (one of the Shark's lieutenants), "nothing happens."

In episode 5 (written by Roberto Aguirre-Sacasa), while rehearsing for *West Side Story* it is revealed that Rachel is having difficulty with the part of María. Her rehearsals with Tony performer Blaine (Darren Criss) yield "no passion." The directors infer that the reason is because Blain and Rachel are both virgins. Evidently, no such concerns arise with Santana; not only is she already suspected to be a lesbian, but she is also known to have had heterosexual relations with at least two male characters in the glee club in previous seasons. While María's and Rachel's virginal status are unproblematically aligned in character, so to speak, so are Santana's sexual past and spitfire persona made parallel with Anita's typical characterization on stage and on film. This contrast is made quite visible in the first rehearsal scene between Rachel and Santana, when they take a turn at the "A Boy Like That / I Have a Love" duet from near the end of *West Side Story*. Important implications of costume and setting are at play here. Rachel is outfitted in a modest, white, frock type of dress covering her chest and shoulders, while Santana is in a fire-engine-red, low-cut, sleeveless dress. A bright-red rose in Santana's hair gives her a certain "Carmen" aura, another stereotype for hot-blooded, dangerous, "dark" women, as described by Mérimée.[21] The "A Boy Like That / I Have a Love" duet is the tour de force song for both characters, as Anita and María first argue, then agree, that love conquers all obstacles, even after Bernardo and Riff are dead and shortly before Tony is killed by María's jilted would-be beau, Chino. Regardless of the context of the song, the duet brings out the ultimate contrast between the two leads in *West Side Story* as seen through the lens of *Glee*: one virginal, modest, and white; the other sassy, sexy, and brown. Moreover, in contrast to the stage and movie versions of *West Side Story*, where the number is sung in the bedroom after Tony and María have just had sex for the first time, in *Glee* the duet is performed in a nondescript, empty stage. A single wooden chair sits between Rachel and Santana, as opposed to the unmade bed in the original. In the play and film, Anita is mourning her boyfriend's death at the hands of Tony, dressed in a modest light purple frock, her head covered with a black and red stole. María is still in a postcoital stupor, having just agreed to elope with the boyfriend, barely dressed in her slip and nightgown after consummating her sexual relationship with Tony. Clearly, the race issues are swept under the rug, sustaining the stereotypes that characterize the performers and the characters they play in the fictional universe of *Glee*. Here, María is dressed as if she was going to her Sunday catechism classes, while Anita looks as if she was ready for the prom. The limbo set and the lack of all context—remember, the song comes right after María has just lost her virginity and agreed to elope with her murderous boyfriend— neutralize all the anger, energy, and meaning of the song in its original form. Yet, it is consistent with the *Glee* appropriation of *West Side Story* in its insistence to showcase Rachel's virtue and safe-playing centrality, in contrast to her sassy, sexy, marginal, colored subordinates, especially Mercedes and Santana (see Figure 13.2).

When we finally get to the opening night of *West Side Story*, about midway through episode 5, the question of Rachel's virginity and with it her suitability to play her character with passion continues to sidetrack the context of the musical numbers, that is, those that the *Glee* producers decide to show. In anticipation backstage, Rachel is wearing the usual pastel, modest dress, while Santana is in the same dress seen in the rehearsal of "A Boy Like That / I Have A Love," though she's not scheduled for that scene until near the end of the second act. Perhaps not surprisingly, the first number featured during opening night in the *Glee* version of *West Side Story* is "America," skipping over, among others, the thunderous "Prologue," and the "Mambo" number at the gym. Not only do these two numbers establish the turf rivalry, the racial tensions, and the displays of violence between the Jets and the Sharks,

FIGURE 13.2 Santana López as Anita (Naya Rivera), left, and Rachel Berry as María (Lea Michelle) are contrasted in attitude, race, and dress, the former "sexy, sassy and brown," the latter "virginal, modest, and white." *Glee*, season 3 (2011).

ostensibly important to the plot, they also offer, along with "Cool," the most vigorous displays of choreography and dance talent in the whole show. However, the role of María is not a dancing part in *West Side Story*; in fact, she and Tony are the most passive in terms of dancing of the main five characters. Yet, "America" is soon set up and becomes the *Glee* signature number in the show's *West Side Story* arc. Only at this time is the TV audience introduced to Bernardo in character. Surprisingly or not, he is played by Puck, a natural bad boy in the *Glee* universe who has previously impregnated the goody-two-shoes cheerleader Quinn and had a sexual affair with Rachel's birth mother, Shelby Corcoran. As with the case of Anita and Santana, we never see Puck audition for any role. As a professional bad boy, sexual activity and mohawk haircut included, Puck is a natural for the switchblade-toting, machista Puerto Rican gang leader Bernardo, though unsurprisingly for *Glee*, he is also ethnically identified, however vaguely, as Jewish. That said, the cast of *Glee*, and the New Directions in particular, features a conspicuous absence of Latino male characters. But, clearly, someone *has* to play Bernardo, and Puck's history, like Santana's presumably, is enough to qualify him for the role. The spoken prelude to the song is played with heavily exaggerated Hispanic accents, giving the glee club director, Mr. Schuster, the opportunity to state, "We have to work on their diction." As a Latinx cliché, the accent is played "for yuks," with mispronunciations and peppered here and there with Spanish words.

The Sharks, which include assorted, though heretofore unseen ethnic types, as well as the Jewish-Asian character Tina Cohen-Chang (Jenna Ushkowitz) in the role of Rosalía, appear on stage all in red and black costumes, in keeping with certain color schemes typically associated with gang loyalties in *West Side Story*. Inexplicably, however, the *Glee* Sharks here plunge into a significantly abridged version of "America" as heard in the movie. As I have argued elsewhere, screenwriter Ernest Lehman insisted that lyricist Stephen Sondheim change the lyrics and structure of the song "America" to make it more palatable, and less openly insulting to Puerto Ricans. Not only were the most offensive lyrics softened down for the film, but the structure was changed into a call and response between the girls, defenders of the Puerto Rican experience in the United States, and more eager to assimilate, and the boys, whose lyrics underscored, in contrast, a dark, unsettling "immigrant" experience of abuse, racism, and ethnic violence.[22] What is more, the movie version of "America" has been historically limited to the film. The immense majority of *West Side Story* productions, from Broadway revivals to opera companies, from local summer stock and regional theater, to university and high school productions, all adhere to the original theater lyrics and staging of the song. In the theater version is it performed only by the Sharks girls, and Rosalía is the sole dissenter who dreams of going "back to San Juan." The copyright holders of the *West Side Story* songbook, Boosey & Hawkes, in fact grant permission for the lyrics only as featured in the original stage play. Thus, the decision of the *Glee* producers to use lyrics as rewritten for the movie, though abridged, as well as the structure as a call and response between the boys and the girls, is not only ahistorical but also controversial. On one hand, it suggests the show's catering to movie and TV audiences, likely to be familiar with the movie, as opposed to the presumably more sophisticated theatergoing public. On the other hand, along with the editing to a shorter version, it sanitizes *West Side Story* for its millennial audience. Paradoxically, the movie lyrics are more political, as they allow for dissent with the fallacy of the American dream, and for an indictment of the naïveté of the girls' assimilationist attitude. While the Sharks girls sing "I like to be in America / OK by me in America / Everything free in America," the boys' biting counterpoint concludes with the lines "Everywhere grime in America / Organized crime in America / Terrible time in America." The *Glee* version purposely manages to deflate that political angle. The abridged lyrics conspicuously do not include the most politically charged lines (quoted above), opting in their stead for the repetition of more tame verses ("Poor as can be in America") and, as a refrain, the recapped, endlessly meaningless phrase "La la la la la la America. . . ."

In yet another seemingly unmotivated revision, the *Glee* version of "America" introduces the Jets. They inexplicably crash the Sharks' party and take over part of their resistant, politically charged lyrics. The Jets appear from within the audience and respond to the girls' verses in lieu of the Sharks. The camera cuts back and forth over the following exchange:

> Sharks' girls: Here you are free and you have pride
> Jets: 'Long as you stay on your own side
> Sharks' girls: Free to do anything you choose
> Jets: Free to wait tables and shine shoes

Paradoxically, the Jets' prejudices against the Sharks *are* voiced here, perhaps to make up for *Glee's* sidetracking of the "Prologue," the "Jet Song," and the "Mambo" challenges. But the hijacking of those specific lyrics from the Sharks' own voices effectively undermines the Puerto Rican's own, real, fact-based grievances against the fallacy of the American dream, which is what the song is about in its movie version. In other words, the producers of *Glee* opt for the movie version of the song, which, as I have argued elsewhere, is evidently more effectively political, even a song of protest. But the potential political content is defused by the intervention of the Jets and their muting of the Sharks' many genuine grievances. In a typically postracial move, their plight, like all racial tensions in *Glee*, is rendered unexplored, unproblematic.

Unexpectedly, this is the highlight of the *Glee* appropriation of *West Side Story*. After the "America" showcase, no mention is made of landmark songs. The "Tonight" quintet, which would have given other performers a chance to show off, the rumble, which emphasizes the inevitability and endlessness of the circle of racial violence, the "Somewhere" ballet, which is not a María solo or duet in the play, are all again sidetracked to get back to what this narrative arc seems most concerned about: Rachel's virginity.

After a somewhat flat performance on opening night, and some suspense about whether the boyfriend is content operating as an acting booster for

Rachel, the virginity "issue" is resolved. She and the boyfriend, Finn (who is not in the show), consummate their sexual relationship, and Rachel/María and Blaine/Tony perform "One Hand, One Heart" with much emotion, on the second night. Naturally, Rachel and the TV spectators are rewarded by the theater audience with a standing ovation. Unbeknownst to them, though not to *Glee*'s fans, it is for her sexual bravery rather than her acting passion that Rachel is rewarded. In *West Side Story*, on the professional stage and the 1961 movie, María's sexual awakening comes at a time of trauma: her brother has been killed by her own boyfriend. Numbed by the events, they fall in each other's arms in a desperate act of grieving. She emerges from the sex act, however, with a regained sense of narrative agency, taking charge, giving Tony instructions for their elopement. Shortly thereafter, after Chino kills Tony, María delivers what is ostensibly the play's moral: "You all killed him, and my brother, and Riff. But not with guns and knives, but with hate. Well, now I can kill, because now I too have hate . . . ."

In the *Glee* version of *West Side Story*, with no narrative context for the songs and the sanitization of the political content, the matter of Rachel's virginity becomes the major plot point, especially given the show's attention to Rachel's relentless quest for, and assertion of, her diva status. In fact, Rachel's stardom comes at the expense of the rest of the New Directions, especially the three women of color: Mercedes Jones, Santana López, and Tina Cohen-Chang.

At the end of the year, the New Directions are whole, back together after the several defections, tensions, and jealousies highlighted through the season. The New Directions win the National Show Choir competitions in Chicago, where Rachel is once again given center stage so that she can make up for a failed audition to the New York Academy of Dramatic Arts (NYADA). Rachel's dreams of NYADA, a fictional school seemingly modeled after NYU, is temporarily derailed when she chokes at her audition in front of the admissions official (Whoopi Goldberg). But she convinces both the glee club members to let her have the solo part at nationals and the admissions official to attend the show. Naturally, her performance at nationals wins her the spot at NYADA, aided by her lead in *West Side Story*, and by all the sacrifices incurred by her teammates. In the season finale, the entire glee club comes to see Rachel off at the train station, New York and NYADA bound. Tellingly, Santana, like Mercedes before her and Tina Chang in the end, have all clearly been brought into the fold. Santana is now sweet, softened by the shows of support for her newly outed status. She has been rendered submissive, aware of her place, or whitened as Dubrofsky may argue. In the postracial fantasy of *Glee*, there is place for only one diva, and the third season narrative arc relentlessly reserves that place for the club's white star, directly at the expense of potentially more talented women of color, particularly Mercedes Jones and Santana López. The fact that the assertion of the centrality of the white diva occurs over the casting of *West Side Story* cannot be ignored. As with the history of casting for *West Side Story*, race, ethnicity, and identity are color blind when it comes to reasserting white privilege.

The *Glee* appropriation of *West Side Story* arguably introduced many of the songs to a new generation of fans, yet failed to correct the historical repression of Puerto Rican talent in national productions or adaptations of the show. The *Glee* emphasis on its own drama, rather than *West Side Story*'s, and its stress on out-of-context musical numbers neutralized whatever political, racial, and political tension existed in the original property. The *Glee* intersection of *West Side Story* continues to blunt the impact of a theatrical property once considered edgy and controversial, and perpetuates the marginalization of its political and cultural context.

NOTES

1. Rachel E. Dubrofsky, "Jewishness, Whiteness, and Blackness on *Glee*: Singing to the Tune of Postracism," *Communication, Culture and Critique* 6, no. 1 (2013): 82–102, 83.

2. Louisa Ellen Stein, *Millennial Fandom: Television Audiences in the Transmedia Age* (Iowa City: University of Iowa Press, 2015), 12–14.

3. See Jason Jacobs, "Raising Gays: On *Glee*, Queer Kids, and the Limits of the Family," *GLQ: A Journal of Lesbian and Gay Studies* 20, no. 3 (2014): 319–352. See also Michaela D. E. Meyer and Meghan M. Wood, "Sexuality and Teen Television: Emerging Adults Respond to Representations of Queer Identity in *Glee*," *Sexuality and Culture* 17, no. 3 (2013): 434–448.

4. Brian C. Johnson and Daniel K. Faill, eds., *Glee and New Directions for Social Change* (Rotterdam: Sense, 2015), xi.

5. Pew Research Center, *Millennials: A Portrait of Generation Next* (Social and Demographic Trends; Washington, DC: Pew Research Center, 2010).

6. Margaux Lippman-Hoskins, "*Glee* and 'Born This Way': Therapeutic and Postracial Rhetoric," in Johnson and Faill, *Glee and New Directions for Social Change*, 111–122, 112.

7. Lippman-Hoskins, "*Glee* and 'Born This Way,'" 122.

8. Dubrofsky, "Jewishness, Whiteness, and Blackness," 98.

9. Dubrofsky, "Jewishness, Whiteness, and Blackness," 83.

10. Dubrofsky, "Jewishness, Whiteness, and Blackness," 85.

11. Ernesto R. Acevedo-Muñoz, West Side Story *as Cinema: The Making and Impact of an American Masterpiece* (Lawrence: University Press of Kansas, 2013), 38.

12. Frances Negrón-Muntaner, *Boricua Pop: Puerto Ricans and the Latinization of American Culture* (New York: New York University Press, 2004), 68.

13. Dubrofsky, "Jewishness, Whiteness, and Blackness," 96–97.

14. Elizabeth A. Wells, West Side Story: *Cultural Perspectives on an American Musical* (Lanham, MD: Scarecrow Press, 2011), 70.

15. Acevedo-Muñoz, West Side Story *as Cinema*, 86–88.

16. Stein, *Millennial Fandom*, 34–35.

17. Negrón-Muntaner, *Boricua Pop*, 228–246.

18. Katherine Hobson, "Sue Sylvester, Coach Beistie, Santana Lopez, and Unique Adams: Exploring Queer Representations of Femininity in *Glee*," in Johnson and Faill, *Glee and New Directions for Social Change*, 95–107, 102–104.

19. Acevedo-Muñoz, West Side Story *as Cinema*, 88–89.

20. Rosa Linda Fregoso, "Lupe Vélez: Queen of the B's," in *From Bananas to Buttocks: The Latina Body in Popular Film and Culture*, ed. Myra Mendible (Austin: University of Texas Press, 2007), 51–68, 51.

21. Prosper Mérimée, *Carmen* (Urbana, IL: Project Guttenberg, 2006), chap. 4.

22. Acevedo-Muñoz, West Side Story *as Cinema*, 161–164.

14 · HIP-HOP "HEARTS" BALLET

Utopic Multiculturalism and the *Step Up* Dance Films (2006, 2008, 2010)

MARY BELTRÁN

It is a scenario and a romantic pairing that have become familiar to the point of cliché to fans of the multicultural dance film. Amid a performing arts backdrop, two young talented dancers, often of different ethnic backgrounds but always from "different sides of the tracks" and with familiarity in contrasting dance traditions, one in ballet and the other in a popular style such as jazz or hip-hop, are paired. They train, they challenge each other, and they make discoveries about themselves and their worlds from doing so. And of course, they fall in love. Clichés of a genre, or in this case subgenre, provide viewer pleasures, while also often working through many of the social issues that are intrinsic to the genre terrain. In multicultural dance films, these romances, key conventions of the subgenre, also support other, timely thematic concerns. In the subgenre's origins in the 1980s and in more recent iterations in the 2000s and early 2010s, narratives of romance, friendship, training, performance, and competition illuminate what it means for youth and particularly working-class youth to have agency and opportunity. As Angela McRobbie has noted, "some of the most richly coded class practices in contemporary society can be observed in leisure and particularly in dance,"[1] with public dance spaces offering youth and young adults settings for the expression of their unique identities, concerns, and frustrations. As cinema's version of the public dance hall, multicultural dance films work through myths of meritocracy and realities of opportunity powerfully intersecting in young adults' lives and futures. However, as the multicultural dance film has evolved over the decades, American notions and social discourses have also shifted on these issues, particularly with respect to race and class. How has the subgenre evolved in relation to these social shifts over the last two decades; what does it mean, in recent films, when hip-hop "hearts" ballet and vice versa?

I begin with a historical survey that illuminates the aesthetic and narrative conventions of the subgenre and the ways in which it has developed apace with national imaginings of race and race relations, class, and its impact on the so-called American dream of achievement through hard work and merit. The multicultural dance film is a subset of the dance musical, Hollywood musicals with a focus on dance, which can be traced back as far as *Applause* (1929) and *Whoopee* (1930), the first known early sound films that incorporated movement and dance as central narrative and aesthetic elements.[2] I define the multicultural dance film as dance musicals with a multicultural (and often mixed-class) cast and urban settings; in my estimation, these films have been released in two main cycles. The first multicultural dance films arguably included *Saturday Night Fever* (1977), about working-class youth such as Tony Manero (played by a young John Travolta) entering the world of disco dancing in 1970s Brooklyn, which focused on ethnic and class distinctions rather than racial differences. *Fame* (1980) and *Flashdance* (1983) soon followed to major box office success, establishing many of the tropes of the subgenre, as I elaborate below. *Fame* in fact was adapted into a television series twice, as *Fame* (1982–1987) and *Fame L.A.* (1997–1998), and was also remade as a film in 2009. Early cycle multicultural dance films also included the first films to focus on hip-hop culture and break dancing, such as *Breakin'* (1984), *Beat Street* (1984), and *Breakin' 2: Electric Boogaloo* (1984), and the Sidney Poitier–directed *Fast Forward* (1985). I focus here on the films that received the widest release and success at the box office, namely *Fame* and *Flashdance*.

Is the more contemporary cycle of dance films a continuation of the narratives, aesthetics, and racial and class politics found in *Fame* and *Flashdance*, or are the films from the two cycles radically divergent in some regards? My research here involves a comparative narrative and textual analysis of these films with a focus on the films' narratives and dance performances and their embedded discourses about race, class, national identities, mixed-race romance, meritocracy, and leadership. Ultimately, I explore a few recent films, namely *Step Up* (2006), *Step Up 2: The Streets* (2008), and *Step Up 3D* (2010), and place them in comparison to the most successful multicultural dance films of the 1980s, *Fame* and *Flashdance*. First, I survey the development of the subgenre broadly through a brief summary of the narratives of the films in these two cycles. As noted, they relate stories of teens or young adults in urban environments striving to achieve success as professional dancers, often despite challenges posed by class or race-related disadvantages.

DANCE AS REMEDY FOR SOCIAL BARRIERS: THE MULTICULTURAL DANCE FILM

Fame (1980), directed by Alan Parker, came in many ways to define the multicultural dance film. Shot in a gritty documentary style, it tells the story of a diverse group of students at the School of Performing Arts (now the High School of Performing Arts) in New York City, and features a number of the school's real-life students as extras. The teen protagonists, who are followed from their auditions until their graduation four years later, include electronics-obsessed musician Bruno Martelli (Lee Curreri), aspiring, angsty actors Doris Finsecker (Maureen Teefy), Montgomery MacNeil (Paul McCrane), and Raul Garcia / Ralph Garci (Barry Miller), troubled dance students Leroy Johnson (Gene Anthony Ray) and Lisa Monroe (Laura Dern), and triple threat Coco Hernandez (Irene Cara), who excels in all three performing arts. As might be surmised from their names and these brief descriptions, the main characters and their classmates hail from different neighborhoods and social worlds of New York City, but many become friends in the course of their challenging years at the school. The narrative does not gloss over the personal struggles, hardships, and obstacles that students at performing arts schools actually face, and also foregrounds the dreams that motivate them to attend their school and pursue professional careers in the performing arts. This motivational quality is especially evident in the soundtrack, and most noticeably the hit song "Fame." It included lyrics by cast member Irene Cara, a Bronx native of Afro-Puerto Rican and Cuban descent and an alumna of a performing arts school: "I can catch the moon in my hand /

Don't you know who I am / Remember my name, fame / I'm gonna live forever / I'm gonna learn how to fly, high."[3] Cara also sang and cowrote the theme song for *Flashdance* (1983), "Flashdance—What a Feeling," released a few years later.

Flashdance took a much more fantasy-based approach to the subject of a young adult striving to become a dance professional. A film driven by its producers (Don Simpson and Jerry Bruckheimer), *Flashdance* is centered on the young, racially and ethnically ambiguous woman Alex Owens (played by Jennifer Beals, now known to be of mixed African American and Italian American heritage). Alex, who lives alone in industrial Pittsburgh and apparently has no family ties, dreams of becoming a ballet dancer but cannot afford to go to ballet school. Instead she trains on her own and works as a welder at a factory and as an exotic dancer at night. Ultimately, she decides to audition for the city ballet company despite her lack of training, encouraged by an older white mentor who had once been a ballerina. The world of Pittsburgh ballet, notably, is presented as overly white in scenes in which Alex has to pass through groups of dancers waiting to audition in order to get an application. Alex is tomboyish and incongruently dressed (in dark, baggy clothes and dark work boots, compared to the other dancers' pink, white, and black ballet outfits), ethnic (with dark curly hair, as opposed to the dancers' controlled buns), and untrained, compared to the other women's seeming comfort within the world of ballet. Alex finally succeeds in auditioning and does surprisingly well because of her energetic and unique dance style forged from watching and practicing break dancing on the Pittsburgh streets. In her audition, she dares to incorporate break dancing moves into her dance routine; her choice to be herself gives her the competitive edge she needs. As McRobbie notes in describing the treatment of jazz dance and break dance in *Flashdance* and *Fame*, popular dance styles are posed as more authentic and vital than ballet in these and other films.[4] In the process these films and dance performances posit a contrast of not just "high" versus "popular" culture, but of class associations as well.

The multicultural dance film reappears two decades later but to discursively different ends, namely in pointing to the importance of social context and the evolving racial and class politics of genre films. In films such as *Center Stage* (2000), *Save the Last Dance* (2001), *Honey* (2003), the youth-oriented *High School Musical* films (2006–2016), the PG-13 remake of *Fame* (2009), and the *Step Up* dance films and television series,[5] plot lines of overcoming economic disadvantage, friendships, and romances that cross social borders and the assertion of meritocracy continue to define the subgenre. However, in these more recent iterations of the multicultural dance film the racial and class politics of the films have shifted dramatically. At the level of aesthetics, the millennial films bring the genre to a utopic imagined locale known as postracial America.[6] Very few darker skinned actors are cast, while light tan actors of ambiguous heritage are favored. More straight-appearing male performers also seem to be favored in the 2000s and 2010s films than were cast in the original *Fame*. At the visual level, the casting and art direction fit definitions of what has been described variously as the multiculti film or mixploitation film.[7] In such films, diversity is foregrounded as a utopic playground in which a rainbow-hued group of vaguely ethnic individuals easily form a happy and harmonious community. Hip-hop dance also takes on a new valence in comparison with the 1980s films. Mastery of hip-hop dance is important to the new films' narratives and dance performances for white youth as well as youth of color, as a kind of performative glue that holds the diverse community together. With respect to the financial incentives for screenwriters, producers, and film financiers, hip-hop music also is likely seen as a lucrative element that attracts American and international youth audiences.

The theme of personal empowerment through dance and fairness in this process, which McRobbie points to as a central element of the 1980s dance films, are dominant discourses in the later cycle of films as well.[8] As John M. Chu, director of *Step Up 2: The Streets* and *Step Up 3D*, notes in a director's featurette on the *Step Up 2: The Streets* DVD, "Dance is the one language that everybody speaks. We all have a heartbeat, it's from that core part of our bodies that we feel music, that we feel dance. I think we have a really strong message, about the world is what we make of it. That it's not what you've got, that it's what you make of what you've got."[9] Dance thus is posited as a utopian equalizer built on meritocracy that further eradicates race and class barriers. For example, the first three films of the *Step Up* film franchise highlight many of the same social concerns. With much of the narrative carried by dance performances at performing arts schools, night clubs with large dance floors, and outdoor spaces where hip-hop dance battles are regularly staged, these three films are concerned with cultural clashes, but also clashes between old and new ways of defining popular culture, its meanings for contemporary youth, and its conferral of status to youth of various class backgrounds and ethnicities. In *Step Up* (2006), directed by choreographer Anne Fletcher, Tyler Gage (Channing Tatum), a white teen and talented hip-hop dancer who has grown up in an African American neighborhood in Baltimore, ends up having to do community service at the performing arts high school, which has a vibrant, ethnically diverse student population. He meets an equally talented and plucky white modern dancer, Nora, and soon they end up training together. They challenge each other and grow from their pairing, culminating in a yin-and-yang dance number that helps Nora professionally and allows Tyler to become a bona fide student of the school.

Step Up 2: The Streets, directed by John M. Chu, explores similar themes with a new female protagonist, Andie. She is another white teen raised in Tyler's neighborhood who also faces new challenges and possibilities in her life after becoming a student at the performing arts school. Meanwhile, battles between dance crews at the popular dance club the Dragon are just as significant as training at the school. Andie and her wealthy and white across-the-tracks love interest, Chase, put together a multiethnic crew of their fellow students, which is ultimately triumphant in the competition because of their hard work and passion for dance. Finally, *Step Up 3D* follows Moose, one of Andie's crew members from the previous film, who is ethnically ambiguous but white, after he moves to New York City for college. He soon finds that he cannot put his love of hip-hop dance to rest in order to study engineering as his father wishes. He is drawn into a creative world of global hip-hop dance competition and joins a multicultural but white-dominant dance crew; he helps lead them to victory at the ultimate, concluding dance battle.

Clearly there are many parallels between the films of the two cycles described above with respect to the kinds of teen realities, dreams of professional careers and stardom and dancers, labor (through dance education and training), and competition that is being addressed, and the substantial, real-life consequences and rewards that come from being seen as winning those competitions. There also are parallels in that all of these films allude to class and racial disparities that can exist with respect to whether young adults can access the training, education, and other support needed to pursue dreams of a career in professional dance. However, many distinctions can be found when comparing films of the two cycles as well.

SAME DANCE, DIFFERENT MEANINGS:
THE MILLENNIAL DANCE FILM

The new border-crossing romance, highlighted in the title of this essay, fore-grounds in both film cycles narratives of attraction, romance, and friendship for the youthful protagonists across racial and class lines. Romances of oppo-sites attracting are not new to the dance musical, of course, with the pairing of Fred Astaire and Ginger Rogers perhaps the most popular permutation in Hollywood's studio era.[10] What has been unique to the multicultural dance film of both cycles is the additional social tension explored through romances that cross social and cultural borders. Films of these two cycles treat these romances quite differently, however. We can begin exploring this narrative element in the original *Fame*. During auditions for acceptance into the per-forming arts school, talented but untrained African American dancer Leroy (Gene Anthony Ray) is viewed by the dance instructors as a somewhat dan-gerous object of desire as he dances for them in a streetwise, sexualized style. He is gifted, but very unsocialized to the expectations of a performing arts school. Later he has a romance with Hilary Van Dorne (Antonia Franceschi), a wealthy white ballerina at the school who flirts with him. While the depth of Hilary's feelings for Leroy are unclear—Leroy would likely be read as potentially gay if he were cast in a more contemporary film[11]—she brings him home to her family's luxurious apartment, knowing that it will upset her rich father and stepmother. Their romance is presented as temporary but destructive. We never learn why the relationship does not last, but Hilary's dreams of ballet stardom are threatened when she later finds herself pregnant and alone.

In contrast, in the more recent cycle of films, *Save the Last Dance* (2008) appears at first to upend the subgenre's 1980s notions of opportunity as only given to white student performers. It focuses on a white ballet dancer, Sara Johnson (Julia Stiles), still coming to terms with her mother's death and hav-ing to live with her father in Chicago. She is now the only white student at an African American high school, where mastery of hip-hop dance is vital to social capital. Luckily, Sara is romanced by her friend Chenille's responsible and kind brother Derek (Sean Patrick Thomas), who guides her in this new environment and most importantly teaches her about hip-hop dance. Their romance helps her grow as a person and in fact have the confidence to successfully audition for Juilliard's dance program. In an audition reminiscent of Alex's in *Flashdance,* Sara showcases a confident and culturally hybrid style that she fully owns, as she blends hip-hop and ballet steps in her routine. While the film highlights a warm and nurturing interracial relationship in comparison to Leroy and Hilary's doomed romance, it still privileges Sara's experience and growth over Derek's. Derek and Chenille fit Krin Gabbard's description of "magical" African American characters, or characters that exist primarily to teach or mentor a white character, given that Chenille or Derek serve as Sara's mentors with respect to how they teach, enlighten, and encourage her development.[12] Admittance into a ballet company is also still the ultimate goal for Sara. Hip-hop dance thus is ultimately a tool to achieving this goal; it has value but not equal value to ballet, associated with whiteness and upper-class status.

The *Step Up* films, moreover, offer new twists on the cross-racial romance, by positioning white protagonists as stand-ins for nonwhiteness in these romances. In *Step Up,* Tyler Gage is positioned within the narrative as symbolically African American. He has been raised in foster care with African American foster siblings, and his friends are African American as well. He has a great love of hip-hop dance based on his upbringing. We see him busting moves in a local dance club and outdoors with his friends in the neighborhood. Because of his background he is initially ill at ease at the performing arts school, which feels like an upper-class, privileged space. It is there, however, where he meets his love interest, ballet and modern dancer Nora. Nora is white and economically privileged, which comes to stand in for unambiguously white within the formula of the subgenre. Tyler and Nora's pairing thus serves within the story line as the stand-in for a mixed-race romance. There are parallels in *Step Up 2: The Streets. Step Up 2* protagonist Andie (Briana Evigan), who is also white, ultimately falls for a white male dance student, Chase. Chase, who loves hip-hop dance, but has to prove himself in this arena because he grew up with economic privilege. Their differing class backgrounds and Andie's ambiguous racialization because of her upbringing are the social divides that they bridge as a couple. In sum, we begin to see both subtle and dramatic shifts in the central romance in the millennial dance films as working-class status becomes racialized in the imagined post-racial environment. The *Step Up* films actually feature few cross-racial romantic relationships despite their veneer of racelessness. Ultimately, they do little to illustrate that their viewers would grow from moving beyond their comfort zone and gaining knowledge of other cultures, beyond of course, gaining mastery of hip-hop dance.

DANCE PERFORMANCES AND UTOPIC MULTICULTURALISM

A common element of these dance films, and one that emphasizes the subgenre's focus on fantasy, both in the 1980s and the 2000s, is a shared trait in dance performances in what I term utopic multiculturalism. While the story premise of a multicultural dance film typically foregrounds the upbringing, class status, and ethnic and racial identities of its protagonists, in performance scenes that foreground utopic multiculturalism, differences are bridged as the young performers bring their voices, bodies, and musical instruments together in song and dance. The spectacle offers a fantasy of utopic harmony between various racial and ethnic groups centered around music, particularly hip-hop music, and dance. Richard Dyer similarly highlights a common focus of Hollywood musicals on utopic scenarios and ideals. As Dyer notes, musicals often provide "the image of 'something better' to escape into, or something we want deeply that our day-to-day lives don't provide."[13] Likewise Erica Chito Childs's concept of multiracial utopia describes film and television scenes in which "different races and colors mesh."[14] However, I suggest, multicultural utopia is a more apt term to describe millennial media narratives that embrace a vaguely racialized or postracial aesthetic rather than addressing race directly. Millennial dance films express utopic multiculturalism not just through the narrative and choreography, but also through films' aesthetics, for instance, choices made regarding the casting, costumes, art direction, and music.

In the original *Fame*'s musical number "Hot Lunch," for instance, the students of the Performing Arts School in New York spontaneously perform a song and dance in the cafeteria on the protagonists' first day. The number begins as student dancers in casual ballet and jazz dance rehearsal clothes and student musicians begin informally improvising together while eating and talking with their friends. The students are widely diverse—Latino, Asian American, African American, white, and ethnically ambiguous—and encompass a wide range of styles, from adventurous and creative in appearance to

FIGURE 14.1 *Fame*'s (1980) "46th Street Jam" showcases youth of color and gay student dancers, highlighting that anyone can be a ballet dancer.

buttoned-down. They are spurred into a full-on musical and dance performance when Bruno plays a song on the piano and Coco sings along, leading the group into what becomes "Hot Lunch." Soon almost everyone is up dancing, typically in ballet and modern dance style, or playing a musical instrument, contributing to the performance and community of their making. Among the many meanings that might be derived from this scene is that art knows no boundaries, and there is great art to be made through sharing. When another spontaneous song and dance spills onto 46th Street, stalling cars unlucky enough to be there at the time, the dance students have even more room to strut their ballet-trained bodies. In the "46th Street Jam," many of the dancers are dark skinned, and some are clearly gay young men (see Figure 14.1). We see a world of New York City in 1980s in which gay liberation and growing racial pride were being felt. Given that ballet is the dance style stressed, the implication is that teens of all races and skin colors can be ballet dancers.

The performances of "Hot Lunch" and "46th Street Jam" encapsulate several of the major ideological takeaways of the film and of the multicultural dance film as a whole. Photos of both dance scenes were used for the film posters for both *Fame* and its 2009 remake. In more recent iterations of the multicultural dance film, these types of scenes are even more codified as part of the subgenre's narrative structure. In the *Step Up* films, for instance, the celebration of utopic multiculturalism comes to be grounded in a location, a bar called the Dragon, where young people seemingly of all economic and class backgrounds come to mingle and compete in hip-hop dance-offs. Andie and Tyler, for instance, amiably dance with friends and face off against rivals at the bar. Compared to the performers in "Hot Lunch" and "46th Street Jam," they are noticeably whiter, much more middle class, and straighter, in a variety of ways, however. These moments in recent dance films have jibed with what has been taking place elsewhere in millennial, youth-oriented popular culture. In previous research, I noted a "raceless" aesthetics, divorced, from the racial politics of films such as *The Fast and The Furious* (2001-) franchise and other millennial action films that featured diverse casts, mixed-race actors, and portrayals of harmonious, multiethnic communities.[15] Dance performances in the multicultural dance film similarly embrace an aesthetics of racelessness as well as emphasizing the possibility of utopic multiculturalism as a social ethos, while not embracing race in a meaningful way.

It is useful to note that in relation to dance performances in the millennial films, hip-hop dance also performs timely symbolic work. In films such as *Save the Last Dance, Honey*, and the *Step Up* pictures, hip-hop dance is given equal and often more value than ballet or modern dance within the main characters' social worlds. This makes sense when viewed from the perspective of the films' producers and distributors, given the global popularity and economic importance of hip-hop music. Whether the incorporation of hip-hop music into the narratives actually supports notions of bridging social and racial divides is debatable, however. In the first three *Step Up* films, the protagonists, Tyler, Andie, and Moose, bring viewers in to vicariously compete and master this seemingly raceless and classless arena. They face their fears, master hip-hop dance, and become leaders (and, in the realm of competitions, winners) within the diverse cultural milieu. Protagonists of color, on the other hand, largely do not.

Dance performances that highlight utopic multiculturalism are one of the main pleasures of the more recent multicultural dance film. In *Step Up, Step Up 2: The Streets*, and *Step Up 3D*, protagonists' friends and dancers of color contribute to an aesthetic of racelessness, smoothing tensions of racial and class divides within the narratives. However, these characters and the actors portraying them are not as well developed as their whiter counterparts. Most of the characters of color in *Step Up*, *Step Up 2: The Streets*, and *Step Up 3D* serve as largely one-note friends, or as underdeveloped fellow classmates, teachers, or rivals to the protagonists. In other words, their perspectives and goals seldom factor in to the narratives even while they add to the utopic fantasy regarding American race and class relationships and the ability of all to achieve their career goals through talent and hard work.

Some distinctions can be found in comparisons between films of the two cycles. In *Fame* (1980), its characters of color are at times more fully developed than those of more recent dance films. However, at times their narratives also reinforce notions of well-deserved white success and nonwhite failure. Two richly drawn characters of color, Coco and Leroy, are among the cast of students, but their narratives are discouraging at best. Even while they both are initially foregrounded as naturally talented and with promising futures ahead, their family stories are notably absent from the story line and they are presented as "problem people," creating and suffering from social problems. Leroy is a star dancer but has never learned to read. He refuses to admit it, which prevents him from being able to join Alvin Ailey's dance company when he is invited in his senior year. We see him in a derelict neighborhood, but never learn about his family. Coco, seemingly head of the class in terms of talent and savvy, lets herself be taken advantage of by a pornographer posing as a legitimate film producer in the concluding moments of her narrative. While there are moments when it is implied that they experience economic disadvantages that many of the white students do not experience, it also is made clear by their actions that their challenges within the competitive world of the performing arts are of their own making.

In a different kind of elision of raced bodies, actress Jennifer Beals's actual biracial heritage was glossed in her character's construction in *Flashdance* and completely submerged during the film's promotion in 1983. With curly, dark brown hair and light tan skin, Beals as Alex Owens might be read as Italian, Puerto Rican, or of mixed ethnic or racial heritage; it appears that Paramount and Adrian Lyne decided the film would have greater appeal if the audience was kept in the dark about the actress's actual heritage. The actor's dance doubles further add to the ethnic and racial elisions of the film. Three dancers subbed in for Jennifer Beals's ambiguously raced body in dance scenes; they included French dancer Marine Jahan, gymnast Sharon Shapiro, and a Puerto

Rican male break dancer, Richard "Crazy Legs" Colón.[16] Nevertheless, the film aesthetics often emphasizes contrasts between the ethnically and racially ambiguous Alex and the pale white dancers at the ballet academy within the narrative, resulting in confusing messages about race and class. In the millennial films, the negation of nonwhite bodies and perspectives continues, but in more subtle ways. In *Step Up 2: The Streets*, African American, Latina/o, and Asian American characters and characters from other countries who do not mingle with white Americans are the villains within the narratives. For example, the 410, Andie's original dance crew and initial friends in *Step Up 2: The Streets*, are constructed mainly as obstructions to peace, safety, and diversity in their communities. They are shown to have a penchant for criminal activity, as in their masked menacing of subway riders in impromptu dances. In *Step Up 3D* we see more of the same with dance crews from around the world. We learn little about these dance crew members that is not already obvious from their glowering demeanor. It is as if conformity is the enemy.

MULTIRACIAL UTOPIA: WITHOUT RACE

Nonwhite bodies are utilized in distinct ways in the contemporary iterations of the dance film, with multicultural aesthetics and notions of diversity and equal opportunity deployed in overlapping and at times contradictory ways. Meritocracy is one of the underlying utopic fantasies of the multicultural dance film. On closer look the dynamics of meritocracy in such narratives have distinctly evolved. One of the major distinctions between films of these different time periods concerns the presentation of diversity, race relations, and racial and class inequities. *Flashdance* notably presents an overwhelmingly white and privileged world of ballet to which Alex, of unclarified but clearly nonwhite (Latina or mixed) descent, did not have easy access. However, she surpasses that obstacle. As Adrienne McLean notes, "The race of the ballet dancer is no longer treated as any sort of barrier."[17] The original *Fame* also acknowledges that Leroy and Coco enter the performing arts school with economic disadvantages. The *Step Up* films, in contrast, while not condemning characters of color as problem people, fail to acknowledge that young people of color might face an unlevel playing field in the performing arts and professional worlds and gloss over the distinctly raced and classed roots of these worlds as well as of hip-hop culture. Black and white become shades of gray, and race is supplanted with the slippery stand-in of "postrace." This view is reinforced through casting practices, as mixed-race and ethnically ambiguous actors are increasingly cast in ambiguously white roles. Moreover, in *Step Up 3D*, which features some of the world's top hip-hop dancers, the villains now have become ethnically ambiguous as well, with a rival crew cast with actors of vaguely Latino, Asian American, and mixed descent, such that race seemingly has no meaning. The film's concluding World Jam Competition features Moose's diverse but predominantly white crew easily outperforming the homogeneous and hostile groups from other countries. By comparison, Moose's group is heterogeneous, good-hearted, fun-loving, and hardworking. Postracial interpretations of urban social life in the *Step Up* films present social divisions as easily bridged through embracing racial ambiguity and a hip-hop-centric, white-dominant, but somewhat diverse dance scene. This utopic discourse about racelessness exists alongside others that pointedly contradict ideals of racial equality.

The protagonists of the *Step Up* films are positioned as natural fits for the leading role in the new postracial environment. This predisposition for leadership is shown to be for multiple reasons. It includes their superior dance skills, work ethic, and also cultural adaptability, which allows them to more easily move between culturally defined spaces and to occupy several at once. It is facilitated in part through casting actors of mixed heritage and ethnically ambiguous appearance in the roles. The choice to have Jennifer Beals promote *Flashdance* as a white rather than mixed-race actor in 1983 highlights the social shifts that have taken place since the previous cycle of multicultural dance films. This is a far cry from how young mixed heritage actors typically are promoted today.[18] Vanessa Hudgens of *High School Musical* (2006) and Zoe Saldana of *Center Stage* (2000) are examples of the ethnically ambiguous look desired in these films, as race and race relations are increasingly presented in shades of gray. The *Step Up* films continue this trend with the casting of actors Briana Evigan, of Polish and Italian descent, in *Step Up 2: The Streets*, and Adam G. Sevani, of Armenian and Italian descent, in the last four films of the franchise. While their roles are white characters, given the unique corporeality of these actors and their characters' cultural liminality within their narratives, they arguably serve as surrogates for mixed-race and nonwhite identity within their story worlds. It is useful to consider how and why. Arguably, their ambiguity harkens back to the first cycle of multicultural dance films with respect to notions of breaking down formerly racialized

FIGURE 14.2 Andie (Briana Evigan), seen here doing a head stand, leads a diverse, but not too diverse, dance crew to victory in *Step Up 2: The Streets* (2008).

barriers in the performing arts. In addition, in the process they may help white viewers identify and see themselves within the story world as well. Literature in performance studies and particularly that of Joseph Roach provides insight into how actors can enact a performative racial surrogacy in film narratives in this manner. Roach notes actors bodies are "possessed of . . . social memory" and can work through both past and present racialized meanings for audiences during performances.[19] Bearing this in mind, we can better understand how ethnically ambiguous protagonists in the *Step Up* films allow these films to explore tensions of color lines that still exists today, even while they seemingly negate them (see Figure 14.2).

Romantic pairings in the multicultural dance film, then and now, have been about much more than romance or the blending of dance traditions; they and their larger narratives also explore what it means for youth, and particularly working-class youth, to have agency and a voice in the language of dance, *a body that matters* within the popular culture. As this comparative analysis illustrates, the social questions and tensions addressed in these films not only still exist but have taken on new meanings since the 1980s. In the purported postracial world constructed in the *Step Up* franchise, racial and class divides are deliberately minimized. This removal of race and class barriers is achieved in part through the narrative integration of hip-hop music, dance, and culture. While hip-hop dance and culture are equated with black, Latino, and working-class identities and urban hipness in these films, they also stand in for actual protagonists of color and their perspectives. Actors and dancers of color are not well developed, celebrated characters but are utilized primarily to add to an aesthetic and narrative vision of utopic diversity.

At the same time, mastery of hip-hop dance by white characters lends them cultural cachet and showcases their growing confidence, drive, leadership abilities. It is within this formulation that Tyler, Andie, and Moose and the racial politics of *Step Up*, *Step Up 2: The Streets*, and *Step Up 3D* can best be understood. As ethnically ambiguous but white protagonists, they serve a dual function, reminding viewers of racial and class obstacles to be overcome while also reassuring viewers of a raceless and classless reality of meritocracy. Examples can be seen in Andie and Moose in the second and third *Step Up* films, respectively, who face their fears, master hip-hop dance, and become leaders (and, in the realm of competitions, winners) within the diverse cultural milieu. Similarly, group dance performances that evoke utopic multiculturalism both highlight racialized differences and can remind audiences of racialized obstacles and also deny their continued existence of race-related inequities. In incorporating these narrative and aesthetic conventions, these films support the notion that competition is always fair and that the most talented and hardworking person will always be recognized and supported to pursue her or his career goals. In the end, ambiguously white protagonists move forward as dreamers, actors, and leaders of the postracial milieu, while hip-hop and "the streets" are made safe (again) for white, middle-class viewers.

NOTES

1. Angela McRobbie, "Dance Narratives and Fantasies of Achievement," in *Meanings in Motion: New Cultural Studies of Dance*, ed. Jane C. Desmond (Durham, NC: Duke University Press, 1997), 189–219, 211.

2. Virginia Brooks, "Timeline: A Century of Dance and Media," in *Envisioning Dance on Film and Video*, ed. Judy Mitoma, Elizabeth Zimmer, and Dale Ann Stieber (New York: Routledge, 2002), xix–xxx.

3. "Fame," written by Michael Gore and Dean Pitchford (music) and Irene Cara (lyrics), performed by Irene Cara, 1980.

4. McRobbie, "Dance Narratives and Fantasies of Achievement," 210. See also Adrienne McLean, *Dying Swans and Madmen: Ballet, the Body, and Narrative Cinema* (New Brunswick, NJ: Rutgers University Press, 2008), 245.

5. The *Step Up* franchise includes *Step Up* (2006), *Step Up 2: The Streets* (2008), *Step Up 3D* (2010), *Step Up Revolution* (2012), *Step Up All In* (2014), and the YouTube Red television series *Step Up: High Water* (2018–).

6. Scholars of postracial rhetoric and media narratives have argued that the term's usage in the news media reached a peak in the late 2000s and began to be used less in the 2010s. See Catherine Squires, The *Post-racial Mystique: Media and Race in the Twenty-First Century* (New York: New York University Press, 2014).

7. Mary Beltrán, "The New Hollywood Racelessness: Only the Fast, Furious (and Multiracial) Will Survive," *Cinema Journal* 44, no. 2 (Winter 2005): 50–67; Gregory T. Carter, "From Blaxploitation to Mixploitation: Male Leads and Changing Mixed Race Identities," in *Mixed Race Hollywood*, ed. Mary Beltrán and Camilla Fojas (New York: New York University Press, 2008), 203–222.

8. McRobbie, "Dance Narratives and Fantasies of Achievement," 210–213.

9. John M. Chu, "Through Fresh Eyes: The Making of *Step Up 2*," on *Step Up 2: The Streets* (Dance-Off Edition DVD; Touchstone Home Entertainment, 2008).

10. Fred Astaire and Ginger Rogers were paired in ten films from 1933 through 1949, beginning with *Flying Down to Rio* in 1933. For further information, see Arlene Croce, *The Fred Astaire and Ginger Roger Book* (New York: Outerbridge & Lazard, 1972).

11. The film captures the ethos of the early 1980s with respect to sexual orientation and homophobia. It includes a story arc about Montgomery struggling to come out as gay and his friends doing little to encourage him. It also includes a number of male dancer extras, many of color, who appear to be proudly gay. The millennial dance films notably do not include main characters who identify as gay or questioning.

12. Krin Gabbard, *Black Magic: White Hollywood and African American Culture* (New Brunswick, NJ: Rutgers University Press, 2004), 6.

13. Richard Dyer, "Entertainment and Utopia," in *Movies and Methods: An Anthology*, vol. 2, ed. Bill Nichols (Berkeley: University of California Press, 1976), 220–232, 220.

14. Erica Chito Childs, *Fade to Black and White: Interracial Images in Popular Culture* (Lanham, MD: Rowman & Littlefield, 2009), 159.

15. Beltrán, "New Hollywood Racelessness"; and Beltrán, "Fast and Bilingual: *Fast & Furious* and the Latinization of Racelessness," *Cinema Journal* 53, no. 1 (Fall 2013): 75–96.

16. Margaret Fuhrer, "Our Favorite Dance Doubles of All Time," *Dance Spirit*, February 29, 2018, www.dancespirit.com/movie-dance-doubles-2540397639.html.

17. McLean, *Dying Swans and Madmen*, 245.

18. For more on mixed race actors' publicity in recent years, see Mary Beltrán and Camilla Fojas, "Introduction: Mixed Race in Hollywood Film and Media Culture," in *Mixed Race Hollywood*, ed. Mary Beltrán and Camilla Fojas (New York: New York University Press, 2008), 1–20.

19. Joseph Roach, *Cities of the Dead: Circum-Atlantic Performance* (New York: Columbia University Press, 1999), 209.

15 · *FAKIN' DA FUNK* (1997) AND *GOOK* (2017)

Exploring Black/Asian Relations in the Asian American Hood Film

JUN OKADA

Independent films about black/Asian relations are few and far between, but they do exist. Those produced within the Asian American media networks of the 1990s to today necessarily reference black cinema in the 1990s, in particular, the so-called hood film.[1] John Singleton's *Boyz n the Hood* (1991), a coming-of-age film about young black men amid the struggles of surviving the unpredictable, racialized violence, and rampant poverty of the inner city, exemplifies the hood film. Originally a film genre specific to the black experience, hood films

share a number of similarities: all represent the artistic output of a group of young, film-literate African American directors; all, with the exception of *New Jack City* and possibly *Do the Right Thing*, detail the hardships of coming of age for their young protagonists; and all place their narratives within the specific geographic boundaries of the hood. Within this context, the hood inhabits precise coordinates: South Central Los Angeles, Watts, Brooklyn, and Harlem. At the same time, it also encompasses a range of possible metaphorical meanings as an urbanscape, meanings which extend beyond the domain of the contemporary hood-film genre.[2]

In response to this definition of the black hood film, I shed light on its alternative, Asian American film and video's own hood films, which serve as something of a response, and possibly a corrective to the deeply injurious and traumatizing wounding of the LA Riots. Specifically, I discuss two Asian American independent films that respond to the LA Riots, *Fakin' da Funk* (1997), directed by Tim Chey and starring Dante Basco and Margaret Cho, and the more recent festival favorite *Gook* (Justin Chon, 2019).[3] This essay discusses how Asian American feature films have riffed on the 1980s and 1990s hood films to examine interracial relations as well as on the relationship between black independent cinema and Asian American independent film and video. In other words, how do Asian American hood films attempt to solve or heal the wounds of the 1990s enmities between minorities groups, especially between Asian Americans and African Americans? Also, what does it mean to compare two independent film movements working outside of Hollywood that similarly critique white privilege but do not, at the same time, cross paths in productive ways? After all, as Paula Masood, Ed Guerrero, and others point out, the hood film finds its origins in the black independent action or Blaxploitation film of the 1970s. In a similar yet less known fashion, the Asian American hood film also traces back to a familiar point in the early 1970s when grassroots Asian American filmmakers first produced films outside of the Hollywood system. Ultimately, it is in the comparison between black and Asian American grassroots film traditions that one may find a shared vision, both about the ideology of race relations as well as in their aesthetics.

There have been intense debates around the cultural poaching of hip-hop by Asian American artists as well as push back on hip-hop's lack of openness to nonblack artists. Does Asian American hood film reach a similar kind of impasse? In thinking about the ongoing scholarly problem of black-Asian relations, I trace the discursive threads that run through the Asian American hood film that touch upon cultural comparison, and the problem of the encroachment of public space, indeed, the space of the hood, itself, not merely to understand the meaning of black/Asian antagonisms and affinities through cinema, but to examine if these films project what Min Hyoung Song has professed as a fundamental break from the idealism of the past to one of pessimism.[4] Ultimately, I argue that as a response to the profound pessimism regarding the LA Riots and black/Asian enmity, *Fakin' da Funk* overcorrects through an attempt at generic comedy, an attempt to be not only optimistic about the future of black/Asian relations, but perhaps equally optimistic about the future of minority independent cinemas and their ability to assume white Hollywood genre forms without critique. By comparison, the twenty-four years of so-called actual future that the film *Gook* has witnessed since the 1992 riots offers perhaps a more measured pessimism, not only about the riots and the possibility of racial healing, but also about the viability of an independent Asian American film aesthetic that more authentically expresses its uniqueness in meaningful historical and political ways. This essay intervenes in the scholarship on black/Asian relations in cultural productions not only through a comparative close textual reading, but through the comparison of larger institutional contexts, specifically, of the relationship between grassroots independent film to Hollywood.

Even in 2018, in the age of hashtags and an intensified public debate about race and representation over social media, the issues about who gets represented and whether it is done correctly or not continues to roil. For example, the discourse of colorism and casting in the 2018 blockbuster *Black Panther* included a notable one about the actress Amandla Stenberg, star of *The Hunger Games* (2012), who claims that she decided, even at the late stages of the casting process when she was in competition for a featured role in the film, to recuse herself from the process "after she realized the film was better suited for darker-skinned actors of color."[5] What is ironic about Stenberg's decision in 2018 is that a previous casting decision involving the actress had been the subject of a Twitter controversy in 2012, when her portrayal of the character of Rue in *The Hunger Games* produced a wave of criticism from readers of the original novel. Specifically, on Twitter these readers protested the casting of Rue, who was assumed to be "the little blonde innocent girl you picture" and not "some black girl."[6] That the discourse of race, color, and casting, as filtered through Stenberg over the era of #blacklivesmatter and #oscarssowhite seemed to occupy opposite extremes, that is, not white enough, but not black enough, is telling of an era that is on the one hand hypervigilant about the meaning of racialized representation in our most hallowed texts, the movies, but on the other echoing familiar, if less recognized, debates.

In a similar vein, the preproduction discourse of an all-Asian cast feature film, the adaptation of *Crazy Rich Asians* (2018), a best-selling novel by Kevin Kwan about a Chinese American woman marrying into a wealthy Singaporean

Chinese family, was met with consternation about the correct way in which to represent Asian Americans. Jaime Chung, a Korean American internet celebrity and actress who auditioned for the big-budget Hollywood film, which starred the first all-Asian cast since *The Joy Luck Club* (Wayne Wang, 1993), twenty-five years previous, complained that she was turned down for a role in the film because she was not ethnically Chinese. A mixed Chinese British actor, Henry Golding, was ultimately cast as the film's leading man.[7] Many in the social media universe voiced the opinion that Golding's casting was overall a positive move, especially considering the actor's own roots in Singapore and Britain, which mirrored the character's, despite his being half white and half Malaysian, hence adding ethnic authenticity in casting. Yet, in addition to Golding, the mixed-race Japanese British actress Sonoya Mizuno was also cast in a supporting role in the film, which further problematizes the politics of racial casting in Hollywood. On the one hand, the issue of Hollywood representation of Asians and Asian Americans as well as authentic ethnic casting in 2018 had become an important improvement in race relations in Hollywood. On the other, the practice of casting Eurasian actors, despite their closeness to the ethnic specificities of the role and context, seemed to echo the troubling history of the centrality of whiteness in racist Hollywood casting practices of the past. Therefore, the politics of ethnic versus racial authenticity had become a new discourse in the ongoing debate over race and representation in Hollywood cinema.

THE HOOD FILM

Much of 2018's media landscape has clearly moved beyond the concerns of the earlier fight to gain even a modicum of black and Asian representation on Hollywood screens, especially in films that incorporate fully black or fully Asian casts. Yet, importantly, questions about how the representations of these groups may or may not intersect, persist. And that, despite the desired narrative of racial progress that, simply, *more* representation seems to suggest, issues like cross-racial integration or lack thereof, in media, persist. In order to bring light to this issue, I historicize the hood film, both the black and Asian American versions. Despite the seeming uniqueness of the African American hood film, upon closer examination, the city, the centrality to which the hood film refers, has figured prominently in both black independent and

Asian American film and video. Paula Masood's historicization of the hood film, for example, begins with the silent films of Oscar Micheaux and the "two-ness" of black experience as represented through the city/country dichotomy, one that has thoroughly influenced later genres like Blaxploitation, which itself emerged as a reflection of black migrations in the post–World War II environment that anticipated urban rebellions in major American cities in the 1960s. She says, the "cityscape of the hood film is largely determined by and firmly entrenched in this multilayered historical and cultural legacy. It is a legacy in which the city has been mythologized as both a utopia-as a space promising freedom and economic mobility-and a dystopia-the ghetto's economic impoverishment and segregation."[8]

Thus, hood films, which include *Do the Right Thing* (dir. Spike Lee, 1989) *New Jack City* (dir. Mario Van Peebles, 1991), *Boyz n the Hood* (dir. John Singleton, 1991), *Straight Out of Brooklyn* (dir. Matty Rich, 1991), *Juice* (dir. Ernest Dickerson, 1992), *Menace II Society* (dir. Allen and Albert Hughes, 1993), and *Just Another Girl on the I.R.T.* (dir. Leslie Harris, 1992), among others, represent a new "two-ness," of the city as both a utopia and dystopia for African Americans, a primary metaphor for black experience. One powerful narrative resolution to hood films, therefore, is the taking back of economic power from white America and the immigrant communities that have benefitted from their proximity to whiteness, and to reestablish and re-root themselves on the shifting ground of urban space. This narrative offers a formidable critique of American capitalism, into which racism has been embedded. For example, the infamous speech by Furious Styles, the embattled, quasi-Marxist, truth-talking patriarch played by Laurence Fishburne in *Boyz n the Hood*, demonstrates this critique. Furious begins his monologue to the neighborhood denizens who stop to listen to his sermon in the hood, standing under a billboard that reads "CASH FOR YOUR HOME. SEOUL TO SEOUL REALTY." Furious explains to his son and fellow hood residents about gentrification and the racist practices that have left the black hood vulnerable to outsiders bent on destroying the community. He explains, "They bring the property value down. They can buy the land cheaper. Then they move the people out, raise the value and sell it at a profit. What we need to do is keep everything in our neighborhood, everything, black, black-owned with black money. Just like the Jews, the Italians, the Mexicans and the Koreans do."[9]

The discourse of self-determination, critique of the investment in whiteness, and valuing of community against the tides of institutional racism holds up a model of the hood genre in ways that others in the genre and its predecessors like Blaxploitation are not able to do. Furious Styles's monologue is especially important in that it is passed from the original "woke" figure, the good black father, onto his only son and future hope of the hood, Tre, played by Cuba Gooding Jr. The role of the father, whether absent or active, provides a crucial narrative anchor in the hood film, which itself borrows from melodrama and all of its attendant Oedipal structuring around families and especially the father. Ironically though, in *Boyz n the Hood*, an exemplary hood film, "the final paradox and tragedy of the film lies in the fact that even though Furious works to instill a sense of responsibility and community in Tre, this influence ultimately equips Tre with the mobility he needs to leave the hood for college in Atlanta, a space defined and verbally signified within the film as a utopia in comparison to L.A.'s dystopia."[10] It is precisely this tension between staying in the hood to keep everything "black owned" as a way to fight racism versus the liberation of characters away from the corruption of the hood to save oneself from it that maintains the crucial significance of the hood as a spatial trope in the genre. This trope is carried over into Asian American independent feature films that feature the hood to inform a discourse of the hood as both a shared and contested, racialized space.

THE CITY IN ASIAN AMERICAN FILM

Before embarking on an analysis of the Asian American hood film, I want to point to the important context of the city, which, as in black hood films, has formed an important emblem and discourse for Asian American independent film. Wayne Wang's *Chan Is Missing* (1982), for example, uses film noir and multicultural urbanity as its world and is therefore perhaps the obvious example of the representation of the city for narrative Asian American feature films. But even earlier than this film, grassroots Los Angeles filmmakers in the 1970s were equally committed to the representation of Downtown Los Angeles as the setting for an Asian American visual, cultural, and narrative legacy. The grassroots film collective Visual Communications made films that evoke the multicultural urbanity of Little Tokyo as a structural basis for Asian American film and video. This otherness of the city, therefore, seemed crucial to be taken back on Asian Americans' own terms. Some of the first Visual

Communications films, *Wong Sinsaang* (dir. Eddie Wong, 1971), *Cruisin' J-Town* (dir. Duane Kubo, 1975), and *City City* (dir. Duane Kubo and Donna Deitch, 1974), for example, relied on a range of representational styles, from a documentary/nonfiction style to an experimental/avant-garde one, to depict Los Angeles as one inhabited and uniquely owned and experienced by Chinese and Japanese Americans who had lived there for generations.[11] As a general rule, these films emphasize multicultural diversity and pride in the Asian American community. And still, as an analogue to the dualistic, ambivalent representation of the black city, the representation of the Asian American ghettos—Chinatowns, Little Tokyos, Manilas, and Saigons—was equally fraught with Hollywood's transposition of Orientalist, othering fantasies established in Yellow Peril literatures and Hollywood genre films.[12]

Even before contemporary Asian American filmmakers began to visualize the city on their own terms, it was the site of charged representational space. Cinematic comparison of Chinatown and the black hood is illustrative of the parallels of the relationship of the city to black and Asian Americans, as both utopic and dystopic, and a primary metaphor for dealing with racial others in public space. The representation of Chinese Americans in silent films about "slumming" in Chinatowns, for example, reveals how a "fascination with mobility, mutability, and bodily transformations" marked the representations of Asian bodies in silent cinema.[13] For white viewers, films like *Deceived Slumming Party* (1908) provided not only a sign of the presence, despite the Chinese Exclusion Act of 1882, of Chinese bodies but also "a fundamentally modern subjectivity not grounded in concepts of identification or stable identity." Moreover, both New York's Chinatown and Harlem "suggest a different concept of non-white physicality, one that is much more grounded in the sensuous materiality of the body."[14] The urban space of the racial other, thus, offered a similar "out-of-body" experience for white Americans as a mode of modernity.

Visual Communications, or VC, was formed in the early 1970s by Asian American film students Eddie Wong, Bob Nakamura, and others, who graduated from UCLA's Film School, which at the time created "Ethno-Communications," an initiative to admit black, Asian American, Native American, and Latino students. Many of the black LA Rebellion filmmakers such as Haile Gerima, Charles Burnett, and Julie Dash were also graduates of this program. Films from this productive period of independent filmmaking by both black and Asian American filmmakers, especially in the more realistic and poetic depictions of urban Los Angeles, required an open rather than a more rigid approach found in the classical narrative confines of genre cinema. Films like *Killer of Sheep* (dir. Charles Burnett, 1978), with its relaxed neorealist visual style, challenged the ways in which the hood was often represented in genre films. Likewise, the experimental nonfiction film *Wong Sinsaang* shows the city through an impressionistic, if sharply observed, racialized perspective. Interestingly, the space of the city as represented in the 1970s films made by both Asian American and black Ethno-Communication directors is one of a nonjudgmental and fluid continuity. The fact that the hood becomes a more charged, contested space in genre cinema reveals, perhaps, the division that continues to exist between grassroots filmmaking practices and the more profit-driven ones of genre cinema.

THE LA RIOTS

With urban space being the charged narrative trope that it is, the LA Riots would seem to offer the perfect storm as a representational crossroads for black independent cinema and Asian American independent film and video. Min Hyoung Song has looked at literary and cinematic representations of the LA Riots as one primarily of dystopia centered largely on bodily trauma: "The presence of the strange—as I will be calling the bearers of a materiality that demands narrative invention—discourages thinking about collective solutions to widely shared problems."[15] Song continues, "When we follow the combined turn of these tropes, they lead us to a particular vision of the future that is replete with uncontrollable change, social disorder, and wholesale violence."[16] Yet, when looking at Asian American independent films as responses to the riots as well as hood films of the 1990s, it seems that they at first seem to encourage collective solutions. Both *Fakin' da Funk* and *Gook* look back on this violence, from varying distances, seemingly as an attempt at reconciliation, but in vastly different, possibly oppositional, ways. *Fakin' da Funk* sees the hood as being salvageable only through the coming together of Asians and African Americans through romantic/sexual bonding, and *Gook* sees the hood in a more somber, but no less reconciliatory, way as a space that needs to be burned clean to make way for new ground.

In many ways, the Asian American hood film responds to the black hood film. It attempts to rectify its fundamental tragic elements, namely the cycle of poverty, death, and destruction, and the anti-black racism that shapes the genre's narrative. For example, *Fakin' da Funk* seeks to displace the centrality of whiteness in narratives of interracial romance by featuring two black/Asian American couples. Director Chey, a devout Christian, Harvard-educated, former Hollywood film executive turned independent filmmaker, is somewhat of an outlier in Asian American independent film and video. Though his first feature film made the rounds at Asian American film festivals, Chey has largely sidestepped an association with the historical community of Asian American filmmaking, which, as outlined previously, began in grassroots community media in Los Angeles.[17] Unlike the fluid cityscapes of the first Asian American films, *Fakin' da Funk* clearly adheres to a melodramatic classical Hollywood narrative structure. The film also clearly riffs on the racialized parameters of LA and Atlanta, the journey traversed by the original prodigal son of the black hood film, Tre, in *Boyz n the Hood*, by having its own main character, Julian, make the ironic journey in the opposite direction, from Atlanta back to Los Angeles. Julian, played by Filipino American actor Dante Basco, is a teen of Chinese descent who has been adopted by black parents Annabelle (Pam Grier) and Joe (Ernie Hudson).

In some ways, *Fakin' da Funk* is a positive response to the Hollywood conception of interracial relationships that feature Asian and African Americans simply due to the fact that "romance and sexual relationships for young people of color within the world of the racially 'integrated' teen comedy films are for the most part nonexistent."[18] Moreover, by putting black/Asian couplings front and center, the film's casting seems to solve the rampant issue of Hollywood genre films in which invariably "Asian/Pacific American, Native American, Latino/a, and Other ethnic groups like those of Arab descent are rendered practically invisible." As Frances Gateward explains, "Because mainstream American media myopically see race as meaning black or white, if a nonwhite character appears in a romantic teenpic context, it is almost invariably a male and he is almost invariably black."[19]

Chey's superficially sunny, classical happy ending in multiple couplings gives in to the neoliberal, neoconservative resolution, in which the market becomes the solution to racism's ills. This speaks directly to Song's notion of the importance of pessimism in 1990s cultural productions. As a late 1990s

FIGURE 15.1 Julian Lee (Dante Basco) and Karyn (Tatyana Ali) reconcile in *Fakin' da Funk* (1997).

film, *Fakin' da Funk* tries to warm over the death and destruction of the LA Riots that intensified pessimism during an earlier part of that decade. As a cure, the film suggests, interracial black/Asian romantic couplings will fundamentally heal the past (see Figure 15.1). Julian's hooking up with an upwardly mobile, Japanese-speaking, sushi-eating black paramour, Karyn, ensures this success story at the narrative's close.

Fakin' da Funk uses John Singleton's debut feature and classic of black independent cinema, *Boyz n the Hood*, as a touchstone. Specifically, *Boyz n the Hood* was significant in showing the tension between the responsibility of black masculinity and the desire for socioeconomic mobility. Massood states,

> The final paradox and tragedy [of the film] lies in the fact that even though Furious Styles (the film's beleaguered patriarch) works to instill a sense of responsibility and community in [his son] Tre, this influence ultimately equips Tre with the mobility he needs to leave the hood for college in Atlanta, a space defined and verbally signified within the film as a utopia in comparison to L.A.'s dystopia. The film thus explores the limits placed on the hood's residents and allows for the possibility of increased movement, but does so only within he strictly defined parameters of South Central Los Angeles and/or Atlanta.[20]

Fakin' da Funk clearly revisits this racialized passage between LA and Atlanta. Crucially, by making LA the utopian destination of the film rather than the dystopia Tre leaves in *Boyz n the Hood*, *Fakin' da Funk* suggests the possibility of racial harmony as an essential part of the solution. The film begins with a backstory/exposition in Atlanta, in which the black patriarch dies of a heart attack, which sets into motion the move to Los Angeles, the contested space wherein many of the original hood films take place. Moreover, *Boyz n the Hood* promotes "the not-so-subtle message of the healing power of the father to the virtual exclusion of the mother."[21] The absence of the black patriarch is similarly significant in *Fakin' da Funk*. The subplot of the film has Julian's younger brother Perry, who is black, involved with a gang in their new home in South Central, and it is implied that this decision is caused by the trauma of the absent father. In a revision to *Boyz n the Hood*, it is Annabelle, Julian's mother, rather than the father, who is able to be the anchor and "native informant" of hood culture for Julian.

Not only does Julian quite literally travel back west into the fire of the epicenter of the LA Riots—South Central Los Angeles—but he arrives there to heal the rift in the ensuing aftermath. *Fakin' da Funk* tries to ameliorate the enmity between Asian Americans and blacks intensified during the LA Riots, and it does so by suggesting that interracial black/Asian romantic couplings will fundamentally heal the past. In taking Furious Styles' speech in *Boyz n the Hood*, in which he exhorts the black community to fight white capitalism's control over black spaces, to heart, *Fakin' da Funk* flips the script of *Boyz n the Hood* and explores an outcome in which people of color stay willingly in their beleaguered communities and contribute to making them better through black ownership. Julian answers this exhortation by coupling with the black heroine and choosing to stay, erecting the classic melting pot ending of all's well that ends well. What is even more problematic is how Julian repeatedly announces that he is as black as, if not more black than, his love interest, Karyn, because she "live[s] in Baldwin Hills and drive[s] a Lexus." Julian asks her, "What do you know about living in the hood?" She answers, "Well, you know I don't have to live in the hood to be black." And Julian has the last word, and the overall message of the film, by saying, "Yeah, well I don't have to live in the hood to be black either." The film takes pains to depict both Julian and Karyn as outliers for their respective races in various clichéd ways. For example, Julian reveals that he is "more black" by being good at basketball, and Karyn, by contrast, speaks Japanese and knows how to properly eat sushi, despite being black. Julian talks in a southern black drawl like his mother, while Karyn speaks in a white standard English accent.

Despite the remarkable protestations against racial stereotypes, and the refreshing lack of white people in the film, Julian problematically and predictably ends up essentially being a white savior come to heal the hood. In other words, in a narrative that is borrowed from white Hollywood genre structure, Julian ends up taking over the role of white savior, despite the fact that he can sort of pass for black because he literally isn't white. By coupling up Julian with the white-acting Karyn, the film ensures a superficially harmonious neoconservative future of the hood.

Likewise, Margaret Cho's character, a Chinese exchange student named May-Lee who provides the comic relief to the melodrama of the film, unwittingly gets placed in the home of a black family in South Central, and by the film's end, she has coupled with a black man who helps her break free from her conservative Asian upbringing. She effectively apes an Ebonics-spouting woman of the hood while schooling a new Asian immigrant to South Central LA, demonstrating to the newcomer that assimilation to black culture, the answer to white racism, is possible and the solution to the race problem of America. It is achieved through upward mobility and acting black or racial masquerade. Therefore, both Asian characters, Julian and May-Lee, effectively become black through affiliation and cultural appropriation, which is what Oliver Wang has described as the misguided, politically naïve Asian American romanticism of achieving solidarity with black people.[22]

As in the original black hood films, *Fakin' da Funk* represents the hood as a space of negotiation but sees it as morphing into a space that could be shared by blacks and Asians through a process of cultural and familial assimilation. The film resolves the racial impasse of Asians and blacks through the suggestive coupling of two interracial couples. However, as Song points out, despite much optimistic research showing how intermarriage is dissolving racial lines, "even as this has occurred, race continues to be a source of conflict. Perhaps what needs to be refuted here is the assumption that intermarriage automatically means the diminishment of racial prejudice. For to offer just one possibility, it should be obvious that someone married to a person of a different race can still remain a racist."[23]

GOOK (2017)

Unlike *Fakin' da Funk*, *Gook* looks back at the LA Riots from a more distant future. Released in 2017, this black-and-white independent film explores black/Asian relations from a much more nuanced, more somber perspective. The narrative tells the story of Korean Americans Eli (played by the film's director Justin Chon) and Daniel, who run a discount shoe store far on the outskirts of the epicenter of the Riots in Paramount, California. In a setup that duplicates the geo-economic situation of Korean American immigrants in LA in 1992, the store's clientele is African American. Within this black community, a parentless young black girl, Kamilla, comes to Eli's shoe store and befriends both him and Daniel, despite her adult brother and sister having reservations about this friendship and the idealism of black/Asian harmony. Kamilla expresses what Song has described as "the deep desire for social interaction that persists despite the risks," a political naïveté that *Gook* takes seriously.[24]

Gook sets up this deep desire through the friendship between Eli and Kamilla. Kamilla was ironically orphaned by the killing of her mother during a robbery in the store owned by Eli's father, who also dies, a scenario that echoes the murder of Latasha Harlins by an LA Korean shop owner, and yet she repeatedly tells Eli that they are family. When Eli tells Daniel and Kamilla that he wants to sell the shoe store and leave, Kamilla protests and tells him that he told her that she could go to the shoe store whenever she wanted and that now she won't have a place or a home. Of course this one small gesture of positivity and love in the film ends tragically and attests to the pessimism surrounding the LA Riots and its aftermath.

One aspect of *Gook* that echoes a key debate in the scholarship on black/Asian relations is the appropriation of black music by Asian Americans. One of *Gook*'s subplots has Eli's brother Daniel passionately pursuing secret aspirations to become an R & B singer. Daniel makes a clandestine demo tape at a makeshift recording studio, the journey to which is plagued by violence. He gets jumped in an alley by a gang headed by Kamilla's brother, therefore risking his life in the endeavor. The idea of expressing himself through a black art form is an authentic, if misguided, attempt at connection on Daniel's part. Yet when he plays the demo tape for his brother Eli, it is a ridiculous notion to him. It is not that Daniel is a bad R & B singer; quite the opposite. When Eli first hears the demo tape, he mistakes it for R & B singer Babyface, then

when realizing that it is Daniel singing, he laughs uproariously at the ridiculous suggestion that a Korean American could make it as an R & B star. Daniel
throws the tape away and starts to laugh hysterically at the absurdity himself.

Oliver Wang, who writes on Asian American studies and music, relates
that space can be literal geographical terrain or metaphorical cultural space.
In his writing on Asian American hip-hop artists, he writes about "hip hop
as a social space where African Americans and Asian Americans encounter
one another in both constructive and cautionary ways."[25] In thinking about
productive ways in which blacks and Asian Americans may share cultural
space, Wang, echoing George Lipsitz, asks, "Which kinds of cross-cultural
identification advance emancipatory ends and which ones reinforce existing
structures of power and domination?"[26]

Wang argues that "the concern over Black/Asian cultural relations is not
that Asian American rap artists or fans hold viciously derogatory views of
African Americans, but rather the reverse: that some Asian Americans roman-
ticize the African American experience and believe that their participation
in hip hop brings them closer in solidarity to African Americans."[27] This is
clearly true with the optimistic view of both 1997's *Fakin' da Funk* and, more
cautiously, 2017's *Gook*. However, in the latter film, Daniel tries desperately
to hold on to this sense of romanticism despite being viciously jumped and
assaulted by Kamila's embittered brother lashing out at Asian Americans
because of the death of his mother needlessly endangered by Eli's and Daniel's father and storeowner. Despite this violence, Daniel records his R & B
track. And yet the fact that Daniel appears to abandon his dreams of an R&B
singing career, not because of the violence he experiences by black men, but
because of the recognition of his own objectifying lens of romanticism, demonstrates the absurdity of usurping the narrative trajectory of black enter-
tainers rising out of the hood and abject poverty.

It is clear that the independent aesthetics of *Gook* appropriate the style
and ideology of the bygone era of grassroots black and Asian American independent film, specifically the city films of Visual Communications and, of
course, the LA Rebellion. One look at the hazy black-and-white, neorealist
images of an abandoned inner-city LA enclave recalls similar scenes in the
rich, evocative, visual blues of Charles Burnett's iconic masterpiece, *Killer of
Sheep*. It is true that, as Wang has contended, hip-hop and genre cinema are
not the same art forms and do not occupy the same plane in American culture. Hip-hop holds deeper, more organic roots to the central role of black

FIGURE 15.2 Eli (Justin Chon) and Kamilla (Simone Baker) hang out on the roof in *Gook* (2017).

people in the history of American popular music, which precedes the moving image. Hip-hop, R & B, jazz, and their relatives find their roots in slave spirituals and the blues and have all been prey to white appropriation. Black cinema, on the other hand, has more youthful roots that begin with Oscar Micheaux, who in the early days of cinema arguably planted the seeds for the eventual emergence of Blaxploitation in the 1970s. Asian American film and video began somewhat like Blaxploitation, in the 1970s, as a grassroots phenomenon, but notably less invested in aspirations toward Hollywood genre cinema. And yet Asians have notoriously been an important part of cinema's young history, with stars like Anna May Wong, Sessue Hayakawa, and others, since the silent cinema days of Micheaux. If indeed Asian American film and video and black cinema have roughly similar historical trajectories, the possibilities for relationality between the two and their creative mining and recombination of generic and representational tropes together might be endless. The somber symbiosis found in the poetic *Gook*, therefore, more effectively and meaningfully intervenes in the impasse between black and Asian American art and culture (see Figure 15.2).

In short, the comparison of black/Asian representation in cases of self-representation by black and Asian filmmakers opens up the discussion about race and representation in more nuanced and expansive ways than in Hollywood and Hollywood-style narratives. Paula Masood has said that "the practice and use of urban spaces such as the hood or the ghetto as a metaphor for African American experience is not a new phenomenon in African American cultural production, nor does it point to the emergence of 'new' problems existing in these areas. Rather, the hood's roots are deeply planted within a tradition of African American writing dating from the turn of the century."[28] I would also argue that the technology of cinema and all of its formal and industrial differences from literature would allow for the parallel historical beginnings and trajectory of cinema to be fairly similar to both black cinema and Asian American film and video, at least in how race has formed each group's participation both within and without Hollywood cinema.

ASIAN/BLACK RELATIONS IN FILMMAKING

In conclusion, a comparison of a film like *Fakin' da Hood* and *Gook* illustrates something else beyond their narratives, namely the potential use of style, form, genre, and institution as effective strategies for the articulation and expression of black/Asian relations in film. First, the black-and-white, art cinema aesthetic of *Gook* and its productive pessimism form a more authentic aesthetic for Asian American film and video even at this historical stage of Asian American independent media's evolution. The film harkens back in time, as argued earlier in this essay about the fluidity and openness of depictions of cities and urban spaces in grassroots Asian American film as well as the films of the LA Rebellion. In other words, in these seemingly handcrafted films, no one needs to own the hood or its representation. Asian American film and video is ill equipped to enter the problematic arena of Hollywood genre cinema. Therefore, while neither *Fakin' da Funk* nor *Gook* has left the indie ghettos, if it is the desire of Asian American filmmakers to collaborate with black cinema, the strategies of art cinema offer perhaps better possibilities than those provided by the assurances of the Hollywood genre film.

Second, the strategy of Asian American independent feature films set in the hood in the 1990s has been to deconstruct the space of the hood as delineated in the black hood film, a project that seems unfinished and could potentially yield more. Interestingly, the black hood film genre of the 1980s and 1990s provided a path for black filmmakers to move out of the cinematic ghetto into the mainstream: John Singleton, Matty Rich, the Hughes Brothers. This has not been the case for Asian American independent cinema's take on the hood films. Neither *Fakin' da Funk* nor *Gook* has enjoyed the cultural attention of black hood films. A similar relationship exists between hip-hop and Asian American hip-hop, as Oliver Wang demonstrates. However, one thing that differentiates the analogy of hip-hop and independent cinema is that unlike cinema, hip-hop belongs to African Americans in a way that it will only awkwardly and suspiciously be available as a form of expression to non-black Americans. Cinema arrived, conveniently, during a time of immigration to the United States and became a language available, supposedly, to anyone. Therefore, the cross-pollination between Asian American film and black cinema could potentially be a space of equal footing, a shared productive aesthetic and political discourse unlike the experiment of Asian American hip-hop beyond appropriation and toward collaboration.

NOTES

1. Asian American media networks include films, film festivals, television films, and other institutions that composed grassroots and state sponsored filmmaking from the early 1970s to the current era. Specific institutions include the Ethno-Communications film program at UCLA, Visual Communications, CAAM (Center for Asian American Media), and others. For more on this history, see Jun Okada, *Making Asian American Film and Video: History, Institutions, Movements* (New Brunswick, NJ: Rutgers University Press, 2015).

2. Paula J. Massood, "Mapping the Hood: The Genealogy of City Space in *Boyz n the Hood* and *Menace II Society*," *Cinema Journal* 35, no. 2 (Winter 1996): 85–97.

3. Although *Fakin' da Funk* deals with Chinese and Chinese American characters and *Gook* deals with Korean Americans living in a black hood, this essay considers all ethnic Asians as Asian Americans by virtue of the political definition of what it means to be Asian Americans, despite the linguistic, geographic, historical, and ethnic difference among Americans of Asian descent.

4. Min Hyoung Song, *Strange Future: Pessimism and the 1992 Los Angeles Riots* (Durham, NC: Duke University Press, 2005), 1.

5. Zack Sharf, "Amandla Stenberg Removed Herself from 'Black Panther' Casting Because the Movie Deserved 'Dark-Skinned Actors,'" *IndieWire*, March 2, 2018, www.indiewire.com/2018/03/amandla-stenberg-black-panther-casting-dark-skinned-actors-1201934575/.

6. Anna Holmes, "White Until Proven Black: Imagining Race in *Hunger Games*," *New Yorker*, March 30, 2012.

7. Kimberly Yam, "'Crazy Rich Asian' Star Claps Back at Criticism That He's Not Asian Enough," *Huffington Post*, November 30, 2017, www.huffingtonpost.com/entry/crazy-rich-asians-henry-golding-casting_us_5a1f172ce4b0d52b8dc2632e.

8. Massood, "Mapping the Hood," 87.

9. *Boyz n the Hood* (dir. John Singleton, 1991).

10. Massood, "Mapping the Hood," 22–23.

11. David E. James and Adam Hyman, *Alternative Projections: Experimental Film in Los Angeles, 1945–1980* (Bloomington: Indiana University Press, 2015).

12. For more on "yellow peril" discourse in Hollywood, see Gina Marchetti, *Romance and the Yellow Peril: Race, Sex, and Discursive Strategies in Hollywood Fiction* (Berkeley: University of California Press, 1994).

13. Sabine Haenni, "Filming 'Chinatown': Fake Visions, Bodily Transformations," in *Screening Asian Americans*, ed. Peter X. Feng (New Brunswick, NJ: Rutgers University Press, 2002), 21–52.

14. Haenni, "Filming 'Chinatown,'" 51.

15. Song, *Strange Future*, 3.

16. Song, *Strange Future*, 3.

17. "Tim Chey: Director of 'The Genius Club' Speaks Out," *Christian Cinema*, November 6, 2008, www.christiancinema.com/catalog/newsdesk_info.php?newsdesk_id=845.

18. Frances Gateward, "In Love and Trouble," in *Where the Boys Are: Cinemas of Masculinity and Youth*, ed. Frances Gateward and Murray Pomerance (Detroit: Wayne State University Press, 2005), 157–182, 157.

19. Gateward, "In Love and Trouble," 158.

20. Massood, "Mapping the Hood," 91.

21. Massood, "Mapping the Hood," 91.

22. Oliver Wang, "These Are the Breaks: Hip-Hop and AfroAsian Cultural (Dis)Connections," in *AfroAsian Encounters: Culture, History, Politics*, ed. Heike Raphael-Hernandez and Shannon Steen (New York: New York University Press, 2006), 146–166.

23. Song, *Strange Future*, 255.

24. Song, *Strange Future*, 133.

25. Wang, "These Are the Breaks," 148.

26. Wang, "These Are the Breaks," 148.

27. Wang, "These Are the Breaks," 157.

28. Massood, "Mapping the Hood," 85.

16 · "LET US ROAM THE NIGHT TOGETHER"

On Articulation and Representation in *Moonlight* (2016) and *Tongues Untied* (1989)

LOUISE WALLENBERG

There is a sequence in Isaac Julien's poetic film *Looking for Langston* (1989) depicting American poet Langston Hughes reciting his poem "Night and Morn" for television, as he stands backed up by a band of five musicians. This televised sequence was recorded in the mid-1950s, some ten years before Hughes died, and within Julien's film it is used to loosely glue together three different time periods: the politically riveting 1960s, the decade when Hughes dies; the late 1980s, a decade much colored by HIV and the decade when Julien, the film maker, is in his present; and the artistically thriving era of the Harlem Renaissance, when Hughes together with other Harlem-based artists came to revolutionize African American art.

While the poem may be interpreted in various ways, especially its connection to the blues offers many possible readings, its placement within Julien's film steers the reading of the poem in one direction. Placed within his *Looking for Langston*, a film that serves to queer not only the Harlem

Renaissance but also many of its front figures, the poem must be read as an utterance through which Hughes decides to stop "being blue." To the beat of the music, he proclaims that this is the time when he is ending his own suffering, his hiding, and all the silence with which he has surrounded himself. "Night and Morn" here turns into a coming out poem: having "been blue all night long" all his life, he finally decides, as the sun rises, to come out and be who he really is.[1]

Barry Jenkins's award-winning film *Moonlight* from 2016 reminds one of Hughes's poignant voice as he reads his hopeful and decisive poem, and of his image, his serious face turning into a smile as the poem reaches its final line. It is as if there is a link between Hughes, the real poet, and Chiron, the fictive character of Jenkins's film. Yet, *Moonlight* may also remind one of Marlon Riggs's *Tongues Untied* (1989), made the same year as Julien's film. Jenkins's film, built as a triptych as we follow Chiron over a period of twenty years, constitutes, one can argue, a kind of humble, yet engaging and proud, response to Riggs's documentary film. Riggs too focuses on his childhood memories and experiences as they give meaning to who he is as an adult and how his very young self is still present and reflected in his adult self.

Before focusing on the relation between *Moonlight* and *Tongues Untied*, let me explain first the connection between the televised sequence of Hughes reading his poem in *Looking for Langston* and *Moonlight*. Like Hughes, Chiron (Trevante Rhodes), the main character in Jenkins's film, will also reach a point when he decides to stop being blue, and like the televised sequence in which we can see Hughes smile, Jenkins's ending of the film will focus on the content and happy relief that Chiron's face conveys after he has spoken up and articulated his confession and desire. But there is also an obvious connection between Hughes's poem and Jenkins's film in terms of the color *blue*: the very blueness that Hughes finally has decided to leave behind, a blueness that we may reckon has up until that moment (partly) defined him, is in *Moonlight* present both as a color and as a state of mind, a painful mood indigo. Chiron wears his pain throughout the film. It is highly visible in the facial expression and in the body posture of him as a delicate child, it is consciously hidden away but still very detectible in him as a lanky teenager and seeping through his sad eyes and his exclusion as an adult. And blue, both as a color and as a mood, is recurrently being referred to, both visually and vocally. Blue is present in the childhood memory recounted by Juan (Mahershala Ali) to Little (Alex Hibbert), Chiron's nickname as a small as boy. Juan tells him how he, as he grew up in Cuba, was once being called out by an old lady to look "blue" in the moonlight: "In moonlight, black boys look blue. You blue, that's what I'm gon' call you. 'Blue.'" Blue is hence the term for referring to a certain blueish skin hue made possible in a certain light. Blue is also present in certain scenes: in the blue moonlight-lit sequences filmed at the beach, showing children bathing, and in the scene portraying Chiron (Ashton Sanders) as a teenager experiencing his first intimate encounter with Kevin (Jharrel Jerome), his school mate and friend. It is there in the third and last part, in the form of an icy-blue electric light as the adult Chiron, now calling himself "Black," washes his face in a basin filled with water and ice. And it is there in the very ending medium shot of Little that ends the film, with his face and body being lit by a clear blue light as he turns and faces us and the camera. Yet while blue is a color that is constantly present and referred to, the color of black is also present.

In what follows, I offer a reading of Jenkins's *Moonlight* through Riggs's *Tongues Untied*, while also, but to a lesser extent, engaging with Julien's *Looking for Langston*. The three films are connected through their joint subject matter, that is, representing and problematizing gay and black identities in a world that is dominantly heteronormative, racist, and masculinist. But while the two films from the late 1980s are explicit in terms of representing gayness, masculinist pressure, racism, and identity, *Moonlight* is much subtler in portraying these intersecting issues. And while the visual representations in *Tongues Untied* and *Moonlight* will be discussed, it is the apparent silence of *Moonlight* versus the ferocious vocalism and expressivity of *Tongues Untied* that will take up most of my focus. They both speak of (in)visibility, silence, desire, and pain in relation to identity, and they both portray in different forms how these are being constricted and expressed.

Together with Julien's *Looking for Langston*, *Tongues Untied* came to lay the foundation not only for the New Queer Wave, or New Queer Cinema, but also for black and gay film, and although there are almost three decades separating Julien and Riggs's films and Jenkins's *Moonlight*, they are clearly aligned.[2] And while Hughes's poem in Julien's film constitutes a reference point for *Moonlight*, it is *Tongues Untied* more than *Looking for Langston* that creates the more direct lineage to Jenkins's *Moonlight*. Reading the triptych *Moonlight* through *Tongues Untied*, I loosely rely on discussions aligned with identity politics, that is, discussions on gay and/or black identity issues. Relying on these discussions, I bridge academic thinking on identity politics and the two films' representations of intersectional identities with the aim of pointing out how they may be understood to support one another. As for identity politics, this has been a most important political and theoretical liberation movement, starting with the civil rights and feminist movements, but it is one that today has come under attack.[3] Jenkins's *Moonlight*, however subtle in its portrayal and message, must nevertheless be read as a powerful continuation of this liberation movement, as it reminds us of how identity issues and politics still matter. The practice of *reading* one film *through* another may sound more structured and formalized than it actually is: what I intend to do in what follows is to discuss and analyze the two films in tandem, linking them to one another via sequences that speak together, as if in dialogue, despite the fact that a period of almost thirty years separates them in time.

BLUE AND BLACK

Let me return to the colors that are constantly present and referred to in Jenkins's film, and which are also present in Riggs's film. I have already touched upon how blue figures within the film as a label in the case of Juan being called out by an elderly, unknown woman; as a skin hue that comes out via the moonlight; and as an emotional mood that is being emphasized by the moonlight that informs several of the scenes. As for black, it is a color that dominates the film and its narrative: besides telling the coming-of-age story of a black man in a black cultural setting, *Moonlight* has an all-black cast. These two facts make it a black film and, as such, rather unique because more than 70 percent of all speaking parts in Hollywood cinema (to which Jenkins's film belong) are white.[4] Narratively and representationally, *Moonlight* deals with black, gay *identity* but also with black experiences in a certain *place* (Liberty City, Florida, and, to a lesser extent, Atlanta, Georgia) and in certain *times* (the late 1990s, the middle part of the millennium's first decade, and the mid-2010s). Blackness is present in the renaming and self-naming of the film's main character, Chiron, when he has become an adult, and the name is also used as the title "Black" for the third part of the film. The name/color is, in fact, already present in the previous part, in the second part titled "Chiron." Chiron has already been named "Black" by his only friend Kevin. It is interesting to note that it is only Kevin who calls Chiron "Black." Although Chiron seems not too happy about it and at one point confronts Kevin about the name, he eventually accepts it.[5] He probably does so, we will come to realize, because he is in love with Kevin, the only other boy in school who is kind to him, and who actually engages with him in conversations.

The other boys and girls in school either only abuse him verbally or physically or treat him as invisible and nonexistent. In an early scene in the film's first part "Little," Kevin (Jaden Piner) is introduced as someone who stands out from the rest: at a football game the two boys are left behind after the other boys have gone, and after playfully fighting in the grass, they walk home, side by side, talking. It is only later, long after years of harassment, Chiron has decided to leave Florida for Georgia and starts calling himself "Black." In re-creating himself he *becomes* "Black," possibly as a way to keep the only friend he is leaving behind present in his memory. But "Black" can also be understood to be an expression of a strong emotional alignment with the loving substitute father figure Juan (who in the second part of the film has already died). Juan was "Blue," and Chiron, modeling himself after Juan, now becomes "Black." Escaping his painful past, the adult Chiron/"Black" transforms himself into another version of Juan/"Blue": he becomes Juan in terms of appearance, driving a similar car, adorning himself with golden jewelry, and building a muscular body, but also in terms of becoming a drug dealer. Yet, in contrast to Juan, "Black" has also chosen isolation and loneliness, and the only other people we see him engage with are his mother Paula (Naomie Harris) and Travis (Stephon Bron), a younger man working for him on the streets. Whereas Menaka Kannan, Rhys Hall, and Matthew W. Hughey in their article on *Moonlight* choose to refer to Chiron's becoming "Black" as a "triumphant emergence," I am less inclined to see this transformation as triumphant. Rather, becoming "Black," that is, becoming Juan, is a survival strategy and a flight from what he is, or, as will become clear, what he is going to be.[6]

And becoming, as in becoming identity, or identities, is a central issue in *Moonlight*. It is also a most central issue in *Tongues Untied*, a film in which exhibiting, vocalizing, and performing a multitude of various black and gay voices and experiences are at its center. The film is performative in the way it combines poems, songs, music, and personal accounts with imagery both nonfictive and fictive. *Moonlight*, like *Tongues Untied*, represents a multitude of black masculinities, hence refusing to let this social group be represented in the stereotypical characteristics that most popular texts employ.[7] Yet these characteristics, while also present, are often turned on their head, as in the case of the character Juan. The multitude of black masculinities makes the text rich, but it also brings about the contradictory and the unexpected. In the words of Kannan, Hall, and Hughey, "[*Moonlight*] is a tour de force in contradictions, as the diversity of the all-black cast makes clear. *Moonlight* also revels in the complexity and multiplicity of black masculinities."[8] And, as they argue, *Moonlight* is "an epic in the way it is a sweeping homage to social transformation (both positive and regressive) and to the nobility and negativity of the human condition."[9]

Music plays a central role, just as it does in *Tongues Untied*: the music on the soundtrack follows Chiron in his three ages and helps enforce and explain his situation, his struggle, and his emotional state of mind. Whereas the first two parts use subtle music, most of which is orchestrally scored with piano and strings, beautifully composed by Nicholas Britell, the third part uses more contemporary music, both more expressive and sensual (e.g., lyrical Brazilian pop music by Caetano Veloso when Black drives to Miami or Barbara Lewis's mellow R&B hit "Hello Stranger," when Black meets up with Kevin at his diner). The soundtrack also relies on hip-hop (e.g., Erykah Badu's "Tyrone") but uses a southern form that is "chopped and screwed" with a deep, slow voice, adding yearning and longing to the music while also making it somehow poetic. The hypermasculinity that characterizes much of hip-hop is here being neutralized to allow for more emotional expression.[10] These chosen music tracks point toward the direction Chiron is going to take as he will finally come to decide for himself who he is going to be.

IDENTITY ISSUES

Identity, then, constitutes a main issue in both films, and in relation to identity, of finding one's place, and of coming home. In *Tongues Untied*, Riggs talks upfront of his long-term exclusion before finding home, namely being excluded from the dominant white, racist, and homophobic society as a black man, and excluded from a black, homophobic society as a gay man, and further excluded from gay white society as a black man (while also being exotified and hypersexualized within this culture). The triple exclusion that he alludes to clearly recalls the testament made by one of the social actors in Jennie Livingston's *Paris Is Burning* from 1991, explaining how "as a gay black man you have three strikes against you." Here, race, sexuality, and gender

FIGURE 16.1 Marlon Riggs and Essex Hemphill in *Tongues Untied* (1989).

together make up a kind of otherness that can lead only to exclusion in a dominant white, heteronormative, and masculinist society. Yet these identity aspects intersect with one another, and as such they demand equal expressivity and presence.

It is not until Riggs turns toward his own "kind" that he will find acceptance and pride. And through this turn, he realizes that black gay love is powerful because it is political (see Figure 16.1). In fact, a claim made in the film is the recurring sentence "black men loving black men is *the* revolutionary act." This sentence is expressed over and over, both in written words (black on white) and shouted out loud at a gay parade, and as the film ends, this is the one sentence that will echo in one's mind. The exclusive essentialism that is being advocated throughout the film and through its various voices is one that is nonhesitant and nonapologetic. This essentialism is one that is political and *strategic*, and hence it is only temporarily essentialist, as in the sense advocated by Gayatri Spivak.[11]

Closely related to the strategic essentialism that we find in *Tongues Untied*, as well as in Julien's *Looking for Langston*, is the aim to rediscover and retell a black, gay past. British cultural critic Stuart Hall positions these two practices or approaches as opposite, ascribing a more positive meaning to the latter, retelling, than to rediscovering. Yet he acknowledges the importance of a more essentialist stance that we find in rediscovery, arguing, "We should not, for a moment, underestimate or neglect the importance of the act of imaginative rediscovery which this conception of a rediscovered, essential identity entails. 'Hidden histories' have played a critical role in the emergence of many of the most important social movements of our time—feminist, anti-colonial and anti-racist."[12] Both Riggs's film and Julien's were very much part of a larger identity politics movement characteristic of both theory and film production in the 1980s and 1990s. Jenkins's *Moonlight* continues to discuss identity but in a different, more subtle way. Here, the issue of identity, although always present, is delicately conveyed since there are no explicit utterances that break the forced muteness that has surrounded much black and gay history. The protagonist Chiron is in fact silent throughout the film, whereas Riggs is expressive and loud. Yet there are many reference points between Riggs's and Jenkin's films: both depict how identity is being negotiated as a label or a box that is being forced on the individual by his or her social and cultural surrounding, and how it may work as a shield or a mask that the individual can decide to perform by his or her own will. And in both films the love of another black man will help our protagonists escape their mental and physical prison, stuck in identities they never claimed were their own.

In *Tongues Untied*, Riggs, together with other social actors, uses various forms to emphasize the variety of identity aspects that make up a black gay community, all along emphasizing a certain political essentialism through the recurring exclamation that black men loving black men is *the* revolutionary act. In *Moonlight*, identity in the environment in which Chiron grows up is presented as a dual, yet closed and narrow, category. There are only two identity options given to him: either he is to be soft and hence at the receiving end of other, more masculine men's hatred and violence, or he has to be hypermasculine and threateningly violent to others. It is easy to see how these two options clearly relate to the choice he has to make between being either *gay* (soft and nonmasculine) or *black* (hard and masculine). Black, according to the societal standards regarding sex, gender, and race that seek to define him, can only equal straight. Or rather, black is only *allowed* to equal straight. From an early age, Chiron, referred to as Little—"My name is Chiron. [But] People call me 'Little'"—is being labeled "soft" and "weak" by his surrounding, and hence viewed as (possibly) gay. The bullying at school is motivated by him being perceived as gay, and his mother Paula's ambivalent relation to her son must most likely be seen as one informed by the fear and dislike of homosexuality.[13] Her fear is to be read not only as a pure expression of homophobia but also as a realization that she, as his parent, will not be able to protect him from the violence and social exclusion that his gayness will cause him. Here, Juan and Teresa come in as a comfort to Chiron as they do not judge him, but fully accept him as he is, *when* he is. As he asks how he can know if he is gay, Juan tells him, "You just do," and Teresa, not wanting to put pressure on him, follows up and says, "You will know when you know."

IDENTITY LABELS AND NAMES

When we first are introduced to Little, he is about eight years old, yet he looks younger because of his physical smallness, and it is made clear, from the very first scene in which he appears, that (homo)sexuality is already being attached to him. Taken that male homosexuality and femininity are being equated within the interpretative framework of heteronormativity and homophobia, Little's smallish features make him girl-like in the eyes of his physically more developed peers and hence, possibly, that is probably, gay. Long before he himself even knows what a "faggot" is, a label that is being thrown his way by the other boys, he is being *made* gay. This labeling is given emphasis in the film. For example, at the opening of the film he is being introduced vocally as a "faggot ass," the label being repeatedly shouted by his predators trying to hunt him down and beat him up.

This type of injurious labeling of Little is mirrored by Riggs in *Tongues Untied* as he tells the spectator of his own childhood, and how he, when growing up, was being called "faggot," "punk," and "freak" by the other boys long before he even understood what these labels meant. He did clearly understand, however, that these labels were severely negative, and hence injurious. In a close-up, seated against a black background, Riggs talks directly to the camera: "I heard my calling at age 6: we had a word for boys like me: 'punk!' At age 11 we moved to Georgia, I graduated to new knowledge—'Homo!' What's a 'homo,' I asked. 'Punk,' 'faggot,' 'freak.' I understood." But as a black boy in a predominantly white school, and as one of only two black boys in an otherwise all white class, Riggs was also being called other injurious labels–racist labels coming from his white schoolmates and accusatory labels thrown at him by his black peers. Interwoven with the medium close-up of Riggs as he recounts his precarious childhood are quick montage sequences showing extreme close-ups of men's mouths shouting out these homophobic, racist, and accusatory labels, making up a rhythmic flow of abusive invectives: "Mother fucking coon, Uncle Tom, punk, faggot, freak, homo, mother fucking coon, Uncle Tom, punk, faggot, freak, homo, Mother fucking coon, Uncle Tom." All these invectives clearly serve to emphasize the harmful power in labeling. Looking straight into the camera, Riggs tells us, "I was confused, I was afraid and alone. Cornered by identities I never wanted to claim. I ran . . . fast . . . hard . . . deep. Inside myself where it was still silent, safe. Deception."

Without a doubt, Riggs's story mirrors Chiron's story. After years of both physical and vocal abuse from his peers, but also from his mother, he too decides to run. Not only does Chiron run away from his predators by leaving the state, he also runs away to re-create or reinvent himself as "Black." Making himself hypermasculine, changing his physical appearance by spending hours lifting heavy weights to make his body more muscular and hence invulnerable and by fashioning himself to look like Juan, he becomes untouchable. The stereotypical notion of black masculinity as untouchable, hard, and latently violent and of black men as prone to criminality becomes his shield. And this shield allows him to run deep inside himself where it is still and silent and safe. The solitude that he forces upon himself, excluding and detaching himself from the world and from intimate relationships with other people, constitutes a second protective shield. It is interesting to note that while Chiron reconstructs himself in order to protect himself from the world, he is molding himself after the only adult male with whom he has had a loving relationship, Juan. Chiron, by becoming the drug dealer "Black," becomes Juan, but he is now a Juan who is without the love and affection of a loved one. And then there is a third shield behind which he hides to protect himself: his *silence*.

"SILENCE IS MY SWORD. IT CUTS BOTH WAYS."

Silence is also constantly being referred to in *Tongues Untied*, and it is so especially through the inclusion of poetry by Essex Hemphill (1957–1995), the American gay activist poet who came to play an important part for visualizing and vocalizing black and gay life in the 1980s and 1990s.[14] Hemphill talks about silence as both protector and a kind of slayer. It "slays" because it suffocates and circumscribes the individual who feels forced to hide a part of herself or himself, hindering her or him from being a full person. But he also articulates silence as a real threat in a time, the 1980s, when HIV indeed was a deadly threat, not least to black gays. Silence, then, is a "deadliest weapon." Hemphill appears in *Tongues Untied* as one of the more prominent voices, reading his own poems in close-ups or on the sound tape. The problem of silence is also addressed by Riggs and in one sequence, as he looks straight into the camera while reading: "Silence is my cloak. It smothers. Silence is my sword. It cuts both ways. Your silence is costing. Your silence is suicide."

Moonlight, filmed some thirty years after *Tongues Untied*, takes place in an era that could be referred to as a post-AIDS-crisis era, and there is within the film no mentioning of HIV.[15] Yet silence dominates and constantly characterizes Chiron; all three parts portray him at different ages as a silent person, afraid of speaking up and afraid of engaging with other people. It is as if his constant violent maltreatment by others has rendered him silent and also invisible. The labels that are forced upon him when he fails to be invisible (which is more or less every day when school is over and he sets out to walk home) are apparently both confusing and harming him. Seeing him struggle with his identity, and how he is being bullied, Juan tells Little, "At some point, you gotta decide for yourself who you're going to be. Can't let nobody make that decision for you." It is going to take a long time before Chiron makes his first decision though, and when he does, it will lead to untouchability, but also to isolation, while still being silent, almost mute. Later, as he is unexpectedly reunited with his first love and childhood friend Kevin (André Holland), he makes the decision that will free him as a person. His becoming himself is carried out and realized through one single utterance: "You're the only man who's ever touched me." His decision to end his blues and his coming out to Kevin beautifully echo Hughes's lines from "Night and Morn": "*This is gonna be ma song. I could be blue but, I been blue all night long.*"[16]

BLACK AND GAY

Identity, in both films, boils down to being able to define oneself. In *Tongues Untied*, this definition is very much about embracing being both black and gay, and hence refusing to choose one over the other, that is, being either gay *or* black. In an interview from 1991, Riggs states, "The way to break loose of the schizophrenia in trying to define identity is to realize that you are many things within a person. Don't try to arrange a hierarchy of things that are virtuous in your character and say 'This is more important than that.' Realize that both are equally important; they both inform your character."[17] Riggs's words are clearly in tandem with the writings made by several black and gay scholars, many of whom were contemporary with Riggs.

In fact, the dilemma of the either/or decision defined many early queer voices on what it meant to be black and gay in a white, racist, and homophobic society, as well as within black homophobic society. For example, British art critic Kobena Mercer deserves to be mentioned here. He has discussed this *duality* in his work as one that came to define black lesbian and gay struggles in the 1980s and 1990s. This duality, he has argued, informs the working on both fronts at all times. These fronts are of course the racist white gay community and the homophobia of the black community, two fronts that in themselves create "the difficulty of constantly negotiating our relationships to the different communities to which we equally belong."[18] Hence, Mercer is referring to a constant twofold struggle, which means that the queer black subject has to locate herself or himself "in the spaces *between* different communities—at the intersections of power relations determined by race, class, gender, and sexuality."[19] Habitually, Mercer continues, we think of identity in "mutually exclusive terms, based on the either/or logic of binary oppositions."[20] This means that one often feels compelled to make a choice. And to have to choose between two sides of one's being amounts, according to Stuart Hall, to an "essentializing of difference into two opposed either/or's."[21] And following British cultural theorist Paul Gilroy, who has argued that black people in the diaspora must refuse the binary black *or* British, Hall argues further that any such binary must be made invalid: "They must refuse it because the 'or' remains the sight of *constant contestation* when the aim of the struggle must be, instead, to replace the 'or' with the potentiality of an 'and.'"[22] The potentiality of "and" is palpable, given that we are "always in negotiation, not with a single set of oppositions that place us always in the same relation to others, but with a series of different positionalities."[23] And each of these "has for us its point of profound subjective identification."[24] Mercer too finds the question whether one is either black *or* queer ridiculous and unhelpful because no one can separate different aspects of his or her identity, certainly not if the individual values both or all of these various aspects.[25] None of us, Mercer claims, "very rarely ever belong exclusively to one homogenous and monolithic community" (even though some of us are definitively less aware of our hybridized belonging than are others). Hence, for many people "everyday life is a matter of passing through, travelling between, and negotiating a plurality of different spaces."[26]

I referred earlier to the strategic essentialism in Riggs's *Tongues Untied*. It is also present, although to a lesser degree, in Isaac Julien's *Looking for Langston*. Both films serve to celebrate and advocate a black and gay experience and make visible and audible a black and gay legacy. The essentialism advocated in these two films takes on different forms to celebrate plurality and openness, yet both break with a single-minded and uniform essentialism. In Riggs's *Tongues Untied*, the men who speak up have all come to embrace their identity as being both black and gay and are vociferous and expressive in their constant outings. *Moonlight* is subtler in its message. Chiron does not artic-ulate his identity until the very end, and when he does so, it is rather subtly. Up until that moment, he hides by being silent and invisible, and when he still is not left in peace by his predators, he decides to transform himself. Becoming a hypermasculine man, and taking up one of few available profes-sions that can keep him safe, he resides within himself. The physical differ-ence between the younger Chiron and the untouchable Black he transforms into is complete, but it is hardly a transformation that is triumphant. Until he comes out to himself and to Kevin, embracing himself for what he is and is becoming, he stays mute and invisible, in Atlanta as in Liberty City, or as Riggs would experience it, "here [San Francisco] as in Hephzibah."

Coming home, for both Chiron and Riggs, means accepting and embrac-ing being black and gay. This acceptance means also that being soft is given another meaning. The end scene, according to Eric A. Jordan and Derrick R. Brooms, "shifts the movie's original meaning of the word 'soft' from weak to sincere, genuine, and loving with other Black men."[27] And Chiron's new soft-ness, exhibited nakedly as he confesses his feelings for Kevin, makes him not only genuine and sincere, but also strong and free (see Figure 16.2).

Identity politics has brought forward the possibility of deciding for one-self what one is while trying to combat the inequalities and domination that come with sexism, racism, and homophobia. For groups at the receiving end of oppression and exclusion due to their ethnicity, sex, class, sexuality, and/or race, a strategic essentialism may be a most valuable and powerful strategy

FIGURE 16.2 Black (Trevante Rhodes) and Kevin (André Holland) in *Moonlight* (2016).

because it may bring individuals together to fight oppression. Yet as post-structuralist theory has taught us, identity is never fixed. It is always *situational*, and even though it can be experienced as stable, its stability is only temporary. Hall, when describing cultural identity and how it comes to be constituted, argues that identity is a form of *being* and *becoming*. Identity, then, belongs both to the past and to the future because it is always *in the making*: "Cultural identities come from somewhere, have histories.... But, like everything which is historical, they undergo constant transformation."[28] The same holds true for Chiron and Riggs. Both films demonstrate how their main characters have their youthful experiences and stories present within their adult self. To paraphrase in Hall's words, one's identity belongs to one's past, one's present, and one's future. Hall hence claims that identity is always *in process*, and further that it is always constituted within, and not outside of, representation, that is, within the representations made in favor of the discourses in power, but also in relation to and within the very counter discourses that upset the hegemonic images.[29] To Hall, identity is never identical to two individuals, nor is it fixed and ready to the one individual.

In *Moonlight* with Kevin lovingly holding Chiron as he strokes his head softly, we are left with a happy ending, yet it is an ending that is subtle, emotional, and silent. After eons of silence, Chiron finally confesses to Kevin, "You're the only man who's ever touched me. The only one. I haven't really touched anyone, since." It is here that Chiron becomes the agent of his own masculinity and sexuality, and it is now through this utterance that he is setting himself free to love and be loved for the first time. Little has finally come home. As Chiron, he is now able to be both gay and black, and his troublesome story of humiliation, pain, and exclusion has come to an end. In this way, the film is indeed epic. The loud and engaging intensity of *Tongues Untied* is mirrored by the almost silent expression in *Moonlight*, yet both films convey a message about being black and gay that is as convincing and as powerful. Riggs telling us "Now, I hear. I was mute, tongue-tied, burdened by shadows and silence. Now I speak and my burden is lightened, lifted, free," is applicable to Chiron's coming out to Kevin; he too is now free, lifted, and lightened.

NOTES

1. Langston Hughes, "Night and Morn" (Smithsonian Folk Ways Recordings, Smithsonian Institution, Washington, DC, 1995), https://folkways.si.edu/langston-hughes/night-and-morn/african-american-spoken-poetry/track/smithsonian.

2. See B. Ruby Rich, "New Queer Cinema," *Sight and Sound* 5, no. 5 (1992): 31–34. See also B. Ruby Rich, *New Queer Cinema: The Director's Cut* (Durham, NC: Duke University Press, 2013). For a discussion on *Looking for Langston* and *Tongues Untied*, see Louise Wallenberg, "New Black Queer Cinema," in *New Queer Cinema: A Critical Reader*, ed. Michele Aaron (Edinburgh University Press, 2004), 128–143.

3. The attack on identity politics is coming from both outside and within the academia. From within, author and academic Mark Lilla can be mentioned. See Lilla, *The Once and Future Liberal: After Identity Politics* (New York: HarperCollins, 2017). For an insightful discussion on how neoconservatism and neoliberalism converge and on how they both lead toward de-democratization, see Wendy Brown, "American Nightmare: Neoliberalism, Neoconservatism, and De-democratization," *Political Theory* 34, no. 6 (2006): 690–714.

4. In a report published by the University of Southern California's Annenberg School for Communication and Journalism in 2017, led by Stacy L. Smith, numbers show how exclusion in Hollywood is still the norm. Of the speaking characters surveyed in Hollywood films made in 2016, 70.8 percent were white; 13.6 percent black; 5.7 percent Asian; 3.1 percent Hispanic; and less than 1 percent American Indian, Alaska Native, or Native Hawaiian. And only *one* film in 2016 featured a gay and black character: *Moonlight*. See Lindsey Bahr, "Movies Still Dominated by White Male Actors Despite Talk of Diversity," *Daily News*, July 31, 2017, www.dailynews.com.

5. Asking Kevin why he insists on calling him "Black," Chiron expresses how he is obviously feeling both confined and defined by the name, yet, yearning for Kevin's affection, he accepts:

Why you always calling me that?

What, "Black"?

Yeah, "Black."

That's my nickname for you. You don't like it?

Naw, it's just, what kinda dude goes around giving other dudes nicknames?

6. Menaka Kannan, Rhys Hall, and Matthew W. Hughey, "Watching *Moonlight* in the Twilight of Obama," *Humanity & Society* 41, no. 3 (2017): 287–298, 288.

7. On the representation of black masculinity in film and media, see, e.g., Donald Bogle, *Toms, Coons, Mulattoes, Mammies, and Bucks: An Interpretive History of Blacks in American Films* (New York: Viking, 1973); Ed Guerrero, *Framing Blackness* (Philadelphia: Temple University Press, 1993); Kobena Mercer, *Welcome to the Jungle: New Positions in Black Cultural Studies* (London: Routledge, 1994); Todd Edward Boyd, *Am I Black Enough for You? Popular Culture from the Hood and Beyond* (Bloomington: Indiana University Press, 1997); and bell hooks, *We Real Cool: Black Men and Masculinity* (New York: Routledge, 2003).

8. Kannan, Hall, and Hughey, "Watching *Moonlight*," 290.

9. Kannan, Hall, and Hughey, "Watching *Moonlight*," 287.

10. Jenkins explains, "It's this Southern form of hip-hop called 'chopped and screwed,' where the voice is really deep and it's really slowed down and lines are repeating. I grew up listening to it; it started in Houston *and* Tampa . . . but Houston claims it. It makes hip-hop almost hypermasculine, but it opens up all this yearning in the lyrics. Hip-hop is usually moving at such a high bpm that you don't catch that not only is this poetry, but it's really pained. If you chop and screw it, you allow all of that pain to come through. I worked closely with the composer, Nick Britell. We also have a lot of violin, cello, and oboe. It's almost like taking someone's heartbeat and slowing it down. Putting it on full display. Which I think is sort of what the actors did with the characters." See Nicholas Rapold, "Interview with Barry Jenkins," *Film Comment*, September/October 2016, 44–45, 44.

11. "Strategic essentialism" is a term coined by feminist and postcolonial philosopher Gayatri Spivak in the 1980s and refers to the strategy that nationalities, ethnic and / or other minority groups can use to unite and present themselves. See Gayatri Chakravorty Spivak, *The Post-colonial Critic: Interviews, Strategies, Dialogues*, ed. Sarah Harasym (London: Routledge, 1990).

12. See Stuart Hall, "Cultural Identity and Diaspora," in *Colonial Discourse and Post-colonial Theory*, ed. Patrick Williams and Laura Chrisman (London: Harvester Wheatsheaf, 1994), 392–403, 393.

13. In the first part of the film, titled "Little," young Chiron explains and tries to convince to Kevin that he is not soft: "I ain't soft," he says, and after the two boys amicably have wrestled in the grass, Kevin turns to Little and says, "I knew you wasn't soft." Soft here holds only negative connotations in a world dominated by ideal male hardness and invulnerability.

14. On the role of silence in Hemphill's work, see Charles I. Nero, "Introduction," in Essex Hemphill, *Ceremonies: Prose and Poetry* (San Francisco: Cleis Press, 2000).

15. It is also interesting to note that Jenkins makes no reference to the phenomenon of the "down low." In recent years, black men who desire other black men, at least in the United States, have come to be defined, or labeled, as men who are on the "down low." In his book *Nobody Is Supposed to Know: Black Sexuality on the Down Low* (Minneapolis: Minnesota University Press, 2017), C. Riley Snorton offers a rich analysis on how the down low is constructed and mirrored in American society, focusing on how popular culture has embraced the phenomenon by making black queerness, which had earlier been hidden, hypervisualized, hence reinforcing problematic perceptions of black sexuality.

16. Hughes, "Night and Morn."

17. Marlon Riggs interviewed by Ron Simmons in "Tongues Untied: An Interview with Marlon Riggs," in *Brother to Brother: New Writings by Black Gay Men*, ed. Essex Hemphill (Boston: Alyson, 1991), 189–199, 191. Simmons partakes in the film as a member of the cast, as field producer, and as director of still photographs.

18. Kobena Mercer, "Dark and Lovely Too: Black Gay Men in Independent Film," in *Queer Looks: Perspectives on Lesbian and Gay Film and Video*, ed. Martha Gever, John Greyson, and Pratibha Parmar (London: Routledge, 1993), 238–256, 239.

19. Mercer continues, "What follows from this is a recognition of the interdependence of different political communities, not completely closed off from each other or each hermetically sealed like segregated bantustan but interlocking in contradictory relations over which we struggle." Mercer, "Dark and Lovely Too," 239.

20. Mercer, "Dark and Lovely Too," 239.

21. Stuart Hall, "What Is This 'Black' in Black Popular Culture?," in *Representing Blackness: Issues in Film and Video*, ed. Valerie Smith (New Brunswick, NJ: Rutgers University Press, 1997), 123–134, 128.

22. Hall, "What Is This 'Black'?," 128.

23. Hall, "What Is This 'Black'?," 129.

24. Hall, "What Is This 'Black'?," 129.

25. Mercer, "Dark and Lovely Too," 239.

26. Mercer, "Dark and Lovely Too," 239. It would be unforgivable to assume that we all experience our identity as hybrid and fluent. For the white, straight, and middle-class subject, there is probably little notion of a plural identity as she or he can pass through life with a sense of being "intact" in her or his identity.

27. Eric A. Jordan and Derrick R. Brooms, "Black and Blue: Analyzing and Queering Black Masculinities in *Moonlight*," in *Living Racism: Through the Barrel of the Book*, ed. Teresa Rajack-Talley (Lanham, MD: Rowman & Littlefield, 2017), 137–156, 149.

28. Hall, "Cultural Identity and Diaspora," 394.

29. Hall, "Cultural Identity and Diaspora," 392.

ACKNOWLEDGMENTS

This anthology fermented as an idea over a considerable span of time. My late dissertation adviser Miriam Hansen pointed in her own work to a new hermeneutic approach to film as featured in this volume long before the terminology of intersectionality became commonly known. My prior mentor, the late philosopher Angel Medina, has given me a solid foundation in understanding the importance of representation, the terrain where cultural battles are fought. Since then various platforms at professional conferences such as the American Studies Association, the Association of Asian American Studies, the Society of Media and Cinema Studies, the Popular Cultural Association/American Cultural Association and the Critical Ethnic Studies Association have given me the opportunity to meet up with peers engaging in a similar effort to study film in a new fashion. When I presented the idea of an anthology of intersectional studies of film to Leslie Mitchner, former editor-in-chief at Rutgers University Press, I received her enthusiastic support for this project. I would like to thank Leslie Mitchner, Executive Editor Nicole Solano, and Lisa Banning for lending continuing support to this project, and Alissa Zarro and Trudi Gershenov for the volume's amazing cover design. Special thanks to Joseph Dahm and his always superb copyediting. I appreciate the daily inspirations provided by members of my Department of English chaired by Rachel Trubowitz as well as the Program of Women Studies chaired by Siobhan Senier at the University of New Hampshire. I would also like to thank all the contributors to this volume for embracing this project with great creativity and originality. Finally, Matthias Konzett has been invaluable with help, suggestions, and advice.

BIBLIOGRAPHY

Aaron, Michele, ed. *New Queer Cinema: A Critical Reader*. Edinburgh: Edinburgh University Press, 2004.

Acevedo-Muñoz, Ernesto R. *West Side Story as Cinema: The Making and Impact of an American Masterpiece*. Lawrence: University Press of Kansas, 2013.

Adams, Samuel Hopkins. *The Gorgeous Hussy*. New York: Grosset and Dunlap, 1934.

———. "The Slave in the Family." *New Yorker*, December 13, 1947, 32–33.

Agee, James. *Agee on Film*. Vol. 1. New York: Grosset & Dunlap, 1967.

Altman, Rick. "Moving Lips: Cinema as Ventriloquism." *Yale French Studies* 60 (1980): 67–79.

Andersen, Kenneth. "Character Portrayal in *The Ox-Bow Incident*." *Western American Literature* 4 (Winter 1970): 287–298.

Anderson, Benedict. *Imagined Communities: Reflections on the Origin and Spread of Nationalism*. New York: Verso, 1983.

Anderson, Thom. "Red Hollywood." In Ferguson and Groseclose, *Literature and the Visual Arts in Contemporary Society*, 141–196.

Andrews, Dana. "The Role I Liked Best." *Saturday Evening Post*, March 16, 1946, 94.

Anzaldúa, Gloria. *Borderland/Frontera: The New Mestiza*. San Francisco: Aunt Lute Books, 1987.

Aptheker, Herbert. "American Negro Slave Revolts." *Science and Society* 1, no. 4 (Summer 1937): 512–538.

Bahr, Lindsey. "Movies Still Dominated by White Male Actors Despite Talk of Diversity." *Daily News*, July 31, 2017.

Bakhtin, Mikhail. *The Dialogic Imagination: Four Essays*. Translated by Michael Holquist and Caryl Emerson. Austin: University of Texas Press, 1983.

Baldwin, James. *The Devil Finds Work*. 1976. New York: Vintage, 2011.

Balio, Tino. *Grand Design: Hollywood as a Modern Business Enterprise, 1930–1939*. Berkeley: University of California Press, 1995.

Bascara, Victor. "The Case of the Disappearing Filipino American Houseboy: Speculations on *Double Indemnity* and United States Imperialism." *Kritika Kultura* 8 (2007): 35–56.

Basinger, Jeanine. *Silent Stars*. Hanover, NH: Wesleyan University Press, 1999.

Basten, Fred. *Max Factor: The Man Who Changed the Faces of the World*. New York: Arcade, 2008.

Baudry, Jean-Louis. "The Ideological Effects of the Basic Cinematographic Apparatus." In Corrigan, White, and Mazaj, *Critical Visions in Film Theory*, 34–45.

Bean, Jennifer M., ed. *Flickers of Desire: Movie Stars of the 1910s*. New Brunswick, NJ: Rutgers University Press, 2011.

Becker, Howard. *Outsiders: Studies in the Sociology of Deviance*. London: Free Press of Glencoe, 1963.

Beltrán, Mary. "Fast and Bilingual: *Fast & Furious* and the Latinization of Racelessness." *Cinema Journal* 53, no. 1 (Fall 2013): 75–96.

———. *Latino/a Stars in U.S. Eyes: The Making and Meanings of Film and TV Stardom*. Urbana: University of Illinois Press, 2009.

———. "The New Hollywood Racelessness: Only the Fast, Furious (and Multi-racial) Will Survive." *Cinema Journal* 44, no. 2 (Winter 2005): 50–67.

Beltrán, Mary, and Camilla Fojas, eds. *Mixed Race Hollywood*. New York: New York University Press, 2008.

Benjamin, Walter. "The Work of Art in the Age of Technological Reproducibility." In Corrigan, White, and Mazaj, *Critical Visions in Film Theory*, 230–252.

Benstock, Shari, and Suzanne Ferriss, eds. *On Fashion*. New Brunswick, NJ: Rutgers University Press, 1994.

Berg, Charles Ramírez. *Latino Images in Film: Stereotypes, Subversion, and Resistance*. Austin: University of Texas Press, 2002.

Berg, Jan van den. *The Changing Nature of Man*. New York: Norton, 1961.

Berger, John. *Ways of Seeing*. London: Penguin, 1972.

Berlant, Laurent. *The Female Complaint: The Unfinished Business of Sentimentality in American Culture*. Durham, NC: Duke University Press, 2008.

Bernardi, Daniel, ed. *Classic Hollywood, Classic Whiteness*. Minneapolis: University of Minnesota Press, 2001.

———. *The Persistence of Whiteness: Race and Contemporary Hollywood Cinema*. New York: Routledge, 2007.

Bick, Ilsa J. "*Stella Dallas*: Maternal Melodrama and Feminine Sacrifice." *Psychoanalytic Review* 79, no. 1 (Spring 1992): 121–145.

Black, Cheryl. "Looking White, Acting Black: Cast(e)ing Fredi Washington." *Theatre Survey* 45, no. 1 (May 2014): 19–40.

Blackwelder, Julia Kirk. *Styling Jim Crow: African American Beauty Training during Segregation*. College Station: Texas A&M University Press, 2003.

Bogle, Donald. *Toms, Coons, Mulattoes, Mammies, and Bucks: An Interpretive History of Blacks in American Films*. New York: Viking, 1973.

Bordwell, David, Janet Staiger, and Kristin Thompson. *The Classical Hollywood Cinema: Film Style and Mode of Production to 1960*. London: Routledge, 1985.

Bourne, Stephen. *Butterfly McQueen Remembered*. Latham, MD: Scarecrow Press, 2008.

Bowser, Pearl, Jane Marie Gaines, and Charles Musser, eds. *Oscar Micheaux and His Circle: African-American Filmmaking and Race Cinema of the Silent Era*. Bloomington: Indian University Press, 2001.

Boyd, Todd Edward. *Am I Black Enough for You? Popular Culture from the Hood and Beyond*. Bloomington: Indiana University Press, 1997.

Brasch, Ilka. "'Let Me See Her Face When He Kisses Her, Please': Mediating Emotion and Locating the Melodramatic Mode in *Stella Dallas*." *Film-Philosophy* 19 (2015): 289–303.

Brooks, Virginia. "Timeline: A Century of Dance and Media." In Mitoma, Zimmer, and Stieber, *Envisioning Dance on Film and Video*, xix–xxx.

Brown, Wendy. "American Nightmare: Neoliberalism, Neoconservatism, and De-democratization." *Political Theory* 34, no. 6 (2006): 690–714.

———. *Walled States, Waning Sovereignty*. New York: Zone Books, 2010.

Burroughs, Edgar Rice. *The Return of Tarzan*. New York: Signet, 1990.

———. *Tarzan of the Apes*. New York: Signet, 1990.

Butler, Judith. *Gender Trouble: Feminism and the Subversion of Identity*. London: Routledge, 1990.

Byrd, Ayana D., and Lori L. Tharps. *Hair Story: Untangling the Roots of Black Hair in America*. New York: St. Martin's, 2001.

Calhoun, John. "*The Ox-Bow Incident*." *Cineaste*, Summer 2004, 55–56.

Callahan, Dan. *Barbara Stanwyck: The Miracle Woman*. Jackson: University Press of Mississippi, 2012.

Callahan, Vicki, ed. *Reclaiming the Archive: Feminism and Film History*. Detroit: Wayne State University Press, 2010.

Campbell, Alice Kamokila. "Text of Kamokila's Testimony: Senator Discusses Objections in Detail; Cites Racial Issues." *Honolulu Advertiser*, January 17, 1946.

Carter, Gregory T. "From Blaxploitation to Mixploitation: Male Leads and Changing Mixed Race Identities." In Beltrán and Fojas, *Mixed Race Hollywood*, 203–222.

Cartwright, Angela, and Tom McLaren. *Styling the Stars: Lost Treasures from the Twentieth Century Fox Archive*. New York: Simon & Schuster, 2017.

Cassano, Graham. "Critical Pragmatism's Status Wage and the Standpoint of the Stranger." In Krier and Worrell, *Capitalism's Future*, 217–239.

———. *A New Kind of Public: Community, Solidarity, and Political Economy in New Deal Cinema, 1935–1948*. Chicago: Haymarket Press, 2015.

Childs, Erica Chito. *Fade to Black and White: Interracial Images in Popular Culture*. Lanham, MD: Rowman & Littlefield, 2009.

Chilton, Karen. *Hazel Scott: The Pioneering Journey of a Jazz Pianist, from Café Society to Hollywood to HUAC*. Ann Arbor: University of Michigan Press, 2008.

Civille, Michael. "'Ain't Got No Chance': The Case of *The Breaking Point*." *Cinema Journal* 56, no. 1 (Fall 2016): 1–22.

Clark, Walter Van Tilburg. *The Ox-Bow Incident*. New York: Modern Library, 2001.

Coffman, Tom. *The Island Edge of America: A Political History of Hawai'i*. Honolulu: University of Hawai'i Press, 2003.

Cohan, Steven. *Incongruous Entertainment: Camp, Cultural Value, and the MGM Musical*. Durham, NC: Duke University Press, 2005.

Collins, Patricia Hill. "Learning from the Outsider Within: The Sociological Significance of Black Feminist Thought." In Harding, *Feminist Standpoint Theory Reader*, 103–126.

———. "Learning from the Outsider Within: The Sociological Significance of Black Feminist Thought." *Social Problems* 33, no. 6 (October–December 1986): S14–S32.

Collins, Patricia Hill, and Sirma Bilge. *Intersectionality*. Malden, MA: Polity, 2016.

Cooley, Charles Horton. *Human Nature and the Social Order*. New York: Charles Scribner, 1902.

Copjec, Joan, ed. *Shades of Noir*. London: Verso, 1993.

Corrigan, Timothy, Patricia White, and Peta Mazaj, eds. *Critical Visions in Film Theory*. Boston: Bedford/St. Martin's, 2011.

Courtney, Susan. *Hollywood Fantasies of Miscegenation: Spectacular Narratives of Gender and Race, 1903–1967*. Princeton, NJ: Princeton University Press, 2005.

Couvares, Francis, ed. *Movie Censorship and American Culture*. Amherst: University of Massachusetts Press, 2006.

Crafton, Donald. *The Talkies: American Cinema's Transition to Sound, 1926–1931*. Berkeley: University of California Press, 1999.

Crain, Mary Beth. "The Ox-Bow Incident Revisited." *Literature/Film Quarterly* 4 (July 1976): 240–248.

Crenshaw, Kimberlé. "Demarginalizing the Intersection of Race and Sex: A Black Feminist Critique of Antidiscrimination Doctrine, Feminist Theory, and Antiracist Politics." *University of Chicago Legal Forum* 8, no. 1 (1989): 139–167.

———. "Mapping the Margins: Intersectionality, Identity Politics, and Violence Against Women of Color." *Stanford Law Review* 43, no. 6 (July 1991): 1241–1299.

Cripps, Thomas. *Making Movies Black: The Hollywood Message Movie from World War II to the Civil Rights Era*. Oxford: Oxford University Press, 1993.

Croce, Arlene. *The Fred Astaire and Ginger Roger Book*. New York: Outerbridge & Lazard, 1972.

Crowther, Bosley. "The Screen." *New York Times*, May 10, 1943, 15.

———. "The Screen in Review; 'Go for Broke!,' Tribute to War Record of Nisei Regiment, Opens at the Capitol." *New York Times*, May 25, 1951.

Cullen, Frank, Florence Hackman, and Donald McNeilly, eds. *Vaudeville, Old & New: An Encyclopedia of Variety Performers in America*. New York: Routledge, 2006.

Dávila, Arlene. *Latinos, Inc.: The Marketing and Making of a People*. Berkeley: University of California Press, 2001.

De Beauvoir, Simone. *The Second Sex*. Translated by Constance Borde and Sheila Malovany Chevallier. New York: Knopf, 2009.

Delamater, Jerome. *Dance in the Hollywood Musical*. Ann Arbor, MI: UMI Research Press, 1988.

Deleuze, Gilles, and Félix Guattari. *Kafka: Toward a Minor Literature*. Translated by Dana Polan. Minneapolis: University of Minnesota Press, 1986.

Deren, Maya. "Cinematography: The Creative Use of Reality." In Corrigan, White, and Mazaj, *Critical Visions in Film Theory*, 146–156.

Desmond., Jane C., ed. *Meanings in Motion: New Cultural Studies of Dance*. Durham, NC: Duke University Press, 1997.

Diawara, Manthia. "Noir by Noirs: Toward a New Realism in Black Cinema." In Copjec, *Shades of Noir*, 261–278.

Dixon, Wheeler Winston, ed. *American Cinema of the 1940s: Themes and Variations*. New Brunswick, NJ: Rutgers University Press, 2006.

Doherty, Thomas. *Pre-code Hollywood: Sex, Immorality, and Insurrection in American Cinema 1930–1934*. New York: Columbia University Press, 1999.

Du Bois, W. E. B. *Black Reconstruction of Democracy in America*. New York: Harcourt, Brace, 1935.

Dubrofsky, Rachel E. "Jewishness, Whiteness, and Blackness on *Glee*: Singing to the Tune of Postracism." *Communication, Culture and Critique* 6, no. 1 (2013): 82–102.

Durkheim, Émile. *The Rules of Sociological Method*. Translated by W. D. Halls. New York: Free Press, 1982.

Dyer, Richard. "Entertainment and Utopia." In Nichols, *Movies and Methods*, 220–232.

———. *Stars*. London: British Film Institute, 1979.

———. *White*. London: Routledge, 1997.

Eagle, Jonna. *Imperial Affects: Sensational Melodrama and the Attractions of American Cinema*. New Brunswick, NJ: Rutgers University Press, 2017.

Emami, Gazelle, Matt Zoller Seitz, and Jen Chaney. "Rita Moreno on Why She Asked for Her One Day at a Time Character to Be Sexual, Marlon Brando, and Her First-Ever Scene Sans Makeup." *Vulture*, January 11, 2017. www.vulture.com/2017/01/rita-moreno-one-day-at-a-time-sexuality.html.

Eyman, Scott. *Empire of Dreams: The Epic Life of Cecil B. DeMille*. New York: Simon & Schuster, 2013.

Factor, Max. "The Art of Motion Picture Make-Up." *Cinematographic Annual* 1 (1930): 157–171.

Fanon, Frantz. *Black Skin, White Masks*. Translated by Richard Philcox. 1952. New York: Grove, 2008.

———. *The Wretched of the Earth*. Translated by Richard Philcox. New York: Grove, 2004.

Felsenstein, Frank. *Anti-Semitic Stereotypes: A Paradigm of Otherness in English Popular Culture, 1660–1830*. Baltimore: Johns Hopkins University Press, 1995.

Ferguson, Suzanne, and Barbara Groseclose, eds. *Literature and the Visual Arts in Contemporary Society*. Columbus: Ohio State University Press, 1985.

Foner, Eric. *Gateway to Freedom*. New York: Norton, 2015.

Foster, Gwendolyn Audrey. *Class-Passing: Social Mobility in Film and Popular Culture*. Carbondale: Southern Illinois University Press, 2005.

Foucault, Michel. *The History of Sexuality*. New York: Vintage, 1990.

Franklin, John Hope. *From Slavery to Freedom: A History of African Americans*. New York: McGraw-Hill, 2000.

Fregoso, Rosa Linda. *The Bronze Screen: Chicana and Chicano Film Culture*. Minneapolis: University of Minnesota Press, 1993.

———. "Lupe Vélez: Queen of the B's." In Mendible, *From Bananas to Buttocks*, 51–68.

Freud, Sigmund. *Group Psychology and the Analysis of the Ego*. Translated by James Strachey. New York: Norton, 1989.

———. "On Narcissism: An Introduction." Gay, *Freud Reader*, 545–562.

Friedman, Lester D., ed. *Unspeakable Images: Ethnicity and the American Cinema*. Urbana: University of Illinois Press, 1991.

Friedman, Ryan Jay. *Hollywood's African American Films: The Transition to Sound*. New Brunswick, NJ: Rutgers University Press, 2011.

Fuchs, Cynthia. "*Taxi Driver*: 'I Got Some Bad Ideas in My Head.'" In Geiger and Rutsky, *Film Analysis*, 748–766.

Fuhrer, Margaret. "Our Favorite Dance Doubles of All Time." *Dance Spirit*, February 29, 2018. www.dancespirit.com/movie-dance-doubles-2540397639.html.

Fujitani, Takashi, Geoffrey M. White, and Lisa Yoneyama, eds. *Perilous Memories: The Asia-Pacific War(s)*. Durham, NC: Duke University Press, 2001.

Fusco, Katherine. *Silent Film and U.S. Naturalist Literature: Time, Narrative, and Modernity*. New York: Routledge, 2016.

Gabbard, Krin. *Black Magic: White Hollywood and African American Culture*. New Brunswick, NJ: Rutgers University Press, 2004.

———. *Jammin' at the Margins: Jazz and the American Cinema*. Chicago: University of Chicago Press, 1996.

Gaines, Jane. "*Lady Be Good*: Do Dogs Dance?" *Jump Cut: A Review of Contemporary Media* 31 (March 1986): 19–23.

Gates, Philippa. "The Assimilated Asian American as American Action Hero." *Canadian Journal of Film Studies* 22, no. 2 (Fall 2013): 19–40.

Gateward, Frances. "In Love and Trouble." In Gateward and Pomerance, *Where the Boys Are*, 157–182.

Gateward, Frances, and Murray Pomerance, eds. *Where the Boys Are: Cinemas of Masculinity and Youth*. Detroit: Wayne State University Press, 2005.

Gavin, James. *Stormy Weather: The Life of Lena Horne*. New York: Atria Books, 2009.

Gay, Peter, ed. *The Freud Reader*. New York: Norton, 1989.

Geiger, Jeffrey. *Facing the Pacific: Polynesia and the U.S. Imperial Imagination*. Honolulu: University of Hawai'i Press, 2007.

Geiger, Jeffrey, and R. L. Rutsky, eds. *Film Analysis: A Norton Reader*. New York: Norton, 2013.

Gever, Martha, John Greyson, and Pratibha Parmar, eds. *Queer Looks: Perspectives on Lesbian and Gay Film and Video*. London: Routledge, 1993.

Ginsberg, Elaine K., ed. *Passing and the Fictions of Identity*. Durham, NC: Duke University Press, 1996.

Gledhill, Christine. "Dialogue: Christine Gledhill on '*Stella Dallas*' and Feminist Film Theory." *Cinema Journal* 25, no. 4 (Summer 1986): 44–48.

———, ed. *Home Is Where the Heart Is: Studies in Melodrama and the Woman's Film*. London: British Film Institute, 1987.

Goffman, Erving. *The Presentation of Self in Everyday Life*. Norwell, MA: Anchor, 1959.

Gordon, Rita Moreno. *Rita Moreno: A Memoir*. New York: Celebra, 2013.

Gramsci, Antonio. *Selections from the Prison Notebooks*. Edited and translated by Quintin Hoare and Geoffrey Nowell Smith. New York: International, 1971.

Green, Laurie B. *Battling the Plantation Mentality: Memphis and the Black Freedom Struggle*. Chapel Hill: University of North Carolina Press, 2007.

Griffin, Mark. *A Hundred or More Hidden Things: The Life and Films of Vincente Minnelli.* Cambridge, MA: Da Capo Press, 2010.

Griffin, Sean, ed. *Hetero: Queering Representations of Straightness.* Albany: State University of New York Press, 2009.

Guerrero, Ed. *Framing Blackness.* Philadelphia: Temple University Press, 1993.

Guglielmo, Jennifer, and Salvatore Salerno, eds. *Are Italians White? How Race Is Made in America.* New York: Routledge, 2003.

Gunning, Tom. "The Cinema of Attraction: Early Film, Its Spectator and the Avant-Garde." *Wide Angle* 8, nos. 3–4 (Fall 1986): 63–70.

———. "Systematizing the Electric Message: Narrative Form, Gender, and Modernity in *The Lonedale Operator.*" In Keil and Stamp, *American Cinema's Transitional Era,* 15–50.

Haenni, Sabine. "Filming 'Chinatown': Fake Visions, Bodily Transformations." In *Screening Asian Americans,* edited by Peter X. Feng, 21–52. New Brunswick, NJ: Rutgers University Press, 2002.

Hagedorn, Jessica. "Introduction." In *Charlie Chan Is Dead: An Anthology of Contemporary Asian American Fiction,* edited by Jessica Hagedorn. London: Penguin, 1993.

———. "Introduction." In *Charlie Chan Is Dead 2: At Home in the World (An Anthology of Contemporary Asian American Fiction—Revised and Updated),* edited by Jessica Hagedorn. London: Penguin, 2004.

Hall, Stuart. "Cultural Identity and Diaspora." In Williams and Chrisman, *Colonial Discourse and Post-colonial Theory,* 392–403.

———, ed. *Representation: Cultural Representation and Signifying Practices.* London: Sage, 1993.

———. "What Is This 'Black' in Black Popular Culture?" In Smith, *Representing Blackness,* 123–134.

Handlin, Oscar. *Immigration as a Factor in American History.* Englewood Cliffs, NJ: Prentice Hall, 1959.

Hansen, Miriam. *Babel & Babylon: Spectatorship in American Silent Film.* Cambridge, MA: Harvard University Press, 1991.

———. "The Mass Production of the Senses: Classical Cinema as Vernacular Modernism." *Modernism/modernity* 6, no. 2 (April 1999): 59–77.

Hanson, Patricia King, and Alan Gevinson, eds. *American Film Institute Catalog of Motion Pictures Produced in the United States, Feature Films, 1931–1940.* Berkeley: University of California Press, 1993.

Harding, Sandra, ed. *The Feminist Standpoint Theory Reader: Intellectual and Political Controversies.* New York: Routledge, 2004.

Hawaii Statehood Commission. *Hawaii and Statehood.* Honolulu: Hawaii Statehood Commission, 1951.

———. *Hawaii, U.S.A., and Statehood: History, Premises and Essential Facts of the Statehood Movement.* Honolulu: Hawaii Statehood Commission, 1948.

Hegel, G. W. F. *Phenomenology of Spirit.* Translated by J. N. Findlay. Oxford: Oxford University Press, 1977.

Hemphill, Essex, ed. *Brother to Brother: New Writings by Black Gay Men*. Boston: Alyson, 1991.

———. *Ceremonies: Prose and Poetry*. San Francisco: Cleis Press, 2000.

Hicks, Heather. "Hoodoo Economics: White Men's Work and Black Men's Magic in Contemporary American Film." *Camera Obscura* 18, no. 2 (2003): 27–55.

Higashi, Sumiko. *Cecil B. DeMille and American Culture: The Silent Era*. Berkeley: University of California Press, 1994.

———. "Ethnicity, Class and Gender in Film: DeMille's *The Cheat*." In Friedman, *Unspeakable Images*, 112–139.

Hobson, Katherine. "Sue Sylvester, Coach Beistie, Santana Lopez, and Unique Adams: Exploring Queer Representations of Femininity in *Glee*." In Johnson and Faill, *Glee and New Directions for Social Change*, 95–107.

Holmes, Anna. "White Until Proven Black: Imagining Race in *Hunger Games*." *New Yorker*, March 30, 2012.

hooks, bell. *Ain't I a Woman: Black Women and Feminism*. Boston: South End, 1982.

———. "The Oppositional Gaze: Black Female Spectators." In Thornman, *Feminist Film Theory*, 307–320.

———. *Reel to Real: Race, Class and Sex at the Movies*. London: Routledge, 1996.

———. *We Real Cool: Black Men and Masculinity*. New York: Routledge, 2003.

Horak, Laura. *Girls Will Be Boys: Cross-Dressed Women, Lesbians and American Cinema, 1908–1934*. New Brunswick, NJ: Rutgers University Press, 2016.

Horkheimer, Max, and Theodor W. Adorno. *Dialectic of Enlightenment*. Translated by John Cumming. 1944. New York: Continuum, 1990.

Huang, Yunte. *Charlie Chan: The Untold Story of the Honorable Detective and His Rendezvous with American History*. New York: Norton, 2010.

Huh, Jinny. *The Arresting Eye: Race and the Anxiety of Detection*. Charlottesville: University of Virginia Press, 2015.

Ignatiev, Noel. *How the Irish Became White*. New York: Routledge, 1995.

Jacobs, Jason. "Raising Gays: On *Glee*, Queer Kids, and the Limits of the Family." *GLQ: A Journal of Lesbian and Gay Studies* 20, no. 3 (2014): 319–352.

Jacobs, Lea. *The Wages of Sin: Censorship and the Fallen Woman, 1928–1942*. Madison: University of Wisconsin Press, 1991.

James, David E., and Adam Hyman, *Alternative Projections: Experimental Film in Los Angeles, 1945–1980*. Bloomington: Indiana University Press, 2015.

Johnson, Brian C., and Daniel K. Faill, eds. *Glee and New Directions for Social Change*. Rotterdam: Sense, 2015.

Jordan, Eric A., and Derrick R. Brooms. "Black and Blue: Analyzing and Queering Black Masculinities in *Moonlight*." In Rajack-Talley, *Living Racism*, 137–156.

Josephson, Barney, with Terry Trilling-Josephson. *Café Society: The Wrong Place for the Right People*. Urbana: University of Illinois Press, 2009.

Jung, Moon-Kie. *Reworking Race: The Making of Hawaii's Interracial Labor Movement*. New York: Columbia University Press, 2006.

Kannan, Menaka, Rhys Hall, and Matthew W. Hughey. "Watching *Moonlight* in the Twilight of Obama." *Humanity & Society* 41, no. 3 (2017): 287–298.

Kaplan, E. Ann. *Motherhood and Representation: The Mother in Popular Culture and Melodrama*. London: Routledge, 1992.

———. "Mothering, Feminism and Representation: The Maternal in Melodrama and the Woman's Film 1910–14." In Gledhill, *Home Is Where the Heart Is*, 113–137.

Keil, Charlie, and Shelley Stamp, eds. *American Cinema's Transitional Era: Audiences, Institutions, Practices*. Berkeley: University of California Press, 2004.

Keyser, Catherine. *Playing Smart: New York Women Writers and Modernist Magazine Culture*. New Brunswick, NJ: Rutgers University Press, 2010.

Kim, Jodi. *Ends of Empire: Asian American Critique and the Cold War*. Minneapolis: University of Minnesota Press, 2010.

King, Rob. *The Fun Factory: The Keystone Film Company and the Emergence of Culture*. Berkeley: University of California Press, 2009.

Knight, Arthur. "Star Dances: African-American Constructions of Stardom, 1925–1960." In Bernardi, *Classic Hollywood, Classic Whiteness*, 386–414.

Kobal, John. "Interview with Eleanor Powell." *Focus on Film* 19 (Autumn 1974): 24–31.

Kojève, Alexandre. *Introduction to the Reading of Hegel: Lectures on the Phenomenology of Spirit*. Translated by James H. Nichols Jr. Ithaca, NY: Cornell University Press, 1969.

Konzett, Delia Malia. "The Belated Tradition of Asian-American Modernism." In Matthews, *Companion to the Modern American Novel*, 496–517.

———. "Classical Hollywood, Race and Casablanca." In Plath, *Critical Insights: Casablanca*, 97–113.

———. *Hollywood's Hawaii: Race, Nation, and War*. New Brunswick, NJ: Rutgers University Press, 2017.

Kotani, Roland. *The Japanese in Hawaii: A Century of Struggle*. Honolulu: Hawaii Hochi, 1985.

Kracauer, Siegfried. *The Mass Ornament: Weimar Essays*. Translated and edited by Thomas Y. Levin. Cambridge, MA: Harvard University Press, 1995.

Krier, Daniel, and Mark P. Worrell, eds. *Capitalism's Future: Alienation, Emancipation, and Critique*. Chicago: Haymarket Press, 2017.

Kroeger, Brooke. *Fannie: The Talent for Success of Writer Fannie Hurst*. New York: Times Book, 1999.

Krüger, Gesine, Ruth Mayer, and Marianne Sommer, eds. *Ich Tarzan! Affenmenschen und Menschenaffen zwischen Science und Fiction*. Bielefeld: Transcript, 2008.

Lacan, Jacques. *Écrits: A Selection*. Translated by Alan Sheridan. New York: Norton, 1977.

Lastra, James. *Sound Technology and the American Cinema*. New York: Columbia University Press, 2000.

Lautier, Louis. "Capital Spotlight." *Afro-American*, September 19, 1936, 3.

Leibman, Nina. *Living Room Lectures: The Fifties Family in Film and Television*. Austin: University of Texas Press, 1995.

Levette, Harry. "Thru Hollywood: Follow the Movie Stars and Players Weekly with Harry." *Chicago Defender*, July 4, 1936.

Lewis, Alfred Henry. *Peggy O'Neal*. New York: American News Company, 1903.

Lilla, Mark. *The Once and Future Liberal: After Identity Politics*. New York: HarperCollins, 2017.

Lindsay, Richard. *Hollywood Biblical Epics: Camp Spectacle and Queer Style from the Silent Era to the Modern Day*. Santa Barbara, CA: Praeger, 2015.

Lippman-Hoskins, Margaux. "*Glee* and 'Born This Way': Therapeutic and Postracial Rhetoric." In Johnson and Faill, *Glee and New Directions for Social Change*, 111–122.

Locan, Clarence A. "The Lon Chaney I Knew." *Photoplay*, November 1930, 58–60, 106–108.

Lott, Eric. *Love and Theft: Blackface Minstrelsy and the American Working Class*. London: Oxford University Press, 1993.

———. "The Whiteness of Film Noir." *American Literary History* 9, no. 3 (Autumn 1997): 542–566.

Love, Heather. *Feeling Backward: Loss and the Politics of Queer History*. Cambridge, MA: Harvard University Press, 2007.

Lubin, David. *Flags and Faces: The Visual Culture of America's First World War*. Berkeley: University of California Press, 2015.

MacDonald, William, ed. *Selected Documents Illustrative of the History of the United States. 1776–1861*. London: McMillan Press, 1898.

Maland, Charles J. "*Film Gris*: Crime, Critique, and Cold War Culture in 1951." *Film Criticism* 23 (Spring 2002): 1–26.

Marchetti, Gina. *Romance and the Yellow Peril: Race, Sex, and Discursive Strategies in Hollywood Fiction*. Berkeley: University of California Press, 1994.

Massood, Paula J. "Mapping the Hood: The Genealogy of City Space in *Boyz n the Hood* and *Menace II Society*." *Cinema Journal* 35, no. 2 (Winter 1996): 85–97.

Matthews, John T., ed. *A Companion to the Modern American Novel*. Oxford: Wiley-Blackwell, 2009.

Maurice, Alice. *The Cinema and Its Shadow*. Minneapolis: University of Minnesota Press, 2013.

Mayer, Ruth. *Artificial Africas: Colonial Images in the Times of Globalization*. Hanover: University of New England Press, 2002.

Mayer, Vickie, Miranda J. Banks, and John Thornton Caldwell, eds. *Production Studies: Cultural Studies of Media Industries*. New York: Routledge, 2009.

McGee, Kristin A. *Some Liked It Hot: Jazz Women in Film and Television, 1928–1959*. Middletown, CT: Wesleyan University Press, 2009.

McLean, Adrienne, ed. *Costume, Makeup, and Hair*. New Brunswick, NJ: Rutgers University Press, 2016.

———. *Dying Swans and Madmen: Ballet, the Body, and Narrative Cinema*. New Brunswick, NJ: Rutgers University Press, 2008.

———. "Putting 'em Down Like a Man: Eleanor Powell and the Spectacle of Competence." In Griffin, *Hetero*, 89–110.

McRobbie, Angela. "Dance Narratives and Fantasies of Achievement." In Desmond, *Meanings in Motion*, 189–219.

Mendible, Myra, ed. *From Bananas to Buttocks: The Latina Body in Popular Film and Culture*. Austin: University of Texas Press, 2007.

Mercer, Kobena. "Dark and Lovely Too: Black Gay Men in Independent Film." In Gever, *Queer Looks*, 238–256.

———. *Welcome to the Jungle: New Positions in Black Cultural Studies*. London: Routledge, 1994.

Mérimée, Prosper. *Carmen*. Urbana, IL: Project Guttenberg, 2006.

Meyer, Michaela D. E., and Meghan M. Wood. "Sexuality and Teen Television: Emerging Adults Respond to Representations of Queer Identity in *Glee*." *Sexuality and Culture* 17, no. 3 (2013): 434–448.

Michelakis, Pantelis, and Maria Wyke, eds. *The Ancient World in Silent Cinema*. Cambridge: Cambridge University Press, 2013.

Minh-Ha, Trinh. *When the Moon Waxes Red: Representation, Gender and Cultural Politics*. New York: Routledge, 1991.

Miola, Robert S., ed. *Hamlet: Text of the Play, the Actors' Gallery, Contexts, Criticism, Afterlives, Resources*. New York: Norton, 2011.

Mitchell, Esther. "Editorial: Senator Campbell and Race Relations." *Honolulu Advertiser*, January 23, 1946.

Mitoma, Judy, Elizabeth Zimmer, and Dale Ann Stieber, eds. *Envisioning Dance on Film and Video*. New York: Routledge, 2002.

Moon, Krystyn. *Yellowface: Creating the Chinese in American Popular Music and Performance, 1850s–1920s*. New Brunswick, NJ: Rutgers University Press, 2005.

Myrdal, Gunnar, with Richard Sterner and Arnold Rose, *An American Dilemma: The Negro Problem and Modern Democracy*. New York: Harper & Row, 1944.

Naremore, James. *The Films of Vincente Minnelli*. Cambridge: Cambridge University Press, 1993.

Negrón-Muntaner, Frances. *Boricua Pop: Puerto Ricans and the Latinization of American Culture*. New York: New York University Press, 2004.

Nichols, Bill, ed. *Movies and Methods: An Anthology*. Vol. 2. Berkeley: University of California Press, 1976.

Noriega, Chon A. *Shot in America: Television, the State, and the Rise of Chicano Cinema*. Minneapolis: University of Minnesota Press, 2000.

Okada, Jun. *Making Asian American Film and Video: History, Institutions, Movements*. New Brunswick, NJ: Rutgers University Press, 2015.

Okihiro, Gary Y. *Island World: A History of Hawai'i and the United States*. Berkeley: University of California Press, 2008.

———. *Margins and Mainstreams: Asians in American History and Culture*. Seattle: University of Washington Press, 1994.

———. *Pineapple Culture*. Berkeley: University of California Press, 2009.

Ouellette, Laurie, and Jonathan Gray, eds. *Keywords for Media Studies*. New York: New York University Press, 2017.

Ovalle, Priscilla Peña. *Dance and the Hollywood Latina: Race, Sex, and Stardom.* New Brunswick, NJ: Rutgers University Press, 2011.

Parchesky, Jennifer. "Adapting *Stella Dallas*: Class Boundaries, Consumerism, and Hierarchies of Taste." *Legacy* 23, no. 2 (2006): 178–198.

Patterson, Orlando. *Slavery and Social Death.* Cambridge, MA: Harvard University Press, 1982.

Pauly, Thomas. "The Cold War Western." *Western Humanities Review* 33 (1979): 265–273.

Pettey, Homer B., and R. Baron Palmer, eds. *Film Noir.* Edinburgh: Edinburgh University Press, 2014.

Petty, Miriam J. *Stealing the Show: African American Performers and Audiences in 1930s Hollywood.* Berkeley: University of California Press, 2016.

Pew Research Center. *Millennials: A Portrait of Generation Next.* Social and Demographic Trends. Washington, DC: Pew Research Center, 2010.

Plath, James, ed. *Critical Insights: Casablanca.* Ipswich, MA: Salem Press, 2016.

Pollack, Queena. *Peggy Eaton: Democracy's Mistress.* New York: Minton, Balsch and Company, 1931.

Presley, Cecilia DeMille, and Mark Vieira. *Cecil B. DeMille: The Art of the Hollywood Epic.* Philadelphia: Running Press, 2014.

Prince, Sabiyha. *African Americans and Gentrification in Washington, D.C.: Race, Class and Justice in the Nation's Capital.* New York: Routledge, 2016.

Rajack-Talley, Teresa, ed. *Living Racism: Through the Barrel of the Book.* Lanham, MD: Rowman & Littlefield, 2017.

Ramsey, Walter. "Five, Fifty, and Fate." *Photoplay*, December 1930, 69–70.

Randell, Karen. "Masking the Horror of Trauma: The Hysterical Body of Lon Chaney." *Screen* 44, no. 2 (Summer 2003): 216–221.

Rapf, Joanna. "1948: Movies and the Family." In Dixon, *American Cinema of the 1940s,* 200–221.

Raphael-Hernandez, Heike, and Shannon Steen, eds. *AfroAsian Encounters: Culture, History, Politics.* New York: New York University Press, 2006.

Rapold, Nicholas. "Interview with Barry Jenkins." *Film Comment*, September/October 2016, 44–45.

Regester, Charlene. *African American Actresses: The Struggle for Visibility.* Bloomington: University of Indiana Press, 2010.

Rich, B. Ruby. "New Queer Cinema." *Sight and Sound* 5, no. 5 (1992): 31–34.

———. *New Queer Cinema: The Director's Cut.* Durham, NC: Duke University Press, 2013.

Riggs, Marlon. "Tongues Untied: An Interview with Marlon Riggs." In Hemphill, *Brother to Brother,* 189–199.

Roach, Joseph. *Cities of the Dead: Circum-Atlantic Performance.* New York: Columbia University Press, 1999.

Robinson, Cedric J. *Forgeries of Memory and Meaning: Blacks and the Regime of Race in American Theater and Film before World War II.* Chapel Hill: University of North Carolina Press, 2007.

Roediger, David R. "Afterword: DuBois, Race, and Italian Americans." In Guglielmo and Salerno, *Are Italians White?*, 259–264.

———. *Working toward Whiteness: How America's Immigrants Became White*. New York: Basic Books, 2005.

Rogers, George. "His Comment on Kamokila Campbell's Attitude." *Honolulu Star-Bulletin*, January 22, 1946.

Rogin, Michael. *Blackface, White Noise: Jewish Immigration in the Hollywood Melting Pot*. Berkeley: University of California Press, 1996.

Rony, Fatimah Tobing. *The Third Eye: Race, Cinema, and Ethnographic Spectacle*. Durham, NC: Duke University Press, 1996.

Rubin, Martin. *Showstoppers: Busby Berkeley and the Tradition of Spectacle*. New York: Columbia University Press, 1993.

Ryan, Michael, and Douglas Kellner, *Camera Politica: The Politics and Ideology of Contemporary Hollywood Film*. Bloomington: Indiana University Press, 1990.

Said, Edward W. *Orientalism*. New York: Random House, 1978.

Sangster, Margaret E. "Lon Chaney." *Photoplay*, October 1930, 40.

Schatz, Thomas, ed. *Boom and Bust: The American Cinema in the 1940s*. Vol. 6, *History of the American Cinema*. Berkeley: University of California Press, 1997.

Schickel, Richard. *Double Indemnity*. London: British Film Institute, 1992.

———. "Serving Up Subversion." *Wilson Quarterly* 29, no. 4 (Autumn 2005): 114–116.

Schrader, Paul. "Notes on Film Noir." *Film Comment* 8, no. 1 (Spring 1972): 8–13.

Schultz, Margie. *Eleanor Powell: A Bio-Bibliography*. Westport, CT: Greenwood, 1994.

Scott, Ellen C. *Cinema Civil Rights: Regulation, Repression, and Race in the Classical Hollywood Era*. New Brunswick, NJ: Rutgers University Press, 2015.

———. "More Than a 'Passing' Sophistication: Dress, Film Regulation, and the Color Line in 1930s American Films." *Women's Studies Quarterly* 41, nos. 1/2 (Spring/Summer 2012): 60–86.

Scruggs, Charles. "'The Power of Blackness': Film Noir and Its Critics." *American Literary History* 16, no. 4 (Winter 2004): 675–687.

———. "The Subversive Shade of Black in Film Noir." In Pettey and Palmer, *Film Noir*, 164–181.

Sedgwick, Eve Kosofsky. *Between Men: English Literature and Male Homosocial Desire*. New York: Columbia University Press, 1985.

Sharf, Zack. "Amandla Stenberg Removed Herself from 'Black Panther' Casting Because the Movie Deserved 'Dark-Skinned Actors.'" *IndieWire*, March 2, 2018. www.indiewire.com/2018/03/amandla-stenberg-black-panther-casting-dark-skinned-actors-1201934575/.

Shohat, Ella. "Ethnicities-in-Relation: Toward a Multicultural Reading of American Cinema." In Friedman, *Unspeakable Images*, 215–250.

Shohat, Ella, and Robert Stam. *Unthinking Eurocentrism: Multiculturalism and the Media*. London: Routledge, 1994.

Showalter, Elaine. "Representing Ophelia: Women, Madness, and the Responsibilities of Feminist Criticism." In Miola, *Hamlet*, 281–297.

Singer, Ben. "Feature Films, Variety Programs, and the Crisis of the Small Exhibitor." In Keil and Stamp, *American Cinema's Transitional Era*, 76–100.

Smith, John David. *Introduction to Ulrich B. Phillips's Life and Labor in the South*. Columbia: University of South Carolina Press, 2007.

Smith, Valerie, ed. *Representing Blackness: Issues in Film and Video*. New Brunswick, NJ: Rutgers University Press, 1997.

Snead, James. *White Screens, Black Images: Hollywood from the Dark Side*. London: Routledge, 1994.

Snorton, C. Riley. *Nobody Is Supposed to Know: Black Sexuality on the Down Low*. Minneapolis: University of Minnesota Press, 2017.

Song, Min Hyoung. *Strange Future: Pessimism and the 1992 Los Angeles Riots*. Durham, NC: Duke University Press, 2005.

Southern, David. *Gunnar Myrdal and Black-White Relations: The Use and Abuse of an American Dilemma, 1944–1969*. Baton Rouge: Louisiana State University Press, 1987.

Spivak, Gayatri Chakravorty. *Can the Subaltern Speak?* Basingstoke: Macmillan, 1988.

———. *The Post-colonial Critic: Interviews, Strategies, Dialogues*. Edited by Sarah Harasym. London: Routledge, 1990.

Squires, Catherine. *The Post-racial Mystique: Media and Race in the Twenty-First Century*. New York: New York University Press, 2014.

Staiger, Janet. "*Les Belles Dames sans Merci*, Femmes Fatales, Vampires, Vamps, and Gold Diggers: The Transformation and Narrative Value of Aggressive Fallen Women." In Callahan, *Reclaiming the Archive*, 32–57.

Stein, Louisa Ellen. *Millennial Fandom: Television Audiences in the Transmedia Age*. Iowa City: University of Iowa Press, 2015.

Stewart, Jacqueline Najuma. "What Happened in the Transition? Reading Race, Gender and Labor between the Shots." In Keil and Stamp, *American Cinema's Transitional Era*, 103–130.

Still, William. *Underground Railroad*. Philadelphia: Porter and Coates, 1872.

St. Johns, Ivan. "Mr. Nobody." *Photoplay*, February 1927, 136.

Studlar, Gaylyn. *This Mad Masquerade: Stardom and Masculinity in the Jazz Age*. New York: Columbia University Press, 1996.

Sutherland, Jean-Anne, and Kathryn M. Feltey. "Here's Looking at Her: An Intersectional Analysis of Women, Power, and Feminism in Film." *Journal of Gender Studies* 26, no. 6 (2017): 618–631.

Szalay, Michael. *New Deal Modernism: American Literature and the Invention of the Welfare State*. Durham, NC: Duke University Press, 2000.

Taccone, Tony. *Life Without Makeup*. Unpublished playscript, 2011.

Takabuki, Matsuo. *An Unlikely Revolutionary: Matsuo Takabuki and the Making of Modern Hawai'i*. Honolulu: University of Hawai'i Press, 1998.

Takaki, Ronald. *A Different Mirror: A History of Multicultural America*. New York: Little, Brown, 1993.

———. *Strangers from a Different Shore: A History of Asian Americans*. New York: Penguin, 1989.

Thomas, Dan. "Lon Chaney Talks in Makeup." *Santa Cruz News*, May 10, 1930, 7.

Thornman, Sue, ed. *Feminist Film Theory: A Reader*. New York: New York University Press, 1999.

Thornton, Edie. "Fashion, Visibility, and Class Mobility in *Stella Dallas*." *American Literary History* 11, no. 3 (Autumn 1999): 426–447.

Trask, Haunani-Kay. *From a Native Daughter: Colonialism and Sovereignty in Hawai'i*. Honolulu: University of Hawai'i Press, 1993.

Turim, Maureen. "Seduction and Eloquence: The New Woman of Fashion in Silent Cinema." In Benstock and Ferriss, *On Fashion*, 140–158.

Valdivia, Angharad N. *A Latina in the Land of Hollywood and Other Essays on Media Culture*. Tucson: University of Arizona Press, 2000.

Velie, Lester. "You Can't See That Movie: Censorship in Action." *Collier's*, May 6, 1950, 11–12.

Wald, Gayle. *Crossing the Line: Racial Passing in Twentieth-Century U.S. Literature and Culture*. Durham, NC: Duke University Press, 2000.

Wallenberg, Louise. "New Black Queer Cinema." In Aaron, *New Queer Cinema*, 128–143.

Wang, Oliver. "These Are the Breaks: Hip-Hop and AfroAsian Cultural (Dis)Connections." In Raphael-Hernandez and Steen, *AfroAsian Encounters*, 146–166.

Warshow, Robert. "Movie Chronicle: The Westerner." In *The Immediate Experience: Movies, Comics, Theatre and Other Aspects of Popular Culture*. Garden City, NY: Doubleday, 1962.

Weaver, William R. "Skelton Starts Here." Review of *I Dood It*. *Motion Picture Herald* 152, no. 5 (July 31, 1943): 1453.

Weber, Brenda R. "Intersectionality." In Ouellette and Gray, *Keywords for Media Studies*, 112.

Wells, Elizabeth A. *West Side Story: Cultural Perspectives on an American Musical*. Lanham, MD: Scarecrow Press, 2011.

Westbrook, Max. "The Archetypical Ethic of *The Ox-Bow Incident*." *Western American Literature* 1 (Summer 1966): 105–118.

Whitehead, John S. "Anti-statehood Movement and the Legacy of Alice Kamokila Campbell." *Hawaiian Journal of History* 27 (1993): 49–50.

Whitney, Allison. "Race, Class, and the Pressure to Pass in American Maternal Melodrama: The Case of *Stella Dallas*." *Journal of Film and Video* 59, no. 1 (Spring 2007): 3–18.

Wiegman, Robyn. "Black Bodies/American Commodities: Gender, Race, and the Bourgeois Ideal in Contemporary Film." In Friedman, *Unspeakable Images*, 308–328.

Williams, Linda. *Playing the Race Card: Melodramas of Black and White from Uncle Tom to O.J. Simpson*. Princeton, NJ: Princeton University Press, 2001.

———. "'Something Else Besides a Mother': 'Stella Dallas' and the Maternal Melodrama." *Cinema Journal* 24, no. 1 (Autumn 1984): 2–27.

Williams, Patrick, and Laura Chrisman, eds. *Colonial Discourse and Post-colonial Theory*. London: Harvester Wheatsheaf, 1994.

Williams, R. John. *The Buddha in the Machine: Art, Technology, and the Meeting of East and West*. New Haven, CT: Yale University Press, 2014.

Williamson, Joel. *New People: Miscegenation and Mulattoes in the United States*. New York: Free Press, 1980.

Willis, Sharon. *The Poitier Effect: Racial Melodrama and Fantasies of Reconciliation*. Minneapolis: University of Minnesota Press, 2015.

Wood, Amy. *Lynching and Spectacle: Witnessing Racial Violence in America, 1890–1940*. Chapel Hill: University of North Carolina Press, 2011.

Woodson, Carter G. *The Negro in Our History*. Washington, DC: Associated Publisher, 1922.

Yam, Kimberly. "'Crazy Rich Asian' Star Claps Back at Criticism That He's Not Asian Enough." *Huffington Post*, November 30, 2017.

Yumibe, Joshua. *Moving Color: Early Film, Mass Culture, Modernism*. New Brunswick, NJ: Rutgers University Press, 2012.

Žižek, Slavoj. *The Pervert's Guide to Cinema*. Directed by Sophie Fiennes. DVD. Microcinema, 2008.

———. *Trouble in Paradise: From the End of History to the End of Capitalism*. London: Allan Lane, 2014.

NOTES ON CONTRIBUTORS

ERNESTO R. ACEVEDO-MUÑOZ is professor of cinema studies and chair of the Department of Cinema Studies & Moving Image Arts at the University of Colorado, Boulder. He is the author of *West Side Story as Cinema: The Making and Impact of an American Masterpiece* (2013), *Pedro Almodóvar* (2007/2009), and *Buñuel and Mexico: The Crisis of National Cinema* (2003). His works have appeared in many journals and edited collections such as *Quarterly Review of Film & Video, Film & History, Lit, Letras peninsulares, Short Film Studies, After Hitchcock, Authorship in Film Adaptation, Contemporary Spanish Cinema and Genre, A Companion to Luis Buñuel,* and *Genre, Gender, Race and World Cinema.*

MARY BELTRÁN is associate professor of media studies in the Radio-Television-Film Department and an affiliate of Mexican American & Latina/o Studies and Women's and Gender Studies at the University of Texas at Austin. She is the author of *Latina/o Stars in U.S. Eyes: The Making and Meanings of Film and TV Stardom* (2009) and coeditor of the anthology *Mixed Race Hollywood* (2008). Her new book in progress is titled *Bronzing the Box: Latina/o Images, Storytelling, and Advocacy in U.S. Television.*

CHRIS CAGLE is associate professor of film and media arts at Temple University in Philadelphia. His research interests include documentary film, classical Hollywood, and the history of cinematography. His book *Sociology on Film: Postwar Hollywood's Prestige Commodity* (Rutgers University Press, 2016) examines the social problem film of the 1940s both as a form of popular sociology and as a strain of middlebrow cinema. He has published essays in *Cinema Journal, Screen,* and *Quarterly Review of Film and Video,* and in a number of edited volumes. His newest book project is an examination of an international festival film style in contemporary documentary.

GRAHAM CASSANO is associate professor of sociology at Oakland University, Michigan. He is the author most recently of *A New Kind of Public: Community, Solidarity, and Political Economy in New Deal Cinema, 1935–1948* (2015). He has published in multiple journals such as *Critical Sociology, Teaching*

Sociology, Journal of American Studies, and *Rethinking Marxism.* His work focuses on urban sociology, theory, labor history, mass media, race, gender, and class.

JONNA EAGLE is associate professor of film/media in the Department of American Studies at the University of Hawai'i at Mānoa, where she teaches on American cinema, war and media, critical and cultural theory, and American cultural and social history. Prior to UH, she taught in the Program in Women's Studies at Duke University. She is the author of *Imperial Affects: Sensational Melodrama and the Attractions of American Cinema* (Rutgers University Press, 2017).

RYAN JAY FRIEDMAN is the director of the Film Studies Program and associate professor of English at The Ohio State University. He is the author of *Hollywood's African American Films: The Transition to Sound* (Rutgers University Press, 2011) and *The Movies as a World Force: American Silent Cinema and the Utopian Imagination* (Rutgers University Press, 2018). He teaches courses in American film, film theory, and American and African American literature, and his scholarship on race and American film and literature has appeared in *Quarterly Review of Film & Video, Journal of American History, Historical Journal of Film, Radio and Television, English Literary History,* and *Arizona Quarterly.*

DELIA MALIA CAPAROSO KONZETT is professor of English, cinema studies, and women's studies at the University of New Hampshire. Her publications include the book studies *Ethnic Modernisms* (2002) and *Hollywood's Hawaii: Race, Nation, and War* (Rutgers University Press, 2017) as well as numerous essays in anthologies and film and literary journals. Her new work focuses on the representation and performance of race in Hollywood cinema.

MATTHIAS KONZETT, formerly associate professor at Yale University, is currently a senior lecturer in English and cinema studies at the University of New Hampshire. His publications include the monograph *Rhetoric of National Dissent* (2002), the first multicultural *Encyclopedia of German Literature* in English (2002), several anthologies, as well as recent essays on global cinema and science fiction film.

ALICE MAURICE is associate professor of English and cinema studies at the University of Toronto, Canada. She is the author of *The Cinema and Its*

Shadow: Race and Technology in Early Cinema (2013). Her work focuses on race and technology in early U.S. cinema. She has also worked in documentary film production and was associate producer of two award-winning films, *A Healthy Baby Girl* (1997) and the Academy Award–winning short *Defending Our Lives* (1994).

RUTH MAYER is professor and chair of American studies at Leibniz Universität, Hanover, Germany. Her research focuses on aspects of popular culture, particularly seriality and serialization, media history, globalization, science studies, and cultural contact. She is the author of *Artificial Africas: Images of Colonialism in the Times of Globalization* (2002) and *Serial Fu Manchu: The Chinese Super-Villain and the Spread of Yellow Peril Ideology* (2013).

JUN OKADA is associate professor of film studies and English at SUNY Geneseo and author of *Making Asian American Film and Video: History, Institutions, Movements* (Rutgers University Press, 2015). She has published articles and reviews in *Journal of Cinema and Media Studies* (*Cinema Journal*), *Velvet Light Trap, Screen*, and *Film Quarterly*. Her recent research concerns the histories of institutional relations between Asian American and African American media.

PRISCILLA PEÑA OVALLE is associate professor and associate director of the Cinema Studies Department at the University of Oregon. She is committed to accessible scholarship that operates at the intersection of theory and practice. In *Dance and the Hollywood Latina: Race, Sex, and Stardom* (Rutgers University Press, 2010), she asked why nearly all Latinas in mainstream Hollywood films danced on screen or gained fame as dancers. Her current scholarship, tentatively titled *The Hair Project*, explores the relationship between hair, race, gender, sexuality, and agency in music videos and television commercials.

CHARLENE REGESTER is associate professor in the Department of African, African American, & Diaspora Studies at the University of North Carolina at Chapel Hill. She is author of *African American Actresses: The Struggle for Visibility, 1900–1960* (2010) and coeditor of *The Josephine Baker Critical Reader* with Mae G. Henderson (2017). Her articles have been published in a number of journals, including *Film History, Journal of Film and Video*, and *Screening Noir*. She has appeared in several documentaries, including *Birth of a Movement* (2017), PBS *North Carolina Bookwatch* (2011), *Movies of Color:*

Black Southern Cinema (2002), AMC *Hattie McDaniel* (2000), and PBS *I'll Make Me a World: African American Artists from the Harlem Renaissance to the Present* (1998).

DEAN ITSUJI SARANILLIO is assistant professor of Asian/Pacific/American studies in the Department of Social and Cultural Analysis at New York University. His teaching and research interests are in settler colonialism and critical indigenous studies, Asian American and Pacific Island histories, and cultural studies. Currently he is working on a manuscript on the admission of Hawai'i as a U.S. state, titled *Unsustainable Empire: Colliding Futures of Hawai'i Statehood*. His essays have been featured in the *American Quarterly*, *Journal of Asian American Studies*, *Settler Colonial Studies*, and several anthologies.

ELLEN C. SCOTT is associate professor and chair of UCLA's Cinema and Media Studies Program. Her research focuses on the cultural meanings and reverberations of film in African American communities and, more broadly, the relationship of media to the struggle for racial justice and equality. Her first book, *Cinema Civil Rights* (Rutgers University Press, 2015), exposes the classical-Hollywood-era studio system's careful repression of civil rights but also the stuttered appearance of these issues through latent, symptomatic signifiers. She is currently working on two projects, one that has been funded by the Academy Scholars grant, examining the history of slavery on the American screen and another on the history of black women's film criticism.

LOUISE WALLENBERG is associate professor in film and fashion studies and former director of the Centre for Fashion Studies at Stockholm University. She has published on queer cinema, gender theory, organization theory, and fashion. Her publications include the coedited volumes *Fashion and Modernism* (2018), *Fashion, Film and the 1960s* (2017), *Harry bit för bit* (2017), *Modernism och mode* (2014), and *Nordic Fashion Studies* (2011). She has published widely in anthologies and journals.

INDEX